Southern Hospitality

Tourism and
the Growth of Atlanta

Southern Hospitality

TOURISM AND
THE GROWTH OF ATLANTA

HARVEY K. NEWMAN

The University of
Alabama
Press

Tuscaloosa and
London

∞

The paper on which this book is printed meets the mini-
mum requirements of American National Standard for
Information Science–Permanence of Paper for Printed
Library Materials, ANSI Z39.48-1984.

Library of Congress Cataloging-in-Publication Data

Newman, Harvey K.
Southern hospitality : tourism and the growth of Atlanta /
Harvey K. Newman.
p. cm.
Includes bibliographical references (p.) and index.

ISBN 0-8173-0961-6 (alk. paper)
ISBN 0-8173-0972-1 (paper : alk. paper)
1. Tourist industry—Georgia—Atlanta—History. 2. Hospitality
industry—Georgia—Atlanta—History. 3. Heritage
tourism—Georgia—Atlanta—History. 4. Atlanta (Ga.)—Social life and
customs—History. I. Title.
G155.U6 N49 1999
338.4′791758231—dc21
98-58014

British Library Cataloguing-in-Publication Data available

CONTENTS

Contents

TABLES

Preface

ONE CAN LEARN ABOUT THE CULTURE OF A REGION from both experience and study. I was fortunate to be born and raised in the South, where I learned the lessons of hospitality in a household that represented both sides of the Mason-Dixon Line. This gave me a perspective on the South that was shaped by the region but also was sufficiently detached to observe its way of life with fascination. My ambivalent perspective toward the South was reinforced by the experience of being an outsider in the small North Carolina town where my family lived for most of my youth. In a community with no hotels, our house seemed like a stopover for the constant stream of people who received bed and board from my family. From this experience, I developed the interest in hospitality that fired my curiosity for this project.

My experience had to be combined with a great deal of research. In the process, I was assisted by colleagues and students at Georgia State University. Their suggestions and questions helped me along the way. One former colleague, Dr. Harold Davis, was especially encouraging with his comments on the early drafts of the book. This friend, who was so generous with his time and gracious in his hospitality, did not live to see the completion of my work; however, I will always appreciate his kindness. Another person who was invaluable in the completion of this work was

Martha Martin, administrative coordinator in the Department of Public Administration and Urban Studies. Other help was provided by the Georgia State University librarians in the reference, interlibrary loan, and circulation departments. The librarians at the Atlanta History Center and the Atlanta–Fulton County Library's African-American Research Center also provided much-needed research assistance. Special thanks are also offered for the patience and assistance shown by Nicole Mitchell and the staff at The University of Alabama Press.

My deepest gratitude goes to my family, each member of which has made special contributions to this project. My wife's mother, Elsie Bane Hewitt, is a member of our household and has provided much of the Southern food that gave me both sustenance and inspiration. To my son, Nathan, I extend my thanks for his devotion to Southern culture—its food, art, and music. Most of all, I thank my wife, Patricia Hewitt Newman, for her love and unfailing support as well as her skills as an editor. Without her help, I would not have understood Southern hospitality; and, so, to her this book is dedicated.

Southern Hospitality

TOURISM AND
THE GROWTH OF ATLANTA

Introduction

URBAN SCHOLAR LEWIS MUMFORD HAS REMARKED that one finds in the history of a city the concentration of the culture of a community. He acknowledged the role that larger influences such as economics and politics might have on an urban area, but emphasized that the city "accumulates and embodies the heritage of a region."[1] This implies an ongoing relationship between a city and its rural hinterland. The urban and rural are not a dichotomy of distinct ways of life, as sociologists such as Louis Wirth have suggested.[2] Instead, rural folk carry their cultural patterns with them as they move to the city; once there, they become part of a continuing relationship between the urban area and the region.[3]

It has been observed by urban scholars that the culture of a region distinguishes one city from another.[4] These cultural patterns are based on the daily routines and the shared patterns of belief and behavior of the people within a region—routines and patterns they carry with them as they move from the countryside to the city. In the Old South, many cultural patterns revolved around the production of staple crops such as tobacco and cotton. For example, slaves were imported from Africa to cultivate the crops. The cities that developed in the South reflected the distinctive way of life based on agriculture, providing the connecting points between the rural hinterland and markets located

1

elsewhere. Towns and cities developed initially along coastal areas and rivers as shipping points for agricultural products and distribution centers for goods imported from outside the region. Atlanta was an interior city that served as a gateway to the agricultural areas of the South, but unlike the older coastal and river cities of the region, it was a new place built astride "rivers of steel"—the railroads.

In a perceptive essay, historian Blaine Brownell reminds us that cities have always been repositories of regional culture. He adds, "The process of urbanization doubtless heightened the contrasts between older customs and newer habits, and the inconsistencies that always existed in the South—hospitality and violence, racism and tolerance, ingenuity and fatalism—were apparent in the region's cities."[5] Numerous writers have explored the cultural influences described by Brownell on the cities of the South. For instance, historian Don Doyle examines the ingenuity of the men who led the New South movement in Atlanta, Nashville, Charleston, and Mobile.[6] Racism in the South has been the subject of works by C. Vann Woodward and Howard Rabinowitz.[7] Dickson Bruce and Bertram Wyatt-Brown have written about violence in the region.[8] Sociologist John Shelton Reed discusses tolerance as a Southern cultural trait in his essay "The Same Old Stand?"[9] Fatalism is a dominant idea in William Alexander Percy's autobiography,[10] and it is a recurring theme in Southern fiction such as William Faulkner's *Absalom, Absalom!*[11] One aspect of Southern culture that has received scant attention, however, is hospitality. Other than Joe Gray Taylor's history of eating, drinking, and visiting in the region and Wyatt-Brown's discussion of hospitality as part of the code of honor, there has been little written on the topic of Southern hospitality.[12] This work proposes to address that gap by focusing on hospitality and the commercial application of this value in the history of Atlanta and its tourism businesses.

Throughout much of its history, the South has enjoyed a reputation for warmly welcoming its visitors. Among the first to describe hospitality among colonial Virginians was Robert Beverley in 1705. Beverley, a first-generation native of the colony, described hospitality in these words:

> The Inhabitants are very Courteous to Travellers. . . . A
> Stranger has no more to do, but to inquire upon the Road,
> where any Gentleman or good House-Keeper Lives, and there
> he may depend upon being received with Hospitality. This
> good Nature is so general . . . that the Gentry when they go
> abroad, order their Principal Servant to entertain all Visitors.
> . . . And the poor Planters, who have but one Bed, will very
> often sit up, or lie upon a Form or Couch all Night, to make
> room for a weary Traveller. . . . If there happen to be a Curl,
> that either out of Covetousness, or Ill-nature, won't comply with
> this generous Custom, he has a mark of Infamy set upon him,
> and is abhorr'd by all.[13]

English parson Hugh Jones, sent as a minister to Jamestown, Virginia, provided another description of Southern hospitality. In his 1724 observations on the Virginia colony, Jones wrote, "No People can entertain their Friends with better Cheer and Welcome; and Strangers and Travellers are here treated in the most free, plentiful, and hospitable Manner; so that a few Inns or Ordinaries on the Road are sufficient."[14] The extending of hospitality during the colonial period was not only an obligation but also a source of intense personal gratification. Even though most houses were cramped and small, they were the centers of hospitality for family, neighbors, and guests.[15]

Most colonial settlement in the South took place in the tidewater areas of the coast, first in Virginia and then in the Carolinas and Georgia. The cultivation of tobacco, rice, indigo, and cotton in these areas was centered in large plantations, with smaller farms scattered on less desirable land. Even though three-fourths of the families in the antebellum South owned no slaves, the small minority at the top of society shaped the culture of the region. Slaves were imported from Africa to provide labor for the larger estates. While slave labor was considered essential for the cultivation of the staple crops that dominated the colonial economy, blacks also made possible the gracious entertaining that characterized the plantation owners. Those whites occupying lower stations imitated as best they could the manners of those at the top of society.

The culture of colonial Virginia described by Beverley, Jones, and others was a mixture of elements taken from England and adapted to the economy and social conditions of the region. Historians Clement Eaton and William R. Taylor have described this transformation of the ideals of the English country gentleman to the Old South. This English culture included the practice of hospitality among the "Cavaliers" of colonial Virginia.[16] One facet of that Cavalier heritage was the domination of society by the white male heads of plantation households. Men dominated the extended families of wives, children, and slaves, exercising a pattern of paternalism that intensified the subordination of women, making it difficult for Southern females to escape from positions of inferiority.[17] This meant that much of the work of providing hospitality fell on women, which has been a pattern in Southern society since the colonial period.

Other influences also contributed to a distinctly Southern way of life. From the native inhabitants, the colonists learned the cultivation of tobacco and corn, the twin staffs of life for the Virginia settlers. Tobacco was the cash crop that provided the livelihood for most, and corn provided bread for everyone except the wealthiest, who could afford wheat flour. The variety of foods reflected the many components of the culture of the South. English livestock provided pork, beef, and chicken. Other meat came from game and fish. Indian corn was made into the hominy, mush, pone, and hoecake that were staples in the colonial diet. Slaves had regular rations of corn, bacon, and salt that could be supplemented with potatoes, greens, fruit, and chickens raised near their quarters.

In spite of their position at the bottom of colonial society, slaves made significant contributions to the culture of the region. Their dwellings reflected African communal living patterns shaped by their inhabitants for their needs. On Sunday, the day of rest, slaves gathered in their quarters for relaxation, which often included singing and dancing. The routine existence of slaves was segregated from their masters so that some aspects of life evolved separately, but with many influences shared by both blacks and whites.[18] For example, slaves who cooked for white masters influenced the types and preparation of food in the South. Whites also imitated the music and dances performed by slaves. Both races influenced Southern culture, even though blacks and whites were segregated during the colonial period.

The interior of the South formed a vast frontier that was sparsely settled until after the Revolutionary War. As farmers moved upland to the interior, they carried their way of life, including hospitality, with them. In his history of the growth of Southern civilization, Clement Eaton noted that emigrating Virginians and Carolinians carried this way of life to remote corners of the South, including the interior of north Georgia.[19] Travel through Georgia's interior was difficult, but made bearable by the hospitality of frontier settlers. In 1828 Scotchman Basil Hall journeyed from Savannah to Darien, Macon, and Columbus on his way to Montgomery, Alabama. Shortly after leaving Darien on the Georgia coast, Hall writes,

> we fairly plunged into the forest, from which we did not emerge for many a weary day of rugged travelling. Towards sunset, we came to a spot where three roads branched off. After a pause, we took the wrong one, as it afterwards proved. It cost us twelve very hard hours' work to make out between thirty and forty miles on this day, and we were right glad, at last, to find ourselves in a solitary log-house, kept by a widow, who welcomed us with all she had, and though she kept no public house, she very cheerfully took us in, according to the universal custom of those wild countries where no regular accommodations are to be found. Of course, these poor people cannot afford to entertain travellers for nothing, but their charges were always as moderate as their means would allow.[20]

Another careful observer of the culture of the South was Alabama lawyer Daniel R. Hundley, who came from a Virginia family and had been educated at the University of Virginia and Harvard

College. In 1860, as a response to what he regarded as many false depictions of the South, Hundley wrote his own analysis of the social structure of the region in *Social Relations in Our Southern States*. He described the hospitality of Southern gentlemen as a crucial aspect of their way of life. While he conceded that the houses of the upper classes lacked some of the elegance of the homes of the wealthy in the North, Hundley insisted that the visitor to the home of a Southern gentleman would find "a much heartier welcome, a warmer shake of the hand, a greater desire to please, and less frigidity of deportment, than will be found in any walled town upon the earth's circumference." Hundley also observed that, while they lacked some of the polished manners of the upper class, middle-class folks in the South were also "extremely hospitable."[21]

As in most matters of behavior, this tradition of hospitality in the antebellum South had both limits and rules of conduct. Most hospitality was family-centered, since few agencies of any kind were available to welcome or care for visitors. The rules of hospitality to strangers in the Old South were somewhat different from the obligations to members of the family. Wayfarers who stopped for the night, for example, could be greeted with considerable suspicion, especially if they arrived unexpectedly. However, a traveler who came with a special claim to hospitality through a letter of introduction or a kinship was cordially received.[22] One who came without these but rode a good horse, wore good clothes, and had the speech of a gentleman would similarly be hospitably received by equals and inferiors. But the traveler who lacked these was likely to be received grudgingly if at all.

Widespread regional poverty meant that standards of cleanliness in homes or public accommodations were frequently not up to travelers' requirements. Even among the planter class, living quarters were uncomfortable for residents and visitors alike, with dust, heat, and insects to endure. Travelers not staying with relatives or close friends in the South were expected to pay for their lodging. Frederick Law Olmsted wrote perhaps the most extensive accounts of travels in the region before the Civil War. During his journeys, he stayed more often in private homes than in hotels but was obliged to pay for his lodging in both settings: "Only twice, in a journey of four thousand miles, made independently of public conveyances, did I receive a night's lodging or a repast from a native Southerner, without having the exact price in money which I was expected to pay for it stated to me."[23]

While paying for lodging surprised some visitors to the South, it seems to have been necessary to defray the expenses of hosts whose standards of living were not high. The practice seems to have been a widely accepted part of the rules of hospitality in the region. These rules created a relationship of obligation between the guest and host. Each was supposed to show respect for the other, and failure to do so severed the code of honor that governed the giving and receiving of hospitality. In this system of obligations surrounding the custom of hospitality in the Old South, Bertram Wyatt-Brown suggests there was an undercurrent of deep mistrust, anxiety, and personal competition.[24] For instance, hosts were often suspicious of the status of the traveler who arrived seeking hospitality. Was the visitor of at least an equal status and, therefore, entitled to receive hospitality? There was also the anxiety of worrying about the suitability of the welcome being provided. What would the guest think of the house, the accommodations, or the food? The hosts also endeavored to keep up with the level of hospitality provided by friends and neighbors. How would the house and its furnishings compare with the ones offered by those who were now guests? Wyatt-Brown says these concerns reflect three components of the Southern code of honor. First, there is a sense of graciousness to others that is part of the sense of self-worth for residents of the region. Second, hospitality is the claim of this graciousness before the public so that Southerners long to appear gracious and hospitable to others. Finally, hospitality is also the assessment of behavior by others. It is part of the reputation of the community. The great charm of the South has been the willingness to create good times with others.[25]

In 1914 an Atlanta journalist and orator of some renown, Colonel John Temple Graves, welcomed the national convention of the Shriners to the city with these words: "Every Southern city and every Southern state is joined in a new confederacy, not of arms, but of hospitality."[26] Graves's welcome to the convention delegates captured the importance of hospitality to a city that earlier had taken up arms against the United States, but now welcomed visitors to the capital of Georgia and the New South.

From Atlanta's earliest days, Southern hospitality was expressed in commercial activities designed to welcome visitors and to provide diversions for residents. This led to the development of tourism businesses as important components of the local economy. Such businesses include boardinghouses, hotels, restaurants, convention and meeting facilities, and a variety of amusements—some legal, some illegal.[27] If we use Clare Gunn's definition of tourism as encompassing *all travel* with the exception of commuting, tourism businesses exist to serve not only visitors from elsewhere but also local residents.[28] This definition does not distinguish between those who travel for business and those traveling for pleasure. It also means that tourism businesses include all tourism-related activities, such as going to a luncheon meeting or an evening of dinner and entertainment before returning home.

This book will examine several major themes entwined within the history of Atlanta. First, hospitality is firmly rooted in the culture of the South. While individuals in other regions could certainly be hospitable, this characteristic is firmly rooted in the unique history of the South, forming part of the way of life for most residents in the area. This widely shared belief in hospitality has also had a strong influence on Atlanta's history, finding commercial expression in the city's tourism businesses. Since the city's founding as a transportation center, Atlanta's tourism businesses have been a vital part of the city's growth. The hospitality extended by these businesses to visitors has helped establish and promote Atlanta as a place to visit and to do business.

The growth of Atlanta and its tourism businesses continued through the hosting of a series of expositions in the late nineteenth century. Early in the twentieth century, a combination of Atlanta's rail connections, the promotional skills of its leaders,

8

and the city's growing reputation for hospitality enabled the city to host national conventions such as the National Association of Retail Druggists in 1906, the National Association of Automobile Manufacturers in 1909, and the Shriners in 1914. Regional and state conventions were also recruited to bring their meetings to Atlanta. These expositions and conventions, as well as other efforts to boost Atlanta's economic growth, resulted from a strong partnership between the leaders of the business community and local government. This partnership has continued to encourage the growth of Atlanta in a variety of ways that have also contributed to the expansion of the city's tourism businesses. In all of these efforts, Southern hospitality remained part of the shared culture that united residents behind the process of urban growth.

Throughout Atlanta's history, hospitality has been conditioned by race, gender, ethnicity, and class. In the antebellum period, much of the labor in hotels was provided by slaves. After the Civil War, African-American men and women continued to perform most of the menial tasks of carrying baggage, cooking, and cleaning in the city's tourism businesses. Recently, Hispanic and Asian immigrants have begun to enter these hospitality business jobs. Gender also affected the types of employment available in the tourism industry. For example, men were more likely to be managers of hotels, while women more often operated boardinghouses. In the early twentieth century, black women were limited in their employment options, and 90 percent worked as maids either in hotels or in private homes.[29]

Segregation of the races by custom as well as by law led to the development of a separate set of tourism businesses to serve African Americans. After the Race Riot in 1906, these black tourism businesses were located in segregated parts of town, of which the most important was "Sweet Auburn" Avenue. Black-owned hotels, restaurants, and amusements served local residents and promoted a segregated convention business with the same enthusiasm as their white counterparts. The pattern of segregation changed as a result of the sit-ins and other demonstrations of the early 1960s and the passage of the public accommodations section of the 1964 Civil Rights Act. As a consequence of change in the relations between the races, many of the African-American tourism businesses closed after desegregation.

As we enter the twenty-first century, Atlanta is a national leader in the convention and tourism industry. Commercial application of Southern hospitality, made possible by the continued patterns of civic cooperation developed in the nineteenth century, has influenced recent events such as the Democratic National Convention in 1988 and the Super Bowl in 1994. Southern hospitality was also emphasized in the promotion and production of the most elaborate event in the city's history—the 1996 Centennial Summer Olympic Games. The Olympic Games were a "hallmark" or mega-event that required years of preparation and focused international attention on the host city.[30]

Strategies to promote growth have had significant consequences for the City of Atlanta. Not only have the tourism businesses contributed to the growth of the city, they have also provided large numbers of jobs for residents of the area. The state and local governments have aided this process by providing the infrastructure to facilitate the welcoming of visitors and the hosting of conventions by constructing amenities such as the Georgia World Congress Center and Underground Atlanta, which are considered crucial for the success of the private-sector tourism businesses. Clearly, Southern hospitality has played an important role in the growth and development of Atlanta as a major city. In this book we will examine and explore how the cultural norm of Southern hospitality and Atlanta's tourism businesses have helped the city become a metropolitan area recognized around the world as a place to visit and do business.

1

The Early Years

ATLANTA IS A RELATIVELY YOUNG CITY. It got its start only after a final treaty removed the native tribes of Creeks and Cherokees in 1825 and the state of Georgia decided to build a railroad from a point near the Chattahoochee River northward to Tennessee.[1] In 1837 the surveyors for the Western and Atlantic Railroad drove a stake in the ground to mark the end point for the rail line, and they named the place Terminus. The log cabins of pioneer settlers gave way to slab houses for the men who worked to build the rail line, and by 1842 the first two-story dwelling was built to serve as a boardinghouse for the railroad workers. The railroad company built the house and hired a man named L. V. Gannon to operate it, giving Gannon the distinction of being the first of many who would earn a living welcoming folks to the community later designated "Atlanta."[2]

Building the Gate City

Local residents disliked the name Terminus, as it connoted a "dead-end" place, and in 1843 sought incorporation as the village of Marthasville. This name was chosen to honor the daughter of the former governor, Wilson Lumpkin, who had promoted

11

the construction of the Western and Atlantic Railroad. When the first train arrived on the new line in September 1845, the three hundred or so residents of Marthasville realized that they had no hotel in which to house the railroad executives who came for the opening ceremonies. With a burst of energy that would become characteristic, they built the town's first hotel, the Washington House, which opened less than two months later. The two-story building had eight bedrooms and no baths, but advertisements boasted of "meals served in time for cars and stages."[3] By 1846 two more rail lines connected Marthasville with Macon to the south, Augusta to the east, and Chattanooga to the north.

In addition to the steady stream of railroad workers, the town attracted people arriving to buy and sell produce. This growth led to the opening of a second hotel, known as the Atlanta Hotel. Both of the new hotels were located on main streets near the rail lines.[4] The Atlanta Hotel, the more elaborate of the two, was a large brick structure built by the Georgia Railroad Company— which, no doubt, saw the importance of providing a place for weary travelers to stay.[5] In response to its competition, the Washington House was enlarged, so that both the town's hotels could accommodate 150 guests. The operator of the Washington House, H. C. Holcombe, charged his patrons $12.50 per month.[6]

Hotels of this type were as dependent upon the rail passengers as the earlier inns had been upon the horse-drawn stagecoaches. Inns were also generally smaller in size since many were converted residences. The first building in the nation constructed for use as a "hotel" contained seventy-three rooms and was built in 1794 in New York. Others followed in major cities such as Boston, Philadelphia, and Baltimore after the turn of the century. By most standards, these earliest hotels were little more than large inns. The first true modern hotel, the Tremont, opened in Boston in 1829. Its large size, distinctive architecture, and amenities for the comfort of guests set it apart from earlier lodging places.[7] Atlanta's two earliest hotels were not as luxurious as those in older Eastern cities, but they were improvements over the older stagecoach inns both in size and in the comfort provided to visitors. Both also featured dining and meeting rooms on a larger scale than was possible in smaller inns.

The railroads were the foundation on which Atlanta and its hotels were built. One of the pioneers in the study of the South's urban history, Rupert Vance, described culture as the nexus of place, work, and people.[8] For Atlanta the railroads provided the location of the town as well as employment for most of its early residents. The construction of the rail lines also brought remarkable growth to the small settlement as it expanded from a mere handful of people in 1840 to more than 2,500 residents ten years later.

The connection between the residents of Atlanta and the culture of the South was strong, as 92 percent of the town's population in 1850 were born in the region, with more than two-thirds of these from Georgia. As the railroads brought travelers to the town, the business of providing hospitality to these visitors was part of the local culture. By 1850 the census report showed that Atlanta had two boardinghouse operators and four innkeepers who managed the town's hotels. All four of these innkeepers were born in Georgia or South Carolina.[9]

The culture and traditions of the South also influenced the way visitors were welcomed to Atlanta's hotels. Hotelkeepers such as Joseph Thompson of the Atlanta Hotel and James Loyd of the Washington House both provided Southern hospitality to travelers. In addition to a cordial welcome, Thompson and Loyd utilized the South's "peculiar institution"—slavery—to operate their businesses. In 1850 they were the owners of the largest numbers of slaves in Atlanta—twenty-three and twenty-four, respectively—whom they employed to cook, clean, carry bags, shine shoes, and perform other menial hotel duties. While slaves comprised only 19 percent of the 1850 population of the city, they were an integral part of the tourism industry, as they were in cities throughout the South. Little is known of the living conditions of African-American slaves in Atlanta's hotels. Reports from other Southern cities indicate that, at best, slaves were given such small spaces as "boot rooms" where they generally slept in their clothing. The status of slaves in hotels and boardinghouses was so low that they were typically not provided with either beds or bedding. Many slept in hallways, where they could be kicked or tread upon with impunity.[10]

Slavery and the railroads were not the only determinants of Atlanta's culture. The town was also a part of a region dominated by agriculture. Although the soil on which Atlanta was located was mostly clay and considered too poor to produce abundant crops, it was on the border between the cotton belt of the state and the heavily forested and mineral-rich area of north Georgia. As the forests were cleared for farms, the land to the north of Atlanta produced food and grain. Hence both cotton and food products found their way to Atlanta for shipment on the railroads to markets elsewhere. Most of these cotton bales were shipped to the North, where textile mills turned the cotton into cloth and finished goods. Some of the manufactured products were then returned to the South by rail for distribution in the region. This pattern gave the South a colonial economy, retarding economic development and limiting the growth of its cities. As Southern leaders increasingly recognized their region's colonial position, many grasped at schemes to stimulate growth and, hence, lessen dependency.[11]

Efforts to promote Atlanta and its growth prompted a group of citizens to approach the Southern Central Agricultural Society to hold its 1850 fair in the town. Previous agricultural fairs had been held in the nearby village of Stone Mountain, including the 1849 fair highlighted by the appearance of P. T. Barnum's traveling show. Capturing the 1850 fair required a high degree of cooperation among residents, businessmen, and city officials. The Atlanta City Council, for example, formed a special committee to raise the application fee of $1,000, and businessmen joined with others in the community to amass the funds. Business leaders also set aside ten acres of land at the edge of town for the use of the Southern Central Agricultural Society "so long as the association should continue to hold their annual meetings in the city of Atlanta."[12]

Agricultural fairs such as these were traditionally held in late summer at the end of the harvest season. This schedule provided farmers an opportunity to display their best produce and livestock as well as farm machinery and craftwork. Fair promoters hoped that Atlanta's railroad connections would enable people to come from neighboring states. As a promotional handbill stated, "the facilities of getting to this central point [Atlanta] induce us to invite, and to expect the presence and contributions of many of our fellow citizens of Carolina, Alabama, Tennessee, and Florida."[13] Evidence indicates that the predictions of the promoters were not fulfilled, however. The list of prize winners, for example, suggests that most were from the immediate area. Perhaps even more telling is the fact that in the following year the society held its fair in Macon. Despite these failures, the staging of the fair was a significant event for Atlanta because it represented one of the first large-scale cooperative efforts between business and political leaders to promote the city.

By the early 1850s, Atlanta was the center of a network of rail lines that connected south and east to the Gulf and Atlantic coasts as well as north and westward to the Ohio Valley. In a region with few railroads, the strategic intersection of so many lines gave Atlanta the basis for rapid population growth. By 1854 there were more than 6,000 residents in a town bustling with sixty stores engaged in wholesale and retail trade.[14]

By 1857 it was possible for connections to be made to move goods by rail all the way from Memphis to Charleston, and many Atlanta businessmen and residents were concerned that the rail lines would enable commerce simply to pass through the young town on its way elsewhere. A party of Memphis businessmen decided to celebrate the Memphis-to-Charleston connection by bringing Mississippi Valley produce and a barrel of water from the river to Charleston. When the group arrived in Atlanta, they were given such a gracious welcome that the mayor was invited to continue to Charleston as part of the celebration. Once they arrived, an elegant banquet was prepared with many toasts offered to the future prosperity of Memphis and Charleston. Near the end of the evening someone also proposed a toast to Atlanta in which he described Atlanta as "The Gate City: The only tribute she levies is the affection and gratitude of those who partake of her unbounded hospitality."[15] Local leaders were so enamored with the description of Atlanta as the "Gate City of the South" that they used this slogan well into the next century as they promoted both the city's railroad connections and its reputation for hospitality.[16]

With its increasing importance as a commercial center, Atlanta continued its rapid growth. By the time of the 1860 census, the population had reached 9,000. With this growth came new hotels as the older Washington House and Atlanta Hotel were joined by the City Hotel, the Planter's Hotel, the Tennessee House, and the Trout House. In addition to lodging, the growing young town had other types of tourism businesses such as saloons and brothels, which according to the 1860 census employed twenty-three barkeepers and forty-nine prostitutes to serve the needs of travelers and residents.[17]

These census data serve as a reminder that Atlanta was still much like a frontier town in those days. The livelihood of the town depended upon the railroads to bring the increasing flow of both people and goods. People residing in the rural areas came to town to buy and sell and were met by local merchants as well as by travelers. The visitor stepping from the train was never more than a block from the hotels, which were built along the main streets adjacent to the tracks. Poor-quality rails and track-laying techniques made early train travel an adventure. And walking about the streets of Atlanta presented its own hazards as well, especially after rain turned the dusty red clay of the un-paved streets to mud.

Many of those who traveled to Atlanta did not stay in the hotels or boardinghouses. The farmers of north Georgia and the state's Piedmont region brought their produce to town in covered wagons drawn by oxen or mules. Coming from as far away as 150 miles to buy and sell in the young town, they often slept under their wagons in one of several wagon yards located in the town. Many brought cotton, but others carried foodstuffs which were bought by local residents as well as by the growing number of Atlanta's wholesale merchants. The farmers helped local commerce by purchasing goods from retail stores and took advantage of the saloons and other hospitality businesses established for their amusement.

The visits to town by these farm people often ended in drunken and disorderly behavior. As a result, the city council passed an ordinance requiring the owners of each wagon yard to post a sign on their gate saying "Drunkenness, violence, and indecent or obscene language forbidden, under the penalty of not exceeding one hundred dollars' fine, or not exceeding thirty days imprisonment, or both." The town marshal and his deputies were also required to supervise the wagon yards at ten o'clock each night to enforce the ordinance and arrest anyone guilty of breaking it.[18] Hence although the railroads connected to distant cities, the constant flow of people in the wagon trade into and out of town kept Atlanta firmly rooted in the economy and culture of the rural South.

As is the case with most crossroads towns, the travelers who came to Atlanta were a diverse lot. While most came on business related to the production of cotton or other agricultural commodities, others were salesmen who served the town's steadily growing retail and wholesale trade. Some guests were also political dignitaries, such as Senator John C. Calhoun of South Carolina, who predicted future greatness for the small community, and former president Millard Fillmore, who was entertained at the Atlanta Hotel in 1854.[19] One early historian noted that, along with decent folks, Atlanta also attracted "a liberal sprinkling of desperate characters, ever hunting opportunities to better their fortunes by playing upon the ignorance and passions of men."[20] This diversity of immigrants gave the place a widespread reputation as "wild and wooly." Among those who inspired this reputation was a widely renowned actor from Rome, Georgia, who came to Atlanta to perform in 1858. Reacting to what he saw as an insult while drinking in the bar of the Atlanta Hotel the night before, the tragedian awoke with a hangover and a pistol. He walked into the street, addressed his antagonist, and fired twice. The first shot missed, but the careful aim of the second resulted in the death of the local bailiff. Although found guilty of the crime, the tragedian was released shortly thereafter since he was, after all, under the influence at the time of the shooting.[21]

This type of reaction to insult, especially after drinking, was part of a pattern of violence in Southern culture that has been described by numerous scholars. While Southern men could be described as gracious and hospitable, they could also be touchy and belligerent. This pattern of behavior was based on a code of honor that included the mannerliness usually described as part of Southern hospitality. Historian Edward Ayers observes that in the antebellum period Southern honor produced an overween-ing concern with the opinions of others which led people to pay particular attention to manners and to ritualized evidence of respect. When that respect was not forthcoming, violence was often the result. Thus, the culture of honor in the South pro-duced extremes of behavior for which the region became equally well known—hospitality and violence.[22]

The Civil War

The Civil War, perhaps more than any other event, changed the town of Atlanta. The year before hostilities broke out, there was great uncertainty over the potential effects of the Southern states' leaving the Union. Besides defending slavery and states' rights, many Atlantans thought that independence from the North would enable the South to become more economically self-sufficient. Southern states could, after all, trade among them-selves as well as increase commercial relations with Europe. Mer-chants and others recognized the dependence of Atlanta upon trade with Northern wholesale merchants and the potential im-pact of being isolated from these relationships. However, when the matter of secession was put to a vote early in 1861, a majority of the county's residents favored leaving the Union.

In the beginning, the war seemed distant. Young men marched off to fight, women pledged their support, and the town pros-pered. Between the census of 1860 and the evacuation of Atlanta in 1864, the population more than doubled, to over 22,000. The strategic location as well as the rail lines made Atlanta a logical choice to serve as both a manufacturing center for war materials and a supply depot. When the work of manufacturing was added to the commercial base already in existence, Atlanta grew explosively. There was a great deal of money to be made producing goods for the Confederate army in addition to the existing economic base of the community.

The hustle and bustle produced by the war was at first good for Atlanta's hotels. The expanding economic activity filled rooms and restaurants, and the city attracted Confederate dignitaries such as Vice President Alexander Stephens and President Jefferson Davis, who stayed at the Trout House in 1861.[23] Later that year, Atlanta also hosted a convention of bankers from throughout the Confederate states.[24] Business and political leaders did not fail to recognize the growth taking place in the city. Before the capital city of the Confederacy was chosen, Atlanta issued its bid: "This city has good railroad connections, is free from yellow fever, can supply the most wholesome foods, and as for 'goobers' [boiled peanuts], an indispensable article for a Southern Legislator, we have them all the time."[25] At the time, however, the reach of the town's leaders exceeded their grasp, and Richmond became the Confederate capital instead.

As the conflict intensified, travel restrictions were imposed, and in 1862 Atlanta was placed under martial law. On August 12, a special order by the provost marshal required hotel and boardinghouse keepers to lodge only those travelers who could produce a permit for their visit. The order further required a daily list of all visitors carrying permits to be turned in to the military authorities.[26] Commercial travel was dramatically reduced under these restrictions, and a further blow to the hotels came when several were converted into hospitals for the wounded soldiers brought to Atlanta by the railroads.[27]

Chattanooga, Tennessee, fell to Federal troops, and by the fall of 1863 General William T. Sherman's army stood poised and ready to invade Georgia, heading south toward Atlanta. The city's strategic importance as a rail center and supply depot made it a natural military objective. Sherman followed the route of the

Western and Atlantic Railroad south from Chattanooga. Confederate defenders fought a series of delaying battles through the mountains of north Georgia, but each time they were forced to retreat and avoid capture as Sherman and his army continued southward in a series of strategic flanking maneuvers. As Sherman's army approached, preparations for the defense of Atlanta began with the construction of fortifications dug around the perimeter of the town by slave labor. In July 1864 Sherman arrayed his troops in front of these fortifications and the Battle of Atlanta began.

The Federals began flanking movements to the east and west sides of Atlanta in order to cut off its railroad connections. Throughout August the Union forces shelled the city, causing many residents to abandon their homes and leave town. After this siege failed to accomplish its objective, Sherman moved troops south of the town, cutting off the rail lines and forcing the Rebel commander, General John B. Hood, to evacuate Atlanta on September 1. Before leaving, the Confederates destroyed all the ammunition and military stores to keep them from falling into enemy hands. This caused some of the destruction later attributed to General Sherman. The mayor and a group of citizens rode out to meet the oncoming Federal troops on the morning of September 2, and Atlanta formally surrendered.

Sherman ordered all citizens of Atlanta to leave as he rested his army before moving across Georgia to Savannah. He left Atlanta in mid-November 1864, after ordering the destruction of anything that could be of military value to the Confederates. The resulting fire destroyed all the railroad buildings and equipment, manufacturing facilities, and warehouses. The fire also consumed most of downtown Atlanta, including all of the hotels except one.

Reconstruction

Following General Lee's surrender in 1865, the era of Reconstruction began. Confederate soldiers headed for home, while

Federal troops moved into major towns to begin restoring Union control over the South. Atlanta became the administrative and military headquarters for Georgia and, as a result, was quickly reoccupied by the Federal army. Atlantans, glad the fighting was over and eager to return to their businesses, began their city's restoration. The railroads were quickly put into operation again, and construction began on new hotels, boardinghouses, restaurants, and saloons. The old Planter's Hotel reopened in 1865 as the American Hotel. During the war, the three-story brick building had been used as a hospital by both armies and was the only hotel spared from destruction.[28] By 1866 newspaper ads indicated that the American Hotel had competition from the National Hotel and the Calhoun House.[29] Names like "American" and "National" indicate how much the local citizens wanted to demonstrate their loyalty to the United States.

A special municipal census in 1867 indicated a total of 20,288 persons resided in Atlanta—a number equal to the city's peak population during the war.[30] Atlanta now boasted nineteen businesses open to lodge the weary travelers. Of this number, fifteen were boardinghouses and four were hotels. There were, in addition, three restaurants and three "eating saloons." As Atlanta rebuilt there were numerous makeshift arrangements, such as the Opera House Saloon Restaurant and Barber Shop located in the basement of the post office.[31] Popular amusements of the day included the performances of traveling theater groups, baseball games in the park, and shows at the opera house (next door to the post office).

Atlanta was one of several inland railroad cities in the South that rebuilt quickly following the war. The older port cities, such as Charleston, Mobile, and New Orleans, were much slower to recover from the effects of the war and the increased use of the rail lines to market cotton through the inland cities. The way of life for the people of these inland cities was shaped by the combination of their location, their ties to the railroads, their role in the transport of agricultural commodities, and the flow of migrants from nearby small towns and rural areas. Atlanta shared this common Southern culture with places like Memphis and

Montgomery as these cities grew in importance and size during the postwar years.

The inland cities of the South were affected by the region's culture in other ways as well. The Southern economy relied upon staple crop agriculture and the continued dependence of the region on the North.[32] The production of cotton and tobacco did not encourage the growth of large cities in the region, and the antebellum plantation system did not even promote the development of small towns. Northern capital was needed to finance the crops, and the small towns that did exist in the South largely served as collection points for the staple crops, which were then shipped to the North for manufacture into finished goods.[33] The breakup of the plantation system after the Civil War and the increased number of smaller farm landholdings created hundreds of rural communities and towns in the South. But the size of these communities was severely limited by the production and marketing system of the cotton belt.[34]

Atlanta's rail lines made it a major transshipment point for cotton and a distribution center for Northern manufactured goods needed to supply the increasing number of small country stores in the region. Many of these small towns were stops along the railroads, whereas other country stores had to be visited by salesmen traveling along dirt roads by horse and buggy. Atlanta's railroads carried the cotton bales to distant markets and returned with produce and manufactured products to be sold to the country merchants. Agents and drummers crowded into Atlanta's hotels at night before taking off the next day to supply the country stores of the area. Livery stables did a brisk business supplying rigs to the salesmen who faced the hardship of roads that always seemed to be either dusty or muddy.

While many Southern historians have described the harshness of political and economic conditions imposed upon the South following the end of the war, the Reconstruction period was actually beneficial to Atlanta. The presence of Union soldiers boosted the local economy, and when the new Georgia state constitution was ratified in 1868, Atlanta became the state capital. This event increased the political importance of the town and brought additional outside attention. Within other Georgia towns there was considerable resentment toward the upstart city. The residents of Milledgeville felt the capital had been stolen from their town and suggested Atlanta would be an ideal location for the state's penitentiary since "it is an institution that will not come amiss to many of her population."[35]

In the North, many saw the conditions after the war, recognized the economic opportunities, and packed their belongings in carpet suitcases to move South. Atlanta attracted more than its share of these "carpetbaggers," and one of them was to have a lasting influence on the tourism business in the young city. Born and raised in New England, Hannibal I. Kimball came to Atlanta in 1867 as the Southern agent of a Chicago company that produced railroad sleeper cars. He quickly established a close relationship with Rufus Bullock, the Reconstruction-era Republican governor of the state. Using his political connections, Kimball convinced the state legislature to finance his purchase of an unfinished opera house so that he could complete the construction, after which the state could rent the building from him for use as its new capitol. This complicated (and probably illegal) scheme worked, and Georgia received a capitol building which it occupied for more than twenty years.[36]

Amid all the bustling activity of Atlanta in the Reconstruction era, Kimball saw additional opportunities for profit. Using highly leveraged financing, he purchased the old Atlanta Hotel, tore it down, and built a structure that was to become an ornament to the community. The day after the Kimball House Hotel opened for business in October 1870, the *Constitution* carried the following front-page story:

> We do not exaggerate when we say that this is an era in Atlanta's history. It marks saliently her city maturity. The cursory thinker does not properly estimate the significance of such an improvement in a growing place, nor its value to the place. It requires large capital to erect such a structure, and large capital fails to seek such an investment unless encouraged by the prospect of large travel and the certainty of a bright future for

the city. An investment like this, therefore, is a brilliant augury of our assured development and commercial importance. It means that the swaddling clothes are cast off, and the place is booked among the capitalists and business men for a steady journey in the direction of metropolitan importance.

While its effect is thus upon the world, its influence reacts at home. It adds to the value of city property and it encourages investment. It draws travel. People will pass through cities to stop at fine hotels. In the selection of routes, the choice is given to those that pass through places having the finest hotel facilities.

About Kimball himself the normally Democratic newspaper added: "A man who projects and carries through such an enterprise as this magnificent hotel in a city, at such a stage in its growth as this is in the history of Atlanta, is a public benefactor, and whatever private returns he may reap, the thanks of his fellow-citizens are due to him for contributing to their private and general interests."[37]

The Kimball House towered six stories above Atlanta and was the city's tallest building. It boasted the town's first steam elevator, as well as 307 rooms and lavish furnishings. John S. Wilson, the author of what may be Atlanta's first history, provided nine pages of detail about the interior of the Kimball House, describing everything from the amount of coal stored in the basement to the decorations in the bridal suite. The hotel was proud of the fact that in its basement laundry—a "wonder of art and invention"—a garment could be washed, dried, and ironed in fifteen minutes. A traveler could count on almost any need being satisfied in the hotel, as there were also sixteen businesses leasing space in the building, including a Turkish bath "for the comfort and restoration of invalids who may desire to avail themselves of the advantages of Atlanta as a health resort."[38] Although a physician, Wilson wrote his history in order to promote the advantages of Atlanta as a place to do business and to enjoy healthful amenities (such as the baths he operated in the Kimball House).

Gender played a significant role in the patronage of Atlanta's tourism businesses. Most of the patrons of grand hotels such as the Kimball House were white males. The hotel served as a home away from home for politicians, judges, cotton brokers, bankers, lawyers, and other businessmen and professionals. Smaller, less expensive hotels catered to the commercial travelers who rode the trains with their suitcases and trunks of sample wares. These traveling salesmen—known as "drummers" because they were always trying to drum up business for their firms—were the mainstays of commercial hotels in cities like Atlanta.[39] Public hostelries and restaurants were generally male domains, with black male employees serving male patrons. Middle- and upper-class white women rarely traveled alone, stayed at hotels, or dined out. When they did, hotels maintained separate "ladies parlors," and restaurants set aside special rooms for women. Only one of the city's restaurants—Allen's Palace Restaurant—advertised itself as a place for ladies to dine, setting aside one of its several dining rooms as a "Ladies' Dining Room and Ice Cream Saloon." The Kimball House provided a ladies' parlor with a private entrance and a small reception room located on the second floor, away from the billiard and bar rooms of the first floor. Women alone or meeting other women could avoid these male entertainments as well as the rough-and-tumble masculine public domain.[40]

Atlanta's promoters could take pride in the growth of the town. The 1870 U.S. census reported almost 22,000 residents (see Table 1.1). The livelihood of many of these citizens depended upon the business of providing hospitality. The city di-

Table 1.1. Atlanta's Population and
Hospitality Business Growth, 1850–1880

Date	Population	Hotels	Boardinghouses
1850	2,572	2	2
1860	9,554	6	14
1870	21,789	5	41
1880	37,409	8	62

Source: U.S. Bureau of the Census and City Directory Collection, Atlanta History Center.

rectory published the following year noted that Atlanta had five hotels, forty-one boardinghouses, ten restaurants, and forty-one saloons.[41] Then, as now, it is difficult to know precisely how many of these establishments served the traveling public rather than local patrons and how many people these businesses employed as clerks, waiters, housekeepers, bartenders, and so on. National-level occupation statistics from the 1870 census indicate that restaurant keepers, hostlers, hotelkeepers, clerks, and saloonkeepers were mostly male, while a majority (55 percent) of boarding-house keepers and many other hotel and restaurant employees (27 percent) were female. In Atlanta, 83 percent of boarding-house operators were female.[42]

This means that while employment opportunities for women in 1870 were generally quite limited in Atlanta, the hospitality business was one area that was open to them. However, within the businesses that provided hospitality, there was a rigid division of labor based on gender and race. The boardinghouses and smaller hotels provided the only significant opportunities for women as business owners in the hospitality industry. There are indications, however, that many of these women were widows for whom the economic necessity of providing for themselves and their families meant taking in boarders after the death of a spouse. Emma Bell, for example, was widowed at age twenty-four and left with two children. In 1878 she opened the Bell House, a boardinghouse for men. Mrs. Bell was strict in screening her prospective boarders but offered them comfortable rooms and excellent food. Her establishment was more successful than most, providing a home for "Bell House Boys" for many years after her death.[43]

As the number of boardinghouses grew, the owners would generally hire black female employees to work as cooks and servants and black men to serve as porters and waiters. During this period, many of the African-American employees resided in the boardinghouses, receiving their lodging and board as part of their pay. These types of service jobs as cooks and cleaners in hospitality businesses and as maids in the homes of wealthy whites were the only jobs available to most black women.[44]

A large hotel such as the Kimball House was a virtual village of employees, most of whom lived on the premises. The largest group of employees was the fifty-five African-American men who worked as waiters (twenty-five), bellhops (eight), and kitchen helpers (twenty-two). These men served the mostly white male customers in the public areas of the hotel and were required to wear uniforms to set them apart from the managers and male patrons. Also residing in the hotel were fifteen white men employed as proprietor, manager, bookkeeper, various clerks, engineer, cooks, baker, and barkeeper. They served in office capacities and in other roles required for the operation of the hotel. Only a few African-American women—eight laundresses and six chambermaids—lived in the Kimball House. The women who worked in the laundry spent their days and nights below ground in the heat of the basement. Like the few chambermaids who lived in the hotel, they had to be on call at all times to respond to customers' needs. The maids were available to answer the bell and clean a room, and the laundresses were expected to provide prompt attention to the guests' apparel. The three or four dozen other maids required to clean the Kimball House were able to live elsewhere. The jobs of the black women in Atlanta's hotels kept them generally out of sight "behind doors and below floors."[45]

The African-American men and women who worked in Atlanta's hospitality businesses were part of a growing black population in the city. In both 1850 and 1860, census reports showed that 20 percent of Atlanta's population were slaves, and there were fewer than twenty-five "free persons of color." Freedom from slavery, exploitation by former owners, and violence in rural areas made Atlanta an attractive destination for many African Americans. The city also offered the possibility of economic advancement as well as the attraction of being with others.[46] In 1870 the city's black population swelled to 46 percent of the total, causing considerable concern among whites whose notions of racial superiority had earlier been enforced by the patterns of a slave society.[47] The presence of Federal troops helped to maintain order, as did restrictive city ordinances that established a curfew and punished vagrants.

After 1870, threats of violence from the Ku Klux Klan and a variety of other measures were used to keep blacks "in their place" within a new pattern of social relations in Southern cities like Atlanta.[48] By 1873, African Americans in cities throughout the South were increasingly segregated into separate galleries in theaters, waiting rooms in railroad stations, and second-class or smoking cars on the trains. They were also excluded from the leading hotels, restaurants, and bars, having to stay in boarding-houses while eating and drinking only in places that served blacks. This rigid segregation created a separate world for blacks and whites in Atlanta.[49] The result was the development of a set of black tourism businesses that would remain separate and segregated from their white counterparts until the 1960s.

Boosterism

One of the traits of Southern culture that Atlanta shared with other cities in the region was its boosterism. A concern with growth—and the promotion of the city to encourage that growth—became one of Atlanta's most enduring characteristics. While cities throughout the United States engaged in promotional activities, Southern urban boosters carried the practice to extremes. Several explanations have been offered for the exaggerated boosterism of Southern cities like Atlanta. Historian Gaines Foster suggests that it resulted from a sense of regional inferiority from the scars of defeat in the years after the Civil War.[50] David Goldfield suggests that the boosterism and growth ethic of Southern cities resulted as a response to the region's "colonial" economy, since the region was dependent upon the North for the processing of agricultural products as well as for credit and commerce.[51]

Beginning in 1870, Atlanta's business leaders attempted to overcome this economic dependence and sense of inferiority by forming several organizations to promote the city. One of these was the Georgia State Agricultural Association, which held annual fairs to promote agriculture in the state. Compared to later events, these agricultural fairs were modest in scale, appealing to area farmers with displays of agricultural products and machinery.[52] They were held on land north of town that was owned by the Western and Atlantic Railroad, and the railroad provided special trains running to the fairgrounds at Oglethorpe Park. Over 20,000 people attended the fair on Saturday, October 21, 1870. This turnout was considered quite successful, as it was nearly equal to Atlanta's population at the time.[53] These annual events provided a rehearsal for later events designed to attract the attention of a much wider audience.

Another promotional group formed in 1871 was the Chamber of Commerce, replacing an earlier Board of Trade that had a more limited membership and function. The new chamber attempted to unite the diverse and often competing interests of the business community behind the pursuit of growth. Few questioned the belief that bigger was better and that the faster a city grew, the more successful its promoters would be. Business leaders and the elected public officials who represented them viewed the city itself as a "growth machine," with each citizen and component contributing to the pursuit of expansion.[54] The Chamber of Commerce served as the organizational voice of the business community.

Atlanta's promoters never seemed to tire of their activities. Residents of other cities in Georgia were less patient with Atlanta's boosterism, with one writer claiming, "If Atlanta could suck as hard as it blows, it would be a seaport."[55] Despite this deficiency, Atlanta's boosters seldom missed an opportunity to promote their city. For example, as an inland city Atlanta never received large numbers of immigrants from overseas. In 1870 only 5 percent of the population were foreign-born. Among these were six hundred Jewish residents, most of them from Germany. Their presence in Atlanta prompted the *Daily Herald* to boast, "We congratulate ourselves because nothing is so indicative of a city's prosperity as to see an influx of Jews who come with the intention of living among you."[56] As there were relatively few Jews in the South and many of these had lived in places like Atlanta since its earliest days, there tended to be less hostility generated by the gentile majority than in other regions of the country. There were also other groups who were much more likely to be subjected to prejudice, such as African Americans.[57] Throughout the remainder of the nineteenth century, Atlanta remained relatively free of anti-Semitism.[58]

Boosterism took a variety of forms. The city advertised itself in the 1870s not only as a place to do business but also as an interesting place to visit. Healthful springs of water were found nearby at Lithia Springs and Ponce de Leon Springs, both of which became resort stops for visitors and residents who took early versions of the street railway for excursions to the mineral springs. In an era when little was known about the causes and treatment of disease, mineral baths at such resorts were highly regarded for their curative properties. Springs located in cooler, more temperate areas at higher elevations than the coastal or river towns became the first resorts in the South. Patients and those simply wishing to escape the heat and waterborne diseases of low-lying cities flocked to the hotels built in these locations. The hotels in places like Lithia Springs remained popular attractions through the first three decades of the twentieth century.[59] Man-made attractions also beckoned travelers to enjoy their stay in Atlanta. For example, beginning in 1873 and continuing for the next nine years, Atlanta held its version of Mardi Gras with parades and balls for the enjoyment of both residents and visitors.[60]

The promotion of growth for Atlanta naturally had a positive impact on the tourism business. Attracting people to the city not only filled rooms and restaurants but also spurred the development of new hotels and saloons. In the fall of 1875 the *Constitution* reported the opening of the "acme of elegance," the Big Bonanza Saloon, located near the Kimball House. From its white marble bar, its hand-woven rug with the name "Big Bonanza" emblazoned on it, and the solid silver bar paraphernalia, the saloon was a source of pride for the tourism business and a major attraction to travelers.[61] In November the Kimball House received new competition with the opening of the Markham House Hotel. The owner put down a rock crossing to the train depot in order for guests to avoid the muddy street. Constructed of brick, the Markham House boasted that all but two of its 107 rooms would be filled with sunshine. These two dark rooms, it was announced, "are adapted for railroad men and the night clerks who sleep in the daytime."[62] Although smaller and somewhat less opulent than the Kimball House, the Markham House was regarded by contemporaries as one of the two best hotels which Atlanta had to welcome visitors.[63] The Markham House elegantly hosted the visit of President Rutherford Hayes to Atlanta in 1877.[64]

The opulence of the city's major hotels was a main selling point in the promotional efforts of local boosters. Just as Atlanta's first "history," by John S. Wilson, had extolled the Kimball House, E. Y. Clarke's *Illustrated History of Atlanta* included drawings of the two most important hotels in the city as an inducement to travelers. Clarke, a local journalist who briefly owned the *Constitution* as well as another local newspaper, also described Atlanta's transportation advantages, its commerce, manufacturing, government, and even churches as part of his promotion of the city. The book was popular when it appeared in 1877, going through three printings by 1881. Clarke's description of the city emphasized its advantages both as a place to live and as a site for business. Regarding the local population, Clarke observed, "A nervous energy permeates all classes of the people and all departments of trade, and the spirit of enterprise never sleeps."[65]

Boosterism of this sort was evidently successful in attracting attention and people to the young city. As one local journalist expressed it, Atlanta's phoenix-like rise from its own ashes gave the city "a great name in . . . [Georgia] and the neighboring states" which lured "every man, young or old, who had $100 or more to invest . . . [like] the pilgrims to Mecca or Jerusalem."[66] By 1880 the U.S. Census recorded a population of 37,409 residents in Atlanta, a growth of nearly 16,000 from the previous enumeration. Most of these new Atlantans were from the South, with 91 percent of the city's residents born in the eleven Confederate states, while just over 5 percent came from the North and less than 4 percent were born overseas.[67] The effects of this growth were reflected in the city's tourism businesses. The city directory for 1881 indicated that eight hotels, sixty-two boardinghouses, twenty-one restaurants, and sixty-six saloons were available to offer Southern hospitality to visitors and residents.[68]

The 1881 International Cotton Exposition

Atlantans faced new challenges in the 1880s. During the past ten years the city had hosted the small state agricultural fairs, but now business leaders moved toward a more impressive scale by hosting the South's first world's fair, the 1881 International Cotton Exposition. This event was to have an impact, not only on Atlanta but also on the entire region. The idea of a cotton exposition came from Boston industrialist Edward Atkinson, whose objective was to hold a fair to demonstrate to Southern farmers how they could improve their methods of cultivating, ginning, and baling cotton. This would make the crop better suited for the manufacture of cloth in Northern mills.[69] Older and larger cities in the South wanted to host the gathering, but Henry W. Grady, managing editor of the *Constitution,* urged Atlanta's business leaders to rally behind efforts to bring the event to the city. Local businessmen changed the purpose of the fair to promote Southern textile manufacturing. Their goal was to use the exposition to make Atlanta into an industrial center that would be known as the "Manchester of America."[70]

Earnest preparations for the event did not begin until February 1881, when the International and Cotton States Exposition Association incorporated a joint stock company to finance and plan the fair. The company selected the energetic H. I. Kimball to be the "Director-General" of the exposition. With only eight months before the scheduled opening, much remained to be done. With his business connections in the North, Kimball conducted a whirlwind fund-raising tour in March that carried him to major cities from Boston to Cincinnati.[71]

Although Atlanta's 1880 population was just over 37,000, exposition organizers anticipated that the event would attract 200,000 to 300,000 people. It would be quite a challenge for the community and its business leaders to host this many people.

With his typical energy, Kimball set up a system of departments with a variety of functions, such as Transportation, Construction, and Protection as well as "Public Comfort." The chief of the Department of Public Comfort was responsible for providing food, lodging, and information for the convenience of visitors to the exposition. The department opened a "bureau of private entertainment and information" near the central train depot and a branch office on the grounds. The organizers also canvassed the city to determine the availability and price of rooms, lodgings, meals, and board. The report indicated over 3,000 rooms in Atlanta, with accommodations for 5,000 guests daily. Prices ranged from $2 to $5 per day for rooms at the luxury hotels such as the Kimball House and the Markham House, to 50 cents to $1 a day (including meals) at some of the boardinghouses.[72]

Still feeling that this number of guest rooms was inadequate to house the 20,000 to 30,000 per day he expected, Kimball directed the building of an Exposition Hotel on the fairgrounds. This hotel would accommodate 1,000 guests in 300 rooms at a charge of $2.50 per day. Its presence was also expected to prevent the others from charging exorbitant rates during the exposition. If there were still not enough rooms, the directors planned to house military organizations and large groups in tents near the exposition grounds. Kimball also prepared a list of individual citizens who agreed to open their homes to visitors.[73] While Kimball called on Atlanta residents to help welcome the exhibition's guests to the community, Atlanta's mayor requested that the townspeople tidy up sidewalks and improve the looks of the city in order to give a favorable impression to visitors.[74]

The International Cotton Exposition opened with a great deal of fanfare at Oglethorpe Park on October 5, 1881, even though many of the exhibits were not completed until several weeks later. Promoters and exhibitors worried about the slim crowds who came during the early weeks of the exposition. Their concern turned to alarm when, by the end of October, the average daily attendance showed little signs of increasing. Finally, after a series of meetings, the railroad companies agreed to establish special excursion fares of one cent per mile in order to attract a greater audience. This must have helped, as the average daily paid attendance climbed from 844 in October to 2,686 in November and 3,936 in December.[75]

Although the gate receipts were much less than anticipated, the exposition received widespread publicity from events such as Governors Day. On this day, cotton growing in a field on the exhibition grounds was picked and ginned shortly after sunrise. Next, the cotton was carded, spun, woven, and dyed in order to make two suits worn by the governors of Georgia and Connecticut to an evening reception.[76] These demonstrations of high technology were impressive to viewers of the fair and to the reporters who publicized the events in newspapers and magazines across the country. The managers of the exposition were willing to lose money on the event if its publicity would attract capital and immigrants to the South.[77]

The fair never generated the overwhelming crowds of visitors its promoters anticipated. The tent city was quickly abandoned, and the Exposition Hotel, though it may have kept prices down at other establishments, was declared "financially unprofitable."[78] But the impact of the International Cotton Exposition of 1881 was far more significant than the immediate returns on the investment in the fair itself would suggest. What was really presented for all to see was the "Atlanta Spirit," the ability of business leaders to organize an event to promote the city. This display of collective entrepreneurship underscored the progress made by the city since the war as well as its eager acceptance of Northern investment. Even old enemies like General Sherman were invited to speak at the exposition to demonstrate that sectional conflict was past and that the South could look forward to a new era.[79] The "New South" that Henry Grady and others promoted was a region open for investment and a people eager to assume jobs in factories instead of traditional agricultural work. Atlanta was also ready to take its place as a regional center of commerce, industry, and transportation in the New South.

In the first six months after the event, approximately $2 million was invested in manufacturing activities in Atlanta. The main building of the fair was converted into the Exposition Cotton Mill, which contained 16,000 spindles and employed 500 people who were housed temporarily in the Exposition Hotel. Northern investors also established several other manufacturing facilities in the city. In addition, the value of real estate in Atlanta rose from $16.2 million in 1882 to $41.5 million in 1893.[80]

Although the exposition returned only $20,000 to its organizers, many of Atlanta's merchants reported huge profits during the three months of the event.[81] The hotels, boardinghouses, restaurants, saloons, and livery stables also benefited from the presence of visitors and reporters. Prominent investors were wined and dined as they were introduced to Atlanta's business leadership. Local boosters such as H. I. Kimball regarded the successful staging of the 1881 exposition as the most important event in postwar Atlanta's history. The exposition launched the New South movement, both as a publicity crusade and as a campaign for economic development, and it placed Atlanta at the vanguard of that movement. Other similar expositions would follow, but according to historian Don Doyle, "it was the Atlanta show of 1881 that established the style and defined the meaning of these New South extravaganzas."[82]

It was no accident that the leadership for the exposition came from one of the city's largest boosters, H. I. Kimball, who was also a major figure in Atlanta's tourism business. More than anyone, Kimball recognized the importance of promoting the city as a place to come and do business. Kimball received praise and recognition throughout the country for his leadership of the exposition and was consulted on many of the other major American fairs, including Chicago's 1893 Columbian Exposition. General Sherman wrote to Kimball, saying that the Atlanta exposition "is your victory." The city's largest cotton broker, Samuel Inman, declared that Kimball was the "one man who, from the first, comprehended the true scope and magnitude of the Exposition."[83] The *Constitution* summed up its praise by saying, "Of all the enterprises Mr. Kimball has undertaken and consummated for Atlanta, as important as they are, none have equaled this in magnitude, in importance, or in its beneficent and far-reaching result."[84]

During the last two decades of the nineteenth century, Atlantans positioned themselves at the center of the New South movement. The city's leaders had a vision that included growth and prosperity based on industry, commerce, and tourism.

2

The New South Era, 1880–1900

AS THE ANTEBELLUM SOUTH WAS CHARACTERIZED by plantations and a rural way of life, the New South era following the Civil War was based in cities, and Atlanta was one of its hubs. Perhaps the major force propelling Atlanta to the forefront in the New South movement was Henry W. Grady, the managing editor of one of the city's leading newspapers, the *Constitution*. Grady not only wrote extensively about a new era for the region but also spoke with eloquence to audiences throughout the country to draw attention to Atlanta and the South. There were four major points to his message about the New South. First, he wanted to industrialize the South, providing factory jobs for those who wanted them. Second, this program of industrialization depended on investment from the North, so Grady actively promoted reconciliation between the sections of the nation. Third, Grady hoped to see improvement in the conditions of Southern agriculture to bring more prosperity to farmers. His recommendations for farmers included diversification of crops and less dependence on commercial fertilizer. Finally, although he believed in white supremacy and segregation, Grady realized that a form of "cooperation" between the races was needed for Southern economic progress.[1]

Throughout the 1880s, Grady worked tirelessly to advance these ideas and to promote Atlanta as the ideal setting for achieving them. He and other Atlanta leaders saw that their newer interior city had two advantages over the older coastal cities that were identified with the agrarian past. First, Atlanta was connected to the rest of the South and the nation by an expanding network of rail lines. Eleven rails passed through the city in 1890, and at peak half a century later there were fifteen rail lines bringing more than 150 trains a day into the city's stations.[2] Although the shipping and processing of cotton was the dominant activity, other important commercial enterprises, such as the retail and wholesale trade, also depended on the city's rail lines.

A second advantage of Atlanta's business leaders was a unified vision of their city as the center of the New South. Grady and his newspaper described this vision as the "Atlanta Spirit"—the "militant expression of Atlanta's personality—forceful, aggressive, intelligent, harmonious, with an abundance of that requisite indispensable in man or city—sleepless initiative."[3] In promoting their city and the ideals of the New South, Grady and other Atlanta leaders borrowed techniques used by other cities—hosting fairs, conventions, and expositions—but did so within a culture that made the welcoming of visitors a responsibility to be shared by the entire city in a way that was unique to Atlanta. Southern hospitality guided their efforts to place the city at the forefront among urban places in the South. This value, shaped in the culture of the Old South, was now placed in the service of the New. Atlanta's leaders would build on the success of the 1881 International Exposition to raise a "brave and beautiful city" out of the ashes of the war.[4] The path toward this goal, however, was not without stumbling blocks.

Major Setbacks

Since its opening in 1870, the Kimball House Hotel was the largest and most luxurious in Atlanta. Built by the carpetbagger Hannibal I. Kimball, the six-story hotel was the tallest building in the city and an object of civic pride as well as a crucial facility among Atlanta's tourism businesses. Whenever Atlanta welcomed the rich and famous, the Kimball House was the place to stay. Political leaders met in its rooms and parlors to plan for the future of the state, county, and city. Before Atlanta had private clubs, the Kimball House was a favorite place for businessmen to gather for conversation and drinks. The splendors of the hotel were noted in the earliest histories of the city. All this gave the Kimball House a reputation throughout the South.

Early on Sunday morning, August 12, 1883, a night watchman noticed fire on the side of the hotel building. The Kimball House was nearly full, with many of the weekend guests being women and children. As a result of swift action by the manager and staff, all the guests were led out of the burning hotel to safety. Atlanta's new paid fire department tried to save the building, but the flames quickly destroyed the entire structure. No one is certain what caused the blaze, but local legend suggests it was the result of a careless cigarette tossed by the operator of a fruit stand beside the hotel. Tissue wrappers used around the fruit were thought to have started what was regarded as the most spectacular fire in Atlanta since Sherman burned the city in 1864. Local newspapers rushed out special editions in order to quiet the rumors that many had perished in the fire, while stories about the destruction of the Kimball House were spread by telegraph and published by newspapers throughout the region.[5]

Word of the fire reached Kimball in Chicago that evening. Displaying his typical energy, he returned immediately to Atlanta, organized a stock company, and set out on a national tour to raise the capital needed for rebuilding the hotel.[6] Although Kimball wanted to have the new hotel reopened within a year of the fire, delays in finance and construction pushed the formal opening of the completed hotel to the spring of 1885.

The opening of the new Kimball House was a grand event for the city's tourism businesses. National publicity was provided by *Harper's Weekly,* which described the hotel and its opening ceremonies:

> The building is of pressed brick, with terra cotta and granite
> trimmings, is thoroughly fireproof, and is located within a few

hundred feet of the center of the city. The house rises seven
stories above the basement, contains 31 stores and general
offices, 357 large airy sleeping chambers, and 22 large public
rooms, not including kitchen, storerooms, bakery and working
apparatus rooms. As it will be seen, the building has a distinct
suggestion of Dutch Renaissance in which the New York of two
centuries ago was built. . . .

The interior decorations and appointments are so disposed
as to give to each and every part of the building an elegant
and artistic feature of its own. The citizens of Atlanta feel a
just pride in the accomplishment of this enterprise. The formal
opening is made the occasion of a congratulatory banquet and
reception that gives it especial interest in the annals of the city.[7]

The new hotel was larger and more grand than the former one,
with its owners also able to boast of electric lights. Although the
destruction of the original Kimball House was a major blow to
Atlanta and its tourism businesses, the energy and activity of business
leaders like Kimball were able to overcome this setback. The
new Kimball House Hotel remained a downtown landmark and
a major fixture among the city's hospitality businesses until it was
torn down in 1955.

As soon as the Kimball House was rebuilt, promoters of the
city were eager to show it off, and Henry Grady suggested that
Atlanta should host a national commercial convention. Four
years earlier the city had shown its availability for investment in
manufacturing with the International Cotton Exposition. The
commercial convention would provide another showcase for Atlanta
as a place for investment in trade and banking. H. I. Kimball
again promoted and directed the affair. The convention
was to attract delegates from boards of trade and chambers of
commerce representing cities throughout the country. It opened
on May 19, 1885, with over three hundred representatives from
thirty states crowding into DeGive's Opera House on Peachtree
Street.[8] Grady welcomed the delegates with a combination of
Southern hospitality and the New South ideal of sectional reconciliation:
"Fifty feet from where we stand . . . our streets rang with

the clamor of battle," he told them, yet "not the slightest trace of bitterness has survived that fearful struggle . . . and . . . the people of Atlanta . . . welcome you in the best way as friends and brothers."[9]

For three days the delegates discussed important commercial issues of the day and, when not in session, attended lavish receptions at the new Kimball House and elsewhere. At the end of the meeting, Kimball predicted that $1 million would be invested in Atlanta as a result of the convention.[10] The event was the first national convention hosted in the city. As early as 1861, Atlanta had been the site for a convention of bankers from the Confederate states. This event was different, though, as it drew attendance from the entire nation and focused attention on Atlanta as a favorable place for both conventions and investments.[11]

Another major setback that affected Atlanta's tourism businesses during the 1800s was the prohibition of alcoholic beverage sales. From its founding, Atlanta had many kinds of businesses providing hospitality to visitors and residents alike, among them numerous saloons and bars. City directories indicate there were three saloons in Atlanta in 1859 and also three in 1867, when the city's population was just over 20,000. As the population grew rapidly after the Civil War, so also did the number of saloons. In 1871 there were 41, while ten years later, with a population of less than 40,000, Atlanta had 66. In 1885 the number had reached 113.[12] In addition to the saloons, most hotels had their own bars, and many restaurants served drinks and wine with meals. Providing liquor to all these establishments was the business of ten wholesale dealers and at least three breweries.

In his study of Southern drinking habits, Joe Gray Taylor says that the consumption of spirits was almost universal by men in the frontier and antebellum South. However, this pattern of consumption began to change in the years after the Civil War.[13] During the 1880s the local option movement spread through rural Georgia, with ninety counties either partially or completely dry by 1884. Southern customs of hospitality that included alcohol came into conflict with another strong cultural value in the South—evangelical Christianity.

Religion had always played an important role in the lives of people in the South. The experience of defeat and poverty made residents of the region anxious to bolster their collective self-esteem, and religion, particularly the evangelical Protestant Christianity promoted by the Baptist and Methodist Churches, became a crucial element in the culture of the South. It was during the last decades of the nineteenth century that Southerners joined churches in large numbers.[14] Whites and blacks formed separate denominations, but both preferred the Baptist and Methodist Churches, giving these groups a domination over the religious life of the region. As cultural historian Charles R. Wilson has shown, religion helped Southerners forge their regional identity in the years following the Civil War, and one of the chief devils to be fought by religious leaders was alcohol. The evangelical churches of the South emphasized individual sin and salvation, and church leaders wanted to eliminate what they regarded as the largest obstacle to being "saved"—drinking.[15]

In Atlanta, as in the rest of Georgia, the leaders of the prohibition cause were Baptist and Methodist preachers, who received strong support from their followers. Prohibitionists circulated a petition and arranged for a referendum on the issue in Fulton County, which was held on November 25, 1885.[16] The campaign was heated, with both sides holding mass meetings and urging voters to support the wets or the drys. Issues of race and class were also involved in the debate, with prohibitionists arguing against the evils of whiskey, particularly as it affected blacks and working-class whites. Liquor was said to stir up the passions of African Americans and absorb the poor man's Saturday night pay, creating premature and destitute widows and orphans. Wets pointed out the damaging effects prohibition would have upon business and produced figures to show that it would be impossible to operate the Kimball House without the revenues made from the bar at fifteen cents a drink.[17]

In spite of the potential harm to tourism businesses, the county voted to end liquor sales by a narrow margin of less than 3 percent of the 7,642 votes cast. The campaign had been divisive, often pitting business partners against each other. Even the ownership of the *Constitution* was divided and did not take an editorial stand on the question. The newspaper did, however, accept advertisements from both sides.[18] Another Atlanta paper, the *Evening Capitol,* strongly favored prohibition. After the victory, the newspaper editorial called for reconciliation between the two factions to make the experiment in temperance a success:

> Our first concern in the matter is for those who have business interests involved. Fortunately our saloon keepers have 7 months in which to close their matters. The change will not be sudden. Let all hands unite in immediate efforts to establish new mercantile and manufacturing enterprises that will give field for investment of the released capital and for employment of the labor.
>
> The hotels, whose bar-rooms will be closed, must have our special aid. Their billiard rooms, free from the entanglement of saloons, will draw more and pay better. Their privilege of furnishing wine at the table will not be interfered with. Let our business men take their noon meals with them when they cannot go home to dinner.
>
> Atlanta's unfailing business sense and resources will come to her in this ordeal to make prohibition a grand moral, humanitarian and business success. Atlanta men have never been known to sulk, and our anti friends are among our best and most potent commercial powers. . . .
>
> Let every tinge of heat or unkindness engendered by the contest be put away. Let the full brotherhood of our peerless city be restored. Let us all recognize in this election the Providence of God, and the exalted destiny of Atlanta.[19]

Despite the editor's pleas, the conflict between the two sides continued to rage. Prior to the deadline, many Atlantans stored as much liquor as they could in jars, jugs, and barrels.

The prohibition of retail sales of beer and liquor began on July 1, 1886. There were both racial and class distinctions in the way the law affected the availability of alcohol. Hotels and restaurants catering mostly to travelers and the more well-to-do white residents could continue to sell wine with meals. Wholesale dealers could continue to sell quantities of a quart or more. Although the local wholesale trade would be reduced, there were still country stores throughout the area to keep supplied. Most of the saloons that served either blacks or working-class whites closed as ordered, although several continued as restaurants or set up "blind tigers"—illegal bars that operated in the back of another establishment.[20]

Those white Atlanta residents who could afford to do so established or joined private clubs where the liquor ban did not apply. It may be mere coincidence, but the movement to establish a Gentlemen's Driving Club occurred within six months of the enactment of prohibition in Atlanta. The Piedmont Driving Club, as it was later called, would become (along with the Capital City Club, established in 1883) one of the city's most exclusive and best-known private clubs.[21] Its early history shows how the close ties between business leaders and city government affected the tourism businesses in Atlanta. At the outset it was organized to satisfy several needs. First, the horse lovers among the city's business leaders desired to purchase land for a driving park, where they would build a clubhouse and "make what other arrangements would be necessary for the pleasure of the members."[22] Second, the land for the driving park would be made available to the city for holding annual fairs. The city had $15,000 set aside for erecting buildings for the fair on the land owned by the Driving Club.

By April 1887 the Driving Club had purchased almost two hundred acres of land for the park and fairgrounds. A rail line was extended beside the property, and crews from the Fulton County chain gang were put to work grading and building roads on the property.[23] This mingling of public and private resources was regarded as appropriate because it would enable Atlanta to stage a Piedmont Exposition, which would showcase the resources of the Piedmont region of Georgia. Henry Grady's *Constitution* promoted the event, saying, "The Piedmont exposition, like the Cotton exposition [of 1881], will mark a new era in Atlanta's prosperity and add one more link to her long chain of successes."[24] A month later, the paper reported that the Piedmont Exposition was going to cost $150,000, which was $50,000 more than the 1881 exposition. Supporters argued that this increased cost for the Piedmont Exposition "will make a larger and better show and leave Piedmont Park very much handsomer, both as regards the park and buildings, than Oglethorpe Park was left when the exposition was closed."[25]

In many respects, Grady was the driving force behind the Piedmont Exposition. He realized that the vote on prohibition had divided local business leaders. What better way could there be to bring opponents together than to focus their energy on staging another exposition? Grady not only used the *Constitution* to promote the fair, but he also used his political connections to secure a visit to the exposition by the newly elected Democratic president, Grover Cleveland. To boost attendance in Atlanta, Grady also secretly arranged for President Cleveland *not* to visit other fairs in the Southeast. As a result, Grady was able to introduce the president to a crowd of over 50,000 at the Piedmont Exposition on October 18, 1887.[26]

The exposition itself was an opportunity to display agricultural products from the region, including ten acres of exhibits featuring horse and cattle shows and a mile of poultry coops. Cotton production and manufacturing were also shown, as well as an art gallery and displays by neighboring cities. Events also included bicycle parades, musical presentations, balloon ascensions, and, of course, trotting and horse racing.[27] Nearly 20,000 visitors were on hand for the opening day on October 10, and a week later the numbers swelled when President Cleveland arrived. The president and his wife stayed at the Kimball House and were entertained at the governor's mansion, the Capital City Club, and the Driving Club. When the Piedmont Exposition closed on October 22, civic leaders agreed that it had been a success.[28] The cultural value of hospitality had once again been pressed into the service of the New South ideal of promoting the city for investment. The city's hotels and boardinghouses profited from the exposition and helped the reputation of Atlanta as a place to come, visit, and do business.

Once the fair was over, however, the issue of prohibition sur-
faced again to create conflict among business leaders. Throughout the month of November, the issue was debated between the
wets and the drys. Both sides held mass meetings and parades
while the debate raged in newspapers and on street corners. Opponents of prohibition appealed for working-class support by arguing that the wealthy could do their drinking in private clubs
while the poor could not. Although African-American citizens
were restricted from voting in white-only Democratic Party primaries, those registered could play an important part in local
prohibition elections, and both wets and drys competed for the
votes of black Atlantans. Many prominent African-American
clergy supported the prohibitionists, while other blacks rallied
support for the anti-prohibitionists.[29]

After the vote on November 26, the local option prohibition
in Fulton County was defeated. In this election the African-
American vote was not decisive, since those who favored reopening the saloons carried every ward in the city. Atlanta's experiment in prohibition had failed as the vote to repeal the ordinance
was passed by a 12 percent margin.[30] Religious leaders in the
city were dismayed by the outcome of the election and continued
their opposition to the sale of alcoholic beverages, but business
interests and Southern drinking habits had proved stronger than
religious leaders and their followers.

Development of Amenities

Atlanta's tourism businesses include those providing lodging, food, beverage, and entertainment for visitors and residents
alike. The rapid growth of the city during the last two decades
of the century encouraged the development of amenities for the
entertainment of travelers and local residents. These amenities
reflected regional cultural patterns that provided hospitality according to class and race.

As early as 1870, Laurent DeGive, a native of Belgium, had
opened an opera house where traveling theatrical companies per-

formed. Patronage of art, music, opera, and theater was regarded as a mark of refinement among the city's elite, and DeGive's business was so successful that in 1893 he opened a second, larger Grand Theatre providing an even more opulent home for the performing arts in Atlanta. The opening-night gala filled the Grand's boxes with the city's elite white families, making it "an event in the social world of Atlanta as well as in the world of art." The Grand Theatre remained a popular place of amusement for Atlantans.[31] Theatergoing was a popular activity in late-nineteenth-century Atlanta, and in 1895 the Lyceum Theatre opened, giving the city three playhouses.[32] Blacks were initially excluded from theatergoing in Atlanta and other Southern cities, but by the 1880s they were permitted to sit in segregated portions of theaters such as DeGive's. A separate theater for blacks, the Schell Opera House, opened on Ivy Street by 1894. This provided a stage for traveling African-American entertainers within the prevailing pattern of racial segregation.[33]

Other amusement with more appeal to the working class was provided by traveling circuses. Religious leaders frequently criticized these shows as sinful diversions, but they were, nevertheless, regular events in the city. Seating for the circus was also segregated by race. As a business venture, the circus was not always successful. In 1889 a circus was visiting the city when it went bankrupt and was sold by auction to George V. Gress, a successful lumber dealer. Gress offered the animals to the city for a zoo, and his gift, along with the building to house the animals, provided Atlanta with an attraction for visitors at its newly built Grant Park. Like the theater and the circus, the zoo opened as a segregated facility. The cages were placed in the center of the building, and aisles were provided on each side. The *Constitution* writer observed that white and black patrons entered the zoo in separate doors, so "There is no communication between them."[34] Four years later, Gress also purchased and donated the cycloramic painting of the Battle of Atlanta known as the *Cyclorama,* which was housed at Grant Park.[35] In an era before television and motion pictures, the *Cyclorama* was an object of wonder for spectators. Together the *Cyclorama* and zoo formed tourist attractions that have continued to be major destinations for residents and visitors to the city.

Another attraction opened in 1895 on the property of the old municipal waterworks located south of the city. A private company bought the site and created the Lakewood Amusement Park. The lake was used for boating, a bathhouse was built, a stage was erected for concerts, and part of the grounds was set aside for picnics. The company also operated an electric trolley connecting the park with downtown, making the area an attractive summer destination for city residents. A privately owned facility, the Lakewood Amusement Park was open to whites only.[36]

The Ponce de Leon Springs were owned and operated by a street railway company, which had extended the streetcar line to the springs in 1874. The springs served as both an amusement park and a health spa for those wishing to bathe in the waters. In cities throughout the country during this time, the companies that owned electric streetcars bought land for amusement parks located at the end of their lines. These land transactions were often more profitable for the companies than the revenues from the fare boxes of the trolleys. The street railway companies also developed suburban housing on property along their lines. The city residents taking the weekend pleasure trips to the amusement parks were good prospects for the housing lots along the trolley lines.[37] Even those who were too poor to ride the cars regularly to work could take them to pleasure grounds like the Ponce de Leon Springs. The amusement park there had separate dance halls and refreshment stands for blacks and whites. African-American residents of the city were generally excluded from the few public parks, such as City Hall Park.[38]

Continued Growth

With its transportation lines bringing commerce to the city from every direction and its promotional activities providing recognition, Atlanta experienced rapid population growth. According to the U.S. Census Bureau, the city's 1880 population of

37,409 swelled to 65,533 in 1890, an increase of 75 percent. Local boosters were quick to point to this growth as evidence of their success in promoting the city as Atlanta's 1890 population surpassed that of its longtime rivals Memphis, Charleston, and Savannah. By 1890 only New Orleans, Richmond, and Nashville were larger Southern cities, and Atlanta had come from nowhere to become the forty-second-largest city in America.[39]

Most people who came to Atlanta moved from the rural areas and small towns of the South looking for opportunities they could not find in the countryside. As historian Edward Ayers observed, these migrants formed a constant stream of people who "washed through the towns, moving from the country, moving farther up the line to a larger city, moving to the North or West."[40] Of those who came to Atlanta, many did not stay long. Young Southern-born whites and blacks composed more than 90 percent of the city's population, but they were likely to move within ten years if they failed to find the economic opportunity that had first drawn them to the city. Although foreigners and Northerners represented a small percentage of Atlanta's population, they seem to have been more likely to acquire property and remain in the city.[41]

Atlanta's population growth was mirrored by an increase in tourism businesses. In 1881 the city had eight hotels and sixty-two boardinghouses, but ten years later there were eighteen hotels and ninety-six boardinghouses. These establishments were important sources of employment. In 1890, 95 percent of black female workers were employed in service jobs. While this employment category also included domestic workers in private households, many of these women worked in the boardinghouses and hotels doing the cooking, cleaning, and laundry. In contrast, fewer white females were employed in the city's tourism businesses. With jobs available to white women in the city's growing number of factories as well as in clerical and sales positions, only 18.5 percent of white females worked in service occupations.[42] At this time many of these hotel and boardinghouse employees were expected to live in their places of employment. By the end of the century, fewer employees lived on the premises of the city's boardinghouses and smaller hotels, a change that historian Gretchen Maclachlan suggests was characteristic of the process of rapid urbanization taking place in Atlanta during the period.[43]

Other tourism businesses also experienced rapid growth in the last two decades of the century. For example, the number of restaurants was twenty-one in 1881, increasing to fifty-six in 1891. Even more remarkable is the fact that the number of saloons increased from sixty-six to seventy-eight during this same period. This growth occurred in spite of the closing of all the saloons during the period of local prohibition between 1886 and 1887.[44]

Atlanta's business and political leaders were proud of their city's growth. The expositions of 1881 and 1887 and the convention of 1885 had advertised Atlanta as a place for investment and contributed to the development of manufacturing and commerce. The expositions also publicized Atlanta as a city that had risen from the ashes of its wartime destruction to new splendor. The official seal of the city discarded the railroad locomotive and replaced it with the phoenix as the symbol of this remarkable recovery. Although other Southern cities such as Richmond, Virginia, and Columbia, South Carolina, had suffered equal devastation during the war, only Atlanta chose to use the experience as a way of promoting itself. The symbol of the phoenix joined the idea of Atlanta as the "Gate City" to form two of the most important and lasting images of the city.[45]

Many observers of Atlanta noted that the city did not appear to be typical of the South. Visitors were reminded of the frantic pace of life in Northern cities when they saw local residents madly dashing about the streets. Another difference from other Southern cities was Atlantans' willingness to embrace investment and people from the North. Some compared Atlanta to Chicago, since both cities were known for their recovery from fire, rapid growth, and constant self-promotion.[46] By consciously adopting the rhetoric of the New South to promote itself as a place to do business, Atlanta had distinguished itself from the rural South and the older coastal and plantation-belt cities.[47]

Another interior city that grew rapidly during the 1880s was Birmingham, Alabama. If the rapid pace of growth in Atlanta made it appear different from other cities in the South, Birmingham was even less typical, not only for its rapid growth but also for its manufacturing. Founded in 1871, the town was located near rich deposits of iron ore, coal, and limestone—all needed for the production of steel. In 1880 Birmingham had only 3,086 residents, but ten years later its population had jumped to 26,178. Within the next thirty years, Birmingham added more than 100,000 residents, earning it the nickname "Magic City." Manufacturing made it a major economic center and Atlanta's rival.[48]

Though they were atypical for the South, Atlanta and the other inland cities of the region still lagged far behind the pace of urbanization in other areas of the country. The percentage of the South's urban population was less than 9 percent in 1880, and Southern cities continued to suffer from the region's colonial economy. The orator of the New South, Henry Grady, noted this dependency on the North and denounced the dominion of the New York and Boston moneylenders over the people of his native Georgia. According to Grady, "Georgia gathers from her languishing fields $2,000,000 of interest every year, and sends it away forever. Could her farmers but keep it at home, one year's interest would build factories to supply . . . the farmers' need."[49] This economic dependence on the North helps explain Southern business leaders' constant emphasis on growth as a means to catch up with their counterparts elsewhere.

Despite the city's identification with Northern urban models, Atlanta's business leaders were firmly rooted in the South. James Michael Russell's study of Atlanta's business leadership during the 1880s showed that 64 percent of the city's economic elite were born in the South, and most of them were from Georgia.[50] Atlanta's economic prosperity and sustained growth drew talented individuals to the city. Once they had arrived, these business leaders coalesced into organizations such as the Chamber of Commerce and in private clubs such as the Capital City Club and the Piedmont Driving Club. Historian Don Doyle has shown that this pattern of business and social organization was also taking place in other cities in the South. Atlanta's business leaders were unique, however, in the enthusiasm with which they embraced the New South ideal of growth and in their willingness to work together to achieve it.[51]

The 1895 Exposition

Atlantans were generally pleased with the comparisons between their city and Chicago. In 1893 Chicagoans impressed the world with the staging of the grandest exposition of the century, the Columbian Exposition, which commemorated the four hundred years since Columbus's discovery of the New World. Over one-third of Chicago had been destroyed by fire in 1871, and the fair was an opportunity to show the world that the city had been rebuilt on a grand scale. Like many other U.S. cities, Atlanta sent its delegation to the Chicago World's Fair. Those who made the trip were inspired to imitate the success of the Chicago event. Atlanta had already shown it could host large events such as the 1881 International Exposition, but that exposition had been "international" in name only (although there were displays of the varieties of cotton plants grown in other countries and a few representatives were sent from other cotton-producing nations), its main purpose having been to promote Atlanta as a place for Northern investors to locate cotton-manufacturing facilities. Atlantans returning from Chicago decided to promote an event that, like the World's Fair, could truly be called international.

Henry Grady died in 1889, but his successors at the *Constitution* are credited with originating the idea for another fair. Once again, New South ideals were combined with traditional Southern hospitality to promote the city. As an observer from the North wrote later, "One of the special objects of the promoters was to foster trade between the South American countries and the Cotton States, as well as to show to the North, and to European nations, what are the products and facilities of the Southern States, and to extend the commercial relations and markets of the entire country."[52] These objectives found expression in the name chosen for the event—the Cotton States and International Exposition.

The timing for this proposal could not have been worse. Atlanta in 1895 had about 75,000 residents and an economic outlook that was not as bright as it had been. Two years before, there was a major bank failure, followed in the summer by a nationwide commercial and financial panic. Banks called in existing loans and refused to make new ones. Money became so scarce as to threaten the annual business of moving the cotton crop through Atlanta.[53] During the following two years, Atlanta and the nation experienced a severe economic depression. It was in the face of this prevailing economic gloom that the proposal was made for Atlanta to host another exposition. Given the past successes, the fair was seen as a way of pulling the struggling local economy out of the mire.

Everyone knew that mounting an exposition would require capital. Finding a sufficient amount in these difficult times presented a severe test of the "Atlanta Spirit," that bundle of New South energy that had come to characterize the city. The solution came from a continuation of the same public-private partnership that had made past events possible. City council appropriated $75,000 toward the fund established to finance the exposition, while private citizens formed a corporation known as the Exposition Company and raised $134,000.[54] Fulton County contributed the labor of its convicts, as the chain gang did an estimated $100,000 worth of grading and dirt moving at the site of the earlier Piedmont Exposition.

Realizing that the 1895 exposition needed more support, business leaders turned to the federal government. The representative from Atlanta introduced a bill in Congress for an appropriation of $200,000 for the construction and operation of a federal exhibit at the fair. The city sent a strong delegation of business leaders to lobby for the passage of the bill, but the real credit for the successful passage of the measure belongs to three black leaders who were hastily called to testify on its behalf. The Chicago fair had not received much support or participation by African

Americans. In a remarkable decision for the time, Atlanta's exposition planners decided federal support would be more likely if blacks were included. Booker T. Washington and two bishops from the African Methodist Episcopal Church went to Washington and spoke to the appropriation committee. As a result of their efforts, the bill passed, and a Negro Building was included in the plans for the exposition.[55]

With federal support assured, exposition planning moved forward. The directors of the exposition sent commissioners with letters to invite the participation of each state in the Union as well as countries in South America and Europe. Invitations also went to major corporations with a stake in the cotton business, such as the railroads and textile manufacturers. Tourism businesses were well represented on the exposition's board of directors. Of the forty-two board members, three were hotel owners, including Joseph Thompson, who also owned a large liquor wholesale business. There was also to be a Women's Building at the exposition, with planning to be done by a separate Board of Women Managers led by Mrs. Joseph Thompson.[56] The Exposition Company's leaders hoped that this broad base of support would ensure the success of the fair in spite of the prevailing economic climate.

Following the success in attracting support from the federal government, several states—New York, Pennsylvania, Alabama, Illinois, Massachusetts, and Georgia—accepted an invitation to provide buildings and exhibits at the fair. It is significant that Georgia decided to participate in the 1895 exposition after failing to support the city's earlier fairs. In addition to the Negro and the Women's Buildings, in less than fifteen months the following buildings were constructed on the Piedmont Exposition grounds: Transportation, Manufactures and Liberal Arts, Agricultural, Machinery Hall, Auditorium, Minerals and Forestry, Chimes, Entrance and Administration, Art, Electricity, and a Fire Building featuring the latest in firefighting equipment.[57] Following the success of the Chicago World's Fair, a midway featured a variety of side shows and attractions such as the "Phoenix Wheel." Placed on the highest point in the fairgrounds, the Phoenix Wheel was "the largest wheel of its kind ever built in the world, and will rival the famous Ferris Wheel of the World's Fair, as its location is more commanding and the view more extensive."[58] All of this construction required a tremendous level of effort for a city of only 75,000 residents in the midst of a depression.

Preparations began for welcoming the expected crowds of visitors to the exposition. As in 1881, a Department of Public Comfort was established. Its first task was to determine how many visitors the city could accommodate. The initial survey indicated that 8,000 visitors could stay at boardinghouses and private residences, while the local hotels could house another 5,000. To accommodate more guests, the Exposition Company offered to pay $15 to $35 per room for new hotel rooms built for the event. Real estate developers seized this opportunity and added 1,500 rooms for the exposition.[59]

White business leaders were not alone in making their preparations for visitors to the exposition. Blacks had been excluded from most hotels, restaurants, and bars in the South. The combination of hostility from whites and voluntary action by African Americans led to the formation of a separate set of businesses, churches, and other organizations in cities throughout the region. Even before the passage of laws, de facto segregation or exclusion affected African Americans in public parks, theaters, zoos, and other amusement places.[60] During the 1890s, states and cities added the force of law to keep the races apart in public facilities and accommodations. There were a few lunchrooms, bars, and boardinghouses that served the needs of black residents and visitors in Southern cities like Atlanta, but otherwise African Americans who traveled for business or pleasure had to depend upon the hospitality of family or friends. The 1895 exposition, with its Negro Building, was certain to attract black visitors to the city. This prospect led the Atlanta Loan and Trust Company to open the European Hotel on Auburn Avenue. This was Atlanta's first hotel for African Americans, and it sought to provide a level of service not available in the more modest black-owned boardinghouses.[61]

Trying to anticipate the demand for lodging during the exposition, business leaders added a thousand rooms in the downtown area. All available upper-floor rooms in stores were refinished for this purpose. In addition, private homes were registered and connected to the Department of Public Comfort by a system of bicycle messengers who circulated to each residence twice per day. With this system in place, all the registered rooms in stores and homes "were run as a vast hotel, with bicycle messengers taking the place of bell boys."[62] Atlantans were excited about their ability to host an event of this size, and civic boosters worked overtime promoting the event far and wide. As preparations neared completion, one promotional publication wrote of Atlanta, "Her hotels are the best, both in quality of service and size of any city in the South."[63] The reputation of the city's tourism businesses was again used to promote Atlanta's growth.

The exposition opened with a great deal of fanfare on the evening of September 18, 1895. Grover Cleveland was again president, and this time he pressed an electric key at his home in Massachusetts to start the fair in Atlanta. According to the front-page headline of the following morning's *Constitution*, 25,000 people attended the opening. A large military parade marched three miles from the city to the grounds as part of the grand opening, followed by music and speeches from political and business leaders as well as Booker T. Washington.[64] Many of those present for the opening were invited guests rather than ticket buyers, as fewer than 16,000 tickets were sold during the first four days.

Attendance remained low during the next two weeks, causing great concern on the part of the Exposition Company's board of directors. They responded by staging a variety of special days honoring Civil War veterans and the various cities and states represented at the exposition. Attendance surged during the week of October 6, when the Liberty Bell arrived to go on display as part of the Pennsylvania exhibit. On October 9, officially declared "Liberty Bell Day," the city's public schools were closed and 12,000 children received free transportation on the streetcars that ran to the exposition grounds.[65]

A shortage of money plagued the exposition from the start.

Soon after the opening, the low attendance forced layoffs in order to reduce the payroll. Managers went without pay for several weeks, and at one point some of the employees went on strike briefly. By late November the exposition was $100,000 in debt despite the issuance of bonds to be repaid by gate receipts. In the midst of this situation, the chairman of the finance committee, Samuel M. Inman, stepped forward and contributed $50,000 in order to keep the exposition open. Other members of the committee pledged the rest, and the embarrassment of a bankrupt fair was avoided.[66] This financial crisis took place in spite of increased attendance in late October, beginning with President's Day on October 23. The popular Democratic president returned to Atlanta, where he was greeted by enthusiastic crowds. The highest weekly attendance was between November 24 and 30, when more than 115,000 people visited the exposition. A large delegation came to celebrate Manhattan and New York Days as well as Atlanta and Georgia Days. On Atlanta's day, businesses closed at noon and a number of important speakers drew one of the event's largest single-day crowds.[67]

Careful records were kept on those who attended the exposition. There were 779,560 tickets sold during the entire three months the fair was open. Based on train tickets and other information, it was estimated that the 1895 exposition attracted 333,737 visitors to Atlanta. In addition, local residents purchased about 200,000 tickets. Many who attended the exposition visited more than once, since it would be difficult to see the entire fair and all of its attractions in a single day. Based on the attendance figures, the exposition was more of a "Cotton States" event than an international fair, since most attendees came from the South. It was estimated that 26 percent of the visitors to the exposition came from within 50 miles, 11 percent from within 100 miles, and 16 percent from within 500 miles of Atlanta.[68]

The 1895 exposition included many interesting attractions and events. Buffalo Bill and his Wild West Show performed, an early version of the motion picture was shown, and John Philip Sousa appeared with his band to play a special composition called the "King Cotton March." Even Dwight L. Moody, the foremost evangelist of the day, built a special "tabernacle" near the exposition grounds and conducted a weeklong revival.[69] One of the more interesting events was the opening speech given by Booker T. Washington in which he described a pattern of race relations that was acceptable to the advocates of the New South movement. Putting aside all claims to political power and social equality, Washington suggested that blacks would make progress as agricultural and industrial labor.[70] Perhaps the most remarkable aspect of his speech was the fact that he was invited at all to address a largely white audience in a city in the Deep South. Although the speech was later denounced by other African-American leaders as a compromise to white supremacy, it received national coverage in the newspapers, helping to publicize the Atlanta exposition.[71]

Atlantans were proud of the exposition, as it gave them a chance to demonstrate their hospitality as well as to offer the city as a place to do business. The city's residents had overcome the effects of the Civil War, Reconstruction, and an economic depression to join together in promoting the 1895 exposition. As part of this relentless promotion, one writer described the exposition, saying, "Like her prototype, Chicago, Atlanta has stopped at no half-way grounds, everything like an obstacle has been swept away by the indomitable push and energy of the people, as an evidence of which is the Cotton States and International Exposition, second only to the World's Fair in size and in import."[72] Even allowing for exaggeration, staging the exposition was a remarkable achievement for a city of 75,000.

The total cost for the 1895 exposition was estimated to be $2.5 to $3 million. The Exposition Company spent around $1.5 million, the U.S government $200,000, and the various states and railroads $300,000 for the buildings and exhibits. The remainder was spent by various exhibitors and concessionaires. Fulton County had contributed the labor of its chain gangs for the grading of the site, and Atlanta gave $70,000 to the Exposition Company. Thus the direct cost to the citizens of Atlanta was remarkably low. This is in contrast to the Chicago World's Fair, which cost $28 million, of which the city subscribed $5 million. Never-

theless, Atlanta's exposition faced constant shortages of capital, and even after the fair closed there remained a $25,000 debt
in bonds which was never paid.[73] The exposition buildings had
to be torn down so that the materials could be sold as scrap. It
had been hoped that the 189 acres of land on which the exposition was held would be purchased by the city for use as a park,
but this was not done as the city could not afford the additional
$75,000 for the land.[74]

As the hub of the New South, Atlanta stood poised for the
beginning of the twentieth century and the remarkable changes
that would lead the city toward metropolitan growth.

3

Atlanta Enters the New Century, 1900–1920

THE BEGINNING OF THE NEW CENTURY provided Atlanta residents with an occasion to look forward to the progress promised by the future and to reflect upon the legacies of the past. Most of the city's leaders embraced the ideals of the New South, seeking to promote the growth of a diversified economy and to end sectional rivalries that might hold back commerce and investment dollars for the city. The three expositions hosted by the city late in the nineteenth century had shown the world that Atlanta was a place to be taken seriously in the years ahead, and Atlanta's business and political leaders hoped to continue the rapid growth the city had experienced since its founding.

Yet the city was also shaped by legacies of the past. The vast majority of Atlantans, born in the small towns and rural areas of the South, had brought with them to Atlanta the cultural patterns of the region, patterns that continued to influence many aspects of city life. One of these was the South's continued economic dependence on agriculture. Atlanta had been established to transport the agricultural products of the area, and this role continued to shape the local economy. Many Southerners also shared a tendency for violent behavior which combined with other elements of the regional culture to affect Atlanta in the early years of the new century.[1]

Atlanta and Its Tourism Businesses in 1900

The U.S. Census for 1900 counted 89,872 residents of Atlanta, a fourfold increase over the 1870 total.[2] Atlanta's leaders were pleased with this growth, regarding it as an indication of success in their city-building efforts. They also took pride in their major tourism businesses, such as the stately old Kimball House and the newer Hotel Aragon, located on Peachtree Street in a fashionable area near the governor's mansion. These two hotels welcomed everyone from presidents to business travelers.[3] In 1901, 35 hotels, 201 boardinghouses, and 18 restaurants provided hospitality to Atlanta's visitors. The hotels, like other tourism businesses, served travelers and also provided dining rooms and gathering places for local residents.[4]

Whether the occasion was a meeting of businessmen or a fancy dress ball, the hotels provided hospitality for a variety of local events. One of these meetings was observed by a traveler who passed outside a banquet hall in the Kimball House: "Why during the hour I stood by that door I saw and heard more enthusiasm than I have ever observed in all my life apart from a Confederate Veterans' meeting." Some four hundred businessmen inside, described as "the cream of the business element in Atlanta," had gathered to launch an industrial exposition and were being treated to speeches on Atlanta's past and future. They cheered every time their city was even mentioned. "It was the one word—'Atlanta'—that set the gathering to making a noise, a sort of talisman for a Babylonian confusion." The visitor was amazed at the excitement inspired by the "Atlanta Spirit." He concluded, "Nothing on earth can delay the advancement and growth of a town which has such loyal, loving, devoted citizens as were gathered in that banquet hall last night."[5]

Another important contribution of Atlanta's tourism busi-

Table 3.1. Employment in Atlanta Tourism Businesses, 1900

Occupation	Men	Women
Bartenders	166	1
Bding & Lodging Housekeepers	29	208
Hotelkeepers	30	19
Housekeepers & Stewards	9	117
Restaurant Keepers	68	65
Servants & Waiters	1,209	4,403
Saloonkeepers	75	–
	1,586	4,813

Source: Twelfth Census of the United States, 1900: Occupations, vol. 3.

nesses to the local economy was employment. As Table 3.1 indicates, the U.S. Census report on occupations in Atlanta for 1900 showed that tourism businesses provided nearly 6,400 jobs—15.7 percent of the city's total workforce. Of particular significance is the number of jobs provided for women in these businesses, since the total in this category represents 32.2 percent of all women in the workforce. Employment opportunities for females were extremely limited during this era, with the occupational category of domestic and personal service including over 70 percent of all working women in the city. When household maids are removed from the statistics, there is still an overwhelming number of women employed as servants and waitresses in the lowest-paying jobs in the tourism businesses. Most of these working women were African Americans.

Consistent with earlier periods (see Chapter 1), many women owned boarding and lodging houses in 1900. Many of these women were widows for whom this employment was their only practical option after their spouse's death. In Southern society, women were encouraged to be married and to remain at home to care for their husbands and children. Married women of either race were not often encouraged to work outside their homes, although economic necessity forced some to do so. Hospitality business employment, either as maids or boardinghouse keepers, was regarded as an extension of women's domestic role, since their main activities would be caring for men.[6]

Race Relations

In 1900 Atlanta had 35,727 African-American residents, almost 40 percent of the total population. Blacks and whites were separated from one another as both the city and state enacted Jim Crow laws requiring the segregation of the races. Originating as the name of a stock character in the minstrel shows popular in the United States in the 1830s, the term *Jim Crow* quickly became an adjective used to describe African Americans, and after 1890 was applied to segregation statutes passed in the South. The term was often used more broadly to summarize the political disfranchisement, economic injustices, and interracial violence of the pre–civil rights era.[7] Before the Civil War, African Americans, except for servants, had been excluded from restaurants, hotels, and parks throughout the South and were also barred from most theaters and shows. Reconstruction provided for the official integration of the races in public transportation and facilities such as railroad stations, but hotels and restaurants continued to exclude black customers.[8]

After the end of Reconstruction in the South in 1877, there was little need for Jim Crow laws because most African Americans simply could not afford luxuries such as hotels, restaurants, and theaters. Blacks who sought food or lodging continued to be excluded, but they were sometimes permitted to sit in segregated areas of theaters.[9] Before the end of the century, however, segregation was becoming the law of the South. For example, in 1892 Georgia passed a law requiring the separation of the races on trains. African Americans' efforts to prevent such legislation were limited because few were allowed to vote because of poll taxes and all-white primaries.[10] In 1908 Georgia passed even more restrictive laws that disenfranchised most of the remaining black voters by requiring property ownership, literacy, and other measures that were not enforced on white voters.[11] African Americans who were excluded from many aspects of life in the South began organizing separate black-owned businesses in towns and cities throughout the region.

The extent to which these segregated African-American businesses emerged in Atlanta may be seen in the description of the city's "Black Side" provided by Edward R. Carter in 1894. Another glimpse is provided by a series of annual reports produced by W. E. B. Du Bois, a professor of sociology and history at Atlanta University, who conducted conferences on the condition of the blacks. In 1899, the Fourth Annual Conference reported on "The Negro in Business" with a special section on African-American business ventures in Atlanta. That year the study found sixty-one black-owned businesses, including two restaurants, two saloons, one drugstore, and one pool and billiard parlor.[12] Numerous businesses combined several activities, such as the grocery stores (and even a woodyard) that operated restaurants as side activities. The development of these businesses suggests that by the turn of the century, while blacks could wait on whites in hotels and restaurants, African Americans needed to open their own enterprises for black customers. Du Bois speculated that these tourism businesses may have been started by former slaves who had worked as house servants and for whom the opening of eating, drinking, and lodging establishments would have been a natural evolution.[13] With the exception of one saloon that was reported to have been in business between ten and twelve years, all the black-owned businesses were only one to five years old.

One of the businesses mentioned in the Du Bois report (and most likely also described in Carter's book) was a restaurant owned by Aaron Perry. He moved to Atlanta as a young man and worked in another black-owned restaurant and in a candy company before opening his own restaurant on West Mitchell Street.[14] Another black-owned tourism business described by Carter was the Schell Opera House on Ivy Street, a three-story brick building that provided a stage for traveling African-American entertainers as well as other amusements.[15] In an increasingly segregated society, businesses such as these depended almost entirely on black customers.[16] And because African-American enterprises depended on customers who were, for the most part, poor, they were risky.

Tensions between blacks and whites in Atlanta increased early in 1900 as the city passed an ordinance requiring the separation of the races in all trolley cars. This Jim Crow legislation was resisted by African Americans, who responded with a boycott of the trolleys. After some initial success, the boycott proved to be too much of an inconvenience for those African Americans who depended on the trolley lines to get to their places of work.[17] When the boycott was over, blacks had to take their places in separate cars or in the backs of cars occupied by whites. Other segregation ordinances followed, such as the prohibition of African Americans from using the new public library that opened in 1902.[18]

White Atlantans imposed Jim Crow policies that affected blacks in a variety of ways. For instance, tourism businesses were open only to one race or the other and were required to display a sign indicating which customers would be served. The Atlanta train depot did not permit blacks to enter through the front door. All of the city's parks, including the zoo in Grant Park, were segregated.[19] Other Jim Crow laws kept blacks in an inferior place in society by providing separate and inferior public schools for African Americans. In downtown stores, blacks could buy clothing but could usually not try on garments.[20]

In the face of such discrimination, blacks organized themselves to promote their own businesses. Booker T. Washington formed the National Negro Business League in 1900 and held annual meetings in cities across the country. The league provided opportunities for African-American business leaders to meet and to share their common struggles. It was also a forum for promoting black-owned businesses. Most of the meetings were held in Northern cities, but on August 29, 1906, the league met in Atlanta for the Seventh Annual Convention. The three-day meeting brought together business leaders to present papers describing their successes and problems.[21]

As black tourism businesses developed in Atlanta during the early years of the new century, a separate African-American convention business also arose for meetings such as that of the National Negro Business League. Lodging places like the Thomas Hotel and the Craig House welcomed black travelers, the Royal Palm Café and Morgan's Blue Front Café provided food, and the Vendome and the Red Star Saloons served drinks to black patrons.[22] The African-American newspaper, the *Independent*, exhibited the boosterism typical of Atlanta when it proclaimed that the city was ready to show its "proverbial spirit" to provide a warm welcome for the league's meeting. There had been a great deal of preparation for the event, including fund-raising by a committee of African-American business leaders to provide entertainment for the convention visitors. "We are prepared to take care of everybody that comes," the newspaper editor added. "Atlanta is noted as a convention city for her hospitality and open door."

On the first day of the convention, a standing-room-only crowd of 3,000 packed into Big Bethel Church on Auburn Avenue, where Mayor John S. Cohen and the president of the all-white Chamber of Commerce welcomed the visiting delegates to the city. After the "Sage of Tuskegee," Booker T. Washington, delivered the opening speech, the visiting businessmen were treated to a banquet at Piedmont Park and a special train excursion to visit Dr. Washington's school in Tuskegee, Alabama.[23] Although Atlanta remained a rigidly segregated city, the meeting of the National Negro Business League indicated that there was opportunity for limited cooperation between the races when business and growth were at stake. Financial support for the event came from white and black businesses, both of which stood to profit from the more than 1,000 visitors to the city.[24] The meeting was held in Atlanta's largest black church, but the city provided the use of a municipal park, and white leaders were available to welcome the convention. The display of hospitality to visitors did not conflict with the demands of segregation.

The same year that white leaders welcomed visiting blacks to the city, Atlanta experienced a bitter race riot. One of the causes of the riot was a racist campaign for governor in which the winning candidate promised to deny blacks access to the ballot box and the schoolroom. Emotions were also heated as competing white newspapers tried to boost circulation by printing stories alleging black rapes of white women. On Saturday evening, September 22, 1906, the papers fanned the passions of racial hatred with lurid headlines and stories that blamed the rapes on the "low dives" that served liquor to African Americans, inflaming their passions and causing them to commit assaults on white women.[25] Most of the newspapers' wrath was directed against the Decatur Street area of the city. In contrast to the pride of the city's commercial district on Peachtree Street, Decatur Street was a collection of poorly built wooden structures that served as boardinghouses, restaurants, and clubs, as well as "dime bed dives," pawnshops, gambling dens, and houses of prostitution. The area attracted drifters, the "criminal element," and, for the most part, ordinary black people seeking entertainment.[26] The city council had already passed a new ordinance that gave the chief of police and the license inspector the authority to close down any restaurants on Decatur Street that were operating as illegal saloons.[27]

By ten o'clock Saturday evening, a mob of whites estimated to be as large as 10,000 had armed themselves and were attacking any blacks unlucky enough to be on the streets of downtown. Trolley cars continued to bring unsuspecting victims downtown, where African-American men and women were pulled from the cars, beaten, and killed. Police officers did little to prevent the massacre except to raid all the dives and arrest the "idle Negroes" in the saloons and restaurants along Decatur Street. By Sunday morning at least twenty blacks were dead and many more were wounded.[28] The white mob continued to attack black residential areas on Sunday evening but were repulsed with gunfire. Any blacks who ventured downtown were likely to suffer the fate of the man who was chased by the mob into the Marion Hotel, shot four times, and left for dead. The mayor ordered all saloons closed for the week to prevent African Americans from obtaining access to liquor. Fearing to venture downtowm, black servants, bellmen, cooks, and waiters did not report for work in the city's tourism businesses.[29] Even the white cast members of a minstrel show in their blackface makeup were attacked as they left the Grand Opera House after their performance on Sunday evening.[30] Scattered violence continued through Tuesday in spite of the presence of the state militia as well as additional police officers who were hired for the emergency.[31]

At the city council meeting on Tuesday, September 25, the pastor of the Second Baptist Church spoke to the group and urged that all of the "Decatur Street dives" be closed, as these places were "blots upon the civilization of Atlanta, breeders of vice and crime." The council responded by passing an ordinance requiring a review of the "character" of business transacted by each licensed barroom in the city.[32] Under the new ordinance, the owners of saloons were not even permitted to enter their places of business. All bars in the city would remain closed until they could reapply for a new business license and be reviewed by a special committee. City leaders were so determined to keep alcohol away from blacks that they extended the ordinance to prohibit the sale of wine, whiskey, or beer in all restaurants. Restaurants would also have to reapply for a new license in order to resume sales of alcohol. The new ordinance did not, however, apply to hotel cafés, since these served only white customers. If anyone in Atlanta missed the point of this legislation, the *Constitution* editorial of September 28 made it clear: "Under no conditions should licenses be granted to saloons catering wholly or in part to Negroes." The paper added that it was the duty of the "superior" white race to keep liquor away from "inferior races."[33]

Aftermath of the Race Riot

The Atlanta race riot had a number of significant effects on the city and its tourism businesses. Business leaders were concerned about the mob violence and, above all, wanted to take whatever steps were necessary to prevent it in the future. Their goal was to restore law and order and to return to business as usual in Atlanta. The city's leadership felt that no one should be allowed to tarnish the city's modern, progressive, and metropolitan image.[34] The riot received unfavorable national publicity in newspaper coverage. Business slumped dramatically in the city as bank clearings for the week after the riot were $204,000 less than the same period the year before. This was the sharpest drop since the bank panic of 1893. The "mob of irresponsibles" tarnished the city's image and caused business losses. This, according to the *Constitution*, was the price of one night's "diversion" by the mob.[35]

Atlanta's mayor and many of its citizens were not pleased with the response to the riot by the police and the state militia. One problem noted by the mayor was the lack of any central place for the militia to assemble during the crisis. Consequently, the mayor called for the construction of a combination auditorium-armory for the city.[36] This facility would serve the city for many years as its municipal auditorium, hosting visits from presidents, operas, and a variety of business and civic meetings.

For the city's tourism businesses, the race riot caused severe financial damage. Saloons were forced to remain closed until the review commission could consider new requests for licenses. Sales also declined in restaurants, which were not permitted to sell wine, liquor, or beer. One week after the violence erupted, the newspaper tried to reassure blacks that they would be safe on the streets and could resume their jobs in downtown tourism businesses.[37] Immediately after the riots, visitors to the city had had to carry their own baggage and generally make do without elaborate meals or clean rooms because most African Americans had remained in their homes. Owners of hotels, restaurants, and saloons worried about the longer-term effects of the riot and the damage to the city's reputation as a friendly place in which to conduct business.

A large convention of the National Association of Retail Druggists was to begin on October 1, with over 2,000 delegates expected for the first meeting of the organization in the South. In preparation for the meeting, city council hastily approved the reopening of twenty-seven retail and wholesale liquor dealers. The council also urged the Sanitation Department to hire white replacement workers and clean the city streets in order to make a better impression on the visitors.[38] Elaborate preparations were made to welcome and entertain the druggists. As the maker of a fountain product sold primarily in drugstores, the local Coca-Cola Company played a major role in hosting the convention.[39] Opening sessions were held in the capitol, and the Kimball House Hotel served as headquarters.

When they arrived in Atlanta, the druggists received reassurance that the recent riots were past and "the lawlessness of the comparatively few did not in any way represent the enterprising and progressive 'Atlanta Spirit.' "[40] The convention—regarded as one of the largest ever held in the city—was important as a sign that Atlanta was ready to extend its hospitality once again. Attendance was reported to be larger than for the previous year's meeting in Boston. A lavish reception was held at the Piedmont Driving Club, and the saloons for whites reopened again to serve crowds of both visitors and locals. Thirty-six saloons serving blacks in the Decatur Street area, however, were denied new licenses and closed permanently. Only eighteen restaurants and saloons serving blacks were permitted to reopen.[41] As historian Dwight Fennell has noted, the race riot resulted in the segregation of African-American businesses in Atlanta. In 1890, Auburn Avenue had been a racially mixed area with only five black-owned businesses. One year after the riot there were twenty-nine African-American businesses on the avenue, including five eating places. In the aftermath of the riot, more than two-thirds of all black businesses in Atlanta relocated to predominantly African-American areas.[42]

New Influences

As Atlanta's citizens struggled to put the horrors of the race riot behind them, a group of civic-minded business leaders decided to follow a tactic that had proved successful in earlier years. They organized as a committee to plan for a large exposition in 1910.[43] After all, they reasoned, the expositions of 1881, 1887, and 1895 had brought attention and economic growth to the city. Perhaps of equal importance, the events had forged the partnership between local business and political leaders to boost Atlanta's development. This time, however, there was no Hanni-bal I. Kimball or Henry W. Grady to lead the exposition planning to fruition, and it never happened. The city needed to look forward with new ideas rather than back to the glorious expositions of its past.

Many Atlantans, believing that the race riot was caused by the inflamed passions of those under the influence of alcohol, did not raise much protest when the state general assembly passed a law in 1907 that imposed a statewide prohibition. Most rural counties were already legally dry, so Georgia's urban areas were the ones most affected by the law, which became effective on New Year's Day 1908. The front-page story in the *Constitution* the week before the law was to take effect described the impact on Atlanta. Under the new law, 132 businesses would close, including 86 whiskey saloons (61 for whites and 25 for blacks), 23 beer saloons (17 for whites and 6 for blacks), 21 wholesale liquor houses, and 2 wholesale beer houses. In addition to the jobs and economic activity represented by these tourism businesses, the newspaper argued, the city itself would lose the $131,142.50 in taxes paid by these businesses during the previous year. Under the earlier local option prohibition in Fulton County, retail sales of wine and beer continued, as did wholesale liquor sales. This time the intent of the law was to outlaw the legal sales of alcohol in public places. This would close down the bars in the Decatur Street area completely.[44]

In the last days before the new prohibition law took effect, patrons packed the saloons to fortify themselves while the business owners tried to sell out their stock before midnight and the arrival of the new year. Many Baptist and Methodist churches planned "watch-night" services in which they would smash a bottle of liquor at midnight and welcome in the prohibition law. A *Constitution* editorial urged enforcement of the law so that there would be no "blind tigers" operating as illegal saloons and no drugstores supplying "medicine" to thirsty customers. Meanwhile, saloon owners and wholesale dealers planned either to

71

move their businesses to other cities or to rent their property to some other enterprise.[45]

Like many other aspects of life in Atlanta, the prohibition debate was influenced by issues of race and class. Following the race riot, many whites felt it was necessary to deny blacks access to alcohol, believing that this would help control the passions that liquor was thought to unleash. Upper-class whites generally belonged to unregulated private clubs, which were permitted to remain open and were soon joined by illegal bars operating as "locker clubs" in the upstairs of many office and commercial buildings. For blacks and working-class whites, a few saloons continued to sell soft drinks and "near beer," which was held by a state court of appeals decision to be legal since the alcohol content of less than 3 percent was said to be nonintoxicating.[46] Illegal "moonshine" whiskey was also made and sold to both whites and blacks in many places throughout the city. Even though most saloons closed, alcohol was almost as readily available in Atlanta as before. The net effect was to reduce tax revenues to the city and to make many citizens and business owners evaders, if not breakers, of the new law.

When Atlanta's tourism businesses suffered a loss such as that resulting from the prohibition law, the city usually took vigorous actions to stimulate new economic activity. A year after the prohibition law took effect, Atlanta embarked on a bold new plan. The suggestion came from Clark Howell, the editor of the *Constitution*. With the city's new auditorium-armory scheduled for completion in the fall of 1909, the paper suggested in January that the completion of the new facility would be an ideal time "to mark the christening of the big building with a practical automobile display that will inestimably stimulate the industry in the Southern states to Atlanta's profit; that will, also bring Atlanta aggressively before the nation's eye."[47] Throughout its early years, the automobile industry had shown little interest in the South because of the region's lower standard of living. Automobile shows by the manufacturers were an important way of selling cars, but these shows had always been held in New York or Chicago. It seemed outlandish to expect that the National Association of Automobile Manufacturers would agree to meet in Atlanta, but in April the association agreed to hold its first official showing of the 1910 model cars on November 6–13, 1909, in the new auditorium-armory.[48]

The national automobile show had the potential to bring money to the city from exhibitors and visitors to the event. It also could make Atlanta the center of the automobile business in the South and promote the building of roads converging on the city. Equally important, the automobile industry could bring Atlanta "a great increase of population and influx of capital," giving new life to the city and its residents.[49] The civic leadership of the city spared no effort to make the show a success. The owner of the Coca-Cola Company, Asa Candler, spent approximately $300,000 to build a racetrack for automobiles south of the city. The Central of Georgia Railway Company spent $10,000 to run a special sidetrack near Candler's raceway to shuttle "speed enthusiasts" to the racetrack from downtown. City government illuminated Peachtree Street and three other major streets with hundreds of lights to decorate the downtown.[50] The racetrack provided a major attraction for the auto show and later became the site of the Atlanta airport.

The results of the automobile show were mixed. Automobile sales in the city and region were strong in 1909 and the following year, perhaps in part because cotton prices reached an all-time high and many Southerners had the disposable income needed to purchase their first automobiles. Cotton prices did not remain at that level, however, so the impact on sales was not sustained throughout the years before World War I. The auto show did, however, provide the impetus for the opening of sales offices in Atlanta, which in many cases also served as regional distribution centers. Atlanta's railroad network again gave the city a natural advantage as a distribution point for the new products. Along with the automobile sales offices came jobs and the need for buildings to serve the needs of the new automobile owners. These jobs and buildings to serve the automobile gave a tremendous boost to the local economy. In the eleven years following the auto show the number of automobile dealerships in Atlanta increased from 9 to 80 while automobile-related businesses in the city also grew, from 9 to 236.[51] Thus the "Atlanta Spirit" continued to play a major role in the development of its economy. In this case the hosting of the national automobile show had provided the catalyst for attracting a new form of transportation to Atlanta. The results would literally reshape the city during the next decade.

From its earliest days, Atlanta was a railroad town. The intersecting rail lines that provided the impetus for the founding of the city also shaped the pattern of the downtown streets and the location of most important economic activities. Major hotels such as the Kimball House were literally steps away from the train depot, allowing travelers to walk easily to their accommodations. By 1900 there were a few hotels, such as the Aragon, located to the northeast on Peachtree Street, but most were still centered within a few blocks of the train depot. In 1901 there was only one hotel more than half a mile from the center of town. Of the thirty-five hotels in 1901, 75 percent were located within two blocks of the railroad tracks, and almost half were within one block. The hotel business in Atlanta was rather transitory, since only three of the thirty-five hotels listed in the 1901 city directory were still in operation twenty years later. Eight other hotels were operating at the same addresses, but under new names in the 1921 city directory. Changing land uses in the downtown area meant that the remaining twenty-four hotel sites listed in the 1901 directory were occupied by other activities two decades later.[52]

The "hotel row" on Mitchell Street illustrates the changing pattern of land uses and the transitory nature of the city's hotel business. The old train station on Wall Street (near the present site of Underground Atlanta) was convenient to hotels such as the Kimball House, but the facility was old and outmoded. Three of Atlanta's railroad companies joined together in 1903 to build a new station for the city at Madison Avenue and Mitchell Street. In 1900 the block on the north side of Mitchell Street between Forsyth and Spring Streets had contained two boardinghouses, two "eating places," a drugstore, and several other small businesses. The news of the construction of the new passenger depot set off a wave of speculation on the block, and when the new station opened in 1905 there was a new Terminal Hotel across the street as well as the Child's Hotel. Three years later, a fire destroyed both hotels and twenty-eight other commercial buildings in the area. Within months, the block was redeveloped with four hotels—a new Terminal Hotel, the Scoville Hotel, the Gordon Hotel, and the Sylvan Hotel. The hotels served the business travelers arriving by train but were never as elegant as the Piedmont or the Ansley, "New York–style" hotels located in the fashionable section of Peachtree Street.[53]

By 1910, Peachtree Street was emerging as the focus for more of the city's commercial and financial activities. This expansion outward from the traditional heart of downtown began as the electric trolley lines were extended along Peachtree Street. With more economic activity moving to the northeast, tourism businesses followed. In 1910 construction began on the Georgian Terrace Hotel at Peachtree and North Avenue. Opening the following year, the Georgian Terrace was hailed as "a Parisian hotel on a noted boulevard in a metropolitan city."[54] Its distance from downtown was shortened not only by the trolleys but also by the increasing use of automobiles in Atlanta.

Atlanta's boosters considered the city's hotels a mark of status, and the arts provided them with another claim for municipal recognition. The patronage of serious music and grand opera was a badge of upper-class culture in cities throughout the country during the late nineteenth century, but during Atlanta's youth its residents had been slow to adopt such trappings of sophistication. When they did, however, Atlantans responded with the enthusiasm typical of the city.[55] In 1908, local business leaders and their wives organized the Atlanta Music Festival Association, and the following year a series of operatic performances were held in the city's new auditorium-armory. Special trains brought visitors from nearby towns to join local arts supporters in five nights of sold-out performances. An even larger festival of grand opera, featuring New York's Metropolitan Opera Company, was held in 1910. During one evening the Italian tenor Enrico Caruso performed to an audience of 7,000. The festival proved to be a showcase for the city's cultural elite and the start of an annual series of spring visits to Atlanta by the Metropolitan Opera. Such amenities became not only a part of the city's cultural life but also an important asset to the promotional efforts of local business leaders.[56]

Atlanta's rapid growth during the first decade of the new century spurred the city's outward expansion. From a population of less than 90,000 in 1900, Atlanta grew to 154,839 residents in 1910.[57] The city also extended its boundaries through two important annexations in 1903 and 1910,[58] adding the Piedmont Park area as well as land on the south side. Streetcars and automobiles enabled people to live farther away from their employment and began the process of spreading the city out from its compact circle around the railroad tracks.

U.S. Census reports for 1910 indicated that 12.1 percent of all jobs in Atlanta's labor force were held by those who worked in businesses providing hospitality to visitors and residents. As Table 3.2 shows, tourism businesses provided over 9,200 jobs in

Table 3.2. Employment in Atlanta Tourism Businesses, 1910

Occupation	Men	Women
Bartenders	138	–
Amusement Keepers*	39	39
Bding & Lodging Housekeepers	36	485
Hotelkeepers	55	11
Housekeepers & Stewards	29	190
Restaurant Keepers	165	92
Saloonkeepers	100	–
Servants**	1,278	5,967
Waiters	589	58
	2,429	6,842

*Includes Billiard Room, Dance Hall, & Skating Rink Keepers
**Includes Bell Boys, Chambermaids, Coachmen, Cooks, etc. in nondomestic settings
Source: Bureau of the Census, *Thirteenth Census of the United States, 1910: Occupations,* vol. 3.

1910. In spite of the state's prohibition law, 238 people still listed their occupation as either saloonkeeper or bartender. This figure was practically unchanged since the 1900 census. Employment in tourism businesses continued to be important for women, as the 6,842 hospitality jobs held by women represent 26.5 percent of all females in the labor force. This suggests that other job opportunities in clerical positions and manufacturing were beginning to open for women in Atlanta as the labor force participation rate for women increased slightly (from 37.7 percent in 1900 to 39.1 percent in 1910). At the same time, the percentage of women employed in tourism businesses declined by 5.7 percent. According to the census reports, women working in the hospitality businesses continued to occupy the lowest-paying positions of boardinghouse keepers, housekeepers, and chambermaids.

The business of providing hospitality to visitors and residents also had its illegal aspects. While their numbers were not often accurately recorded, many women in Atlanta earned their livelihood in the illicit side of the tourism business as prostitutes. This "oldest of professions" had flourished in the city since its earliest days. Remarkably little was done to disturb this business, and as a consequence houses of prostitution operated openly in several red-light districts in Atlanta. These districts included the notorious intersection of Decatur and Collins Streets, an area of brothels that had opened in the late 1880s. By the turn of the century Collins Street was well known for its houses of prostitution, which provided living quarters for ten "madames," sixty-five prostitutes, and nine servants.[59] Another location for the sex trade was a row of two-story brick tenements on Mechanic Street, which was between downtown and the campus of the Georgia Institute of Technology.

Despite laws against prostitution, during the late nineteenth and early twentieth centuries most U.S. cities permitted such areas to exist on the fringe of the central business district. The names of these red-light districts in larger cities were well known—the Tenderloin in New York, the Levee in Chicago, the Barbary Coast in San Francisco, Storyville in New Orleans. Of these, New Orleans legally recognized the Storyville district between 1898 and 1917, hoping to keep prostitution out of more respectable neighborhoods and isolated in this one area of the city. Both residents and visitors usually knew the location of these districts, and reformers in most cities frequently called for closing the areas.[60]

In Atlanta the most serious reform effort began in 1912, when a new police chief decided to close down the city's red-light districts. His crusade was backed by most of the local clergy and their supporters, organized into a group called the Men and Religion Forward Movement. On September 24, 1912, Police Chief James L. Beavers delivered an order to the fifty "recognized houses of ill-repute" in the city, demanding that they close by midnight on Saturday, September 28. The president of the Men and Religion Forward Movement announced that "the inmates of the resorts ordered closed could enter a new life, secure desirable homes, and . . . be given incentives to lead useful and Christian lives." Chief Beavers added that although Atlanta was the first city of its size in the South "to eradicate tolerated prostitution, this is only the beginning of a reform wave that will soon sweep Dixie."[61] On Sunday the *Constitution* reported that most of the madames had closed the doors of their houses and that many of the women who lived in the city's two red-light districts had already left town.[62]

The reform efforts by the police chief and the Men and Religion Forward Movement did not have solid support among Atlanta's business leaders. A short time later, the chief was charged with "inefficiency and insubordination" and forced to resign.[63] Although Atlanta's two red-light districts had been closed, police made few subsequent efforts to close the houses of prostitution that continued to operate in locations scattered throughout the city, and the women likely relocated to ply their trade in less visible areas. The same fate awaited Storyville in New Orleans, which was closed in 1917 by order of the U.S. government, and New York's Tenderloin, which closed by 1920 as tolerance for commercial sex declined. As historian Timothy Gilfoyle observed, prostitution did not disappear from New York and other cities, it simply became less visible in recognized red-light districts.[64]

The early efforts by reformers to close Atlanta's red-light districts in 1912 indicate the limits of the clergy's influence on decision making in the city. Generally the city's religious leaders worked in harmony with business and political leaders. In the aftermath of the race riot, for example, the clergy supported the city council's action to close down the saloons that served liquor to blacks. However, when moral issues conflicted with the interests of most business leaders to keep prostitution going in the city, the business influence on local government was stronger. As the mayor of New Orleans said about prostitution when he was forced to close Storyville, "You can make it illegal, but you can't make it unpopular."[65]

Atlanta was built as a transportation center, and its economic development through the nineteenth century depended on the use of the rail lines for the sale and distribution of goods and services to the region. After the turn of the century, the city literally and figuratively moved away from the railroad tracks and became more important as a commercial center. Businesses moved north along Peachtree Street, away from the Five Points area that had been the center of the earlier railroad city. In the first two decades of the twentieth century Atlanta added thirty-six major new buildings, including office buildings, hotels, and stores. Many of these were skyscraper office towers and high-rise hotels that supported the city's new image as a commercial and office center.

As historians Karen Luehrs and Timothy Crimmins have shown, Atlanta's business leaders shared a vision of the city as more than just another Southern railroad junction. The new skyline gave Atlanta the image of a big city like New York or Chicago, unlike many of its regional cousins.[66] These new buildings were used primarily for commerce, tourism, and consumerism. Many of the office buildings housed financial institutions, while the new hotels and theaters catered to both the business and convention crowds. New department stores, such as Rich's and Davison-

Paxon (now Macy's), and the Peachtree Arcade made the down-town a more attractive place for women to shop.

Beginning in 1909, city council began an effort to make down-town safer and more appealing to women by funding the con-struction of the "Great White Way." The project illuminated streets and sidewalks around Peachtree Street and Five Points with bright electric lights, making the stores, theaters, and hotels in the area more attractive to evening patrons. The city and local businesses provided more funding during the next five years for additional lighting and women's restrooms along the way. The Great White Way was intended to encourage women to mingle, stroll, and shop in a downtown area that had heretofore been the domain of businessmen. The Peachtree Arcade, located at Peachtree and Broad Streets, opened in 1918 with a variety of shops and personal services designed to attract middle-class white women. It served for many years as an important down-town meeting place and embodied many aspects of Atlanta as a twentieth-century commercial city.[67]

Tourism was a major part of the new use of space in downtown Atlanta during the first two decades of the century. With its new hotels, theaters, and the auditorium-armory, the city began to establish a reputation for hosting conventions. With charac-teristic "Atlanta Spirit" and Southern hospitality, conventions were invited to meet in the city, and in 1912 the Chamber of Commerce started a separate organization to encourage the process. The head of the chamber, Wilmer L. Moore, is credited with starting this group, which was initially known as the Atlanta Convention Bureau. Ivan E. Allen was its president, and Fred Houser directed day-to-day operations.[68] Under their leadership, the bureau aggressively solicited groups to hold their meetings in the city. Governor Joseph M. Brown wrote letters of invitation to a variety of groups extending the promise of a warm reception and the gracious hospitality of the city,[69] and it was not unusual for public funds from the city to be used to host an important convention. The city council had a standing Committee on Audi-torium and Conventions that would report the need for assistance to the full council, especially if there were delegates coming to the city from all over the country for a convention that would "mean much to Atlanta." On other occasions the mayor and council would agree to "meet the tourists and officially welcome them to Atlanta."[70] Through this collaboration between the Atlanta Convention Bureau, business leadership, and elected public officials, Atlanta was transformed into a national convention center.

Several factors contributed to Atlanta's success in attracting conventions. First, the city was a transportation center, and the network of rail lines connecting Atlanta with other cities in the state and region made it an accessible meeting place. Second, the city had a growing number of tourism businesses, including hotels, restaurants, and places of amusement. Third, the hospitality of its residents had been demonstrated when Atlanta hosted the major expositions of 1881, 1887, and 1895, as well as several early conventions. Fourth, there was a strong organizational capacity to promote the convention business as a result of the long-standing partnership among Atlanta's business and political leaders. And finally, the cultural value of hospitality contributed to Atlanta's success as a convention city, since it added to the city's reputation as a place whose people extended a warm welcome to visitors.[71]

The Atlanta Convention Bureau aggressively sought to attract a variety of organizations to hold their annual meetings in the city. For example, on August 17, 1915, a delegation of fifty businessmen led by Fred Houser went to Birmingham to invite the members of the Southern Cattle Men's Association to hold their meeting in Atlanta the next year. Other cities, such as Shreveport, Louisiana, also extended invitations to the organization, but Atlanta's delegation was determined to prevail, saying beforehand that "boosting material of all sorts will be taken, and a great fight will be put up for the convention."[72] Their efforts to promote the economic growth of Atlanta by attracting the convention, however, were overshadowed by another event that would affect the city's reputation.

More Violence

During the nineteenth century, Atlanta was relatively free of hostility toward its small Jewish population. As the numbers and the diversity of Jews in the city increased, however, the potential rose for violence to be directed toward these "Strangers within the Gate City."[73] The spark that ignited this violence took place in April 1913 when a fourteen-year-old girl, Mary Phagan, was found dead in the pencil factory where she worked. The manager of the factory, a recent arrival in Atlanta from New York named Leo M. Frank, was arrested for the murder and subjected to a sensational trial. Many of the same newspapers that had fanned racial hatred into riot in 1906 now turned their rhetoric against Frank. Passions ran high during the trial, and each evening the jury returned to their hotel amid shouts of "Hang the Jew" from people who lined the streets.[74]

Frank was convicted on circumstantial evidence and sentenced to be executed. Appeals on his behalf stayed the execution three times during the next two years, while Frank was confined to a state prison farm in Milledgeville. Governor John M. Slaton reviewed the evidence in Frank's case and commuted the sentence to life imprisonment. The decision was so unpopular that on August 16, 1915, Frank was dragged from the prison farm by a well-organized mob, driven 175 miles over dirt roads to Marietta (a town just north of Atlanta), and lynched near Mary Phagan's birthplace. The body was brought to Atlanta the next day, where a crowd of an estimated 15,000 filed past to see it in the funeral home. Acting Mayor I. N. Ragsdale appealed for order to "protect the good name of Atlanta." Newspapers published detailed accounts of the lynching, but none of the participants was ever identified.[75] The Southern code of honor apparently required Frank's death as a protection for females such as Mary Phagan. Mayor J. G. Woodward expressed this sentiment when he spoke at a meeting in San Francisco: "Leo M. Frank suffered the just penalty for an unspeakable crime. . . . [W]hen it comes to a woman's honor, there is no limit we will not go to avenge and protect." He was also outraged at the national press, which he believed had poisoned opinion against Atlanta.[76]

As they had in the past, Atlanta's business leaders now rallied in response to the negative publicity surrounding the Frank lynching. The Chamber of Commerce, representing the interests of all types of businesses in the city, passed a resolution calling for a revival of the "Atlanta Spirit." The city had been torn by dissensions, and it was time "for a strong pull toward the upbuilding and re-establishing the prestige of our city." Business groups representing bankers, retail merchants, and manufacturers also endorsed the resolution in the hope that the "Atlanta Spirit" could be revived and bring the city the "harmony that made Atlanta the great commercial and social center of the southeast."[77]

Business leaders focused their attention on plans already under way for an agricultural exposition. In the aftermath of the Frank lynching, the promoters of the exposition wanted to have "one week in which everything will be forgotten but fun, and Atlanta will be stimulated by an influx of visitors from all parts of the state." In typical Atlanta fashion, the city business leaders threw their energy into promoting the exposition. This was not an "international" exposition but would be a harvest festival for Georgia farmers designed to promote agricultural diversity in the state.[78]

During the Frank trial and its aftermath, the members of Atlanta's Jewish community continued to live in fear of the anti-Semitism that had emerged in the city. There was some effort to boycott Jewish merchants, but most were able to continue their business with little disruption. The lynching showed Jews in Atlanta that they were vulnerable to bigotry and that economic success would not protect them. One result of the national publicity surrounding the episode was the organization of the Anti-Defamation League to combat anti-Semitism.

Another outcome of the Leo Frank case was a revival of the Ku Klux Klan in Atlanta.[79] On the evening before Thanksgiving 1915, William J. Simmons, an organizer of several fraternal organizations and a former Methodist minister, gathered twenty men in a meeting room at the Piedmont Hotel. Fifteen members of the group left the hotel and drove to nearby Stone Mountain in a sight-seeing bus hired by Simmons. After climbing to the top of the mountain in the dark, Simmons ignited a cross of pine boards and initiated the men into the Klan. Two weeks later, membership in the Klan grew in response to the excitement generated by the Atlanta premiere of D. W. Griffith's film *The Birth of a Nation*.[80] The movie about the founding of the Klan during the Reconstruction era was so popular that it played in Atlanta theaters for many years. The revived Ku Klux Klan made its headquarters in Atlanta. Simmons held the title of Imperial Wizard in the Klan he directed from the Imperial City of Atlanta, and Klan members promoted racial and ethnic hatred throughout the nation.

The Frank lynching had little economic impact on Atlanta. There were a few Northern companies who said they would refuse to do business in the city until members of the lynch mob were brought to justice, but otherwise business resumed as usual. Four days after the lynching, the Southern Conference of the YWCA announced that its next meeting would be held in Atlanta. One week later, the city's convention recruitment was in high gear as the Southern Nurserymen's Association announced plans to meet in Atlanta in 1916. The next day, the governor addressed the opening of the National Association of Building Managers as their eight hundred delegates met in the city. On September 21, 1915, an important Cotton Convention opened with growers, warehousemen, and bankers gathering to discuss a faraway threat to this Southern staple crop.[81]

Atlanta during World War I

When it began in Europe in 1914, the war seemed far removed from the concerns of most Atlanta residents. This changed quickly as an embargo reduced overseas shipments of cotton. The economy of the Southeast depended heavily upon cotton growing and marketing, and Atlanta's rail lines provided the transportation for much of the region's cotton, which was still shipped elsewhere for manufacturing. With European markets closed because of the war, cotton prices in the South dropped. The low cotton prices continued throughout the war, only to be replaced by a more serious threat to cotton production at the end of the decade when the boll weevil marched across the South, destroying crops along the way. With cotton prices down, farmers and others who depended on the crop had less money to spend. This, in turn, affected the local economy in Atlanta.

The impact on the city would have been even greater if there had not been new activities to stimulate the economy. One of these was provided by the national convention of the Shriners held in Atlanta on May 10–12, 1914. Shriners from all over the continent arrived for the event, filling all available rooms in the city's hotels. An overflow of 4,000 visitors stayed in 250 Pullman cars parked in the railroad yards, and other visitors stayed in private homes.[82] An estimated 45,000 Shriners and their wives were in the city for the convention, generating $3 million in revenues for the economy.[83]

Recognizing the seriousness of dependence on a single agricultural crop, the leaders of Atlanta's Chamber of Commerce decided to rekindle an old idea by staging an agricultural exposition to promote diversified farming. This agricultural fair was also a partnership between business leaders and the local governments of the city and Fulton County. The city owned the 375-acre site south of downtown known as Lakewood Park, which had long been the location for an amusement park that leased the land from the city. Under the new agreement, the city and county each advanced $75,000 and local business leaders promised to raise $75,000 from a stock subscription. The money from the city would be used for the construction of permanent buildings on the fairgrounds, while the county would provide money, labor, and materials for improving the grounds and approaches. The money from the private investors would be used to promote and administer the fair.[84] The partners in this venture rushed to arrange the first Lakewood Agricultural Fair in 1915, which was combined with a weeklong Harvest Festival. Visitors to the festivities filled the city's hotels and crowded into cafés, theaters, and other places of amusement. Some of those turned away from the hotels stayed in private homes in a display of hospitality, which would not allow visitors to the city during the event to be without quarters.[85]

The following year the fair grew to become a major attraction for the city, and it remained an annual event for the next seventy years. Although its goals were more modest than the expositions of the nineteenth century, the Lakewood Agricultural Fair played a major role in promoting the poultry and livestock industry in Georgia.[86] The fair also helped revive the "Atlanta Spirit" among the business community during the months following the Frank lynching.

When the United States entered World War I in 1917, Atlanta became the location of two large military training facilities, one for officers at Fort McPherson and another for enlisted men at the newly constructed Camp Gordon. It is estimated that over 233,000 soldiers passed through Camp Gordon during the war period.[87] Soldiers filled area hotels, restaurants, and amusement places, and several new hotels were constructed during this time to accommodate the crowds of recruits and soldiers who came to Atlanta. One of these new facilities was the Cecil Hotel at Luckie and Cone Streets.[88]

While these crowded conditions were good for the tourism businesses, they also allowed for the spread of disease. In early October 1918, the national influenza epidemic struck Atlanta. The presence of so many soldiers contributed to the flu's spreading among both the military and civilian populations. The board of health responded by closing all places of public assembly, including schools, libraries, theaters, dance halls, motion picture shows, and even churches.[89] Amusement places, restaurants, and hotels were hit hard by the order, which lasted until the end of the month.[90] Overall, however, the war period was good for Atlanta's tourism businesses.

One veteran returning from the war had an idea that was to have a profound impact on tourism businesses in Atlanta and elsewhere. Isadore M. Weinstein was wounded in France, and while recovering in military hospitals conceived the notion of a linen supply service for hotels and restaurants. In 1919 he returned home and with limited capital started the Atlanta Linen Supply Company, which supplied towels for public restrooms, uniforms for waitresses, tablecloths, and other linens for hospitality businesses. The local success of the business led to the formation of the National Linen Service Corporation, which is still headquartered in Atlanta and serves tourism businesses throughout the country.[91]

Two Decades of Growth

Atlanta had begun the new century as a city of just under 90,000 residents. During the next two decades, economic growth brought a rapid expansion of the population to the area as new jobs attracted new citizens. Many of the homes built to house this population were located in new suburban developments outside the city limits, and several annexations expanded the borders of the city and increased its population. This enabled the 1910 census to report almost 155,000 residents in Atlanta, and by 1920, over 200,000.[92] Atlanta's tourism businesses also expanded with the city's increased economic and population growth. In 1901 there were 35 hotels and only 18 eating places in the city; twenty years later there were 48 hotels and 372 eating places.[93] Boardinghouses stopped being enumerated in the city directories during this period, reflecting a shift in housing patterns as apartment buildings were constructed for many of those who did not own or rent single-family housing. There continued to be boardinghouses in the city, however, as the Census Bureau indicated 470 keepers of boarding and lodging houses in 1920, up from 237 at the turn of the century.

As a comparison of Tables 3.2 and 3.3 demonstrates, employment in Atlanta's tourism businesses grew only slightly between 1910 and 1920. Part of the reason for this modest growth in the number of jobs in the hospitality businesses may be the labor shortages caused by the war. This is suggested by the fact that the

Table 3.3. Employment in Atlanta Tourism Businesses, 1920

Occupation	Men	Women
Bartenders	3	–
Amusements	84	–
Bding & Lodging Housekeepers	56	414
Hotelkeepers & Managers	55	9
Restaurant Keepers	225	127
Saloonkeepers	5	–
Servants*	1,196	6,731
Waiters	596	361
	2,220	7,642

*In nondomestic settings
Source: Bureau of the Census, *Fourteenth Census of the United States, 1920: Occupations*, vol. 3.

number of men employed in tourism businesses showed a slight decline between 1910 and 1920, falling from 4.8 percent of all males in the labor force in 1910 to 3.3 percent in 1920. It is interesting that even with a statewide prohibition since 1908, and a national prohibition which took effect in 1920, three men listed their occupations as bartenders and five as saloonkeepers.

The 7,642 women employed in Atlanta's tourism businesses represent 23.7 percent of all females in the labor force. While this is a slight decline from 1910, it shows that women needed the low-paying jobs as maids, cooks, and waitresses in hospitality businesses. Only nine of the sixty-four hotelkeepers and managers were female, while the lower-paying positions as boarding-house keepers continued to be held predominantly by women. The overwhelming majority of women employed in this area, however, continued to be black women working as cooks and maids in Atlanta's hotels and eating places. During the war, many women moved into jobs in tourism businesses usually filled by men, such as waiting on tables. For example, a 1918 survey of thirty-four hotels in the city showed that women filled 15 percent of such jobs. Many of these new positions were lost once the war was won and men returned home.[94]

After the first two decades of the new century, Atlanta had grown considerably, rising from forty-third-largest among the nation's cities in 1900 to thirty-eighth in 1920.[95] Among cities in the South, in 1920 Atlanta ranked second in population behind New Orleans, and just ahead of another city that had grown as if by magic, Birmingham. While Atlanta expanded as a transportation and commercial center, Birmingham thrived as an industrial city, growing from a population of under 40,000 in 1900 to almost 179,000 in 1920. In spite of this rapid growth, urbanization in the South still lagged far behind that of the rest of the nation. For example, the 1920 U.S. Census showed that the nation had become for the first time in its history a majority urban nation, with 51.2 percent of the population living in cities. That same year, however, the urban population of the South was only 25.4 percent.[96] Georgia's urban population was 25.1 percent in 1920 and did not reach a majority until the 1950s, indicating the persistence of the predominantly rural nature of the state and region.[97]

Yet by 1920 Atlanta was part of a growing system of cities in the Southeast, and the largest cities in the region were growing more rapidly than any other cities in the nation. Atlanta could depend upon its location and its rail lines as well as the determination of its leaders to stay at the forefront in what they perceived to be a race for municipal greatness. The decades ahead would provide challenges to the city as the prosperity of the 1920s would be followed by an economic depression that devastated the nation's poorist region.

4

Prosperity, Depression, and War Years, 1920–1945

In 1920, one of the young women who made her debut into Atlanta society amid the whirl of dinners, dances, and fine clothes was the daughter of one of the city's oldest families. Once the round of debutante parties was over, the woman followed the convention of the time and married, after which she might have been expected to give her time to charities and the social life of the city's elite families. Instead, the young woman took a job as a reporter for the magazine section of the *Atlanta Journal*. In other departures from tradition, she divorced her husband in 1924, continued her employment with the newspaper, and re-married the following year while keeping her maiden name, Margaret Mitchell. She gave up her job in 1926, after an automobile accident, and began writing a novel while confined to the apartment on Peachtree Street she shared with her husband, John Marsh. Ten years later, in 1936, her novel *Gone with the Wind* was published.

Mitchell's book was a national best-seller, capturing the imagination of an audience of readers that quickly spread throughout the world. For many the appeal of the novel was captured in its title, which evoked an image of the lost glories of the Old South. As Mitchell described this antebellum era, the social life of the plantation class was based on a code of behavior that featured gracious hospitality depicted in an endless series of fancy balls, hunting parties, and other forms of entertainment. This social life was disturbed only by the talk of fighting a war against the North to defend the Southern way of life. The loss of the war and the horrors of Reconstruction meant the destruction of the plantation way of life and the "Golden Age" it represented. The heroine of the book, Scarlett O'Hara, survives through all of these cruel circumstances. Margaret Mitchell said that Scarlett's survival after the loss of her old way of life was the major theme of the book.[1]

The story of the loss of the Old South and its way of life may account for much of the popularity of *Gone with the Wind,* but it is only part of what Mitchell had to say. In a summary of the novel written to her publisher, Mitchell said, "I thought I would write a story of a girl who was somewhat like Atlanta—part of the old South; part of the new South; [how] she rose with Atlanta and fell with it, and how she rose again."[2] There was a deliberate identification of Scarlett with Atlanta. In the novel, as the young widow Scarlett leaves her plantation home, Tara, to live in Atlanta with her Aunt Pittypat, Mitchell wrote,

> But Atlanta was of her own generation, crude with the crudities of youth and as headstrong and impetuous as herself. . . .
>
> In a space of time but little longer than Scarlett's seventeen years, Atlanta had grown from a single stake driven in the ground into a thriving small city of ten thousand that was the center of attention for the whole state. . . .
>
> Scarlett had always liked Atlanta for the very same reasons that made Savannah, Augusta and Macon condemn it. Like herself, the town was a mixture of the old and new in Georgia, in which the old often came off second best in its conflicts with the self-willed and vigorous new. Moreover, there was something personal, exciting about a town that was born—or at least christened—the same year she was christened.[3]

In this scene Mitchell captured an essential truth about Atlanta—it embraced the ideals of the New South, where the pursuit of

wealth through industrialization and Northern investment triumphed over the old Southern plantation way of life. The older
coastal and river cities were eclipsed by the younger interior city,
where commerce moved by railroads. Scarlett thrived in postwar
Atlanta by embracing the New South. She married for money,
became a hard-nosed businesswoman, collaborated with the car-
petbag-scalawag government, employed convict labor in her saw-
mill, married the wealthy Rhett Butler when her second husband
died, and built an ostentatious Victorian mansion. Atlanta did
these things too, with a spirit of boastfulness and arrogance that
provoked the jealousy of older cities in the state and region. Also
like Scarlett, there was, even in the hustle and bustle of the capital of the New South, a certain amount of nostalgia for the Old
South. After the war, the ladies and gentlemen of Atlanta resumed the social regimen in imitation of the old days. As Scarlett
attended a dance in Atlanta after the war, she reflected on the
men and women of the city: "Everything in their old world had
changed but the old forms. . . . The old usages went on, must go
on, for the forms were all that were left to them."[4]

Mitchell's discussion of the Old South versus the New South
in *Gone with the Wind* says much about the attitudes of Atlantans
toward their past and about Southern cultural values such as hospitality. The world of the Old South was lost along with the Civil
War, and Atlanta became a place of importance as the center of
the New South. Although the chief concern of its leading citizens
was business, the "old forms"—the traditions and culture of the
older rural South—continued. The graciousness of traditional
Southern hospitality was one of these forms that continued to be
carried on by the ladies and gentlemen of Atlanta. Yet even this
form was changed by the commercialism of the New South. The
expositions of the nineteenth century and the conventions of the
twentieth were commercial expressions of Southern hospitality
in Atlanta. Hospitality was expressed in the charm and grace
with which visitors were welcomed to the city, but the invitation
was usually to come and do business. The culture of the Old
South was put into the service of the New. Written in the 1920s,

Mitchell's novel succeeded in describing the *ethos*—the guiding complex of beliefs about the nature and role—of Atlanta in the period after World War I.[5]

A Decade of Prosperity

Following the end of World War I, Atlantans saw the future in terms of peace and prosperity. The war had swelled the city with soldiers passing through on the railroads and training in local military bases. Now that peace was at hand, a spirit of optimism reigned in the city as business boomed and the population continued to grow. As the *Constitution* reminded its readers at the beginning of 1920, Atlanta was "no longer a village nor a town, but a big, prosperous and growing city."[6]

In the midst of Atlanta's success as the center of the New South, there remained a long-standing relationship between the city and the rural areas of the region. A wartime embargo of cotton shipments to Europe had lowered cotton prices since 1915. This was followed by an agricultural disaster in the South caused by the destruction of cotton crops as the boll weevil spread across the region. In 1918 Georgia produced more than 2 million bales of cotton, but two years later production dropped by more than 700,000 bales. As the insect plague spread, the cotton crop continued to decline so that the state produced a total of only 715,000 bales in 1922. While many sharecroppers and tenant farmers left the state, thousands of displaced farmers, both black and white, flocked to Atlanta in hopes of finding jobs in the city's expanding commercial and industrial economy.[7]

The presence of so many native-born migrants from the small towns and countryside continued to influence Atlanta and other cities in the region as these migrants brought with them patterns of Southern rural culture.[8] One of the strongest elements of this regional culture was religion. As Charles Reagan Wilson has noted, the evangelical Protestantism of the rural South has permeated the culture of the region. Wilson quotes William Faulkner's description of religion's role in his upbringing: "My life was passed, my childhood, in a very small Mississippi town, and that was a part of my background. I grew up with that. I assimilated that, took that in without even knowing it. It's just there. It has nothing to do with how much of it I might believe or disbelieve— it's just there."[9] Historian David Goldfield adds to the list of Southern cultural traits, suggesting that when rural folks moved to cities in the region they carried with them tastes for native music—jazz, bluegrass, country, and rhythm and blues; indigenous food—pork barbecue, fried chicken, fried okra, and pecan pie; and a generally slower pace of life that still included manners and etiquette.[10]

Other observers have commented on manners and hospitality as aspects of Southern culture transported by rural migrants to the cities. Josephine Pinckney, a poet from Charleston, noted the contrast between the urban civilization of the North and the "still rural character of Southern society." A Southern woman of higher position in society was "more cordial, more interested in the people she meets, than her equivalent elsewhere, and the working-girl more courteous." Pinckney attributed these differences to the smaller cities in the South and the large percentage of their residents "lately recruited from the plantation and the farm." Part of the pattern of hospitality in the South was kindness toward neighbors, where "you drop in to see them and send them some hot rolls when the cook bakes especially well." Having black servants made the obligations of hospitality easier for the women of the upper class than for their less-well-to-do sisters.[11]

The rural migration to Atlanta and the annexation of neighborhoods on the edge of the city helped Atlanta to record a population of over 200,000 in the 1920 U.S. Census. This represented a growth of more than 45,000 in the last decade. Atlanta's rate of growth was the cause of considerable jealousy in other cities in the region. For instance, Birmingham's *Age-Herald* accused Atlanta of surreptitiously watering its census report: "The Georgia metropolis has a way, it is said, of counting week-end visitors, and in a pinch hotel registers and morgue records."[12] Despite such criticism, the local civic leadership took great pride in the city's growth, seeing it as a validation of their efforts to boost the reputation and the economy of Atlanta.

Eating Places

In 1920 most of Atlanta's 372 eating places were independently operated establishments. Only a few chains operated in the city. The largest number of these businesses (194) were lunchrooms, which were important to people who found themselves away from home at midday. Serving simple food quickly and inexpensively, they were the period's equivalent of today's fast-food hamburger shops.[13] Many of these lunchrooms were sandwich shops, while others were known for their "meat, three sides, and a drink" menus (which remain popular in the South today). Some of these eating places were known as "tea rooms," which were a popular Southern type of lunchroom during the period. Sometimes these specialized in a particular dish, such as Mrs. McRee's Tea Room, which featured chicken dinners with hot rolls.[14] Another regional favorite, the cafeteria, is also included among the listings for both lunchrooms and restaurants in the city directories of the period. One of the largest cafeterias was the S and W, with elegant seating for 750 patrons amid palms, ferns, waterfalls, and fountains.[15] Most of the cafeterias were also independent operations.[16]

In the era of racial segregation enforced by custom as well as Jim Crow laws, blacks and whites had separate eating places. By 1920 Auburn Avenue had become the center for African-American life and commerce in the city. As one elderly black Atlantan recalled, "You could get anything you wanted on Auburn Avenue, and we owned it." The area was a source of pride for African Americans, who could shop without the restrictions and insults often encountered in downtown stores. There were dozens of black-owned businesses and professionals on the street, including restaurants, drugstores, and eating places of all kinds as well as the dining facilities of the James Hotel. Several of the eating places on "Sweet Auburn" were owned by African-American women. One of these, Ma Sutton's Café, was a longtime landmark and well known both to local black residents and visitors. It featured fried chicken, barbecue, ribs, and "good Southern cooking, the kind that satisfies and then lingers on and on in sweet memories of joy and happiness."[17]

Restaurants with table service were few in Atlanta. Those featuring fine dining were even more scarce and were primarily associated with hotel dining rooms rather than free-standing restaurants. Except for these few dining rooms that catered to the traveling public and to locals on fancy occasions, the quality of food generally available in Atlanta's eating places in 1920 was rather poor and designed to appeal to the typical Southern-born resident who was downtown and hungry at noon. The fact that people in Atlanta and the South in general did not eat out often is reflected in the relatively small number of eating places and individuals employed in them.[18] Most important meals were eaten in the home, and for the wealthy there were always private clubs for dining and entertaining. Private clubs for the elite were found in most cities, although eating out was much more common in the more heavily industrialized cities of the North than among the South's working classes. This was because of the availability of diners to serve industrial workers.[19]

Conventions

Atlanta's civic leadership had long recognized the importance of commercial applications of hospitality. Elected public officials such as the mayor or the governor would send formal letters of invitation to prospective organizations at the request of the Atlanta Convention Bureau. Once a group decided to meet in Atlanta, the bureau would be responsible for the follow-up to promote the event, help with finance, arrange the program, and furnish entertainment.[20] Officials of the Chamber of Commerce and the Convention Bureau were convinced that going out and getting conventions to come to Atlanta was good for the town as a whole. As the bureau's assistant secretary explained, "The fundamental reason for desiring to bring Conventions to Atlanta is that their coming means more business. Visitors in town spend money. Hotels spend money to entertain visitors. Transportation companies receive money for transporting visitors from, to and about the town. . . . Merchants receive money from selling to visitors. Every business is more or less directly benefitted by the presence of visitors."[21] While seldom expressed this clearly, this same logic has motivated the commercial hospitality of Atlantans since the city's early days. Railroads, streetcars, and taxicabs benefited from having more passengers. Tourism businesses grew and prospered from the presence of convention visitors. Retail businesses sold goods and services to them, and other businesses profited from the circulation of dollars in the local economy.

The Atlanta Convention Bureau took credit for bringing 2,410 conventions to the city during the first eleven years of its existence. Although many of these were state and regional meetings, the city also hosted national and even international conventions. Some of the larger groups were the International Association of Advertising Clubs of the World, the International Rotary, the International Kiwanis, the National Council of General Federation of Women's Clubs, the National Association of Credit Men, and the National Convention of Elks.[22] The bureau welcomed these organizations to the city with exemplary Southern hospitality. For example, when the American Society of Mechanical Engineers brought its 1,500 delegates to meet in Atlanta in 1922, the Convention Bureau made plans "to give the distinguished visitors an entertainment thoroughly in keeping with Atlanta's reputation for hospitality." The social events of the meeting included an old-fashioned barbecue with "all the fixin's," as well as an exhibition golf match featuring local champion Bobby Jones. Atlantans hoped that showing off the city and its hospitality would bring increased industrial investment to the city.[23]

A much larger national meeting of the fraternal organization known as the Benevolent and Protective Order of Elks was held in Atlanta on July 9–15, 1923. Local business leaders prepared for every detail of the visit with characteristic "Atlanta Spirit," crowding the visitors' schedule with parades, receptions, balls, barbecues, and merrymaking in the streets. After welcoming speeches by the mayor and governor, the grand exalted ruler of the supreme grand lodge of Elks responded to the greetings by saying, "Atlanta has fulfilled every promise she has made. The welcome accorded the visiting Elks has been beyond expectation. Atlanta has taken in and generously provided for every single man and woman of our organization who came to knock at her doors, and she has shown the best of that Southern hospitality which is famed over the length and breadth of the United States."[24] Estimates of the number of visitors to the city for the Elks' convention varied, but it was generally thought that 40,000 Elks and their wives were in town for the event. Overall the convention went smoothly, although there were numerous violations of the national prohibition laws, including one large raid on a "blind tiger" which resulted in twenty-one arrests.[25]

Atlanta hosted 315 conventions during 1923, the seventh-largest number in the nation.[26] Fred Houser, secretary of the Convention Bureau, estimated that conventions brought 80,000 visitors to the city during 1923. If each visitor stayed an average of three days and spent an average of ten dollars per day, then the monetary returns from conventions during the year were estimated to be $2,400,000. The costs to operate the Convention Bureau for the year, on the other hand, were $20,000, and $88,000 was spent to entertain the conventions hosted by the city. According to Houser, this gave a net profit to the city for 1923 conventions of $2,292,000, or a dividend of 2,100 percent for every dollar invested in the bureau.[27] This is the sort of exaggerated claim that was designed to promote support for continuing efforts to attract more growth to the city. Although dollars were injected into the local economy from these events, these estimates actually understated the costs to the city and its residents, such as traffic congestion, higher prices, and the drain on public services.[28]

Part of the credit for Atlanta's success in attracting conventions was given to the local newspapers for their help in "selling" the city to the convention and also marketing the convention to the city.[29] This seems consistent with the role of the local media as prominent participants in the "growth machine."[30] Newspapers are important local property owners and profit from the increased circulation resulting from growth. The Atlanta papers, notably the *Constitution* and *Journal,* frequently acted as "cheerleaders for development," whether that growth came from conventions or outside investment of another sort.[31] Houser described Atlanta's newspapers as "ever on the lookout for an opportunity to serve the city," adding that the newspapers "have in no uncertain way made the effort to secure conventions for this city much easier than it otherwise would have been."[32]

New Hotels

One of the results of Atlanta's growing convention business was an increase in the number of hotel rooms needed for visitors. This led to the expansion of several hotels and plans for the building of new ones.[33] During 1924 three new hotels opened for business—the Biltmore, the Robert Fulton (later known as the Georgian), and the Henry Grady. All three were located to the north of the older hotel district near the railroads. The Biltmore was constructed on West Peachtree, the Fulton on Luckie Street, and the Henry Grady on Peachtree Street.

At the spectacular opening of the Biltmore, more than a thousand people drove up to the entrance in a scene described by the *Atlanta Georgian:* "The building, the majestic portico of the carriage entrance, the gleaming marble terrace, and the carefully planned garden that was like a gem of many facets, all were fairly ablaze with light in which the expensive automobiles shone, the evening gowns of women twinkled with fairy iridescence, and the general effect was one of grandeur."[34] This hotel, like many in the city's past, was built by the alliance of a local entrepreneur and Northern capital. The local component was supplied by William Candler, a young member of the family that had owned the Coca-Cola Company. He served as vice-president and treasurer of the operating company for the Biltmore, which was part of the national Bowman group of hotels.[35]

The neo-Georgian Biltmore was designed by New York architect Leonard Shultz. At the time of its opening the hotel was the largest in the city, with 600 guest rooms, several large halls for banquets and balls, and elegant formal gardens. The Biltmore advertised itself as the "South's Supreme Hotel."[36] Unlike the city's earlier grand hotels, such as the Kimball House and the Markham House, the Biltmore was the result of changing transportation technology, since it was designed with an automobile entrance and located far away from the early center of town near the railroad lines.

During 1925 two more new hotels opened in Atlanta. The first was the Carlton Bachelor Apartment Hotel (later the Cox-Carlton Hotel) on Peachtree Street near the Fox Theater. Providing lodging for men, it served the same function as the boardinghouses of earlier days. One of the city's older boardinghouses, the Bell House, merged with the Carlton, its residents moving into the top three floors of the new twelve-story hotel. The longtime housekeeper of the Bell House, Mrs. Nettie Howard, and her sister also moved into the Carlton as the only women allowed in the hotel. (The Cox-Carlton Hotel property continues in operation as part of the Days Inn chain of hotels.)[37]

The other new apartment hotel was built on the corner of Ponce de Leon and Highland Avenues by Coca-Cola magnate Asa G. Candler. This luxury hotel, called the Briarcliff, was designed by local architect G. Lloyd Preacher and served as the southwest anchor for Candler's new Druid Hills residential development. The Druid Hills neighborhood, featuring a country club with golf course and well-designed streets and parks, had been designed as a suburban enclave for the wealthy by the famous landscape architect Frederick Law Olmsted. The new luxury hotel enabled visitors to stay near the homes of some of the city's most prosperous citizens.[38]

Promoting the City

The prosperity and growth of the early years of the decade began to fade by 1925. Many Atlanta residents were caught up in the booming real estate development in Florida. The effects on Atlanta were perhaps more psychological than actual, but local business leaders began to worry if the city was, indeed, losing ground as people left to take part in the Florida land boom. There was also the threat of competition from Birmingham, located only 150 miles to the west. Birmingham's population in 1920 was only slightly less than Atlanta's 200,000, and business leaders wondered if Atlanta could sustain its growth as a regional metropolis. To counter this sense of malaise, the president of the Chamber of Commerce, W. R. C. Smith, suggested a nationwide advertising campaign to promote Atlanta. During the fall of 1925, the leaders of the chamber planned the program that came to be known as the "Forward Atlanta" campaign. William Candler, part owner of the Biltmore Hotel, led a fund-raising drive to finance the campaign, and Ivan Allen, Sr., chaired the Forward Atlanta Commission. Enthusiasm among business leaders was high, and the campaign raised $268,000 in four days.[39]

Forward Atlanta advertisements stressed the need for industries to decentralize and locate branch manufacturing facilities in the city. Atlanta was already a rail center as well as a financial center due to the presence of the Federal Reserve Bank, making the city a logical transportation and distribution center for the South. Ivan Allen and his commission printed the advertisements more than 43 million times in selected publications during 1926. As a result of this initial year of the promotion, 169 new businesses employing more than 4,000 people and with annual payrolls of more than $7 million opened in Atlanta in 1927. With these phenomenal results, the chamber decided to extend the Forward Atlanta campaign for two more years with an advertising budget of $1 million.[40]

After four years of the campaign, 679 new businesses had located in the city. Many of these were later consolidated, leaving a total of 594 businesses employing nearly 17,000 people with an annual payroll of $30 million by 1930.[41] Some of the larger companies to open Atlanta branches as a result of the Forward Atlanta campaign were Johnson & Johnson, General Motors, Sears Roebuck, National Biscuit Company, Cluett Peabody & Company, and Macy's. Most of the new businesses were regional sales offices, wholesale distribution centers, and retail establishments, adding to Atlanta's role as a regional and increasingly national commercial city. By 1930 Atlanta, the twenty-ninth-largest city in the United States, ranked second in terms of available office space.[42] The promotional efforts were so successful that B. C. Forbes wrote in his business column, "If your city wants to attract industries, ask Atlanta how it is done."[43]

Atlanta's business leadership had once again shown that their spirit of enterprise could spark their city's growth. The organized efforts of the Chamber of Commerce succeeded, while Birmingham lacked an indigenous business leadership. The owners of the Birmingham steel mills lived in Pittsburgh and had no vested interest in local economic development. This slowed Birmingham's growth in its rivalry with Atlanta as both cities competed to become major regional metropolises.

The economic development activities of the Chamber of Commerce did not please all Atlantans, however, as white business leaders had not offered blacks equal participation in the city's plans for economic development. African-American newspapers such as the *Independent* criticized the Forward Atlanta advertising campaign for ignoring blacks, asking, "How can we enter heartily into the movement, when the million dollars are spent among white folks only, and the invitation extended through advertisements are [*sic*] to white people only?"[44] As a result, African Americans focused their attention on the improvement of their own neighborhoods and the economic advancement of their people. Booker T. Washington's National Negro Business League encouraged support for black-owned businesses, and the National Association for the Advancement of Colored People (NAACP) promoted self-help and racial solidarity among blacks. The result was a segregated African-American commercial-civic elite with its own visions of growth and economic development within the black community.

As Atlanta grew as a center for African-American business, Auburn Avenue became the black equivalent of Peachtree Street, while other African-American businesses were established on

Decatur Street and in the newer "westside" commercial development along Hunter Street near Atlanta University.[45] These three areas contained a variety of tourism businesses, including theaters, clubs, hotels, and restaurants, which served black local residents and visitors. African-American tourism businesses hosted segregated conventions such as annual meetings of the NAACP, the Alpha Phi Alpha Fraternity, and the National Baptist Convention.[46]

There was considerable irony in the fact that Atlanta developed as a center for black business during the 1920s, when the city was developing a reputation as the Imperial City, the headquarters of the Ku Klux Klan. Following its revival in 1915 by William Simmons, the Klan had grown to include several thousand members across the South by 1920. That year Simmons had joined forces with two Atlantans, Edward Y. Clarke and Elizabeth Tyler, who brought publicity and organizing skills to the Klan.[47] Within a year the organization had spread to cities outside the region and its membership had grown to almost 100,000.

Besides serving as Klan headquarters, Atlanta was also the home of the Klan's publishing house and a manufacturing company for official Klan regalia.[48] Klan membership was heavily concentrated among blue-collar workers, with some lower-echelon white-collar employees. During the 1920s many members of Atlanta's police force were also Klansmen. Klan membership was strong in other cities throughout the South (except for New Orleans), and the group also showed surprising strength in cities outside the region.[49] Historian Kenneth Jackson has shown that the Klan was popular in urban areas because it reflected widespread discontent with rapid growth and the presumed decline of older moral and religious values. Its members posed no threat to the dominant commercial civic elite that controlled business and politics in cities like Atlanta, and its white supremacist views were thought to keep blacks "in their place" in society. Many of the leaders of business and city government shared these views, and although the newspapers occasionally condemned the Klan's violence, the organization was usually tolerated as beneficial to the order and well-being of the community.

The Chamber of Commerce did little to deter Klan activity because the organization pumped money into Atlanta's economy. The city hosted numerous "klanventions" and "klanvokations," such as the first Imperial Klanvokation, held in May 1922, which attracted nearly 4,000 Klansmen. The meeting included a march down Peachtree Street, a special ceremony atop Stone Mountain, and a reception at "Klancrest," the official home of the Imperial Wizard. A second Klanvokation was held that November and brought representatives of a thousand local Klans to the Imperial City. At this meeting Simmons was made Emperor of the Klan and a new Imperial Wizard, Dr. Hiram W. Evans, was elected. The local press greeted these meetings with the same enthusiasm that other organizations and their conventions received.[50]

With the rekindling of the "Atlanta Spirit" in the Forward Atlanta campaign, local tourism businesses also got a boost. Early in 1925 the Convention Bureau reorganized itself to become the Convention and Tourist Bureau, a change reflecting its new purpose of promoting Atlanta as a tourist destination. The city offered its railroad connections to make it accessible, hotels for accommodations, a pleasant climate, and several points of interest for visitors, including the *Cyclorama,* a huge painting of the Battle of Atlanta for which a special building had been constructed in Grant Park in 1921.[51] Another major attraction was found fifteen miles east of the city at Stone Mountain, the largest body of exposed granite in the world, which offered excellent views of downtown Atlanta. Plans were also under way during the 1920s to carve a monument to Confederate war heroes—Robert E. Lee, Thomas J. "Stonewall" Jackson, and Jefferson Davis—as a symbol of regional pride.[52] Other Atlanta tourist destinations included the Lakewood Fairgrounds and several nearby amusement parks.

Throughout the 1920s business leaders pushed for the paving of roads in the state and region. Early in November 1929 their plans were realized with the opening of the Dixie Highway connecting the Great Lakes and the Florida Keys. Its completion redefined Atlanta as a regional metropolis at the hub of travel by motor vehicle in addition to rail. This was the start of road building into the city, which would make Atlanta the crossroads of three major Southeastern interstate highways.[53] The change to the motor vehicle as the primary means of transportation would support Atlanta's growth and its tourism businesses in the years ahead.

Visitors and residents supported a lively theater district in the downtown area north of Five Points. Within a one-block area were the Howard, Grand, Lyric, Forsyth, Metropolitan, and Rialto Theaters. Most were built with stages for performances by traveling companies and vaudeville shows. In the late 1920s, many changed over to movie houses with the heyday of the Atlanta motion picture theaters.[54] These upscale theaters were designed for white audiences, but most featured separate entrances and seating for black patrons. African Americans wishing to avoid the stigma of segregation could choose among the "81" and the Ritz on Decatur Street, Bailey's Royal on Auburn Avenue, and the Ashby Theater on Hunter Street.[55] Most African-American businesses in the city were concentrated on these three streets.

Business organizations of both races promoted the city as a tourist destination, the National Negro Business League reminding blacks that "Atlanta, the Metropolis of the Southeast, is close to everywhere and within twenty-four hours ride of ninety per cent of the colored population of the U.S."[56] White audiences were also recruited throughout the region by publications such as the Chamber of Commerce's *City Builder,* which featured articles on annual performances in Atlanta by the Metropolitan Opera Company as well as editorials on the advantages of the city's hotels and restaurants.[57]

With the success of these promotional efforts, Atlanta's convention and hospitality businesses enjoyed a decade of remarkable growth. By the end of the decade the city ranked among the country's top ten destinations for conventions and was attempting to become a leisure travel destination as well. Business leaders were aware of the remarkable growth of Miami, which showed the largest percentage population increase of any city in the United States between 1910 and 1920. Its growth was almost entirely based on the leisure travel of tourists, and if tourism would make a city grow, Atlanta did not want to be left out. Officials of the Convention and Tourist Bureau stressed the healthfulness of the favorable year-round climate as well as the high altitude and good drainage of Atlanta in comparison to other cities. At the same time, they knew that the city lacked some amenities needed to attract tourists—a need that has remained a constant theme of Atlanta's tourism business leaders since the 1920s.[58]

Since the 1920s, promoters of Atlanta's hospitality businesses have used exaggerated claims to tout the economic impact of tourism on the city. A constant stream of information from the Chamber of Commerce or its Convention and Tourist Bureau provided glowing reports on the economic benefits to the city as a whole from the tourism businesses. This rhetoric perhaps reached its zenith in a 1929 *City Builder* article by W. G. Hastings, publicity director of the Biltmore Hotel. Hastings began by asking, "What part of Atlanta's development is due to its hotels?" He answered that "the hotels of Atlanta have done as much for her development as the railroads, without which there would have been no Atlanta."[59] With the number of excellent hotels in the city, Hastings suggested, many transients had been encouraged to become permanent residents. At the very least, the hotels made it possible for hundreds of thousands of visitors to come to Atlanta who otherwise would not. Certainly the grand opera and large conventions would be impossible without the city's hotels. Citing a study of the tourism and convention business in Detroit, Hastings argued that the benefits of Atlanta's hotels spread to the city as a whole. He broke down the convention visitors' spending as follows: "Merchandise, 26 per cent; restaurants and cafes, 20.5 per cent; hotels and rooms, 17.3 per cent; automobile accessories, gas, oil, 11.5 per cent; theatres and amusements, 8.5 per cent; transportation, 7 per cent; street railways, taxis, busses, 3.3 per cent; incidentals, 5 per cent." Even the money received by the hotels flowed back into the local economy as the hotels spent it for salaries, food, and supplies.[60]

There is no question that tourism businesses contributed to

the growth of Atlanta. There were, however, other costs that were not evaluated by promoters like Hastings. These included pollution, the inconvenience to residents caused by congestion, the need to provide extra sanitation services, more law enforcement for traffic control and security, and additional municipal services for the use of public buildings and streets. There was also the issue of the distribution of benefits from tourism businesses, since many of those employed in this field worked long hours for low pay. Hospitality business proponents seldom mentioned these issues as they discussed the industry's contributions to the community. Instead, they became caught up in the optimism of an era and assumed that the years of prosperity and growth for their own businesses and the city would go on forever.

The pro-business Atlanta government kept taxes low and services minimal. As a result, schools were usually crowded and inadequate for the task of educating the city's children. The situation was even worse for African Americans, since the first high school for blacks, Booker T. Washington High, did not open until 1927, fifty years after the establishment of the first high school for whites. The city government was also slow in paving streets outside the downtown area and providing services such as water mains and sewer lines in African-American neighborhoods. The horrible living conditions in which most of the city's blacks lived continued to be neglected by the city for several decades to come.

Decisions that would help business were not postponed during the decade, however. For example, in 1925 a young member of the Board of Aldermen, William B. Hartsfield, encouraged the city to lease the old auto racetrack for use as Atlanta's first airport. As a boy Hartsfield was captured by the excitement and the possibilities for the future importance of aviation. As an alderman, and later as mayor, he worked to make Atlanta a regional hub for this new form of transportation, just as earlier leaders had pushed the city to become a rail and highway center. In 1926 the federal government authorized an airmail route from New York to Miami. Atlanta's municipal rival, Birmingham, seemed a natural choice for the route, as airplanes could fly down the

Shenandoah Valley to Birmingham and on to Tampa and Miami. Well aware that the designation of the federal airmail route could determine which city would become the regional center for aviation, Hartsfield arranged to show the assistant postmaster general the hospitality and spirit that had helped shape Atlanta. He arranged for a greeting with an eight-motorcycle escort and motorcade down Peachtree Street, a lavish dinner at a private club with the mayor, governor, and business leaders present, and a deluxe hotel suite for his overnight stay. "No east Indian potentate ever got the attention he did," Hartsfield proclaimed. A week later, Atlanta was designated as a stop on the federal airmail route.[61]

At Hartsfield's insistence, the city purchased the racetrack property in 1929 as its municipal airport, which enabled Atlanta to become a regional leader in both airmail and airline passengers. Before the end of the decade there were already daily flights between Atlanta and Birmingham as well as other cities in the South. This early support for air transportation would be of great significance to Atlanta's future. The city's continued importance as a transportation center was reflected not only in its attention to aviation but also in the inauguration of commercial bus service between Cincinnati and Jacksonville in 1929. The buses took advantage of the city's network of newly paved highways.[62] These and other accomplishments reinforced the spirit of optimism among Atlanta's business leaders. However, these good times would not last forever.

The Depression

Most Atlantans regarded the stock market crash of October 24, 1929, as a temporary setback. Newspaper articles reassured residents that the basic conditions of business in the country were sound and that the depression in stock prices was the result of feverish speculation.[63] These assessments proved to be wrong as Atlanta, like the rest of the nation, experienced declining business activity from late 1929 through the end of 1933. There were losses in construction, real estate sales, and retail trade as well

108

as increased bankruptcies and a decline in the need for transportation.[64] For Atlanta this meant fewer travelers to patronize the city's tourism businesses.

During the prosperity of the late 1920s, Atlanta business leaders planned several huge skyscraper projects for the city. As the depression deepened, they were forced to abandon these plans. Included among the discarded proposals was a thousand-room hotel on Peachtree Street expected to cost $10 million, which was to have been built by the Dinkler Hotel Company.[65] The booming convention business of the previous years might have justified such a project, but with the economy in a downward spiral, there was no financing available and no demand for it as well.

One of the businesses forced into receivership by the depression was the Atlanta Baseball and Amusement Corporation, which operated the Atlanta Crackers of the Southern Baseball Association. The baseball team found itself more than half a million dollars in debt at the end of the 1932 season. Also forced to close for a time in 1932 was the Fox Theater, the lavishly designed Moorish revival movie palace. Its operators were unable to pay taxes for 1930 or 1931 or to meet a note due the next spring, so the theater was placed in the hands of an Atlanta bank.[66]

Other effects of the depression on the city's tourism businesses were immediate. A swift drop in travel reduced the number of visitors to the city. Businesses and organizations found themselves without the cash to afford meetings and conventions, and the number of conventions and attendees dropped from high levels achieved during the previous decade. The low point came in 1933, when only 206 conventions were held in Atlanta. These meetings brought 28,000 convention delegates to the city.[67]

With the decline in business travelers and convention visitors, employment in tourism businesses fell. Table 4.1 lists the levels of employment in tourism businesses from the 1930 census. Despite increases in the number of hotels and restaurants in the city, the number of workers had declined by nearly three hundred since the previous census (compare with Table 3.3). Given the increased numbers of hotels and restaurants, it is not surprising to find increases in the number of managers as well as wait-

Table 4.1. Employment in Atlanta Tourism Businesses, 1930

Occupation	Men	Women
Bding & Lodging Housekeepers	45	547
Hotelkeepers & Managers	89	13
Housekeepers & Stewards	62	395
Restaurant Keepers	468	269
Servants*	797	5,189
Waiters	914	780
	2,375	7,193

*In nondomestic settings
Source: Bureau of the Census, *Fifteenth Census of the United States, 1930: Occupations,* vol. 3.

ers. Substantial drops are found in the lowest echelon of workers (classified as servants) who cleaned the rooms and carried the bags of the city's hotel guests. As a cost-cutting measure, many of these positions were no doubt eliminated as business declined. Even with a 50 percent increase in the number of hotels in the city, the number of servants dropped by nearly 2,000, causing severe hardship among the men and women who were poorly paid even when they had jobs.

The 7,193 jobs provided to women in tourism businesses represents 15.3 percent of all females in the Atlanta workforce in 1930, a decline from 23.7 percent from 1920. The number of men employed in tourism businesses represented only 2.9 percent of all males in the labor force in 1930, a decline from 3.3 percent in 1920. Atlanta's population as a whole showed an increase of roughly 70,000 during the decade, to 270,366. Suburban areas also saw substantial gains. Atlanta tried to augment its growth by devising a plan to include all of its surrounding communities as boroughs of "Greater Atlanta," but since each town retained its political autonomy, the Census Bureau refused to allow the scheme.[68]

Workers in the lower echelons of Atlanta's hospitality businesses quickly felt the effects of the depression. Blacks who held many of these positions were forced out of their jobs by pressure from a white supremacist group known as the Atlanta Black Shirts. This hate group, which appealed to many former Klan members and unemployed whites, pressured the city's hotels to fire African-American bellhops and porters in order to hire whites. The largest hotels were able to resist this pressure and retain their black employees, but smaller businesses, especially those with working-class customers, found the pressure overwhelming. According to a report by the U.S. Employment Service, "in Atlanta practically all the hotels have replaced Negro bell boys with white help." Black maids in the hotels were more successful in holding onto their jobs.[69]

Economic conditions continued to deteriorate from the fall of 1929 until 1933. Competition for the existing jobs was intense among the many residents who had lost jobs and worsened as migrants arrived from the countryside, where agricultural conditions had been declining since 1918. These migrants' hopes of a better life in Atlanta were quickly dashed by the grim realities of the depression era. A police officer later recalled spending his time trying to find relatives of the nameless bodies found dead from hunger in the streets. Men and women also begged the police to arrest them in order to gain a warm night's rest and a hot meal. Private charities were overwhelmed with people needing assistance, and the city used the municipal auditorium as a soup kitchen.[70] To aid drifters, in 1933 the city government created a Transient Bureau, which set aside two older hotels for men passing through the city looking for work.[71] While these facilities stayed full, many more slept in the open.

The economic decline affected local business conditions for both blacks and whites. One response was the formation of the Atlanta Negro Chamber of Commerce in 1932. Many African-American business leaders had participated since 1900 in the Atlanta chapter of the National Negro Business League. Since that was a national organization, many wanted a local group that would promote black businesses hard hit by the depression. With encouragement from the white Chamber of Commerce, J. B. Blayton, the executive vice president of Citizens Trust Bank, or-

111

ganized the Atlanta Negro Chamber of Commerce. Although its resources were limited, this group encouraged blacks to patronize local businesses owned by other African Americans. Ironically, the all-white Atlanta Chamber of Commerce and the Negro Chamber of Commerce were both members of the same national organization.[72] The "Atlanta Spirit" of boosterism was shared by the Negro Chamber of Commerce as it proclaimed that "Atlanta is now number one in the number of stores and new sales per capita of colored population[s]" in the United States.[73]

Many of those who migrated to Atlanta during the depression were former cotton farmers forced by the combination of the boll weevil and decreasing cotton prices to leave the farms in hopes of finding work. The hardships of the depression were not new to these former sharecroppers, since conditions of poverty and poor nutrition were normal ways of life for most. There are numerous descriptions of the diet of the Southern poor during this era. For most poor folks, both black and white, the daily fare consisted of cornbread, biscuits, gravy or molasses to sop the bread, and, on occasion, fatback, which was either boiled or fried. In season there might also be greens, especially collards, which would be boiled with fatback.[74]

The foods of the rural South reflect the combination of Native American, European, and African ingredients from which the distinctive culture of the region evolved. Corn was a gift from the Indians of the South that found its way on the table in many forms. When ground, it became grits; cornmeal mixed with water and bacon grease was baked to make corn pone or hoecake; and corn was distilled to make bourbon (if mellowed and aged) or "white lightning" (if produced illegally). The Europeans brought hogs, which became the favorite meat of the South. Both poor blacks and whites ate fatback, pigs' feet, chitterlings, and other less expensive parts of the hog. The more affluent ate the parts that were literally "higher on the hog," such as ham, bacon, and pork chops. Communal occasions such as political rallies, church socials, and large family gatherings usually featured pork barbecue, although variations in preparation were found throughout the South. Some of the ingredients of Southern cooking arrived aboard the slave ships. Okra, black-eyed peas, watermelons, and peanuts as well as some spices and cooking techniques came from West Africa. ("Goober," the name for boiled peanuts, was African in origin.) These were part of the gardens raised by slaves on the plantations and found their way to the tables of blacks and whites throughout the region.[75]

As people moved from the rural South to the cities, they brought their distinctive foods with them. For many Atlantans a fondness for these foods and the way in which they were prepared by poor blacks and whites survives in numerous households and restaurants as the "soul food" of the region. Southern food preferences reflect a complex blend of cultural influences, but they continue to be shared by both blacks and whites in the region. These foods are part of the culture of the rural South and are important to Atlanta and its tourism businesses.[76]

The New Deal

The presidential election of 1932 brought new hope to Atlantans as a part-time resident of the state, Franklin D. Roosevelt, was elected to replace the unpopular President Hoover. The New Deal programs quickly put into place by the Roosevelt administration helped the morale of Atlanta and the nation by beginning to give people jobs building roads, bridges, schools, and other public works. These projects were important to the city because local and state funds were inadequate to provide them. Many of the buildings and infrastructure improvements remain as lasting contributions of the New Deal emergency relief measures. Other legacies of the period also remained as problems for the city, such as Techwood Homes, the nation's first public housing project, which was completed in 1935.[77]

Another idea to lift the spirits of the nation was the repeal of the national prohibition in 1933. While this effort was resisted by Georgia's more conservative state government, local Atlanta residents and public officials campaigned to allow alcohol sales, and the city passed an ordinance on May 19, 1933, allowing the

113

sale of 3.2 percent beer in Atlanta. The response was overwhelming as forty-nine businesses purchased licenses to sell beer. One waiter complained, "We can't even get it cold. They drink it up almost as fast as we put it on ice."[78] Georgia did not officially permit a local option on the sale of 3.2 percent beer until late in 1934. Conservatives and religious leaders still had enough influence in the state legislature to delay the legal sale of wine and hard liquor. Restaurants and hotels were allowed to sell wine the following year, but the continued ban on hard liquor encouraged bootlegging and the manufacture of illegal moonshine whiskey in the state.[79]

The city offered many places to buy illegal liquor. Many were drive-in restaurants that sold sandwiches and hot dogs, but whose main business was liquor. Customers drove in, placed their order at the curb, and had the illegal pint delivered to the car.[80] Finally, in 1938, voters permitted cities to allow the sale of liquor in package stores. Restaurants could now sell set-ups (mixers for patrons who brought their own bottles), but they still could not serve liquor by the drink.[81] The taste for illegal, inexpensive moonshine whiskey remained strong even after package stores opened, and poor farmers in north Georgia continued to distill their corn and ship the raw, clear liquor to Atlanta long after prohibition ended. Homemade corn liquor was popular among recent black and white migrants from the countryside, and Atlanta maintained its reputation as a white lightning center for many years.[82]

From 1936 until 1940, tourism activity in the city gradually returned to pre-depression levels. The city continued to host a variety of meetings for both black and white organizations. For instance, in 1937 the National Negro Business League met in Atlanta for the first time in more than thirty years. The league's Atlanta chapter published a directory of African-American businesses to promote local patronage as well as to showcase them for convention delegates. One item in the directory, entitled "Atlanta—You Ought to Know Your Auburn Avenue," compared Atlanta's center of black commerce with the bright spots of New York and Chicago. Auburn Avenue offered clubs such as the "Yeah Man" and the Top Hat for music and dancing, as well as eating places like Big Smittie's Grill, the Economy Delicatessen, and "Chop Suey" restaurants. Advertisements in the directory promoted a wide array of African-American tourism businesses to serve a variety of tastes, including hotels, theaters, clubs, restaurants, taverns, pool rooms, soda shops, and ice cream parlors.[83]

With its large variety of tourism businesses, Atlanta was becoming known as a mecca for black as well as white conventions. Convention attendance figures show that in 1939 the number of visitors exceeded the level reached ten years earlier. Table 4.2 indicates the slow recovery of the convention business during this period. The number of visitors to the city in 1939 was unusually high as the city hosted a huge meeting of the World Baptist Congress in July of that year. The crowds were so large that the event had to be held at the Ponce de Leon baseball park.[84]

Although the number of visitors to the city increased, hotel construction did not experience an attendant boom. A special U.S. Census of Business published in 1939 found seventy-one hotels in Atlanta—one fewer than in 1931.[85] The hotel that failed to appear in the 1939 census was the Terminal Hotel, which suffered a tragic fire on the morning of May 16, 1938. Flames had quickly spread from an explosion in the basement or the kitchen, killing thirty-four despite heroic efforts by the fire department. For a city that had experienced hotel fires since the

Table 4.2. Atlanta Conventions and Attendance, 1929–1940

Year	Conventions Held	Attendance
1929	321	57,785
1936	246	38,215
1937	270	38,863
1938	310	51,973
1939	495	134,000
1940	282	51,329

Source: Atlanta City Directories, Atlanta History Center collection, Atlanta Chamber of Commerce, Industrial Bureau reports.

original Kimball House burned in 1883, this was Atlanta's worst disaster in terms of loss of life. Newspaper accounts described the deaths of some of the victims who plunged to the street. Many of the dead were railroad workers, while others were women and children. After the fire the newspapers called for increased safety in the city's hotels and tighter inspections, but the dangers remained. It would take an even greater tragedy for Atlanta to improve the safety of its hotels.[86]

Atlantans have always rebounded quickly from adversity, and despite the tragic fire in 1938, the following year brought glamour and national attention to the city's tourism businesses. In stark contrast to the meeting of Baptists from around the world during the summer, Hollywood arrived on Peachtree Street for the December 15 premiere of the motion picture version of *Gone with the Wind*. Former alderman William Hartsfield had been elected for his first term as mayor of the city in 1936, the year the best-selling novel was published. Hartsfield cared little for the novel itself but saw the potential to make money from the film and its connection with Atlanta. The mayor lobbied the film's producer, David O. Selznick, to stage the world premiere in the city, sending him a box of homegrown magnolia blossoms. When Hartsfield heard a rumor that the event might be held in New York, he "leapt eight feet in the air" and told reporters it was "the worst outrage since Sherman burned the town." Selznick agreed to hold the premiere in Atlanta seventy-five years and one month after Sherman's burning of the city.[87]

The mayor staged a huge event to showcase Atlanta. The stars began arriving at the airport two days before the opening and were carried downtown in a thirty-car motorcade. Most stayed at the Georgian Terrace Hotel, but receptions and social events were held at restaurants, clubs, and hotels throughout the city. The evening of the premiere, all the lights and glitter focused on Lowe's Grand Theater for the arrival of Vivian Leigh, Clark Gable, and other celebrities and cast members, as well as local author Margaret Mitchell.[88] Whatever feelings Mayor Hartsfield and other civic leaders may have had about the image of the Old South portrayed in the movie version of *Gone with the Wind,* they seized the opportunity to publicize Atlanta. They were like the heroine, Scarlett O'Hara, who triumphed in the commercialism of the New South while using the values of the Old South to welcome her guests.[89]

The publicity surrounding the premiere of *Gone with the Wind* helped bring a record number of visitors to Atlanta in 1939. These guests stayed in the 5,616 rooms of the city's seventy-one hotels. The hotels employed 1,792 men and women with a total annual payroll of $949,000. Even including managers and higher-paid supervisors, hotels employed so many low-wage workers that the average income for all of Atlanta's hotel employees in 1939 was just over ten dollars per week.[90] Unions were weak in businesses engaged in manufacturing and nonexistent in tourism businesses, so wage scales in the city generally remained low. This gave organizations holding conventions the advantage of lower costs for hotel rooms compared with other cities.

All things considered, Atlanta emerged from the years of the depression and the New Deal in a better position in 1940 than in 1929. Business leadership was still strong, and the programs of the New Deal era had been used to pay for improvements in roads, sewers, the airport, and other basic infrastructure that would enable the city to grow in the years ahead. There was, however, no challenge to the belief in white supremacy which kept the city's African-American residents in a position at the bottom of the social ladder. Overall, the era can be fairly described as one of some change, and, yet, a great deal of continuity in Atlanta.

Despite the years of the depression and New Deal, Atlanta had continued to grow. The city added nearly 32,000 residents during the decade, reaching a population of 302,288 in 1940. Likewise, a comparison of the 1931 and 1941 city directories shows an increase from 72 to 101 lodging places. There was a change, however, in the types of establishments listed in the directories. Whereas the lodging places in 1931 had all been hotels, the listings for 1941 included the new category of "hotels and tourist camps."[91] Built for the motoring public, these tourist camps were located on the edges of the city along the network of newly paved highways that converged in Atlanta. The increased use of the automobile accelerated the trend toward the decentralization of the city's lodging businesses that had begun early in the century. Just as stagecoach inns were replaced by downtown hotels with the development of the railroad, these tourist camps, which provided only sleeping accommodations, would be replaced by the motor hotel (or motel) as highway travel increased in the early 1950s.[92]

The War Years

The nations of Europe were plunged into war following the 1939 invasions by Hitler's German army. Prior to the entry of the United States into the conflict, increases in defense industries and military preparedness had an effect on the Atlanta area. To the northeast of the city, the old Camp Gordon from World War I was rebuilt into an army hospital and the Atlanta Naval Air Station. An army airfield was also located next to Atlanta's municipal airport. The rail lines that had led to the founding of the city now helped with the location of military bases as an enormous supply depot now known as Fort Gillem was built on a 1,500-acre tract in Clayton County, southeast of town. The army's brick warehouses and elaborate switchyards opened just before the Japanese attack on Pearl Harbor brought the United States into the war. On Atlanta's southwest edge, Fort McPherson became a beehive of activity as thousands of men arrived for induction into the army.[93]

With thousands of soldiers passing through Atlanta on their way to induction and training centers in the South, many spent time in the city during stopovers or while on leave. Military personnel from throughout the country filled the city's hotels, restaurants, and amusements. Many of the visiting soldiers spoke with accents that were unfamiliar to Southerners. As one observer recalled, "If you went to the old Henry Grady [Hotel] to the Dogwood Room for lunch or for an evening, you would hear utterances and sounds of all types of language."[94] The city was

118

especially crowded on weekends, since most of the recruits received training from Monday through Friday and then were turned loose to explore the city.

For soldiers arriving at the Terminal Station, a United Service Organization lounge was located in the depot. In this era of segregation, the USO lounge had separate entrances for whites and blacks. White soldiers could attend dances at the Georgian Terrace Hotel and visit several canteens to relax and socialize. One of these canteens was located in the ballroom and banquet hall of the Kimball House Hotel. The Butler Street YMCA served as a gathering place for black soldiers, providing recreational activities as well as dances. The YMCA was also close to the Auburn Avenue entertainment and commercial district, where African Americans could enjoy restaurants, the Top Hat Club, and other amusements. When the facilities of the Butler Street YMCA became too crowded, a USO center for blacks opened at Washington High School. It is estimated that Atlanta's USO centers served more than 2.5 million men and women in uniform during the war.[95]

Like many other Southern cities, Atlanta received a sizable share of the expanding defense industries. During the early stages of the war mobilization, the region as a whole received a disproportionate share of the nation's large war plants, with a total investment in the South of more than $17 billion.[96] The Atlanta Chamber of Commerce reported that in 1941 alone 116 new businesses were established in the city. The following year brought another 161 new businesses, as well as 37 new federal departments and agencies. This investment created a business boom in the city, reducing unemployment and helping to bring the city out of the depression.[97] The most important new manufacturing facility was the Bell bomber plant located northwest of the city in the town of Marietta. By 1944 the huge factory employed nearly 30,000 workers producing B-29 airplanes. The plant produced seven hundred of the bombers by the end of the war.[98]

Altogether the investment by the military and defense industries brought more money into the area than the programs of the

New Deal. The depot at Fort Gillem made Atlanta the supply center for the eight states of the Southeast. Other federal agencies, including the Federal Reserve Bank, located their regional offices in Atlanta, giving the city a boost as a regional financial center. Other important federal investments in Atlanta included the U.S. Court of Appeals and a large federal penitentiary.[99] This economic activity provided an enormous stimulus to the growth of both jobs and population in the Atlanta metropolitan area, raising the population to over 500,000 by the end of the war.

The war had a mixed impact on Atlanta's tourism businesses. With construction materials and labor reserved for the war effort, no new hotel facilities could be built. Convention activity also declined. In 1941 Atlanta hosted 445 conventions, which brought nearly 76,000 visitors, whereas two years later there were only 193 meetings hosting 55,000 visitors.[100] Even with fewer conventions, however, military personnel crowded Atlanta's hotels, eating places, and amusements, and the city's train depots and bus stations received the full influx of military personnel traveling from one place to another. One observer recalled that the troop trains often seemed to be stacked one on another at the stations.[101] Even older hotels in declining areas—such as the Gordon, the Scoville, and the Sylvan, which formed the "hotel row" on Mitchell Street—were revived by the arrival of soldiers at nearby Terminal Station.[102] The demand for hotel rooms was so great that the owners of a three-story office building on Marietta Street remodeled the upper floors and opened the Hotel Roxy. The sign painted on the building said, "Welcome South Brother," as the Hotel Roxy offered hospitality to working-class guests for $1.00 and up.[103] Military personnel in Atlanta packed the city's tourism businesses, which operated at full capacity in spite of the labor shortages, rationing, and other wartime hardships.

The city government responded to the presence of so many visitors by remodeling the old municipal auditorium, which had been badly damaged in the 1940s by fire. With building materials diverted to the war effort, Mayor Hartsfield had the building patched with wood, so the facility was opened again in 1943. The auditorium hosted dances and concerts as the Metropolitan Opera Company returned to the city for performances. The auditorium was also used extensively for war bond rallies, at which celebrities gave concerts to promote the sale of government bonds in support of the war effort.[104]

With so many servicemen present in the city, the demand for prostitution increased, resulting in an epidemic of venereal diseases. In 1942 Atlanta led the nation among cities of its size in the number of reported cases, prompting a tightening of local laws against prostitution. According to the recollections of the police chief, it was unlawful for a man and a woman to be in a hotel room together if they were not married. The police department established special squads and raided all the hotels on weekends. While there were lots of arrests, the enforcement did not eliminate illegal sexual activity as prostitutes simply scattered into different areas of the city.[105]

For other women, the labor shortages caused by military enlistments created new job opportunities. White women took jobs in the defense industries and pursued promotions within businesses where they previously would have been restricted to the lowest-level clerical or sales clerk positions. As black men entered military service, some new areas of employment became available for African-American females, prompting many well-to-do whites to complain that domestic help was hard to find during the war. African-American men who worked as waiters left their positions for better opportunities in the military or elsewhere, creating additional positions for black waitresses. As one African-American woman recalled, "I would do extra work as a waitress at the Biltmore on the weekends, because men were so scarce. . . . Many women were out there doing waitress work because so many waiters had to go away." These new jobs paid more than their former employment as maids.[106]

In the spring of 1945, residents and visitors alike waited anxiously for the news of Allied victory in Europe. On April 20 an announcement came that the Germans had surrendered. Local bars, liquor stores, theaters, and restaurants closed in fear of what might be a rampage of revelers celebrating the victory, but the report proved to be false and businesses reopened. When

121

victory in Europe was achieved the following month, the celebration was tempered by the recognition that the war still raged in the Pacific. However, the marquee lights returned to the theaters on Peachtree as the fears of bombing vanished and blackouts ended.[107] The celebration of the victory over Japan took place on August 15, 1945. One hundred thousand people jammed Peachtree Street, shouting, cheering, and waving flags as even Mayor Hartsfield urged the crowds to "Tear the roof off."[108]

With the celebration of victory, Atlantans looked forward to the prosperity of an era of peace in which their city could grow into a place of national prominence.

5

The Postwar Era, 1945–1960

AS WORLD WAR II ENDED, Atlanta faced a shortage of housing and hotels. Several factors contributed to this inadequate supply. Following the stock market crash in 1929, no new downtown hotels were built during the depression years, and during the war, despite growth in the city and its economy, materials and personnel shortages had prevented hotel construction. There were, however, the newer tourist camps and motor hotels built to serve the motorists on the edges of town where land prices were lower and where the federal highways came into the city. These motels, as they came to be called, were to have a significant impact on the nature of the tourism businesses in the years ahead as downtown hotels continued to rely primarily on travelers arriving by rail, bus, or airplane.

Recovery

Atlanta's growth as a regional center of finance and commerce brought increased numbers of travelers to the city, aggravating the shortage of hotel rooms in the crowded downtown area. The federal reserve bank helped Atlanta achieve a position of dominance in banking, and several insurance companies located their headquarters or regional offices in the city. Atlanta's rail network and highway system continued to make the city a regional hub for commerce. Almost anyone traveling through the South by railroad had to change trains in Atlanta. The network of transportation lines radiating from the city—including fifteen rail lines—not only moved passengers but also made Atlanta a natural distribution point for manufactured goods and produce.[1] In 1929 the first paved highway had connected Atlanta with Florida and the Midwest, and by 1945 six federal highways intersected in the city, enabling travelers and commerce to move along the roads in virtually every direction.[2]

In spite of Atlanta's position of economic leadership, the surrounding region remained poor and dominated by agriculture. The economy of the South continued to lag far behind that of the rest of the nation. Although cotton continued to be hailed as king, the boll weevil infestation had reduced production and the cultivation of a single crop had worn out the soil. In the years after World War II, the use of farm machinery such as the mechanical cotton picker became more widespread. This mechanization further reduced the demand for farm labor, causing more sharecroppers and tenant farmers to leave rural areas.

This migration not only changed the rural South but also had a profound effect on cities in the region and nation. Between 1920 and 1950 more than 4 million blacks who had lived on Southern farms moved to cities in the Northeast and Midwest. Many also migrated to the larger cities in the South, such as Atlanta. In 1920 fewer than 20 percent of blacks in the South lived in cities; thirty years later this figure had risen to 42 percent, with the vast majority living in the central cities of large metropolitan areas.[3] Although some white farmers also left the South, many others moved to towns and cities within the region. But as African Americans migrated to cities, more whites tended to move to small towns and areas located on the suburban fringes.

The movement of white and black farmers caused a drop of 27.4 percent in the South's rural population during the 1940s. At the same time, urban areas of the region grew by nearly 40 percent, a rate of urbanization more than twice that of the nation as a whole.[4] However, Southern cities grew horizontally, with low-density suburbs sprawling in many directions to form large metropolitan areas. This settlement pattern left a distinctive imprint on the cities of the South and the culture of their residents. As demographers John Maclachlan and Joe Floyd, Jr., have noted, "It seems to be likely that a considerable portion of the region's people may make the transition more or less directly from the older agrarian way of living to the new metropolitan way," without passing through the same urban experience as people in other parts of the nation.[5]

Many of the farmers who moved to the towns and cities of the South sought jobs in textile mills. These jobs generally went to poor whites who were housed in villages built and owned by the mill operators, such as the "Cabbagetown" neighborhood near Atlanta's Fulton Bag and Cotton Mill. These newcomers to the cities of the region brought with them their rural cultural patterns. Though they were derisively called "poor white trash" or "lintheads," cultural historian Idus Newby prefers to describe these white millworkers of the South as "plain folk" whose most common experience was extreme poverty.[6] This poverty contributed to an illiteracy rate in the region twice as high as the rest of the nation's. During World War II, 14 percent of the South's white draftees failed the Army intelligence test.[7] Extreme poverty also kept these plain folk from the enjoyment of tourism businesses in a city like Atlanta. Visiting neighbors and sharing special treats from the kitchens of friends were chances to enjoy hospitality, which was otherwise limited by the hours spent in the mills. Men and boys often played baseball in the mill villages. Drinking illegal moonshine liquor was also a popular diversion among the poor whites in Atlanta as well as other Southern cities and towns.[8] Although these plain folk shared similar economic conditions as blacks, the prevailing patterns of segregation meant that they inhabited two separate societies.

In 1945, Atlanta's black visitors and residents could choose from a wide variety of businesses. Excluded by segregation from the downtown area, these businesses were clustered in secondary African-American business districts and residential areas. According to a study done in 1944–45, Atlanta had 845 black-owned

125

businesses, almost all of which were small establishments serving an exclusive African-American clientele. Among these businesses, the largest group was made up of 222 restaurants. Most of these were owned and operated by family members who could enter this type of business with limited capital. Small retail stores and service establishments made up most of the rest of the city's black businesses. In addition to the restaurants, the survey identified eleven taverns and clubs and seven hotels for African Americans.[9]

Among Atlanta's largest black enterprises were the Atlanta Life Insurance Company, the Citizens Trust Bank, and the *Daily World* newspaper. The owners of these businesses formed the city's African-American economic elite and were involved in many other ventures. For example, the three owners of Citizens Trust Bank also owned a soft drink company, a fire insurance company, drugstores, a radio station, and the Top Hat Club, a dance hall on Auburn Avenue.[10] Clustered near these larger enterprises on "Sweet Auburn" were numerous smaller tourism businesses, including twenty-five restaurants, three hotels, two billiard parlors, a theater, and two other clubs.

Though Auburn Avenue was the largest concentration of African-American businesses, Decatur Street was well known as a black entertainment center in 1945. It offered five hotels and numerous other inexpensive lodging places, many of which were used for illegal activities such as gambling, drinking, and prostitution. The street also contained fourteen restaurants, three billiard parlors, and two theaters to serve African-American customers. Some of the Decatur Street businesses, such as the two theaters, were owned by whites but served a black clientele. Another concentration of African-American businesses was on Atlanta's west side near the Atlanta University Center. Several restaurants, a theater, and a club were located in this area.[11]

In spite of the success of a few black entrepreneurs, most African Americans faced limited economic opportunity as discrimination restricted the jobs available to them. Returning black veterans who were trained for skilled jobs in the military would not be hired in Atlanta except in service employment, semiskilled, and unskilled occupations. This led to high levels of unemployment for African Americans. Poverty caused many blacks to live in poorly built, overcrowded housing, which would be labeled by white observers as slum areas.[12]

Poverty among large numbers of whites and blacks was not the only problem facing Atlanta after the war. Despite rapid urban growth, political power throughout the South remained in the hands of rural-dominated governors and legislatures. In Louisiana the state Democratic Party was dominated by the machine of the "Kingfish," Huey Long, who sought to control politics in New Orleans.[13] In Georgia a "county unit" system of voting gave each of the state's 159 counties almost equal voting strength, regardless of population. As a result, the political machine of Gene Talmadge dominated the Democratic Party and Georgia politics for more than fifty years following his first election as governor in 1932.[14] In each of his four successful gubernatorial bids, Talmadge campaigned against Atlanta and the economic power it represented in the state. As a consequence, Atlanta's politics became increasingly separate from those of the rest of Georgia. In cities throughout the region, local politics was dominated by a commercial-civic elite determined to promote their city's economic growth and a favorable national image.[15] In Atlanta this meant projecting an image of moderation on racial issues—an image that was frequently in opposition to state government policies. The resulting political conflicts would have significant consequences for Atlanta throughout the postwar era.

Tragedy

In November 1919, four people had died in a fire at the Wilson Hotel, a small structure on Peachtree Street near Five Points at the center of downtown.[16] The tragedy brought a demand for stronger building codes to reduce the risk of fire in the city's buildings, but the ordinances passed did not require any refitting of older buildings. When fire struck the thirty-year-old Terminal Hotel in 1938, killing thirty-four guests and destroying the building, it was reported that the proprietors had not been required to build fire escapes or install other safety features after the 1919 tragedy.

Another Atlanta hotel that had opened before the required fire safety ordinances passed was the Winecoff Hotel. The Winecoff rose an impressive fifteen stories above Peachtree Street on a small lot. When the hotel opened in 1913, safety features such as sprinklers, fire escapes, and fire doors were not required unless a building's ground area exceeded 5,000 square feet, so the Winecoff was exempt.

The Winecoff was usually packed in the months after the end of the war. Although it did not feature convention facilities or live entertainment as other hotels in the area did, the Winecoff billed itself as a fireproof hotel that was "Nearer than anything to everything on Atlanta's most famous thoroughfare."[17] Four theaters within a block of the Winecoff showed movies, adding to the hotel's popularity with out-of-town guests. Friday evening, December 6, 1946, found the hotel filled with teenagers from across the state attending a YMCA meeting, as well as returning servicemen, people doing business in town, and families visiting nearby department stores for holiday shopping.[18]

Around three in the morning of December 7, a fire broke out on the third or fourth floor and spread rapidly throughout the building. Acting like a chimney, the tall, narrow building fanned the heat and smoke up the stairs and into the hallways of the crowded hotel. Although firemen reached the building quickly after they were called, they could do little to reach many of the guests. The tallest ladders available to the firefighters were 75 and 85 feet tall, while the hotel was 155 feet tall, preventing the firemen from reaching anyone above the eighth floor. To make matters worse, the west side of the hotel faced a six-foot-wide alley between the Winecoff and the adjacent building, so fire equipment could not reach the rooms on that side. Another problem was created by wooden shutters attached to the windows on one side of the building. Designed to provide privacy and ventilation, these shutters could not be removed, causing many victims to suffocate in their rooms. Some guests died from the flames, others were smothered by the smoke, and many were killed jumping to the street below.[19]

When the flames were out, 119 had died, making the fire the worst hotel disaster in the world at that time. The causes of the fire were the subject of intense debate. Official reports declared that the fire probably started with a mattress catching fire while someone was smoking in bed, but speculation persists that the fire was set by someone involved in an illegal card game taking place on the third floor.[20] Given the rapid spread of the flames through the building, it is not unlikely that some flammable liquid was used to start the fire; however, these suppositions are not supported by the fire department's reports or the resulting grand jury investigation.

Despite the deaths of so many of its occupants, including members of the Winecoff family who were permanent residents of the hotel's top floor, the building itself was not destroyed by the fire. The hotel stood charred and empty until 1950, when it was purchased and remodeled. The following year, with fire escapes and fire doors, it reopened as the Peachtree on Peachtree Hotel. Competition from newer lodging places in the 1960s, as well as memories of the tragedy, forced its closing in 1967.[21]

Mayor Hartsfield acted promptly to repair the damage to the city's image caused by the fire. As the fire department's equipment had been inadequate to prevent the tragedy, the mayor gave the chief of the fire department a blank check to purchase additional trucks with taller ladders so that the department would be one of the best-equipped in the nation. Newspaper editorials focused public attention on the issue of fire safety, urging lawmakers to "see that the victims of the fire did not die in vain."[22] As a result, local and state building codes were changed not only in Georgia but also across the nation. New codes required all hotels to be fitted with fire escapes and sprinkler systems. President Truman even called a special national conference on fire prevention in the spring of 1947.[23]

The families of those who perished in the Winecoff Hotel received little satisfaction in the legal proceedings that followed the fire. Two individuals who had operated the hotel were indicted for their negligence in permitting unsafe conditions in the building and for their delay in calling fire authorities, but neither was convicted. The "fire-proof" building carried little insurance coverage, so claims filed by relatives of the victims were settled with awards averaging less than $1,000.[24] Many of those lucky enough to survive the fire continued to be haunted by the experience. Most Atlantans seemed ready to forget the tragedy and carry on with their business.

Continued Growth

In spite of the tragedy of the Winecoff Hotel fire, Atlanta's tourism businesses were well prepared for continued growth as the South's leading convention city. The following year, 1947, the Convention and Tourist Bureau reported that 219 meetings held in the city had brought more than 89,000 visitors. These attendance figures were the largest for the city since 1939.[25] (The number of visitors attending conventions in Atlanta has risen steadily every year since 1947.)

Nor was growth limited to the tourism businesses. With the depression and the war finally over, Atlanta added two new automobile assembly plants, led the South in bank clearances, and bragged of having the third-largest telephone exchange in the world.[26] This economic growth created jobs and brought record numbers of people to the city. The 1950 U.S. Census recorded this postwar growth by noting that Atlanta's population had reached 331,314. City leaders were cheered by the fact that Atlanta had added almost 10 percent to its population since the previous census, though their enthusiasm was tempered by the fact that the 1950 census also revealed that for the first time Atlanta's suburban population exceeded the central city's. Growth in the suburbs of Atlanta between 1940 and 1950 was extremely rapid, with an increase of almost 30 percent. The Atlanta metropolitan area recognized by the Census Bureau now contained 671,797 residents.[27]

Attempts by Atlanta to expand by annexing its suburban areas had failed in 1938, 1943, and again in 1947. After beginning his third term in office in 1947, Mayor Hartsfield was committed to enlarging the city by annexation. The mayor noted that the black population of Atlanta was growing, while "good, white, home-owning citizens" were migrating out of the city. Failure to support annexation would eventually mean turning political control of the city over to African Americans, which in 1950 was unthinkable to white Atlantans long accustomed to political control.[28] Hartsfield formed a powerful public-private partnership with downtown business interests who were organized into the Central Atlanta Improvement Association. Other business leaders were represented by the Chamber of Commerce, which focused on a broader area. Together the partnership promoted the expansion of the city as part of a broad program known as the "Plan of Improvement." Under the plan, which was approved by voters in June 1950 and took effect on January 1, 1952, the land area of the City of Atlanta increased from 36 to 118 square miles, and the city's population rose about 100,000, to an estimated total of 430,000 residents.[29]

Tourism businesses continued to provide employment to substantial numbers of residents both in the city and in the surrounding metropolitan area. The 1950 census report indicates almost 13,000 people working in various hospitality businesses in the Atlanta metropolitan area. Eight out of ten hotel and lodging place employees worked in the central city. Eating places were more numerous than hotels in the suburbs, but seven out of ten jobs in eating and drinking places were inside the city limits. On the other hand, entertainment and recreation services were more widely distributed throughout the metropolitan area, with 45 percent of these jobs in the suburbs. This reflects the fact that in 1950 most movie theaters were still located downtown, but there were numerous amusement parks and recreation areas outside the city.[30]

As Table 5.1 shows, nearly equal numbers of men and women worked in tourism businesses in the city. The number of men working in these businesses represented 5 percent of the total male labor force in Atlanta, whereas the 4,636 women working

Table 5.1. City of Atlanta, Tourism Business Employment, 1950

Occupation	Men	Women
Eating & Drinking Places	2,314	2,934
Hotels and Lodging Places	1,069	1,086
Entertainment & Recreation	1,042	616
	4,425	4,636

Source: Bureau of the Census, *Seventeenth Census of the United States, 1950: Occupations,* vol. 3.

in this field comprised almost 8 percent of the total for females. Seven of every ten male and female workers in Atlanta's tourism businesses were black, with most of these concentrated in lower-echelon positions as cooks, waiters, waitresses, maids, and bellmen. The low pay associated with these positions is indicated by Table 5.2. Women working in eating and drinking places were paid only 62 percent of the median income for all females in the labor force. Men in this category fared slightly better, earning 83 percent of the median income for all men in the workforce. Both men and women working in hotels earned approximately three-fourths of the median national income for all members of the civilian labor force.[31]

These census data reflect a major characteristic of employment in the tourism industry. Although the businesses in this field provided numerous jobs for residents of the community, many of these individuals had low educational levels and few job

Table 5.2. U.S. Median Income, 1950

Occupation	Men	Women
Eating & Drinking Places	$2,225	$ 983
Hotels & Lodging Places	$1,942	$1,174
All Civilian Labor Force	$2,668	$1,575

Source: U.S. Bureau of the Census, *Seventeenth Census of the United States, 1950: Occupations,* vol. 3.

skills and worked in poorly paying positions with long hours, few benefits, and little opportunity for advancement. The continued growth of tourism businesses in Atlanta would contribute to the growing disparity between those with the limited number of good jobs in the city and the many working poor.

Downtown Decline and Renewal

By 1950 there was a growing awareness among business and political leaders in Atlanta that conditions in the downtown area were deteriorating. First the depression and then the war had brought new construction of buildings in the area to a halt. Immediately after the war, when building materials became available, they were used to meet the booming growth in suburban single-family housing. This lack of growth and development activity in the downtown area troubled the city's leaders. When Floyd Hunter interviewed forty of the most influential individuals in Atlanta in 1950 for his study of decision making in "Regional City," they listed growth and development as the city's critical priorities. Two other related issues were identified as traffic problems and the "Negro question."[32] Downtown needed growth, and it had little room to do so because of the congestion caused by automobile and truck traffic as well as the crowded low-income black neighborhoods surrounding the central business district.

Atlanta's decision makers initially attempted to address the problems of growth for downtown, traffic congestion, and crowded slum housing for blacks in a single effort. In 1945 white business leaders and public officials had proposed north-south and east-west expressways to link downtown with the suburbs. The north-south expressway would curve around the edge of downtown and form a buffer zone between the business district and the black neighborhoods to the east. The African Americans who were going to be displaced by the expressway construction would be relocated to outlying areas to the west and south of downtown.[33] Construction began in 1950 on the north-south expressway, which is now called the downtown connector and carries traffic from I-75 and I-85. Although the roadway has been enlarged and expanded over the years, it still bends around the east side of downtown and separates the downtown area from the eastside African-American neighborhoods.

Urban historian Raymond Mohl has shown that Miami also bulldozed black neighborhoods to make a path for interstate highways in the late 1950s.[34] By the time the expressway construction was completed in Atlanta, more than 7,000 African-American families were displaced from their homes. The vast majority of people displaced were the poor and those with special needs and problems. Seventy-five percent of those forced to move were renters, and virtually none received any relocation assistance.[35]

The downtown connector severed the most important street for black commerce in the city, "Sweet" Auburn Avenue. Since just after the turn of the century, Auburn Avenue had been the center for the largest concentration of Atlanta's African-American businesses. The expressway isolated the residential portion of the street on the east from the commercial part on the west. Several businesses were closed for the path of the expressway, including the well-known Ma Sutton's Café. Others, such as Jenkins Steakhouse in the Rucker Building in the commercial part, closed after the start of construction because its customers were cut off from easy access to the area. The severing of Auburn Avenue for the expressway began a process of economic decline from which the famous street has never recovered. Although the city was able to increase access to the downtown area, the expressway construction contributed to a legacy of distrust within the city's low-income black community that continues to be a problem today.

Solid agreement existed among white business leaders on the need to upgrade the central business district. Together with Mayor Hartsfield, they embarked on a vigorous program to rejuvenate the business core and augment downtown property values. During the 1950s, the federal government sponsored urban renewal programs to help cities identify and renovate substandard areas of residential and commercial property. Local governments would designate areas as slums, acquire the properties using the power of eminent domain, and pay the owners with federal dollars. Like the interstate highway program, the urban renewal program was used by cities throughout the country to change land uses in downtown areas and relocate large numbers of low-income residents.[36]

The process of urban renewal was different in Southern cities from cities elsewhere in the country. In the South, most of those displaced were African-Americans, whereas outside the region it was commercial areas that were cleared. Southern cities also lagged far behind cities elsewhere in replacing the housing destroyed by the urban renewal program. Most of the cleared sites in Atlanta and other Southern cities were used for public buildings, which provided no new taxable value and often required a substantial capital expense by the city.[37] Atlanta's business and public leaders used the urban renewal sites for civic facilities, hospitals and educational institutions, and commercial redevelopment.

The city identified three potential urban renewal areas that would aid tourism businesses. The first was the Butler Street area, a mix of low-income black residential and commercial property just to the west of the new north-south downtown expressway. Since it offered access to the expressway and the opportunity to expand the central business district to the highway, the Butler Street area became the city's first urban renewal site in 1956. The second area was a primarily residential low-income neighborhood north of the central business district known as Buttermilk Bottom. Although the area had been identified as early as 1950 as having serious drainage problems as well as severely blighted housing conditions, it was home to 3,000 African Americans, many of whom worked in the central business district. The area had obvious commercial value owing to its proximity to downtown and an expressway exit. Business groups such as the Central Atlanta Improvement Association regarded Buttermilk Bottom as a prime site for a "continued battle against the ring of blight encircling downtown Atlanta."[38] The third renewal location was the Rawson-Washington area, in a neighborhood known as Summerhill located to the southeast of the central business district.

It was also a poorly drained area of "bottom land" containing a mix of poor blacks and a few poor whites. The clearance of these three areas would have great significance for the expansion of the city's tourism businesses.

Support for the urban renewal plan came from carefully negotiated behind-the-scenes discussions between the mayor, white business leaders, and leadership in the black community. In spite of the dislocation of many low-income blacks, the plan offered business opportunities for some African-American entrepreneurs who stood to benefit from construction and real estate sales opportunities. Low-income African Americans would receive additional public housing, although at a considerable distance from the downtown. Unofficial agreements encouraged blacks to move into west and southside areas of the city, thus keeping the northside reserved as an area for whites.[39]

The purchase of land and clearance of the Butler Street urban renewal site began in 1956. Several new hotels and motels were built in this area, including the Atlanta Central Travelodge, a Holiday Inn (now the Marriott Courtyard and Fairfield Inn Downtown), and a Marriott Hotel (later the Downtown Radisson, now the Spirit of Atlanta Hotel). These establishments added 1,300 new rooms to the downtown area.

In 1962, after serving in office for twenty-three years, Mayor Hartsfield decided against running again. He was succeeded by Ivan Allen, Jr., who was a business leader and president of the Chamber of Commerce, as well as the son of one of the city's leading promoters during the 1920s Forward Atlanta campaign. Allen sought to promote business activity in the city by promising to continue vigorous urban renewal efforts, including the building of a civic center and a stadium for major-league sports.[40] The locations for these activities were the urban renewal areas known as Buttermilk Bottom and Rawson-Washington, respectively. Since the former was adjacent to the Butler Street area, which was the site of several new hotels, the proposed civic center would be near these tourism businesses.

The use of these areas for tourism-related activities would accomplish several objectives. First, they would provide the city with amenities regarded as necessary by business leaders and the mayor who represented their interests. The old civic auditorium had been built in 1909 and, with a seating capacity of 5,200, was too small to host large gatherings or conventions. The Chamber of Commerce noted that cities such as Dallas, Miami, and Des Moines had new auditoriums capable of seating 15,000. Large, sought-after groups such as the Kiwanis, Rotary, American Legion, and Elks had bypassed Atlanta in favor of rival cities with larger facilities. The report added, "Atlanta is definitely minor league in the business of auditoriums. And our competitors, for the most part, are major league in that respect."[41]

Hosting conventions was a fiercely competitive activity among cities. The city with a superior facility enjoyed an advantage over rivals seeking to host the same event. Urban scholar Dennis Judd has observed that the rivalries among cities to provide facilities for conventions was more intense than the cold war among nations.[42] Throughout Atlanta's history, business and political leaders had worked together to provide Southern hospitality to visitors attending fairs, expositions, and conventions. The use of urban renewal land to provide space for a new civic center, as well as hotel rooms and a sports facility, demonstrated again the importance of the cultural value of hospitality in the city's economic development policies.

Atlanta's leaders saw the city as increasingly prominent at the national level and did not want to remain "minor league" in any way. The city had two successful minor-league baseball franchises—the Atlanta Crackers and the Black Crackers—that played to large crowds in the old ballpark on Ponce de Leon Avenue. The old ballfield had a unique charm of its own, with a magnolia tree growing in the outfield near the fence. The all-white Crackers were for many years the champions of the AA-level Southern Baseball League. The urban renewal land offered the opportunity to build a stadium which city leaders hoped would attract major-league baseball and football teams.

As a second goal of the urban renewal program, the use of these areas for tourism-related activities would eliminate the slums near downtown and relocate their low-income African-

American residents. The massive relocation of residents from urban renewal and expressway construction areas near central cities had given the whole urban renewal program the nickname "Negro removal." However, unlike the earlier expressway construction program, the federal urban renewal legislation required assistance for those who were being relocated from both commercial and residential properties. As Table 5.3 shows, the three urban renewal areas targeted for tourism-related activities displaced more than 2,100 families, as well as 219 businesses. The number of families moved from these three areas for tourism-related activities represented nearly half of the total number of families relocated from all of the city's urban renewal areas. In the Rawson-Washington area, 308 white families were moved, making up over 75 percent of the white families relocated from all the city's urban renewal areas. Ninety-one percent of all the families moved in the city's urban renewal program were African-American, giving some validity to the nickname "Negro removal."[43]

The two governmental programs for expressway construction and urban renewal accomplished their objectives of making the downtown area larger and more accessible. These public policies, however, caused a dramatic displacement of more then 21,000 families—more than 67,000 people—between 1956 and 1966. This means that Atlanta's city government moved a population equal to that of the 1960 population of Macon during this pe-

Table 5.3. Displacement by Urban Renewal Program
for Tourism-Related Activities

Area	Businesses Relocated	Families displaced
Butler Street	103	836 (all black)
Rawson-Washington	75	948 (308 white)
Buttermilk Bottom	41	337 (all black)
	219	2,121

Source: Eric Hill Associates, *Report on the Relocation of Individuals, Families, and Businesses,* Atlanta Community Improvement Program, September 1966.

riod. Approximately one-third of all the families who were displaced received relocation assistance.

Little record was left of the hardship caused by the displacement of so many households. In one instance, an elderly black woman had lived in her home on Houston Street for more than thirty-five years. When ordered to move in April 1960 to make way for the hotels in the Butler Street area, she shot herself with a pistol.[44] Some individuals and families were relocated to public housing units, but most simply moved into more densely crowded low-income housing elsewhere. This had the ironic effect of increasing the overall deterioration of housing in Atlanta while clearing the way for the expressways and the expansion of the central business district.[45] The two policies also increased the distrust of government among low-income African-American residents in the city, since these people felt that their neighborhoods had been sacrificed for the improvement of business. These low-income residents lost their neighborhoods and all of the familiar surroundings these areas provided, as well as the proximity to downtown jobs, shopping, transportation, health care, and other vital services.

Most of the small businesses that were moved did not succeed in their new locations, since the customers on which they had depended were no longer nearby. Others were never able to re-open elsewhere. Among those that closed forever were the black tourism businesses located on Decatur Street. After Auburn Avenue, Decatur Street was the most important African-American commercial area in the city. In 1959 the area offered five lodging places, ten restaurants, three billiard halls, and one theater. These black-oriented businesses on Decatur Street were razed to provide land for the expansion of Georgia State University.[46]

For Atlanta's white tourism businesses, the dislocation caused by the urban renewal program provided room for new hotels, convention facilities, and amenities for the amusement of residents and visitors. By 1966 the new hotels that were completed on the urban renewal land added 1,300 new rooms to the downtown area, while the civic center provided auditorium and exhibition space for the expanding convention business. The stadium would provide the site for part of Atlanta's symbolic move toward national visibility with the presence of major-league sports. With the passage of time, few would recall the dislocation that provided space for these new facilities, which promoted Atlanta's traditional role as the "Gate City."

Hartsfield's Legacy

Historian Bradley Rice has observed that Atlanta's boosterism has gone through several stages. Atlanta's first goal was to become the leading city of the state, and by 1868 it became the capital of Georgia. The next objective was to become the metropolis of the South. By 1895 the city of 75,000 residents celebrated its progress toward this goal by hosting the Cotton States and International Exposition, and the Forward Atlanta campaign of the 1920s enabled the city to accomplish its second objective by attracting regional offices for many corporations. After World War II, business leaders were not content to remain residents of a regional city as they aspired to support a city of national prominence. Much of the growth toward this third goal would take place during the 1960s.[47]

As a result of the Plan of Improvement, Atlanta's boosters greeted 1960 with a spirit of enthusiasm, since the Census Bureau reported that over the previous decade the city had grown by more than 47 percent to reach a record population of 487,455.[48] In spite of some population loss owing to the policies of expressway construction and urban renewal, the city grew as a result of the 1952 annexation. The 1960 census report showed that the City of Atlanta's population increase had outpaced that of its suburbs, which still managed just under a 40 percent increase for the decade.

In 1960 the Census Bureau recognized five counties as part of the Atlanta metropolitan area—Fulton, DeKalb, Clayton, Gwinnett, and Cobb. Together these counties had a population of just over a million. The City of Atlanta was almost entirely in Fulton County, and many of those who lived in the suburbs commuted

Table 5.4. City of Atlanta, Tourism Business Employment, 1960

Occupation	Men	Women
Waiters, Bartenders, Cooks & Counter Workers	2,053	3,617
Eating & Drinking Places	5,628	3,387
Entertainment & Recreation Serv.	1,674	658
	9,355	7,662

Source: Bureau of the Census, *Eighteenth Census of the United States, 1960,* vol. 1, part 12, *Characteristics of the Population.*

into the city for employment. Tourism business employment remained strong in Atlanta. As Table 5.4 shows, many men and women were employed in the food and beverage business as part of the city's hospitality industry.

Hotel employees who worked outside food service operations were no longer enumerated as a separate employment category, and so are not included in these statistics. However, the men employed in these three tourism businesses represented 7.6 percent of the total male workforce in the city. The hospitality business jobs were even more important for women, since they represented 9.1 percent of the females in the city's labor force.[49] While some tourism businesses were outside the city in the suburban counties, many people lived outside the city and commuted in for employment. Table 5.5 shows the number of tourism business employees in the five-county metropolitan area that includes the

Table 5.5. Atlanta Metropolitan Area,
Tourism Business Employment, 1960

Occupation	Men	Women
Waiters, Bartenders, Cooks & Counter Workers	2,677	5,707
Eating & Drinking Places	8,654	5,345
Entertainment & Recreation Serv.	2,828	1,033
	14,159	12,085

Source: Bureau of the Census, *Eighteenth Census of the United States, 1960,* vol. 1, part 12, *Characteristics of the Population.*

141

City of Atlanta. The most numerous of these were employees of eating and drinking places who lived outside the city. Since all the counties outside Atlanta were legally dry, many of these individuals obviously commuted to jobs in the city.

As mayor of Atlanta for twenty-three years, William B. Hartsfield shaped many of the policies that prepared the city for its growth toward national prominence. In the early 1950s he began implementation of the transportation plan that created the north-south and east-west expressways ahead of the national interstate highway system. Using available federal funds for urban renewal, he started the slum clearance program that expanded the land area of downtown. In contrast to the political leaders of most other Southern cities, Hartsfield set a tone of moderation in race relations that gave Atlanta a positive reputation. He sought to avoid racial disturbances in order to promote a good business climate for the city. As mayor, his constant theme for promoting business was to proclaim that Atlanta was the "city too busy to hate."

No matter how many times the mayor repeated his slogan, though, the city could not keep away the passions of racism that were swirling in the South during the 1950s. Following the Supreme Court's 1954 decision in *Brown v. Board of Education,* the desegregation of public schools angered most Southern whites as they faced the process of change in established race relations. Blacks and their sympathizers became the targets of bombings as white supremacist organizations were formed to try to halt change. One twelve-month period in 1957–58 saw forty-seven bombings or attempted bombings in the South. Civic leaders hoped it could not happen in Atlanta.

On October 12, 1958, in the early morning hours, an explosion of dynamite blasted one wall of the Temple, the city's oldest Jewish synagogue. The target was probably the congregation's rabbi, Jacob M. Rothschild, who had been outspoken on the subject of race relations. Mayor Hartsfield rushed to the scene and told reporters, "Atlanta has prided itself in being a beacon of tolerance and racial and religious decency in the South. This shocks and amazes us." He went on to add that surely the bombing was the work of out-of-towners. The moderate editor of the *Constitution*, Ralph McGill, wrote a Pulitzer Prize–winning editorial denouncing the bombing as "the harvest of defiance of courts and the encouragement of citizens to defy the law on the part of many Southern politicians." McGill called on all Americans to turn their backs on the "wolves of hatred," whether that hatred was against Jews or blacks.[50] Although several members of the anti-Semitic National States Rights Party were arrested and one member was tried, no convictions followed the Temple bombing. Rabbi Rothschild continued to speak and act on behalf of justice for blacks in Atlanta. The bombing had the effect of reinforcing Atlanta's reputation for moderation in race relations as the mayor, the newspaper, and civic leaders rallied in support of the Temple.

Hartsfield was also responsible for much of Atlanta's expansion as an air transportation center, a role that fueled the continued growth of both the city and its tourism businesses. Air traffic into the Atlanta municipal airport received a boost from the travel demands of personnel and equipment during World War II. However, despite improvements in runways and landing facilities, funds were unavailable for supplies for passenger facilities. These shortages continued after the war as the terminal building was constructed from surplus war materials. This facility served air travelers throughout the 1950s. Hartsfield entered his last term as mayor determined to leave one final mark on the city's air transportation, and he convinced members of the business community to support the largest bond debt ever incurred by the city in order to finance a new airport facility. Work began on the $20 million facility in 1959, and Atlanta's new airport terminal opened two years later during Hartsfield's last full year in office.[51]

Hartsfield wanted Atlanta to have an airport terminal large enough to make a strong impression on visitors, so the architect designed an eight-story international-style office building above the terminal facility. The facility had forty-eight gates and the capacity to expand to sixty, giving it the ability to handle 6 million passengers per year.[52] Aircraft technology was changing rapidly from propeller to jet power, and the new terminal was designed with this transition in mind. Each gate was equipped with a "jetway" that allowed passengers to step directly from the waiting area onto the plane through an air-conditioned passage without going outside and up steps into the airplane.[53]

In May of 1961, a crowd of five hundred joined Mayor Hartsfield for the official dedication of the new terminal. Fittingly, the speaker was Eugene Black, the grandson of Henry W. Grady, the greatest booster of Atlanta and the New South during the nineteenth century. Black reminded the crowd that Atlanta started as a transportation center for the railroads. Over a century later, the technologies had changed, but Atlanta's main reason for being and the engine of its prosperity was still its transportation system. In the past the city had battled with other towns to add rail lines. Mayor Hartsfield and Atlanta's business leaders recognized the importance of air travel and the necessity for the city to attract and hold as much as possible. The *Atlanta Journal* editor wrote, "When jets came in we could handle them. Now we can handle the passengers they bring. . . . In Atlanta we can't rest. We have to keep planning and working in order to maintain our present position and move ahead."[54]

The modern new jet-age airport would help Atlanta remain the regional center for air transportation. In the first issue of a new magazine published by the Chamber of Commerce, the editor noted that

> the famous city of Atlanta is coming of age. This is the town which movies and books have long portrayed as the hub of Southern hospitality, and the Fried Chicken Capital of the World. But Atlanta is changing. . . . This booming nerve center of the South has turned a new face to the nation. And it's a broad-beamed face of fancy new skyscrapers, fast moving expressways, great wealth and plenty of hustle. This is Atlanta in the Sixties. . . .
>
> In short, Atlanta has outgrown its reputation of charm and graciousness. It's still charming, and still gracious—but in a hustling, bustling, booming sort of way.[55]

His words captured much of the way Atlantans regarded their Southern heritage. They wanted to be the center of Southern hospitality and continue the city's reputation for graciousness and charm, yet they also wanted their city to be a booming metropolis with the tall buildings, interstate highways, and the "hustle" that accompanied urban growth. Atlantans also faced the challenges of the civil rights struggle as they tried to live up to the image of the "city too busy to hate."

In 1846 when the young town was still named Marthasville, the Georgia Railroad Company opened the Atlanta Hotel. Slaves owned by the hotelkeeper did most of the work needed to welcome guests in the years before the Civil War. (Courtesy of the Atlanta History Center)

The original Kimball House Hotel opened in 1870 as the city's most elegant place to stay. A fire destroyed this building in 1883, but energetic owner H. I. Kimball quickly replaced the landmark hotel. (Courtesy of the Atlanta History Center)

In October 1887 Atlantans gave a warm reception to President Grover Cleveland as he arrived at the Union Station for the Piedmont Exposition. Spectators crowded the balcony and ledges of the Markham House Hotel to catch a glimpse of the popular president. (Courtesy of the Atlanta History Center)

Aerial view of the 1895 Cotton States and International Exposition grounds. The fair brought attention to Atlanta as a hub of the New South. (Courtesy of the Atlanta History Center)

Mrs. Emma Bell and some of her "Bell House Boys" in front of her boardinghouse c. 1900. Mrs. Bell, a widow, opened her boardinghouse in 1878. (Courtesy of the Atlanta History Center)

Beginning in 1909, city leaders illuminated Peachtree Street, creating the "Great White Way." On this evening in 1917, the lights burned to attract visitors for a stroll downtown. (Courtesy of the Atlanta History Center)

Bailey's 81 Theatre was part of a lively entertainment district for African Americans on Decatur Street. The theater opened in 1910 for vaudeville and picture shows, remaining a landmark showplace until it was demolished as part of the urban renewal program in the 1960s. (Skip Mason Archives)

During the Jim Crow era, African Americans developed a separate convention business. In 1920 delegates to the national meeting of the NAACP met at Big Bethel A.M.E. Church, where they were addressed by Dr. W. E. B. Du Bois. (Skip Mason Archives)

The Top Hat Club on Auburn Avenue opened in 1937 and was known as "Club Beautiful" to its patrons. The Top Hat featured its own orchestra and was a showcase for nationally known African American entertainers. In 1949 Mrs. Carrie Cunningham, the owner of the Royal Hotel and Bailey's Royal Theatre, purchased the Top Hat and renamed it the Royal Peacock Club. (Skip Mason Archives)

On December 15, 1939, Atlantans welcomed the glamour of Hollywood for the world premier of the motion picture version of Margaret Mitchell's *Gone with the Wind*. The entrance of Loew's Grand Theater added a replica of a columned plantation house for the event. (Courtesy of the Atlanta History Center)

From 1939 until 1954 the sign on the Hotel Roxy read "Welcome South Brother" as the owners provided hospitality to working-class visitors. In 1995 the Hotel Roxy was converted to loft apartments and provided the location for several businesses, including Thelma's Kitchen, a popular soul-food restaurant. (Photograph by author)

The Southeastern Fair opened in the aftermath of the Leo Frank lynching in 1915 to provide a week of fun and to promote agricultural diversification in Georgia. Rural folks and city dwellers continued to meet at the fair in this 1943 photograph of the crowded midway at the Lakewood Fairgrounds. (Lane Brothers Collection, Special Collections Department, Pullen Library, Georgia State University)

The Winecoff Hotel, pictured here soon after it opened in 1913, advertised itself as the fireproof hotel that was "Nearer than anything to everything on Atlanta's most famous thoroughfare." Early in the morning, December 7, 1946, a fire swept through the Winecoff, resulting in the deaths of 119 people in the worst hotel disaster in the world at the time. (Courtesy of the Atlanta History Center)

One of the mayor's duties was to welcome conventions to the city. Mayor of Atlanta for twenty-three years, William B. Hartsfield (fourth from right) greeted the 1950 Jewelry Convention at its meeting in the Biltmore Hotel. (William B. Hartsfield Collection, Special Collections Department, Robert W. Woodruff Library, Emory University)

In 1961 entertainment promoter B. B. Beamon purchased the Savoy Hotel on Auburn Avenue and opened Beamon's Restaurant. His restaurant served as a meeting place for planning civil rights marches in the city. (Skip Mason Archives)

On July 3, 1964, the defiant owner of the Pickrick Restaurant, Lester Maddox, turned away one of three black students who attempted to integrate the restaurant. Maddox, armed with a pistol, and a supporter with a pickax handle were arrested under the Civil Rights Act. After losing a U.S. Supreme Court decision, Maddox closed the restaurant in protest, gaining popularity that helped to get him elected governor in 1967. (A Press Wide World Photo, William B. Hartsfield Collection, Special Collections Department, Robert W. Woodruff Library, Emory University)

Architect-developer John Portman's Hyatt Regency Hotel opened in 1967, creating a dramatic addition to the city's skyline. It was part of the Portman-designed Peachtree Center complex that included the Atlanta Merchandise Mart and two other hotels. (Photograph by author)

From 1969 until 1982 the area under the viaducts in downtown was a popular tourist attraction known as Underground Atlanta. The initial success of this historic area faded as rapid-rail construction, fires, and other problems gradually closed the sixty-five businesses operating in Underground. (Courtesy of the Atlanta History Center)

The Georgia World Congress Center opened in 1976, providing 640,000 square feet of exhibition space for conventions and making it the "world's largest hall." (Photograph by author)

The John Portman–designed Marriott Marquis Hotel opened in 1985 with 1,674 rooms, making it the largest hotel in the South. During the 1996 Olympic Games, the Marriott Marquis served as the official "Olympic Family Hotel." (Photograph by author)

In July 1988 Governor Joe Frank Harris of Georgia welcomed the delegates to the Democratic National Convention in the Omni sports arena. (Courtesy of the Democratic Party of Georgia)

The new Underground Atlanta reopened in 1989 as an entertainment complex for visitors and residents but failed to fulfill many of the hopes of its supporters. (Photograph by author)

The round, reflective glass of the Westin Peachtree Plaza Hotel provided a background for the Fountain of Rings in Olympic Centennial Park. The Plaza's seventy stories made it the tallest hotel in North America. (Photograph by author)

At the end of the Opening Ceremony at the 1996 Centennial Olympic Games, fireworks lit up the sky above the athletes assembled from around the world. The ceremony featured an array of Southern culture viewed by 80,000 spectators and an estimated three billion viewers on television. (Courtesy of the Atlanta History Center)

6

Turmoil and Prominence, 1960–1970

THE CULTURE OF THE SOUTH HAS helped to shape patterns of life in Atlanta throughout the city's history. Hospitality, as expressed in the graciousness with which guests were welcomed, was quickly converted into commercial applications as hotels, restaurants, places of amusement, and other types of tourism businesses grew along with the city. Factors such as race and class, however, always influenced the ways hospitality was extended. By the beginning of the twentieth century a rigid pattern of segregation in race relations required that blacks could wait on whites in white-owned tourism businesses, but African Americans could not be customers in these establishments and needed to open their own businesses for black customers. This led to the development of African-American commercial areas located on Auburn Avenue, Decatur Street, and near the Atlanta University Center to the west of downtown.

There had been gradual pressure for change in these patterns of segregation. As mayor throughout the postwar era, William B. Hartsfield set the tone for race relations by carefully negotiating issues such as the urban renewal clearance so that black middle-class leadership could make some gains out of the process. Hartsfield believed in segregation and had, at best, a paternalistic attitude toward African Americans. However, he was also a politician who recognized that he needed black votes to remain in office.[1] Many of his gestures toward African Americans were largely symbolic, such as the hiring of eight black policemen in 1948 (these officers could only arrest other African Americans), but these seemed important in the midst of die-hard segregation in the rest of the state and region. Many of the changes were accomplished slowly—such as the elimination of the "White" and "Colored" signs from the restrooms at the airport. Hartsfield simply ordered the signs gradually reduced in size until they disappeared without public notice. He also negotiated the desegregation of the city's buses in 1958.[2] Hartsfield's pragmatic approach to race relations was good for both politics and business. After the end of the all-white Democratic Party primary in Georgia in 1946, he needed the support of growing numbers of African-American voters. Good race relations were also good for the city's business climate as Atlanta sought investment from other parts of the nation.

Progress toward the desegregation of theaters, eating places, hotels, and other public places was moving slowly throughout the South. In Atlanta, the advances made by careful negotiations between elder white and black leaders seemed painfully slow to a younger generation of African-American students enrolled in the institutions that made up the Atlanta University Center. A new strategy to speed the process was begun by a similar group of black college students in Greensboro, North Carolina. On February 1, 1960, several students sat down at a lunch counter in downtown Greensboro and refused to leave when told that the store did not serve blacks. News of the sit-in spread quickly throughout the South, prompting a variety of responses. African-American students enrolled in Atlanta's six private institutions planned their own demonstrations and sit-ins.[3]

Fearing the spread of the movement in Georgia, the state's general assembly passed a special trespass law that enabled the owners of restaurants and lunch counters to refuse service to anyone they wished. On March 9 the Atlanta University Center students published a full-page advertisement in all the local newspapers in which they called for an end to discrimination in education, jobs, housing, voting, health care, and law enforcement. Entitled "An Appeal for Human Rights," the advertisement also noted that tourism businesses such as movies, concerts, and restaurants discriminated against African Americans: "Negroes are barred from most downtown movies and segregated in the rest. Negroes must even sit in a segregated section of the Municipal Auditorium. If a Negro is hungry, his hunger must wait until he comes to a 'colored' restaurant."[4]

The same week in which the "Appeal" was published, the students took their grievances to the streets in demonstrations and to the lunch counters of the city, where they staged sit-ins to protest the trespass law and force the process of integration. One of their first targets was the lunch counter at the downtown Rich's department store.[5] Rich's was selected because it was locally owned and was the city's leading department store. The following week one hundred students were jailed following sit-ins at ten eating places located in public or tax-supported buildings such as the rail and bus stations, city hall, the Fulton County courthouse, and the capitol.[6]

Although Mayor Hartsfield was concerned that the demonstrations would be harmful to the city's image, he was unable to negotiate a quick settlement to end the conflict. At a meeting between student leaders and white businessmen, the students were told that businesses in downtown Atlanta were not about to end segregation. Faced with this hostility, the students shifted the focus of their demonstrations to stores that depended upon black customers but that did not hire African Americans in any capacity above menial jobs. This decision was criticized by many older blacks, including the editor of the leading African-American newspaper, the *Daily World*.[7] The split among the generations of blacks caused difficulties in negotiations, since the mayor and white business leaders were accustomed to dealing with the older blacks, whom the students now distrusted.

Through the spring and summer of 1960, the Atlanta University Center students focused most of their demonstrations and calls for a boycott against an A&P supermarket located in an

African-American neighborhood. By early September the students had succeeded in changing the employment discrimination against blacks in two stores. The following month the students again directed their protests against downtown businesses. This time they invited Dr. Martin Luther King, Jr., to join them, since he was a Morehouse College graduate and Atlanta was his home. King had tended to remain aloof from the Atlanta demonstrations, concentrating his attention on other parts of the South that needed his leadership and organizational skills. By October 20, however, King and fifty-seven students had been arrested for sit-ins at Rich's and other downtown businesses. The students were well organized and used two-way radios to coordinate their peaceful sit-ins and picketing. These demonstrations brought large numbers of arrests under the state's trespass law, as well as counter-demonstrations led by robed Klan members. Although Mayor Hartsfield was unsuccessful in negotiating an end to the demonstrations, he reacted in typical Atlanta booster fashion by announcing to the press, "Well, at least in the field of lunch counter demonstrations, Atlanta can claim two firsts. With the help of the Ku Klux Klan, it can be the first to claim integrated picketing. And now we have radio-directed picketing. At least we are handling our problems in a progressive way."[8]

With tensions high between the races, holiday sales declined as a result of the success of the boycott and the presence of so many demonstrators. The conflict remained unresolved as the first anniversary of the Greensboro student sit-ins approached. The Atlanta students changed their tactics by seeking arrest and crowding the jails by refusing to post bond. This led to renewed negotiations conducted by the president of the Chamber of Commerce, Ivan Allen, Jr. On March 6, 1961, both sides agreed to a compromise that would end the demonstrations in return for a promise to desegregate lunch counters and restrooms in downtown stores no later then October 15, 1961. The young students were impatient with the delay but were persuaded in a dramatic appeal by Dr. King to suspend their demonstrations. In spite of misgivings on both sides, the agreement held, and the integration of restaurants and lunch counters in downtown department and variety stores took place without incident on September 27, 1961.[9] Atlanta was the first Southern city to take this step toward ending segregation in its tourism businesses. In other cities in the South where there were lunch counter sit-ins, the businesses responded by closing their eating facilities.

Rioting in Little Rock and New Orleans over the desegregation of public schools had tarnished the image of these cities, and Mayor Hartsfield was determined to avoid this kind of negative publicity for Atlanta. In a triumph of symbolism over substance, he carefully negotiated the peaceful desegregation of the city's public schools in the fall of 1961, as he prepared to leave office. Only 9 African-American students out of approximately 45,000 enrolled in previously all-white schools that fall, but more than 200 out-of-town reporters were shown a peaceful day on the first day of classes. The peaceful "integration" of the city's schools was a giant public relations coup for Atlanta, bringing congratulations from President Kennedy and favorable recognition from the nation's press. The schools remained largely segregated, as two years later there were only 54 blacks attending integrated schools in Atlanta. It would take further litigation by the NAACP to hasten the desegregation of Atlanta's public schools.[10] Hartsfield, however, was able to retire from his twenty-three-year tenure as mayor having made a symbolic commitment to desegregation.

With Hartsfield's retirement, the race for mayor came down to two candidates, Ivan Allen, Jr., and Lester Maddox. Allen was the president of the Chamber of Commerce and a member of a socially prominent family, while Maddox was a restaurant owner and a high school dropout whose father was a steelworker. Through most of his early life, Allen had been a segregationist who had little contact with blacks except as servants. As he campaigned for mayor, however, Allen reached out to African-American voters to forge the same coalition of upper-status northside whites and blacks that had won elections for Hartsfield. Allen's change on matters of race was both personal and pragmatic. He recognized the growing political strength of African Americans as well as the potential damage to the city's business if Atlanta became another Little Rock or Montgomery.

Allen campaigned openly in black areas of the city and won the endorsement of most of the older generation of leaders in the African-American community. Maddox was a white supremacist whose newspaper ads for his Pickrick Restaurant promoted both his fried chicken and his segregationist views. His campaign was popular among blue-collar white voters, as Maddox attacked the wealth of his opponent as well as Allen's willingness to seek black votes. Allen had a vision for the economic growth of Atlanta that depended upon harmony between the races.[11] With the solid support of black voters, Allen won the election with 64 percent of the total vote. The new mayor had no sooner turned back the challenge from the conservative racial views of Lester Maddox when he faced more challenges to the long-held pattern of segregation in Atlanta's tourism businesses.

Civil Rights Struggles

Most observers saw Allen's election as a continuation of the coalition that had kept his predecessor in office for so long. Under Mayor Hartsfield the process of desegregating Atlanta's tourism businesses had been marked by gradual change that resulted from carefully negotiated biracial settlements. When Allen took office in 1962, however, the pace of change quickened. There were several reasons for this. First, the sit-ins by black students from the Atlanta University Center which had brought about the integration of many downtown lunch counters had departed from the tradition of slow negotiation. Impatient with their elders and desiring the complete desegregation of tourism businesses in the city, the younger generation of African-American students was not content to wait for white political leaders to work out agreements with the older generation of black leaders. Their well-organized demonstrations kept the pressure on the mayor and business leaders to end segregation in hotels, restaurants, theaters, and other hospitality businesses.

A second reason for change was pressure from within the tourism businesses themselves. Atlantans had long recognized the economic potential of Southern hospitality in attracting conventions to the city. The Atlanta Convention and Visitors Bureau, organized in 1912, was among the oldest such organizations in the nation. With its transportation connections, the promotional efforts of its business and political leaders, and the warmth of its hospitality, Atlanta had been among the nation's leaders in convention hosting ever since the 1920s. However, the policy of racial segregation in Atlanta's hotels, restaurants, and other facilities had made it increasingly difficult to attract some conventions to the city. As the executive vice president of the Convention Bureau, Walter Crawford, said, "More and more convention people are requesting that all of their members—of all races—be handled together. One hotel here has begun to handle limited numbers . . . that is, they will take a few Negroes, for instance, into their private banquet rooms. If the membership of the convention has a small percentage of Negroes they'll handle the banquet."[12]

Some African-American educational, business, and professional organizations decided to avoid meeting in Atlanta or any other segregated city. Several labor unions also followed this policy. When blacks did come to Atlanta to participate in national meetings, such as the Junior Chamber of Commerce in June 1961, they were quickly reminded that they were in the segregated South. As the Jaycees arrived, the Heart of Atlanta Motel refused to honor the reservation of an African-American delegate from Minnesota. Because the motel did not want to be the first to "break the color line," the man was forced to stay in a friend's apartment. The Dinkler Plaza rented a room to the Pennsylvania delegation which was occupied by their black president-elect. Reporters swarmed outside his room, causing considerable embarrassment to the hotel as well as its guest. Another African-American delegate reported that he found the Atlantans he met "friendly and hospitable," but he was disappointed over the segregated accommodations. "Atlanta has missed a marvelous opportunity," he concluded.[13] In the highly competitive convention business, Atlantans could not afford to wait much longer. Hotels in Dallas, Houston, and Miami were already desegregated, giving their convention business an advantage over Atlanta's.[14]

Just two weeks after Allen's election in November 1961, the Atlanta chapter of the NAACP asked for the desegregation of all the city's hotels.[15] The Atlanta University Center students were eager to offer support, in March 1962 they staged a "sleep-in" in the lobby of the Henry Grady Hotel. Several white and black students made reservations by mail at the hotel. When the students arrived as a group, the whites were given their rooms but the blacks were refused. The students announced that they would sleep in the lobby, but they were arrested under the anti-trespass law.

The students continued to apply pressure through 1962 and early 1963. Some restaurants that had desegregated under the 1961 agreement reverted to their racist past, closing their doors to African-American customers. One obstacle to be overcome was the differing ideas of what constituted racial harmony in the city. As Mayor Allen described it, whites tended to define that as absence of disturbance, while blacks pressed for their full rights as American citizens.[16] The students' right to demonstrate peacefully was also increasingly challenged in 1963. As they marched outside city restaurants, the African-American students faced violence from restaurant employees and counter-demonstrators, who would attack before the police could arrive.[17]

Above all, the mayor wanted to keep the peace in the city to avoid any damage to Atlanta's reputation. At his urging, the Chamber of Commerce issued a policy statement in May 1963 asking all businesses to desegregate in order to "maintain a healthy climate." Eighteen leading hotels and motels as well as thirty restaurants responded by voluntarily agreeing to end segregation in their establishments. The mayor took the unusual step of going to Washington that summer and testifying in support of federal legislation that would require the integration of all hotels, restaurants, and facilities engaged in any sort of interstate commerce. Allen was the only mayor from the South to support the public accommodations bill. He recognized that voluntary efforts to desegregate tourism businesses had not worked, and that only federal legislation requiring all to comply would succeed in ending segregation. On July 2, 1964, President Johnson signed the Civil Rights Act into law, making the integration of public accommodations the law of the land. While black Atlantans rejoiced in the victory, some whites were not ready to change old habits.

In a test of the Civil Rights Act, three African-American seminary students from the Atlanta University Center tried to enter Lester Maddox's Pickrick Restaurant. They were met at the door by Maddox, who waved a pistol as he ordered them to leave. Other whites from the restaurant used pickax handles to beat the car in which the three blacks attempted to drive away. Maddox was placed under arrest for his refusal to desegregate the restaurant. In federal court his case was joined by a lawsuit filed by the owner of the Heart of Atlanta Motel, who argued that the Civil Rights Act denied him the "liberty to segregate" his property. The federal court's ruling against Maddox was upheld on appeal by the U.S. Supreme Court. Hotels, motels, restaurants, theaters, sports arenas, and any other places of public entertainment were required to serve all customers, regardless of race.[18] Although the motel owner obeyed the Court's decision, Maddox closed his restaurant in protest. He placed a mock coffin outside his restaurant, declared that free enterprise was dead, and sold pickax handles as souvenirs.

The publicity that resulted from the Maddox trial and its aftermath embarrassed Atlanta's mayor and business leaders but gained support for Maddox outside the city. Maddox became a symbol of white resistance to integration and used his fame to be elected governor in 1967. Journalist Frederick Allen observed that Maddox was good for Atlanta because he made the city's leaders appear more liberal than they actually were. By embodying the most ugly form of white racism, Maddox served as a perfect foil, enhancing the city's reputation for moderation within the climate of bigotry that characterized much of the South.[19]

An opportunity for Atlantans to demonstrate their difference from most other white Southerners was soon at hand. In 1964,

Dr. Martin Luther King, Jr., who was born and raised in Atlanta, won the Nobel Peace Prize for his efforts to win civil rights for blacks in the South. Eager to publicize the event, Mayor Allen and Robert W. Woodruff, head of the Coca-Cola Company, organized a biracial dinner to recognize King's achievement. The event was planned for January 27, 1965, at the Dinkler Plaza Hotel. In spite of efforts by Mayor Allen, former Mayor Hartsfield, newspaper editor Ralph McGill, and local religious leaders, ticket sales for the event were slow. Many white business leaders resented King's role in the sit-in campaign and other local protests. However, to ignore the Nobel winner would sully the city's national image and call into question its commitment to racial progress.[20] A last-minute intervention by Robert Woodruff showed the influence of Coca-Cola in Atlanta and succeeded in selling out the 1,500 seats at the dinner. As expected, the event generated favorable publicity for Atlanta as blacks and whites ended the affair by joining hands and singing "We Shall Overcome."[21]

Throughout the civil rights struggles of the early 1960s, several of the city's African-American tourism businesses served as important meeting grounds for the participants. Just as Atlanta's private clubs often served as informal gathering places for influential white decision makers, two black restaurants, in particular, served the same function as places for African-American leaders to gather, Paschal's Restaurant and Beamon's Restaurant. Paschal's Restaurant on Hunter Street (now Martin Luther King, Jr., Drive) was a gathering place both for the students from nearby Atlanta University Center and for black community leaders. The Paschal brothers, James and Robert, were famous for their fried chicken, as well as for their restaurant's reputation as "black city hall." They also operated a jazz club, La Carrousel, which between its opening, in 1959, and 1964 was licensed by the city for African-American customers only. The musicians who performed at La Carrousel were so popular that the club's clientele was often as much as 60 percent white.[22] Before the signing of the 1964 Civil Rights Act, the jazz club showed that whites and blacks could share the same facilities and demonstrated that

170

music was an aspect of Southern culture that offered a biracial vision capable of being enjoyed by both races.

Another black tourism business owner who played a role in the civil rights struggle was Benjamin Burdell Beamon, the proprietor of Beamon's Restaurant and the Savoy Hotel on Auburn Avenue. In 1961, when Dr. King was helping the students plan lunch counter demonstrations, most of the meetings took place in the private dining room of Beamon's restaurant. Beamon began his career during the depression working as a dishwasher in the Henry Grady Hotel. He worked and saved his money to invest in the hotel and restaurant in the Herndon Building on Auburn Avenue. Most of his investment came from his role as a promoter of entertainment for African Americans as well as the owner of the Magnolia Ballroom, a dance hall. Throughout the 1940s and 1950s, Beamon brought black entertainers to perform at both his ballroom and the city's municipal auditorium.[23]

Mayor Allen's ability to keep the peace and to support some change for African Americans kept his political coalition intact and enabled him to win reelection in 1965. His actions during a period of turmoil enhanced Atlanta's reputation as a different kind of Southern city, one where changes in traditional cultural patterns could be made if they were good for business. Ironically, the end of segregation contributed to the decline of black tourism businesses in Atlanta. In 1960 four hotels had served African Americans on Auburn Avenue; in 1974, ten years after the passage of the public accommodations law, a single motor hotel remained on the avenue. The number of restaurants and clubs on "Sweet Auburn" also declined during this period, from twenty-one to nineteen.[24] While the 1964 Civil Rights Act was an important step, it did not eliminate problems of housing, employment, and discrimination which continued to affect black Atlantans.

Partnership for Growth

On the evening of January 3, 1966, Mayor Allen stood before the city's Board of Aldermen to give his State of the City Address, in which he proclaimed that "the time was most certainly ripe for Atlanta to emerge from a static position of just another American city and move vigorously forward as a regional and national giant."[25] Allen had reason to boast of Atlanta's movement toward national prominence. The Chamber of Commerce had conducted a second Forward Atlanta campaign from 1961 to 1964 to promote the city and had attracted 25,000 new jobs in each of its three years of operation.[26] The new jet-age airport ranked fourth nationally in passenger enplanements and fifth in commercial operations. The number of hotel and motel rooms had more than doubled in the years since World War II. The new Atlanta Stadium was completed, major-league baseball and football were on the way, and a new civic center was under construction. The state had created a Metropolitan Atlanta Rapid Transit Authority to study the feasibility of a rail transit system for the city. Atlanta's desegregation had been peaceful in comparison to other cities in the region, giving the city a favorable reputation for racial moderation. Finally, the city had passed a referendum that permitted the sale of liquor by the drink, ending the hypocrisy of private "locker" clubs and "blind tigers."[27] All of these achievements made Atlantans feel that the city was positioned in 1966 to take its place at the national level.

Throughout the postwar period, the partnership between business leadership and elected officials provided additional room for downtown to expand, land for tourism business facilities, a new airport, and the Forward Atlanta campaign. These accomplishments laid the foundation for the spectacular growth that followed. One of the fruits of this partnership was the convention business. Atlanta had promoted itself as a convention city throughout the twentieth century, and as Table 6.1 illustrates, from 1940 to 1970 both the number of meetings held in Atlanta and the number of people participating in these conventions steadily increased. During World War II the city averaged fewer than 100 conventions per year attended by less than 65,000 persons per year. Each five-year period saw growth in both the number of meetings held and in attendance. The opening of the new civic center in 1965 with its exhibition space provided facilities

172

Table 6.1. Number of Conventions and Attendance,
City of Atlanta, 1940–1970

Year	Number of Conventions	Attendance
1940	282	51,329
1945	271	79,135
1950	198	98,010
1955	216	113,540
1960	251	120,000
1965	330	175,000
1970	525	420,000

Source: Atlanta Convention and Visitors Bureau.

for more and larger conventions, as is reflected in the increases between 1965 and 1970. At a cost of $9 million, the new civic center could seat 4,560 in its auditorium and had an exhibition hall that could seat 10,000 for a meeting or 6,000 for a banquet.[28] This facility gave the city the ability to compete for larger meetings and conventions with its major regional competitors, Miami and Dallas, as well as with national leaders such as Chicago, New York, Washington, D.C., Atlantic City, and Los Angeles.[29]

John Portman's Peachtree Center

Atlanta's development as both a city and a hospitality center has often been advanced by individuals. Shortly after the Civil War, Hannibal I. Kimball built the grand hotel that bore his name. Later, Henry W. Grady promoted the city and its Piedmont Exposition of 1887. In the following century, Ivan Allen, Sr., led the activities of the Atlanta Convention Bureau shortly after its founding in 1912 and, as head of the Chamber of Commerce, directed the initial Forward Atlanta campaign during the 1920s. Another individual who has made a remarkable contribution to the growth of the city and its tourism businesses is John C. Portman. Though born in a small town in South Carolina, Portman grew up in Atlanta and graduated from the architecture program at Georgia Tech. As a young architect working in a downtown office, he sensed the important role Atlanta had played as a commercial center for the region.

During the late 1950s, Portman redesigned an abandoned building for use as a merchandise mart. The success of this project led to the construction of a much larger merchandise mart building on Peachtree Street, with over a million square feet of exhibit space. The new mart opened in July 1961 to serve as "a wholesale shopping center, where buyers from all over the southeast come to see manufacturers' merchandise displayed."[30] Three years later the merchandise mart was drawing crowds and generating demand for an adjacent hotel. Civic leaders were excited about this project because it would be downtown Atlanta's first major new hotel in forty years. The new hotel, the Hyatt Regency, would be unique in several ways. It would be among the largest in the South, with eight hundred rooms, and would contain an exhibition hall of 24,000 square feet and a grand ballroom large enough for 3,000 guests. The hotel would form, along with the adjacent merchandise mart, a "Rockefeller Center–type complex" that would redevelop an entire section of downtown.[31]

Another unique aspect of the project was that Portman not only designed the hotel but also served as its developer. This combination of responsibilities gave him an extraordinary measure of control over the project. The design of the hotel was different from the typical central city hotel. Portman described the traditional urban hotel as a "cramped thing with a narrow entranceway, a dull and dreary lobby for registration, elevators over in a corner, a closed elevator cab, a dimly lighted corridor, a nondescript doorway, and a hotel room with a bed, a chair, and a hole in the outside wall." Portman saw his design objective as the opposite of this. He intended to "explode" the hotel and open it up to create a grandeur of space that would seem like a resort in the center of the city.[32] The result was a huge atrium of 3 million square feet extending twenty-two stories high. For many visitors this was the largest interior space they had ever seen. Portman filled the space with light and movement from the exposed tear-shaped glass elevators that provided visitors with a ride similar to that usually found only in an amusement park. The building was topped with a revolving cocktail lounge of blue glass shaped like a flying saucer.[33]

From the moment the hotel opened in 1967, the Hyatt Regency was a distinctive landmark on the Atlanta skyline. It was a financial as well as an architectural success, with a 95 percent occupancy rate within three months after opening. The Hyatt Corporation had been the only national hotel chain that would take a chance on the innovative design. Soon after it opened, Hyatt wanted more rooms, so Portman added two hundred rooms in a cylindrical glass tower built on top of the ballroom. The openness of the atrium lobby was so spectacular that Hyatt used the design in other hotels across the country. Portman's reputation as both an architect and developer was now established, and in 1968 he doubled the size of the merchandise mart building and added the first office tower to the Peachtree Center complex.[34] Eventually, he would add two more larger hotels to Peachtree Center, the Westin Peachtree Plaza in 1976 and the Marriott Marquis in 1985. Peachtree Center itself would expand to occupy all or part of seventeen city blocks, making it one of the largest private developments in the world.

The Peachtree Center had an enormous impact on the development of Atlanta and its tourism businesses. Like H. I. Kimball, Portman built grand hotels in downtown Atlanta, but Portman did so at a time when growth was moving to the suburbs and central cities in many places were dying. His investments reshaped a major portion of downtown, spurring growth northward along Peachtree Street and away from the traditional center of the business district at Five Points. In the process, Portman also gave Atlanta some of the most distinctive buildings in its skyline. His hotels with their restaurants, lounges, and meeting spaces have helped to transform the tourism business in Atlanta. These businesses are now crucial parts of the economic growth of the city itself rather than magnets to attract investment in other activities. Seen within the context of the 1960s, Portman helped expand the function of downtown as a tourism-oriented area that depends upon visitors from conventions and business travel. Viewed from another perspective, activities once performed to lure additional growth to the city have now themselves become major sources of growth. As both architect and developer, Portman contributed to the changes in Atlanta that have helped make tourism businesses a major part of the local economy.

Portman's contributions to downtown Atlanta have not been without controversy. Large multiple-use structure projects such as Peachtree Center (often called "megastructures") have been criticized both for their design and for their impact on cities.[35] Typical of the architectural criticism of megastructures is that they represent controlled, self-contained environments that tend to seal people inside the buildings. Travel writer Arthur Frommer described Portman's architecture as "fortresses with forbidding walls, opaque exteriors making no contribution and adding no color or light to their city streets, confining their guests 'inside the moat,' so to speak, excluding them from Atlanta instead of introducing them to it."[36] Others have noted that these projects are like suburban developments, since the people inside seldom leave the buildings to be a part of the city. In the Peachtree Center complex, the buildings are connected through a series of glass tubular "skywalks," so occupants can avoid the sidewalks and remain indoors as they move from one building to another. This design has been called "anti-urban" since the buildings fail to relate to what is around them.[37]

In addition to generating controversy surrounding its design, the Peachtree Center project also inflated land values in the area around the complex. This pushed other businesses from the area, reducing employment opportunities for central city residents. Following the initial financial success of Portman's project, several other megastructures were built in downtown Atlanta. Two of these—the Omni complex and Colony Square—were much less successful financially, causing one writer to label them "urban dinosaurs." These huge projects not only drove up the value of surrounding land but also generated an oversupply of office space in the downtown and contributed to the decline of areas between the megastructures. The result was a further deterioration of the downtown the megastructures were supposed to save.[38]

Underground Atlanta

The increased numbers of conventions meeting in the new civic center, along with the business travelers coming to Portman's new downtown hotel and merchandise mart, gave city business leaders renewed hope for the central city. At the same time, they realized that downtown needed some sort of entertainment center for the amusement of residents and visitors alike. This interest coincided with the city's establishment in 1966 of a Civic Design Commission charged with the responsibility of encouraging historic preservation. The members of the commission looked for historic areas that might be restored and noticed the area near the railroad tracks under the city's viaducts. The old storefronts and warehouses of nineteenth-century Atlanta had been left behind as a home for derelicts. According to the commission, "The footings and ground floors of a number of business buildings dating from the 1870s, 1880s, and 1890s presently exist beneath the Pryor Street, Alabama Street, and Central Avenue viaducts."[39] Aware of the potential of restored areas such as New Orleans's French Quarter and St. Louis's Gas Light Square, the commissioners added, "It would be historically desirable and commercially feasible to clean up the area and restore certain of those buildings and lease them to desirable tenants."[40] This was Atlanta's first attempt at "preservation for profit," and it fit perfectly into the city's tradition of commercial hospitality. Visitors and residents could enjoy stepping back into the previous century to experience the charm of Atlanta during the railroad era without the soot and mud.[41]

While the impetus for the project came from the city, the next step was the formation of a private corporation, Underground Atlanta, Inc. Led by two Georgia Tech graduates, Jack Patterson and Steve Fuller, the company set out to obtain rights and leases from the owners of storefronts that were still standing, as well as permission to enclose open spaces. The first event in Underground Atlanta took place on April 16, 1968, when the Dogwood Festival sponsored by the Women's Chamber of Commerce hosted a "Festival of Old Atlanta" under the Central Avenue viaduct. With gaslights ablaze and women dressed in antebellum clothing, the Old South atmosphere of the event was so popular that the corporation was able to raise $4 million to continue the restoration as a permanent tourist attraction. A year later, twenty-two charter tenants were signed up and Underground Atlanta opened with a mixture of restaurants, clubs, museums, and shops.[42]

By 1970, Underground was the best-known and most visited tourist attraction in Atlanta, offering approximately sixty-five establishments appealing to a variety of tastes. The location was within walking distance of the heart of downtown with its daily flow of business and government workers, as well as the students from Georgia State University. At lunches, happy hours, and in the evenings, crowds of local residents were joined by visitors passing through Atlanta en route to Florida, as well as conventioneers. With the state's legal drinking age lowered to eighteen and all the surrounding jurisdictions legally dry, Underground Atlanta drew huge crowds of young people.

Success came almost too easily for Underground Atlanta. The development expanded quite rapidly with little control exercised over the mix of tenants in the area, and by 1973 some observers had noticed signs of trouble from several sources. Because many of the visitors were whites looking for some connection to the culture of the South, souvenir shops charged outrageous prices for cheap goods such as Confederate caps and pictures of Rhett Butler and Scarlett O'Hara. Former governor Lester Maddox opened a store where he sold autographed pickax handles. Local residents became disenchanted and increasingly went only to eat, drink, and listen to music. Public safety became a major concern as the large numbers of teenage drinkers scared away adults. The rising crime rate in the area began to further tarnish Underground's reputation. Another safety issue was the nearby railroad tracks, which posed a constant danger to revelers walking across them. Then, in 1973, the rapid rail system approved by voters destroyed almost one-third of the area to provide right-of-way for its tracks. As the number of visitors declined, the remaining establishments began losing money. Some desperate owners began offering striptease dancing, which attracted attention but only added to the area's seedy reputation. One cynical observer noted that the only thing the entrepreneurs of Underground Atlanta, Inc., proved was that with enough capital they could transform an old deteriorating area into a new deteriorating area.[43] Efforts to increase lighting and security failed to halt the gradual decline, and the last business closed its doors in the old Underground in 1982.[44]

Other Amusements

While Underground Atlanta was planned as a major focus for tourist activity in the downtown area, other amusements were opening throughout the metropolitan area. One of the city's older hotels, the Dinkler Plaza at Fairlie and Spring Streets in the central business district, opened a Playboy Club, creating a sensation with scantily clad "bunnies" serving guests. This reflected a trend toward downtown hotels catering to the convention trade by offering more restaurants and entertainment while the interstate highways served as magnets for the growth of new motor hotels.[45]

The accessibility of the interstates also encouraged the development of amusements in the suburbs. In 1965, Governor Carl Sanders announced that a group of Texas developers was planning an amusement park located near an exit ramp on I-20, west of the city. On June 16, 1967, Six Flags Over Georgia opened on 276 acres of land in suburban Cobb County. For a single entry fee, visitors could enjoy roller coasters and other rides, a music hall, puppet shows, a petting zoo, and other activities located in the simulated English village, the Spanish fort, or the Confederate area. The park was an immediate success and by 1970 attracted more than 2 million people per year.

Six Flags Over Georgia had become one of the top amusement parks in the nation by "constantly increasing the excitement of its rides and shows."[46] The need for constant increases in the attractions of a successful amusement park is characteristic of tourism businesses in general. Added attractions and excitement are necessary in order to keep visitors coming back. This often leads tourism-dependent cities like Atlanta into the development of more projects to add to the appeal of the city and to attract tourists from other places. The constant emphasis on new attractions is important in the competition among cities for conventions but may also be seen in resort areas such as Orlando, Florida.

While many Atlantans and visitors flocked to the new amusement park, others welcomed the 1967 opening of the Memorial Arts Center. Cultural activities have always struggled for support in Atlanta. As a relatively young city, Atlanta lacked the large numbers of extremely wealthy individuals generally needed to underwrite the arts. Those who supported the visual arts suffered an enormous blow in June 1962. A group of 106 members of the Atlanta Art Association flew to France on a chartered plane to visit art museums there. As the plane left Orly Field in Paris to return the group to Atlanta, it crashed, killing everyone aboard. Those who were killed were the backbone of the city's cultural life and the leading patrons of the arts.[47]

Following the tragedy, leaders of the business community pulled together and raised $8 million to build an arts center that would serve as a memorial to those who died. The Memorial Arts Center (now known as the Robert W. Woodruff Arts Center in honor of the city's most generous philanthropist) on Peachtree Street houses the High Museum of Art, the Atlanta School of Art, the Atlanta Symphony, and the Municipal Theater.[48] A prominent feature of the Arts Center is a bronze statue by Rodin which the French government donated to commemorate the tragedy. This multipurpose facility has been a major attraction for cultural activities in the city and has added to the amenities available for residents and visitors. In typical Atlanta fashion, the Arts Center is frequently used by the Chamber of Commerce and the Atlanta Convention and Visitors Bureau to promote the city. The arts in general are part of the cultural attractions frequently cited by tourism studies as a major reason people enjoy visiting a city.[49]

As Atlanta developed its tourist-oriented economy, prostitution flourished in a city where it had always been present. Even the Chamber of Commerce noted the extent of prostitution and other crime in the city in an article in its *Atlanta* magazine. The executive director of the Metropolitan Council on Crime and Delinquency was quoted as saying that tourism-related crimes involving sex, moonshine whiskey, the lottery, sports betting, and other gambling grossed perhaps a million dollars a week in Atlanta. He added, "One hundred prostitutes work in the city full time. Their annual income is well over a million dollars, and others working part-time run the take to one million five hundred thousand per year."[50]

Throughout Atlanta's history there have been only occasional and halfhearted efforts to suppress this illegal activity, as it added to the allure of the city and provided amusement for tourists— both local and visiting. In 1915, Police Chief James L. Beavers was fired after making vigorous efforts to suppress prostitution in Atlanta. His actions were opposed by a business community that had financial investments in houses of prostitution, and at a time when the city was competing to attract conventions. Subsequent public officials, including Mayor Hartsfield, were inclined to discourage vigorous enforcement of vice laws involving drinking, gambling, and prostitution as long as these activities were good for the city's business climate.[51] With this attitude it is not surprising that only a few years later, Atlanta's tourism businesses would capitalize on *legal* sex activity as the city became well known for the number and variety of its strip clubs.

A major step in the transformation of the city into a major center for athletic competition was the construction of Atlanta–Fulton County Stadium. The stadium was built on the edge of downtown on urban renewal property. In the spring of 1966, Atlanta became a big-league city with the arrival of the National

League Braves baseball team from Milwaukee. In the fall the city welcomed the National Football League expansion franchise known as the Atlanta Falcons. These major-league sports teams not only boosted the image of the city as a place of national importance but also provided an important addition to the tourist amenities available in Atlanta. With sports being an important aspect of the regional culture, crowds flocked to the games from throughout the metropolitan area and beyond.[52] Baseball fans were enthusiastic in their support of the Braves, and even the mediocre expansion football team drew sellout crowds of over 50,000 for every home game during the early years of operation.

In spite of the revenue generated from fan support of the two teams, Atlanta Stadium did not take in enough from gate receipts to cover the principal and interest on the $18 million in revenue bonds issued to finance its construction. According to the financial report of the Stadium Authority, the city and county paid almost $500,000 to reduce the debt in 1967, and over $900,000 the following year. In 1969 the city and county were responsible for paying half a million dollars on the debt service.[53] This type of revenue shortfall is common in many cities, causing some to question whether the tangible benefits from the public sector's investment in sports teams and stadiums justify the expenditures.[54]

For Atlanta's boosters, the stadium and its two major-league teams were a validation of the claim that the city had attained national prominence. They were regarded as an important tool for economic development, since professional sports attract media coverage and provide intangible benefits such as an increase in civic pride, community spirit, and collective self-image.[55] Atlanta has never been lacking in civic pride, but the acquisition of professional sports did serve to make Atlantans feel that their city was on a par with New York, Chicago, and other major-league cities. It also increased the perception of the distance between Atlanta and its municipal rivals in the Southeast such as Birmingham, Charlotte, and Jacksonville, which could be regarded as "minor league."

While local fans of the Braves and Falcons did not show the same enthusiasm as soccer fans in Rio de Janeiro, the two franchises did increase a sense of community spirit among Atlantans. Sociologists who study sports observe that the attachment of spectators to a team promotes "social bonding" among local residents. People from different classes, races, and social circumstances share their allegiance to local teams, giving the fans a common experience to discuss which transcends their differences.[56] In the large, diverse metropolitan area Atlanta had become, the benefits of community spirit from its sports teams cannot be dismissed. When the Braves became Western Division champions in 1969, the entire city responded enthusiastically, despite the team's subsequent defeat in the National League Championship Series. This brief success was followed by many years of frustration over losing teams in both baseball and football. This gave rise to a negative collective self-image as Atlanta's sports franchises earned the city the nickname "Losersville"—a label that would follow the Atlanta sports teams for more than twenty-five years.[57]

Central Area Study

As Atlanta ended the 1960s, many changes had taken place in both the city and its hospitality businesses. The expressway system enabled people to live farther from the central city and commute to jobs. This shift also led to an increase in retail activity throughout the metropolitan area and a relative decline in the importance of downtown as the center for retail activity. Without geographic barriers to restrict growth, the metropolitan area of Atlanta was expanding in all directions. With the influence of the automobile and the expressway system, Atlanta was becoming a horizontal city.

The automobile and the interstate highway system had another profound effect on Atlanta as a transportation center. Although the city was built originally as a railroad hub, by the end of the decade passenger train service into and out of Atlanta was almost gone. Nearly 90 percent of all passenger travel in and out of the city now came by automobile, with airplanes carrying 8 percent and trains less than 2 percent.[58] This change made the motor hotel even more important for the convenience it offered to the motoring public.

While these changes in transportation technology were taking place, downtown Atlanta was being reshaped with the construction of tall office buildings, hotels, convention facilities, and the amenities for its tourism businesses. Underground Atlanta, the Memorial Arts Center, and Atlanta Stadium provided a diversity of entertainment and amusements for the enjoyment of both resident and visiting tourists. What was missing was a coherent strategy to tie all of these investments together into a framework to guide the growth of the central city as a part of the emerging metropolitan area.

In 1941, downtown business leaders had organized themselves into a group known as the Central Atlanta Improvement Association. This group shortened its name to Central Atlanta Progress (CAP) as it promoted such projects as the urban renewal program and expressway construction. In 1969, CAP joined with Mayor Allen to undertake a comprehensive study of the past and the development of a plan for the future of the downtown area. The resulting document, known as the "Central Area Study," was significant because it formalized the partnership between business leaders and elected public officials to promote the interests of downtown in the face of metropolitan growth. The study also recognized the growing importance of tourism in the economic future of downtown.

The final report, issued in 1971, identified several economic functions for the Atlanta area as a whole, including the city's traditional role as a transportation and distribution center as well as its growing importance as a financial and administrative center for the Southeast. Added to the list were the concentrations of cultural activities and the largest inventory of conference and hotel and motel rooms in the region.[59] Atlanta had become the

Table 6.2. Hotel and Motel Room Location, 1950–1970

| | Number of Rooms | | |
	Downtown Core	Metropolitan Atlanta	Downtown as Percent of Total
1950	2,008	3,288	61.1%
1960	2,494	4,969	50.2%
1970	4,818	14,202	33.9%

Source: Central Area Study, 1971.

focal point for much of the art, theater, historical, recreational, and entertainment activities in the region, and ranked second only to Miami in the number of visitors it could accommodate in its hotels and motels.[60]

The 1971 report also made some observations about downtown Atlanta's role in the metropolitan area as a center for hospitality business activity. As Table 6.2 indicates, the number of hotel and motel rooms in the downtown area almost doubled during the 1960s. However, the number of rooms located in the suburbs grew at an even more rapid rate, leaving the downtown as a smaller percentage of the total in the metropolitan area. For the first time in the city's history, downtown was no longer the main focus of the lodging business, its share of the metropolitan area's hotel and motel rooms declining to around a third by 1970. The suburban motels primarily served commercial travelers as well as an almost equal number of vacationers and group meetings. In contrast, almost half the downtown hotel visitors were part of the convention trade.[61]

The automobile was the major factor in the rapid growth of motel rooms outside the central business district. The location of newer hotels away from the railroad-oriented downtown, begun early in the century, accelerated with the completion of the expressway system. Most of the new businesses were located near exit ramps on the interstate highways. Nearly 3,000 of the new motel rooms were outside of downtown but still on the fringes of the central business district, so that the Atlanta area still contained more than 44 percent of the total for the entire five-county metropolitan area.

Bolstered by the report of the Central Area Study on the importance of tourism, downtown business and political leaders realized that additional investment in convention, trade, recreation, and sports facilities were needed to keep tourists coming to the area. The study predicted that with these kinds of amenities available, the supply of hotel rooms in the downtown area would increase to 16,000 by 1983 and double again to 32,000 by 1995.[62] Tourism was no longer regarded as an aid to economic growth but as an economic growth strategy in itself. The Central Area Study thus functioned as a planning document endorsed by both business leaders and city government.

The 1970 census confirmed the extent of population growth outside the city. Atlanta recorded a population of 496,973, which represented a gain of 2 percent since 1960. On the other hand, the five-county metropolitan area reached nearly 1.4 million, an increase of 36.7 percent. Most newly arrived whites settled in the suburbs, while previously all-white areas on the south side of town attracted blacks. Whites fleeing from these neighborhoods also added to the population growth of suburban areas and contributed to the city's shift to a black majority of 51.3 percent.[63]

The presence of a large African-American population in the central city changed the balance of voting power in municipal elections. In 1969 the city saw a major change in municipal politics when the candidate favored by the city's business leadership was defeated by a coalition of black and liberal white voters who elected Atlanta's first Jewish mayor, Sam Massell. The same coalition of voters elected a young African-American attorney, Maynard H. Jackson, as vice-mayor. Their presence at city hall marked the beginning of a new relationship between the city's business leaders and local government.

The census report also showed employment patterns in the metropolitan area's tourism businesses. As Table 6.3 indicates, more than 38,000 were employed in the major occupational categories of the tourism businesses. This does not include the 2,468

Table 6.3. Metropolitan Atlanta, Tourism Business Employment, 1970

Occupation	MEN		WOMEN	
	White	Black	White	Black
Cleaning Service Workers	2,485	5,208	504	4,006
Food Service Workers	2,612	2,279	6,427	5,465
Personal Service Workers	1,927	680	5,557	1,528
	7,024	8,167	12,488	10,999

Source: Bureau of the Census, *Nineteenth Census of the United States, 1970,* vol. 1, part 12, *Characteristics of the Population.*

who were listed as "Managers of Restaurants, Cafeterias, and Bars." The 15,191 men represent less than 5 percent of the total number of men in the metropolitan area labor force, while the 23,487 women represent nearly 10 percent of women in the labor force. Because of changes in the occupational classification system used by the Census Bureau, these data are not comparable with earlier census reports. However, the importance of tourism business employment for women represents the continuation of a longer historical pattern.

Table 6.4 documents another long-standing pattern of relatively low wages for those employed in tourism businesses. In every category, the median income for hospitality business occupations is below the median for all full-time workers in the Atlanta area. With one exception, black employees also earned sig-

Table 6.4. Median Income for Tourism Business Employees, 1970

Occupation	Men		Women	
	All	Black	All	Black
Cleaning Service Workers	$4,775	$4,433	$3,016	$3,023
Food Service Workers	4,717	4,274	3,167	2,966
Personal Service Workers	5,915	5,231	4,958	3,247
All Full-time Workers	$8,958	$5,529	$5,085	$3,460

Source: Bureau of the Census, *Nineteenth Census of the United States, 1970,* vol. 1, part 12, *Characteristics of the Population.*

nificantly less than their white counterparts. African-American women working as cleaning service employees were slightly ahead of the median for all women working in this area; however, only 11 percent of the total employed as maids, cleaners, and char-women were white. The occupational category of food service workers includes large numbers of poorly paid women employed as cooks, waitresses, and food counter workers. The personal service workers—porters, bellhops, housekeepers, and recreation and amusement employees—were among the best-paid of those employed in tourism businesses. All of the median income figures are for full-time employees who worked at least fifty weeks during the year. Numerous part-time employees in tourism businesses earned even lower wages.[64] This has always been the weakness of the hospitality business. Although it provides large numbers of jobs, especially for women and minorities, many of these positions pay low wages and provide limited benefits.

After achieving a measure of national prominence during the 1960s, Atlantans would struggle with the image of their city in the years ahead. Many of Atlanta's leaders pushed toward a new goal as an international city.

7

Atlanta Struggles with Its Image, 1970–1990

In 1970, ATLANTA'S WHITE BUSINESS LEADERS worried about the future of their city. For more than three decades the mayor's office had been held by men such as William Hartsfield and Ivan Allen, Jr., who represented the interests of the city's white business elite and consulted with them on important decisions. In 1969, when Allen had chosen not to seek reelection for a third term, Rodney Cook, the candidate supported by the Chamber of Commerce, lost to Sam Massell, whose liberal background and Jewish faith earned him support among black voters (who now composed a majority of Atlanta's population) and distrust from the white and mostly Protestant business leaders.

Fearing the loss of the "Atlanta Spirit" which had unified their efforts to promote the city in the past, business leaders and the Chamber of Commerce launched a comprehensive planning process and forged a willingness to work with the new mayor. Together they promoted the passage of the referendum on a mass transit system in 1971. The new bus and fixed-rail system, known as the Metropolitan Atlanta Rapid Transit Authority (MARTA), included only the two central counties of Fulton and Dekalb and failed to involve the thirteen other counties recognized by the 1970 census as part of the Atlanta metropolitan area.[1] Despite

189

MARTA's limited service area, however, business leaders and the mayor were excited by the image of Atlanta served by the sleek new transit system and regarded it as another sign of municipal progress.

The new partnership between business leaders and Mayor Massell also resulted in the 1971 pronouncement of a lofty goal of making Atlanta "the world's next great international city." As historian Bradley Rice observed, this was a logical progression for a city that had always aspired to climb up the next rung on the municipal ladder.[2] Other than the Coca-Cola Company, however, few businesses in Atlanta were involved in global commerce in 1971. There was also little foreign investment in the city, and international flights from the airport connected only to Mexico City. Critics laughed at the new image for Atlanta as an international city, but few took into account the city's history of promotionalism. The mayor and business leaders, who used the new slogan, were aided by the fact that there was no accepted definition of what it meant to be an international city. The pronouncement was also offered as a future goal for Atlanta and not as a present reality.[3]

As mayor, Sam Massell faced the challenge of maintaining the partnership with white business leaders while representing a constituency of black residents. He increased the number of African Americans employed by the city and created an Office of Affirmative Action within city government. These efforts were not enough to diminish the growing desire within the black community for the election of an African-American mayor, a step regarded as essential to end all vestiges of discrimination and to focus the policies of city government on the needs of the low-income African-American residents who had often been ignored in the past. These citizens found a spokesman in the young attorney who served as Massell's vice-mayor, Maynard H. Jackson.

The grandson of the unofficial "mayor" of Auburn Avenue, John Wesley Dobbs, Maynard Jackson was well connected within Atlanta's black community. He was also an inspiring orator, and as an idealistic thirty-year-old had challenged Herman Talmadge in the 1968 state Democratic primary in the race for the U.S.

Senate. Jackson lost the primary, but won a majority of the votes in Atlanta with support from blacks and liberal whites. His reputation established in the Senate contest, Jackson won the election as vice-mayor the following year, giving notice that he would be a threat in any future election he chose to run. As Massell faced reelection in 1973, everyone anticipated that the campaign would feature the incumbent mayor against the vice-mayor.

Crime

Crime had always been a concern for Atlanta's leaders. The city had all the ingredients for a high crime rate, such as a high poverty rate, high unemployment among young males, a Southern culture predisposed toward violence, and a tourism industry that brought crowds of generally well-to-do visitors to the city. In 1973, the same year that the Atlanta Convention and Visitors Bureau reported that the city ranked third nationally in the number of conventions hosted, Atlanta residents were dying at a record pace with an all-time high of 263 murders—double the national average on a per capita basis. By the end of the year Atlanta had earned the distinction of being the "murder capital of the United States," and other violent crime statistics were also up.[4]

Crime became the major issue of the hotly contested mayoral campaign in the fall of 1973. Sam Massell attempted to appeal to white voters with the slogan "Atlanta's too young to die." This was designed to take advantage of the fear of crime among whites as well as to suggest that black control of city hall would weaken the climate for business investment in the city. Among African Americans, the police department represented a part of the crime problem, as black citizens were frequent victims of police brutality. To them the election of an African-American mayor would mean an opportunity to change the leadership in the police force.

Massell's rhetoric provoked a backlash among white voters who resented his criticism of the city as well as the thinly disguised

191

racism implied in the slogan. Black voters overwhelmingly supported Maynard Jackson, who received 59 percent of the total vote and became the city's first African-American mayor. Once in office, he moved rapidly to make changes in the police department. Jackson created the position of public safety commissioner and appointed his college friend Reginald Eaves. With increased training for police officers and better cooperation from the community, arrest rates went up. This did not immediately lower crime rates, however, so the perception still existed that Atlanta was a city out of control. The *Constitution* added fuel to the fire with a series of articles called "Atlanta: A City in Crisis," which criticized the city's black political leadership.[5] Reports of Atlanta's crime problem reached the rest of the nation, contributing to the Elks' decision to hold their 1976 convention elsewhere. The mayor blamed the newspaper articles for the economic loss to Atlanta.[6]

A closer examination of the city's crime statistics showed that violent crime was not widespread in the downtown area. There were isolated pockets of criminal activity, with most taking place in low-income neighborhoods against persons of the same race. The central business district was well patrolled by police officers, some of whom were mounted on horseback. The horses and their training had been a gift of Central Atlanta Progress, a downtown business group, in an effort to promote the image of security downtown. Unfortunately, the prevailing image of unsafe streets contributed to the decline of entertainment areas such as Underground Atlanta. At the same time, actual crime rates began to decline under Commissioner Eaves's leadership, especially during 1975 and 1976.[7]

During his first term, Mayor Jackson shifted away from the traditionally close relationship between city government and white business leaders. He pressed instead for affirmative action in municipal hiring and required minority participation in firms doing business with the city. This independence made him appear aloof and arrogant to business leaders. Jackson was criticized not only by the newspapers, but also by Harold Brockey, the board chair of Central Atlanta Progress. The focus of their criticism was that effective governance was impossible without cooperation between city hall and the business community.[8] With the gulf existing between the two, it would take a crisis to restore the old cooperative relationship.

The emergency was provided by a baffling series of murders which began in June 1979. Black children and youths began to disappear from the streets, their bodies later found in isolated places. In all twenty-eight murders occurred by May 1981. When residents realized that there was a serial killer of young African-American males loose, fear and panic spread through the city. Many blacks feared the Ku Klux Klan might be responsible for the murders, and in the midst of the crisis an explosion on October 13, 1980, in the day care center of a public housing project killed four children and a teacher. The need to demonstrate swift action in response to what turned out to be an accident from a faulty boiler brought about a reconciliation between the mayor and business leaders. Funds were raised and the day care center was rebuilt almost overnight. Finally, the new public safety commissioner, Lee Brown, and a special task force on the missing and murdered children case arrested an African-American male named Wayne Williams for the crimes. Gradually the city returned to normal, but publicity from the case caused considerable damage to Atlanta's reputation.

In the intense competition to attract conventions, cities with a reputation for crime are sometimes at a disadvantage. Southern cities in general tend to have more violent crimes per capita than cities located elsewhere, and Atlanta is no exception. Edward Ayers, John Shelton Reed, and Christopher Ellison attribute this statistic to a cultural norm of violence which has long been a pattern of behavior in the region. Reed, a sociologist, notes that many Southerners take high levels of violence for granted, especially when it occurs in circumstances considered a "normal" part of the culture. Southern cities do not lead the nation in all categories of violent crime, however. Their rates are higher in homicides and assaults, but lower in robberies and rapes. Reed observes that the higher Southern homicide rates are not because of violent street crime directed against strangers, but are generally the result of killings among family members and acquaintances. Crimes of this sort occasion less comment and produce less fear than random acts of violence against strangers—"street crimes"—which are more common in Northern cities. This cultural explanation for higher crime rates in Southern cities explains why the public generally has less fear of crime in Atlanta than would be expected given the high rates of homicide and assault.[9]

Whenever Atlanta did receive unfavorable publicity for its violence, such as the race riot of 1906 and the lynching of Leo Frank in 1915, city leaders worked to ensure that visitors received a warm welcome for their conventions. They also increased efforts to promote the city. During the 1970s, the Convention Bureau, the Chamber of Commerce, and the leading corporate citizen, the Coca-Cola Company, joined in a new promotional effort designed to make the city appear attractive through an emphasis on Atlanta's hospitality. This helped Atlanta to remain a leading convention destination despite high rates of violent crime. However, the continued presence of a high poverty rate, combined with teenage gangs, drugs, and guns, made crime a constant threat to the city's tourism businesses.

Georgia World Congress Center

Atlanta's civic center was less than five years old when the city's hospitality business leaders realized that a larger facility was needed. Planning began in 1971 for a convention center that would keep Atlanta competitive in attracting major national events. This desire to expand exhibition space for conventions was part of a national trend that saw the amount of space available in the major U.S. convention cities go from 6.7 million square feet in 1970 to 11 million in 1980. These "space wars" represented the use of the tourism business as an economic development strategy among American cities. For decades cities had sought to attract manufacturing as they engaged in a competition known among chambers of commerce as "smokestack chasing." This economic development strategy was especially popular in the South as cities and states followed Henry Grady's vision for a region less dependent upon agriculture. Besides local efforts such as Atlanta's initial Forward Atlanta campaign during the 1920s, there was a variety of state-supported efforts throughout the South to sell the advantages of the region for manufacturing plants.[10]

As more cities began recognizing the advantages of attracting conventions and capturing the dollars spent in the local economy by visiting delegates, the economic development competition shifted to the building of convention centers to attract more and larger groups. Places as diverse as Boston, Miami, San Diego, and St. Louis attempted to lure the convention business as part of a development strategy based on what one former mayor of St. Louis described as "the smokeless industry . . . that cannot move to the suburbs."[11] In this competition, the decisions to build these large public facilities were often made without public support. When convention centers were placed on a ballot, most failed, causing business leaders and public officials to find other financing. The costs were frequently shifted to dedicated taxes that fell on visitors.[12]

Atlanta's business leaders were doubtful of receiving public support for the development of a new convention facility to replace the civic center. They looked instead to the state government, asking Georgia to create an authority to build and operate the $20 million Georgia World Congress Center, thus avoiding local politics. The major obstacle was convincing a general assembly often hostile to Atlanta that this investment in the city would benefit the state as a whole. After intensive lobbying by a pro-business governor and business leaders, approval finally came in 1974, by which time the price had risen to $35 million.[13] When the facility opened two years later, its 640,000 square feet of exhibition space made it the "world's largest hall."[14] Its opening enabled Atlanta to host meetings of 60,000 or more. The facility allowed the city to increase both the number of conventions and attendance between 1975 and 1980. In 1975 the city hosted 710 conventions attended by 545,000 people. Five years later, with the

World Congress Center in operation, 1,090 conventions were attended by 1,002,900 people.[15]

The Georgia World Congress Center was financed by revenue bonds that would be paid off with fees from conventions using the building. A specially created state agency known as the Georgia World Congress Center Authority operated the center. This arrangement avoided the need for any local voter support for the project, and also shifted most of the tax burden to visitors who used the facility. The name of the new facility also indicated the increasing efforts by Atlanta to promote itself as an international city. The World Congress Center represented a new public-private partnership with the state in support of the city's tourism businesses.

The construction of the convention facility stimulated new hotel construction in the downtown area. Closest to the World Congress Center was the Omni complex, developed by Tom Cousins. This complex contained the Omni International Hotel and was adjacent to the Omni sports arena. In addition to the hotel, restaurants, shops, and an ice skating rink, the complex housed a $17 million indoor amusement park called the World of Sid and Marty Krofft.[16] After opening in the spring of 1976, the amusement park closed by November.[17] The hotel and entire complex struggled financially for several years until purchased in 1985 by communications innovator Ted Turner, who converted the Omni into CNN Center, which functioned as the studios and headquarters for his media companies. The 470-room Omni International Hotel continues to operate within the CNN Center.

Developer Tom Cousins wanted to make the Omni complex competitive with John Portman's Peachtree Center. He purchased the National Basketball Association's St. Louis Hawks in 1968. The team played in the Omni sports complex, which was built next to Cousins's development by the City of Atlanta and Fulton County. In 1972 Cousins purchased another sports franchise, the Atlanta Flames of the National Hockey League. While football held a special place in the culture of the South, hockey was new to the region.[18] Despite elaborate promotional efforts and the supply of transplanted fans who had moved from the

North, the Flames failed to sell out their games or generate widespread local enthusiasm. After several years of declining revenue, the team moved to the cooler climate of Calgary, Canada, in 1980. Cousins eventually sold the Hawks to Turner, who also purchased the Atlanta Braves in order to televise the games of both teams as part of his nationwide "superstation."[19]

The development of new hotels as a response to the availability of the Georgia World Congress Center continued in 1976 with the Atlanta Hilton on Courtland Street. Its 1,224 rooms made the Hilton almost as large as the Hyatt Regency. One of the most innovative design features of the Hilton was its accessibility to those with disabilities. The hotel also featured fifty meeting rooms and a total exhibition space of 41,000 square feet. The Atlanta Hilton dwarfed the civic center, constructed only ten years earlier with less than 6,000 square feet of exhibition space.[20]

Not to be outdone, architect and developer John Portman opened the world's tallest hotel on Peachtree Street in 1976. The seventy-three-story Westin Peachtree Plaza Hotel contained 1,100 rooms in a striking new addition to the city's skyline.[21] The tall black cylindrical structure was coated with reflecting glass and featured a revolving restaurant on the top three floors, a dazzling lobby area with a half-acre lake, and a five-level, ninety-foot-high skylit atrium.[22] This addition to his Peachtree Center complex towered above Portman's earlier Hyatt Regency Hotel.

The building of these new hotels indicated the close relationship between the public and private sectors in Atlanta's tourism businesses. The new exhibition space provided by the Georgia World Congress Center represented a public-sector contribution of $35 million to expand the city's convention capabilities. With this added space, private-sector developers followed by increasing the supply of hotel rooms in the downtown area. This growth, as well as competition from other convention cities, led to plans to expand the World Congress Center within two years after its opening.[23] In spite of the center's popularity, the revenues it generated failed to meet the requirements of the outstanding debt incurred to finance it, and in 1979 the facility was operating at an annual deficit of nearly half a million dollars. Somewhat reluctantly, Governor George Busbee agreed to support a bailout of the facility even as plans were under way to expand it.[24]

The New Airport

When Mayor Hartsfield dedicated the new airport terminal in 1961, the building was designed to handle 6 million passengers per year. Within its first year of operation the number of passengers using the airport exceeded 9.5 million.[25] By the aggressive promotion of its location and facilities, Atlanta handled a greater volume of air traffic than many other larger cities. Because it served as the Southern hub for two major airlines, 70 percent of the passengers came to the airport on connecting flights. By 1970 the airport was the world's second-busiest airport, after Chicago's O'Hare. International flights started in 1971 with connections to Mexico City, followed by Brussels, London, and Frankfurt by 1979.[26]

The airport's overcrowding stimulated a debate over the options of expanding the existing facility or building a second airport. This discussion among the city, the airlines, the Federal Aviation Administration, business leaders, and others continued through the mid-1970s without reaching agreement. After taking office in January 1974, Mayor Jackson sought to change the debate by advocating a position that would benefit his black constituency, which was largely concentrated in the city's southside. Jackson's policy proposal was to build a new terminal next to the existing one on the southern edge of the city. The mayor insisted on minority participation in all phases of the airport's construction, despite opposition from business leaders and the newspapers.[27]

The $305 million in bonds required to finance the new terminal was the largest ever issued in Georgia and the largest airport bond issue in the country at that time. Construction began in 1977, with an opening date set for 1980. Additional money was required for parking decks, air freight facilities, and an international terminal, and before the terminal was completed the city issued a total of $450 million in bonds.[28] The new airport opened on time in spite of the earlier misgivings about minority participation in the project. The minority partners in the concessions at the new terminal were James and Robert Paschal, who were 25 percent partners in the Dobbs-Paschal Midfield Corporation. This company leased the snack bars and cocktail lounges at the airport, many of which were minority-owned and operated. Within five years, the Paschal brothers' annual share of the airport business was estimated to be $13 million—ten times more than they earned from their hotel, restaurant, and nightclub businesses.[29]

In addition to providing new restaurants and lounges, Hartsfield International Airport was vital to the city's other tourism businesses. During its first year of operation the new terminal handled 41 million passengers on 600,000 flights, many of them arriving for conventions.[30] According to a study by the Convention Bureau, 73 percent of the city's convention visitors came through the airport. The bureau listed accessibility by air and other transportation modes as the city's number one asset as a convention and meeting site. Other assets noted were the relatively low costs of meals and lodging in the city, as well as Atlanta's pleasant climate and convention facilities such as the Georgia World Congress Center.[31]

Image Problems

For many people who arrived in Atlanta for the first time, the main image of the city was shaped by Hollywood's version of Margaret Mitchell's *Gone with the Wind*. These visitors came from all over the world expecting to see stately plantations like the mythical Tara. The reality was jarring, for there was little connection between the Atlanta they saw and the Old South depicted on the motion picture screen. Most searched vainly for links to *Gone with the Wind*. Besides a downtown restaurant named for Scarlett's Aunt Pittypat, few were to be found.[32]

Even Atlantans struggled with their image of the city. By 1980 the determined effort by business and political leaders had reshaped the central area of the city so that once-familiar downtown landmarks were torn down to make way for gleaming office towers, hotels, and other new facilities. Many residents took pride in having the continent's tallest hotel, the seventy-three-story black cylindrical Peachtree Plaza Hotel, which became a landmark on the city's skyline. However, building it had required tearing down the old, familiar Henry Grady Hotel, which served as the home for many of Georgia's political leaders since its opening in 1934 and was a political and social landmark in its own right.[33]

The replacement of the older and more familiar sights with the gleam and glitz of the new was accompanied by dramatic social change in the city itself, with a majority black population reflected in the political leadership at city hall. The city's image had changed, and both residents and visitors were unsure what to make of Atlanta. Earlier generations had adopted for Atlanta the image of the phoenix, rising in splendor from the ruins of its ashes. The New South rhetoric of Henry W. Grady had appealed to many Atlantans, who saw their city as the capital of that movement in the late nineteenth century. During the 1920s the Chamber of Commerce had proclaimed a progressive image of the city in its Forward Atlanta campaign. Many had embraced the image of a businesslike, progressive Southern city captured in Mayor Hartsfield's slogan "Atlanta, the city too busy to hate" during the turbulent decades of civil rights struggle. By 1980, few were willing to accept the vision of Atlanta as "the next great international city." No unifying image of the city represented Atlanta to its citizens and to others.

A 1982 report on the city's convention industry brought Atlanta's image problem to the attention of business leaders and public officials. Noting that earlier images of the city which linked it to the Old South were no longer appropriate, the report indicated the need for a new central theme to unify marketing for the convention business. The main responsibility for this effort would have to come from an expanded and better-funded

Convention Bureau, which would work with other organizations to promote a new image for Atlanta.[34]

Efforts to fund the promotion came from the familiar partnership between business leaders and city government. Mayor Jackson had introduced friction in this relationship during his first term, but before his second term ended in 1982, he managed to develop better relations with business leaders. Jackson was succeeded by Andrew Young, a minister and former congressman and United Nations ambassador. Young used his considerable diplomatic skills to restore the cordial relationship with business leaders, pledging to make economic development the cornerstone of his service as mayor. In May 1983, Mayor Young and a group of business leaders met and agreed to raise $2.5 million for the new campaign to promote Atlanta's image as a convention city.[35]

This promotional effort was timely because the number of conventions meeting in the city during the first six months of 1983 had dropped by 10 percent from the same period a year earlier. This drop caused considerable alarm among tourism business leaders, who feared a loss of as much as $20 million from the city's economy.[36] The following spring, the Convention Bureau began a nationwide road show to promote the city using the slogan "Look at Atlanta Now." The traveling promotion was followed by a print media campaign using the same theme.[37]

Economic Development

Support for the city's tourism industry continued in other ways. During his second term, Mayor Jackson had established an independent organization called the Atlanta Economic Development Corporation to create public-private partnerships in the area of economic development. A closely related group known as the Downtown Development Authority was also created by the city in order to finance projects in the city for the Atlanta Economic Development Corporation. In 1983 the Downtown Devel-

opment Authority authorized a $9 million industrial develop-
ment bond to finance the construction of a new hotel. The
French-owned Ibis Hotel, which opened in 1986, was built on the
recently renamed International Boulevard.[38] In the same year,
the Downtown Development Authority also approved the financing of a $45 million hotel and shopping center complex at the
site of the old Hartsfield airport terminal. Two years later, the
cost for the project had risen to $65 million, then escalated to
$130 million with plans for an adjoining conference center. An
agreement was finally reached in 1987 with the Stouffer Corporation to operate the hotel at the old airport terminal site on the
city's south side.[39] Partnerships to finance these hotels assured
hospitality businesses of continued support by city government
for the convention and tourism industry.

Atlanta's tourism businesses made sure that their presence
in the city was appreciated by issuing a series of reports during
the 1980s. These reports highlighted the fact that Atlanta ranked
as the third most popular convention city in the nation, trailing
only New York and Chicago.[40] According to a report issued by the
Convention Bureau, the 1,128,000 convention visitors to Atlanta
in 1981 stayed an average of four days each and spent an average
of $110 per day. Thus the total estimated convention delegate
expenditure in the city for the year was $496,320,000. Visitors
spent slightly over two-thirds of that money on food and lodging,
10 percent in retail stores, and 10 percent on entertainment such
as sports events, sightseeing, theater, nightclubs, recreational activities, and hospitality suites.[41]

The City of Atlanta also benefited from the expenditures of
convention visitors. The 3 percent hotel-motel tax enacted in
1976 generated almost $4 million in revenue. This was divided
between the city's general budget and the Convention Bureau,
which received 25 percent of the taxes in order to promote the
industry. In addition, the five major downtown hotels, the merchandise mart, and the Atlanta Apparel Mart paid $6.1 million
in property taxes in 1981, which represented 14 percent of the
total property taxes collected in the city that year.[42] Local and
state governments also benefited from the sales taxes collected

from visitors (although estimates of these sales tax receipts are difficult to make with accuracy since visitors' dollars mingle with the money spent by local residents).

One of the most frequently touted benefits of the hospitality businesses was the number of jobs provided by tourism. Estimating the numbers of people employed in these businesses, however, is fraught with problems. The Convention Bureau reported that approximately 75,300 people were employed in convention-related businesses in 1981. This would represent 9 percent of the workforce in the metropolitan area.[43] By 1985 the employment estimates for the Atlanta area had mushroomed to 208,000 for the convention and tourism trade, making it "the largest industry in the Atlanta area."[44] Claims of this size are difficult to justify, however, given the nature of tourism business employment. First, there is no single occupational category for employment in the field of tourism. Jobs are scattered across many parts of the "service sector" of the economy. These jobs may be included among hotels, restaurants, shops, local transportation, and tourist attractions of all kinds. Employment categories from census data are useful in providing the numbers of people working in service occupations outside private households. These occupations include maids and other cleaning service workers, as well as food service employees such as cooks, bartenders, dishwashers, and waiters. Other personal service workers include bellhops and people working in recreation and amusement businesses.

While these census data give some general indication of hospitality business employment, they by no means include all who earn their livelihoods in tourist-related jobs. Missing are the retail clerks who sell goods to tourists, as well as cab drivers and others who work in providing local transportation. Also missing are management personnel in hotels and other tourism businesses. Completely reliable statistics on hospitality business employment would require extensive survey research, which is both costly and time-consuming. Visitors bureaus such as the Atlanta Convention Bureau resort to shortcut methods of estimating employment in the field, and as a result their figures are of the greatest significance to the promotional activities of the agencies themselves and to local politicians who wish to justify expenditures in support of tourism businesses.[45] These estimates depend upon a knowledge of how many tourists come to a locality, their daily expenditures, and a multiplier effect based on the estimated number of times the dollars spent by tourists circulate through the local economy.

Throughout the years since World War II, Atlanta's private and public sectors invested heavily in tourism businesses as the city's major approach to downtown redevelopment and economic growth. It is not surprising, therefore, to find numerous efforts during the 1980s to assess the impact of tourism and hospitality businesses on the city. Although several research methods were used, none of the reports offered conclusive evidence of the precise numbers of visitors to the city, the amount of their expenditures, or their length of stay.[46] All of these indicators needed to be accurately measured in order to provide more comprehensive and reliable estimates of the number of jobs and revenues generated both directly and indirectly by the tourism industry in the city.

In the absence of direct observation of hospitality business impacts, a number of groups constructed simulation models to provide estimates of tourism business benefits and costs. Perhaps the most comprehensive model was the Travel Economic Impact Model (TEIM) developed during the 1970s by the U.S. Travel Data Center.[47] Using this model, the center estimated that tourism generated 65,000 jobs in Atlanta in 1987, of which 35,000 were created by visitors staying in hotels.[48] Without this kind of comprehensive research, the tourism industry and public officials can provide only estimates based on spending levels by travelers as the only indicators of the economic benefits of tourism businesses on the local economy.

Data on travel expenditures say little about the income and wealth that tourism and hospitality businesses generate in the local economy. If travelers purchased all their goods and services from residents who employed only local labor and purchased supplies that originated solely from the area, then travel expenditures would represent income to the community. In actual

204

practice, many of the goods purchased by convention visitors to a city like Atlanta have a high import content, which means that the money spent for them does not circulate entirely in the local economy. As the former director of the U.S. Travel Data Center observes, "to focus on travel expenditures as the measure of economic benefits to an area's residents is to grossly misstate the actual benefits generated in the area."[49]

Just as it is difficult to estimate the benefits associated with tourism businesses, there are also problems determining the costs of these economic activities to the community. In addition to the private costs generally paid by the tourist, there are public costs that are incidental to the business of providing commercial hospitality. For example, several large conventions regularly meet in Atlanta, such as the Bobbin Show, which is an international exposition showcasing the textile industry. When the 45,000 textile officials arrive in the city for this show, traffic congestion increases dramatically, which increases the time residents spend commuting to work.[50] Another "life quality" cost associated with tourism business activities is environmental damage, which is generally absorbed by local residents. In addition, fiscal costs to the public sector are increased due to the public investments in convention halls, stadiums, and other facilities, as well as the cost of providing services such as increased police and fire protection to visiting tourists.[51] Both the "life quality" costs and the fiscal costs are underestimated or ignored by hospitality industry reports, which tend to stress only the benefits to the city. While tourism businesses do provide economic benefits to places like Atlanta, the costs involved must not be ignored. As Atlanta grows, the benefits and costs of its hospitality businesses are no longer confined to the central city.

Metropolitan-Area Convention Business

Atlanta's population growth in the 1980s took place in its sprawling metropolitan area rather than the central city. The metropolitan area recognized by the U.S. Bureau of the Census included five counties in 1960, fifteen in 1973, and eighteen in 1983. The area's population, which was just over 1 million in 1960, jumped to more than 2 million by 1980. Meanwhile, in 1980 the population of the City of Atlanta registered the first decline in its history, dropping to 425,000, a loss of 14.5 percent from the previous decade.[52] This change largely resulted from white flight to the suburbs, as well as the continued clearing of land for expressways and other projects. The resulting central city population made Atlanta the twenty-ninth-largest city in the nation, while its metropolitan area was the twelfth largest.

While the largest convention facilities were located in the downtown area of the city, the growing population of the suburbs and the economic success enjoyed by the city's convention business made suburban communities eager to host conventions as well. Since many convention visitors came to the city by air, the town of College Park, located in Clayton County near the airport, was among the first to attempt to enter the convention business. In 1983, College Park started planning for the construction of a hotel and convention center. Financed by $45 million in bonds issued by the town's newly created development authority, the Holiday Inn Crowne Plaza and College Park International Convention Center opened the following year.[53]

Other suburban areas joined the competition. Several rapidly growing commercial areas, such as the Cumberland Mall and Galleria Mall area of Cobb County and the Perimeter Mall area of Dekalb County, were becoming "edge cities" in their own right.[54] These areas offered concentrations of homes, shopping centers, and office parks in the suburbs. New hotels followed in the early 1980s with the Doubletree Hotel and the Hyatt Ravinia near Perimeter Mall (now the Holiday Inn Crowne Plaza Ravinia) and the Renaissance Waverly Hotel near the Galleria Mall. New county visitors bureaus were created to promote conventions in these locations. In 1985, for example, Gwinnett County enacted a 3 percent local hotel tax in order to fund its own visitors bureau.[55]

By 1987 there were 10,500 hotel rooms located in the downtown Atlanta convention area, with another 2,000 rooms in

nearby Midtown, just north of the central business district. The
metropolitan area, however, offered more than 46,000 rooms for
convention visitors and other guests.[56] Suburban towns and counties also built convention facilities, such as Cobb County's Galleria Centre, in order to compete more successfully for meetings.
The former mayor of St. Louis was wrong when he described the
convention business as a "smokeless industry . . . that cannot flee
to the suburbs." Although large gatherings needed the facilities
of the Georgia World Congress Center and the concentration of
hotels downtown, many smaller groups moved to the suburbs.[57]

Restaurants

Prior to the 1980s, Atlanta was not noted for the diversity of
its restaurants. With its population largely split between whites
and blacks, the city lacked the ethnic diversity to support a variety
of cuisines. The area offered limited opportunities to enjoy Polish, Hungarian, Russian, or even German food, as relatively few
residents would support these types of restaurants. Since the
early 1980s, Atlanta attracted large numbers of Spanish-speaking
and Asian immigrants, and these have added to the diversity of
the city's restaurant scene. Many of the city's ethnic restaurants
were clustered in enclaves along the Buford Highway, catering
to the immigrant groups that settled there as well as to outside
visitors. These restaurants were added to the mix of traditional
Southern restaurants, such as Mary Mac's Tea Room and the
Colonnade.

Another important type of restaurant in Atlanta was fast food.
These places provide what urban geographer Richard Pillsbury
calls "body food"—a meal that can provide the body's basic need
for food quickly and inexpensively. This is in contrast to restaurants that feed the "soul" by providing food on which to dine
in order to celebrate, reward, impress, or create a mood.[58] Perhaps the favorite Atlanta body food restaurant has been the local
chain known as The Varsity. Founded in 1928 by Frank Gordy, a
former Georgia Tech student, this restaurant specializes in hot

dogs and hamburgers served with fried onion rings or potatoes and fried pies for dessert. The original location across the street from Georgia Tech claimed to be the world's largest drive-in. Another fast-food chain that began locally was Chic-fil-A, which got its start when founder Truitt Cathey began selling fried chicken breast sandwiches at his Dwarf House Restaurant in East Point, located on the south side of metropolitan Atlanta.

Area residents' fondness for fast food was demonstrated by the fact that in 1983 metropolitan Atlanta had the nation's highest per capita spending in this type of restaurant.[59] This standing would be consistent with a metropolitan area of sprawling suburbs where fast-food restaurants would be clustered in "Hamburger Alleys" located in automobile-oriented commercial strips. Restaurants in these areas tend to be dominated by chain operations. One of the largest chains of general restaurants has been the locally owned coffee shop chain known as Waffle House. These restaurants dotted the exits of interstate highways and major intersections of commercial areas.[60]

Two other local chains made significant contributions to Atlanta's supply of fine dining restaurants. In 1973, Stephan Nygren and Dick Dailey opened the Pleasant Peasant on Peachtree Street just north of downtown. The chain eventually expanded to eleven upscale restaurants. The Peasant Restaurants introduced Atlanta's diners to servers who memorized the menu, which was presented to the table on a chalkboard.[61] In 1979, Pano Karatassos and Paul Albrecht opened a restaurant known by their first names, Pano's and Paul's. With a variety of other partners, Karatassos became president and co-owner of the Buckhead Life Restaurant Group, which operated eleven of the city's most successful restaurants. Each restaurant featured its own decor and theme, ranging from Southwestern to Atlanta's ultimate diner. All of the upscale restaurants were located in the affluent northwest area of the city known as Buckhead.[62]

While these chains provided expensive food for fine dining, Atlantans continued to share the culture of the region in their preference for two distinctive types of restaurants, the barbecue restaurant and the cafeteria. Southerners' fondness for these types of eateries was reflected in the fact that in 1984, 4 percent of the restaurants in the Atlanta area were barbecue places and 2 percent were cafeterias. Nowhere outside the South were these two types of restaurants as popular.[63] For the out-of-town convention visitor seeking to experience Southern food, there was Pittypat's Porch on International Boulevard, which attempted to create the mood of the Old South in its food and decor (its name is taken from a character in Margaret Mitchell's novel).

Other restaurants offered the foods and tastes of the region in what might be called "nouveau-Southern" cuisine, devising new ways to serve grits, greens, and pork in upscale settings. For both newcomers and visitors, these restaurants introduced new interpretations of Southern food. For those who wanted a more authentic experience, numerous places still offered okra, a favorite vegetable of the region, and other traditional Southern foods. Two of these, Deacon Burton's Grill and Thelma's Kitchen, were small businesses owned by African Americans that survived the era of desegregation. Both remained popular with blacks and whites, indicating that fried chicken, greens, corn bread, okra, and other Southern foods were a unifying part of the region's culture.[64]

Atlanta's restaurants are a rapidly growing segment of the area's tourism businesses. National as well as local chains have shared in the economic growth of the metropolitan area. According to a 1995 survey by the National Restaurant Association, Atlanta-area residents spent 47.2 percent of their food budget eating out, the highest percentage of any U.S. city.[65] In number and variety, Atlanta's restaurants reflect the tastes of a population that has come to the city from many places but remains rooted in the South.

The New Underground Atlanta

During the early 1970s, Underground Atlanta, near the center of downtown, flourished as a tourist attraction. In 1973 an estimated 4.5 million people visited the area under the viaducts.

However, the combination of rapid rail construction, fear of crime, fires and flood, and competition from suburban attractions gradually diminished its appeal to visitors and residents.[66] When the last business closed in 1982, calls began for a new downtown entertainment complex. For instance, Research Atlanta's 1982 report on the convention industry indicated that the lack of a downtown entertainment area was the greatest weakness in the city's convention business. A report issued the following year said that the city's tourism and convention market would be improved with the addition of more evening entertainment for visitors.[67]

In response, Atlanta joined with Fulton County, the state of Georgia, and Central Atlanta Progress to finance a $400,000 feasibility study on the revitalization of Underground Atlanta. The study, conducted by the American City Corporation (owned by James Rouse, the developer of Baltimore's Harborplace and other festival marketplaces throughout the country), recommended the redevelopment of the Underground area with a mix of restaurants, nightclubs, specialty retailing, and public spaces.[68] Although the revitalization of Underground Atlanta enjoyed the support of Mayor Young and the business leaders of Central Atlanta Progress, the project was expensive and controversial. Initial estimates were $124 million, although final costs would be almost $20 million more. The revitalization effort was essentially a downtown urban renewal project, requiring that land be taken from 150 private owners and sold or leased to others. This provoked resistance from those original owners and considerable skepticism from city council.[69]

Despite opposition, the project had powerful supporters. In addition to the mayor and business leaders, the local newspapers—the morning *Constitution* and evening *Journal*—produced 128 articles between 1981 and 1987 dealing with the revitalization of Underground. A content analysis of these articles indicated that 72 percent recommended the redevelopment.[70] This finding is consistent with John Logan and Harvey Molotch's claim that newspapers serve as important members of the local coalition favoring growth in cities. Other members of the urban "growth machine" described by Logan and Molotch include businesses involving property investing, development, and real estate finance; politicians; utilities; and a group of auxiliary players such as labor unions, small business owners, and universities. The newspaper coverage helped forge the consensus among participants in the growth coalition that was needed to proceed with the project.[71]

The redevelopment of Underground Atlanta involved a continuation of the public-private partnership that had been crucial for the city's growth. The city used its powers of eminent domain to acquire most of the land for the project. The land itself was then conveyed to the Downtown Development Authority, which also issued $85 million in revenue bonds to finance the construction of most of the facility. The Downtown Development Authority leased the land back to the city at an annual rent equal to the debt service on the bonds. The Rouse Company organized a local corporate entity known as Underground Festival, Inc., which formed other partnerships to develop the entire project and manage it after completion. Other public-sector contributions to the project came from $18.5 million in an Urban Development Block Grant and a Community Development Block Grant from the federal government, and $14.5 million from a local sales tax windfall.[72] More than 80 percent of the total funding for the redevelopment of Underground Atlanta came from public sources. Other similar projects, such as Boston's Faneuil Hall, an earlier Rouse Company project, had less than 21 percent public-sector support, with the remainder coming from private-sector investment.[73] Although Atlanta business leaders wanted the project, they were unwilling to assume a large share of the financial risk. For the city, the deal carried considerable risk since both the earlier version of Underground and the Omni's entertainment area, the World of Sid and Marty Krofft, had failed.

What did Atlanta expect to receive in return from its investment in the redevelopment of Underground? First, the city was in a position to profit from the investment if the project proved financially successful. Atlanta assumed the role of entrepreneur, taking much of the risk required by the large initial costs of the project. A revived Underground would provide entertainment for the downtown convention industry, whose steady stream of reports had underscored the need for recreation in the evenings for visiting tourists. There would also be the creation of an estimated 3,000 additional jobs and the fiscal benefits of increased sales and property taxes, as well as parking revenues. Finally, the project would serve as a stimulus for the physical renewal of the southern edge of downtown by increasing economic activity in the area.[74] The city council insisted that the revitalization address the social issues of providing minority business opportunities in the construction and operation of the marketplace itself, as well as among the tenants who were to occupy the project. All of these needs made redevelopment a complex process, lasting from 1982, when the feasibility study was undertaken, to June 15, 1989, when the opening was celebrated.

The resurrected Underground Atlanta accomplished some of its objectives. To assure patrons that the new complex was safe, the city police opened a precinct station on the property in addition to the force of thirty security officers employed by the project's management. During the first year of operation, an estimated 13 million people visited Underground, exceeding the 10 million anticipated. However, only 40 percent of the patrons were visiting tourists, and 60 percent were local area residents. The crowds of convention delegates did not come as hoped.[75] This was perhaps because of the complex's location away from the major convention hotels in other parts of downtown. Another problem was the proliferation of similar festival marketplaces in the downtown areas of cities across the country, effectively reducing the novelty of Underground Atlanta as an attraction to visitors. Although Underground was carefully designed to evoke feelings of nostalgia, very little of the original historic Underground was present for visitors to experience. The result was a site that lacked the authentic qualities to set it apart from similar festival marketplace developments.[76]

While Underground Atlanta did not hold the attraction for out-of-town visitors that its backers anticipated, there were other goals for the project. Underground was projected to create 3,000 new jobs in the city, and a 1992 report indicated that 969 new jobs were actually created, including 552 full-time and 417 part-time.[77] There is little doubt that the redevelopment of Underground also increased property taxes collected by the city. The run-down area had generated only $134,000 in property taxes in 1984, but brought $533,000 in property taxes in 1991 (valued in 1991 dollars). Thus the revitalization increased the annual property tax revenue to the city by almost $400,000 per year. An additional $95,000 in property taxes was collected in 1991 from the value of merchandise and fixtures among tenants in the project. The opening of Underground also generated additional sales taxes (even though there was some shifting of expenditures from one location to the new site). With allowance for shifting in sales taxes, the city received an additional $209,000 in tax revenues in 1991. When alcoholic beverage taxes and license fees were added, Underground Atlanta generated $908,000 in additional tax benefits for 1991.[78]

Concerns about crime and security caused a decline in attendance and sales at Underground following the fatal shooting of a black teen in a gang dispute in August 1990.[79] Many tenants fell behind in rent, causing the Underground management company to be late with a $10 million payment to the city which was needed to repay outstanding debt. During its first five years of operating the facility, Underground Festival, Inc., sustained losses of $28 million. In 1994 the company sought to restructure its debt to the city in order to continue operations.[80] This restructuring enabled Underground's managers to increase marketing efforts and lure new tenants, which were essential to the continued operation of the complex.

Other goals of the Underground redevelopment were to provide an economic stimulus to downtown and to encourage the physical revitalization of the south side of the central business district. One year after Underground's reopening, the Coca-Cola Company opened a pavilion known as the World of Coca-Cola, where visitors could learn about the history of the soft drink as well as sample Coca-Cola products marketed in other countries. A Japanese investor also purchased a nearby building, which was enlarged and converted into the Underground Atlanta Suite Hotel.[81] Additional investment in the area, however, lagged, while many of the above-ground retailers in the Underground complex closed because of declining sales.[82]

Underground Atlanta was helpful to minority business since its inception. Of the design and construction contracts, 25 percent went to minority-owned businesses and 3 percent to female-owned businesses. At the time of the initial leasing, 27 percent of the tenants were minorities and 10 percent female. Among street vendors, the percentages of minority- and female-owned businesses were even higher.[83] After Underground reopened, many of these undercapitalized businesses failed as sales declined. Some were replaced by national chain businesses, causing some racial tension among tenants in the complex.[84]

Overall, the new Underground Atlanta failed to fulfill many of the ambitious goals set for it. The complex was vulnerable to crime and security problems, which weakened its support from suburban patrons. It also did not draw as many convention visitors as had been anticipated.[85] In one significant respect, however, the project succeeded by providing a public space in the heart of the city for people to assemble for festive occasions. The lighting of the city's Christmas tree, New Year's Eve, World Series baseball games, and other special events gave residents an opportunity and a place to come together and celebrate. If Underground serves as the type of ceremonial place once provided by village greens and courthouse squares, it enhances the feeling of community so difficult to achieve in major cities.[86] This provides Atlanta with a qualitative value not easily subjected to cost-benefit analysis.

Underground Atlanta has also posed a dilemma for a city struggling with its image. The earlier version of the entertainment district used the symbols of a predominantly white Southern culture to reflect the city's past. With extensive public support from black elected public officials as well as white business leaders, the new Underground could not market the same cultural symbols of the Confederacy and the Jim Crow era that were displayed in the first Underground Atlanta. As Charles Reagan

Wilson articulated the problem, "We are at a historic moment in which Southerners are struggling to define their public culture in a biracial, postsegregation society." One solution would be to banish all the symbols that suggest a racially divided history into museums and private homes. This offends many white Southerners for whom the Confederacy represents not the defense of slavery, but inherited stories of family danger, adherence to principle, sacrifice, and love of history. On the other hand, many black Southerners find meaning in the cultural symbols in the civil rights movement and the struggle for racial equality in the recent past. Wilson suggested that perhaps the solution is to display the two sets of cultural symbols side-by-side, so that they represent public recognition of a joint history.[87] Underground Atlanta has had difficulty finding an appropriate balance between banishing the symbols of the Old South and finding a way to unify the symbols representing a new Southern culture. Perhaps too much was asked of a commercial entertainment complex, but in many respects the problems of the new Underground Atlanta reflect the struggles of people in the city and the region to understand their common culture.

Major Events

With its convention facility, the Georgia World Congress Center, built and its entertainment complex, Underground Atlanta, being revived, Atlanta residents felt the city was ready to compete for the largest events in the nation. The 1980s saw a boom in hotel construction throughout the metropolitan area, with more than 16,000 new hotel rooms added between 1982 and 1987. This growth, however, contributed to declining occupancy rates throughout the metropolitan area. In 1982 the occupancy rate for the area's 30,000 hotel rooms was 65 percent, whereas five years later it had fallen to 63 percent for the more than 46,000 hotel rooms.[88]

The rapid construction during the 1980s also increased the variety of hotels in the city. In the luxury hotel class, two new

Ritz-Carlton Hotels opened in 1984, with one located downtown and the other in the upscale residential, commercial, and retail area known as Buckhead. The next year, John Portman's Peachtree Center added still another hotel, the Marriott Marquis, the largest hotel in the South, with 1,674 rooms (and the fourth hotel in the downtown area with more than 1,000 rooms). Convention planners could also boast of the tallest hotel on the continent, the Westin Peachtree Plaza, with its seventy-three stories and 1,078 rooms. The Hilton Hotel contained 1,224 rooms as well as 41,000 square feet of exhibition space. The Hyatt Regency had 1,279 rooms, and its architecture was so striking that the hotel set a standard imitated around the world.[89] With facilities such as these, Central Atlanta Progress promoted the convention and hotel industries in the city as "a dominant force in the local and regional economies."[90] During 1985, Atlanta hosted a record number of conventions, with 1,400 meetings in the city attended by 1.5 million people.[91] But city leaders wanted more and larger national events to host.

The type of massive events the city's leaders dreamed of were not long in coming. In 1986, Atlanta's hotels were booked to capacity for the meeting of the Southern Baptist Convention. Although the city's bars did not profit from its presence, the Southern Baptist Convention brought 45,000 delegates for the five-day meeting. An even larger event that year was the first Super Show of the Sporting Goods Manufacturing Association, attended by 55,000 manufacturers and buyers of sporting equipment. The event is a major showcase for sports equipment. Athletes and entertainers come to Atlanta to sell the products they endorse, and industry giants like Nike introduce their latest product lines with glitzy displays and huge private parties for retailers.[92]

The Super Show has grown in size each year. It uses all available exhibition space in the public facilities at the Georgia World Congress Center and the Georgia Dome, as well as the private facilities of Peachtree Center's Apparel Mart and the Inforum.[93] With an attendance of 114,000 at the February 1995 Super Show, the event has become the city's largest regular convention. Sixty-six of Atlanta's hotels set aside all or part of their rooms for those attending the event, and limousine services, restaurants, clubs, and bars do their largest weekend business of the year during the show. In a continuing effort to keep the event in Atlanta, the Convention Bureau, the City of Atlanta, and Underground Atlanta host parties for those visiting the city.

The needs of large trade shows keep the pressure on convention facilities to increase the exhibition space available for them. Cities compete by building larger convention facilities and offering discounted rates in order to attract these major events. In the 1990s Chicago led the race, having invested $987 million in an expansion of McCormick Place to create 2.6 million square feet of exhibit space.[94] In this intensely competitive climate, calls were sounded for the addition of 500,000 square feet to the Georgia World Congress Center. These cries for a larger facility were underscored by the announcement of Atlanta's loss of its second-largest convention, the Comdex computer show. This event brought 90,000 people to the city for the four-day show in April 1995, but after 1997 Comdex moved to Chicago.[95]

Other large groups continued to hold their meetings in Atlanta. In August 1987 the city hosted the national meeting of black Shriners, bringing 70,000 delegates to the city. Preparations were also under way for bringing the largest and best-publicized event the city had ever known, the 1988 Democratic National Convention. The city council increased the hotel room tax in order to raise $15 million, which was the estimated cost of preparing the city for the event. Even though industry promoters feared the increase would hurt the city's convention business, hotels and motels in the city and Fulton County paid the 6 percent tax on room rentals.[96] Having out-of-town visitors to pay most of the expenses for hosting the event was a politically acceptable solution for city residents and their elected officials.

Despite the convention industry's success, concern continued over the lack of attractions in the area for visitors. Clayton County, in the southern part of the metropolitan area, decided to take advantage of the Democratic National Convention by spending $23 million for a theme park centered around Tara, Scarlett O'Hara's mythical family home in *Gone with the Wind*. In

217

spite of promotion by business leaders and county commission members, Clayton County voters defeated a proposed tax increase needed to pay for the theme park.[97]

As the July 19, 1988, opening of the Democratic National Convention drew near, preparations for the event moved into high gear. A specially created nonprofit group known as "Atlanta 88" received a third of the new hotel tax to spend preparing the city to welcome the convention. Making sidewalk, park, and streetscape improvements in the downtown area a priority, "Atlanta 88" planted trees and improved sidewalks along International Boulevard, the major pedestrian corridor between the Georgia World Congress Center and most convention hotels. The Omni sports arena's seating capacity was enlarged, and skyboxes were installed for the use of television crews covering the convention. The final cost for the preparations exceeded $22.5 million.[98]

More than anything else, however, Atlanta's leaders worried about the image that convention visitors and the media would have of the city. This reflects in part what historian Bertram Wyatt-Brown has said in his description of the code of honor surrounding the customs of hospitality in the Old South. Wyatt-Brown notes an undercurrent of deep mistrust, anxiety, and personal competition among those providing Southern hospitality.[99] What would guests think of the welcome being provided? Were the place, the accommodations, and the food adequate? Would the hospitality be equal to that provided by others? These questions worried civic leaders as the city prepared for the convention.

Like a household in the antebellum South, Atlanta as a city had taken great pains to fix itself up for company coming to town, and it did not want anything to spoil the impression made upon its guests. When a *Wall Street Journal* article on Atlanta called the city the "Big Hustle," a place where growth itself was the major industry, the pride of local boosters was offended. It was one thing for Atlantans to promote their city in the finest Southern tradition, but it was another to be criticized for it by a Northern newspaper. The article went on to describe the poverty of the central city and the contrast with the prosperity of the suburbs, noting that Atlanta hosted the third-largest number of conventions in the country but was also the city where convention visitors stayed the shortest time.[100] In response, the editor of the *Constitution* described the article as a "cheap shot" by the "headline-hunting reporters" who would descend on Atlanta for the convention.[101]

Local newspapers took great pains to sharpen the image of the city in response to this and other visiting media scrutiny. They wanted Atlanta to be seen as a "Southern city with a heritage of racial tolerance and a reputation for good business sense."[102] To make sure that the city was shown in a more favorable light, the Convention Bureau and the Georgia Department of Industry and Trade set up the "mythbusters," a group of three women given the task of dispelling myths and providing visiting journalists with a favorable image of the city and the South.[103] Atlanta's traditions of boosterism and Southern hospitality were used throughout the preparations for the convention. According to the *Journal Constitution,* the Democratic National Convention was "a Super Bowl of civic pride, a high-wire prance between hospitality and hype put on for the benefit of more than 5,300 delegates and alternates, 13,500 journalists and 10,000 members of the political and corporate elite."[104]

The city's tourism businesses eagerly awaited the arrival of the Democrats. Hotel rooms in the metropolitan area were booked to near capacity, and restaurants, bars, and clubs anticipated booming business. Most of the lunches, brunches, picnics, and dinners planned for the convention featured traditional regional foods such as pork barbecue, fried chicken, biscuits, and peach cobbler in what one writer, caught up in the event, called "the shining hour of Southern cuisine."[105] Mayor Young officially welcomed the convention in its opening session, saying, "We hope you enjoy our Southern hospitality." He added that he hoped the delegates would have all the greens, ribs, and grits they wanted before returning home.[106]

Perhaps the most interesting welcome to the visiting delegates came from the chairman of the Fulton County Commission, Michael Lomax. His comments spoke to the image Atlanta was attempting to portray as well as the sensitivity to criticism felt by most boosters of the city. Lomax began by saying that cities such as New York, Chicago, and Venice have long ago established their magnificence, while Atlanta is "a great city that is creating its history and evolving its own identity right now." Although older cities have the self-confidence to present themselves to the world "warts and all," Atlanta "has only begun to realize its aspirations to world-class status within the past decade or so. Like the nouveau riche entrepreneur on the block who's always spending money to let you know he's got it, we're forever proclaiming our greatness to the world, constantly seeking affirmation from outsiders, lest we begin to doubt our own self-worth."[107] Events like the Democratic National Convention put the city under a microscope for close examination by journalists and visitors. According to Lomax, Atlantans needed to be less sensitive to the criticisms that come from such scrutiny and develop a "thicker skin," to be able to admit flaws as well as to promote the city's attractions.[108]

A Good Place for Business

As the 1980s came to a close, Atlanta's tourism businesses reached a milestone that was celebrated by industry leaders. With the opening of the Airport Hilton Hotel in 1989, metropolitan Atlanta boasted of having over 50,000 hotel rooms. As Table 7.1 indicates, this represented an increase of more than 20,000 since 1982. However, at the same time room rates were increasing, the occupancy rate had declined 3 percent, falling below the national average for 1989 of 65 percent. Nonetheless, Atlanta boosters were proud of reaching the 50,000-room level—an achievement that moved Atlanta to seventh place among the nation's hotel markets. Table 7.2 shows Atlanta's position in 1989 relative to the other large convention and resort cities.

National hotel chains found that Atlanta was a good location to build hotels in spite of the "soft" market. For instance, the $51 million Airport Hilton was the fifth Hilton property in the Atlanta area, giving the corporation a total of 2,700 rooms. The

Table 7.1. Metropolitan Atlanta Hotel Growth, 1982–1989

YEAR	NUMBER OF HOTEL ROOMS	OCCUPANCY RATE	AVERAGE DAILY ROOM RATE
1982	30,422	65%	$46
1983	32,190	67%	$47
1984	35,087	69%	$51
1985	39,717	67%	$55
1986	42,308	63%	$56
1987	46,437	63%	$58
1988	49,825	63%	$60
1989	51,097	62%	$62

Source: Pannell Kerr Forster, Hospitality Consultants.

Marriott chain was even more bullish on Atlanta, with twenty-eight hotels in the area offering a total of 5,000 rooms—10 percent of the inventory in the metropolitan area.[109] The boom in hotel construction during the 1980s resulted in part from favorable federal tax laws as Real Estate Investment Trusts were created to finance these projects.

The growth of Atlanta's hotel market continued to be a source of some concern among tourism business leaders. With the boom in hotel construction during the 1980s, they felt the city was overbuilt. The city was also dependent upon convention and business travelers for 70 percent of its room rentals, whereas other cities listed in Table 7.2 were resort destinations where leisure travel was more important than commercial visitors. Even New York

Table 7.2. Largest Hotel Markets in the United States, 1989

1. Los Angeles 68,600	6. Las Vegas 51,600
2. Orlando 63,600	7. ATLANTA 51,000
3. New York 63,000	8. Miami 46,000
4. Washington, D.C. 56,500	9. Houston 41,000
5. Chicago 52,500	10. San Francisco 39,500

Source: Pannell Kerr Forster, Hospitality Consultants.

City had a more balanced clientele, with 50 percent of its hotel occupancy dependent upon business and convention travelers.[110] Despite the Convention Bureau's efforts to promote the city and the boosterism of other business groups, Atlanta's hotel business suffered when no conventions were meeting in the city. Occupancy rates in convention hotels often dropped to 15 percent when there were no meetings scheduled, placing tremendous stress upon the Convention Bureau to increase their efforts to bring more conventions and more visitors to the city. The bureau sought out large groups with the seriousness of a military campaign, and efforts continued to add new attractions for visitors to experience as part of their stay in Atlanta. Only with this combination of hard work, new attractions, and boosterism could the city's tourism businesses remain viable.

Throughout the 1980s, the city continued to struggle with its image. The Convention Bureau's promotional campaign urged potential visitors to "Look at Atlanta Now," and in a variety of ways Atlanta sought to project an image of itself as a good place for business. However, outsiders often came away with a different impression of the area. Many visitors criticized Atlanta's traffic and parking problems, while others noted that the downtown area lacked activities for convention visitors. As a consequence, many convention guests did not bring their spouses to the city, nor were they likely to extend their stay.[111] Other influential visitors were also critical of the city's attractions. In January 1987, travel writer Arthur Frommer visited Atlanta and spoke to a local audience about his impressions of the city. "Atlanta itself is characterless and without charm, dull and excessively devoted to business and finance," he said. Frommer observed that 28 percent of the city's population lives below the poverty level, a figure second only to Newark, New Jersey. What, he asked, has the building of office towers and corporate headquarters done for these poor residents of the city? Regarding the city's tourism businesses, "No vital center city area has ever existed on traffic from visitors alone, without assistance from a community of residents inhabiting the very same area or nearby." The downtown area could be a more attractive place for visitors, Frommer suggested, if At-

lanta paid more attention to the preservation of its historic buildings and areas. He proposed the revitalization of the areas of
downtown known as Fairlie-Poplar and Auburn Avenue, emphasizing that preservation of these areas would provide different
types of jobs than the skyscrapers which dominate the downtown. This would not only make Atlanta more attractive to visitors, but would also aid the low-income residents of the city.[112]

Frommer returned to Atlanta in November 1988, just after the
Democratic National Convention. In a speech to local business
leaders, he again criticized the city for failing to make the downtown more livable. He added that this failure would cause the
convention and tourism industry to decline as visitors continued
to be confined to hotels in an area with little life or personality.
Frommer recalled his earlier speech, in which he said that
Atlanta in the evening is a "graveyard, a scene of death and deso-
lation, a nullity as far as the life, culture, and camaraderie present in numerous other cities." Even the revitalized Underground
Atlanta was unlikely to save the downtown, since no festival market project by the Rouse Company had ever saved a central city
on its own. What was needed, he suggested, was public policy to
preserve older buildings and to develop housing in the downtown. Atlanta did not need more high-rise office towers or hotels
to serve visitors. Instead, the downtown needed life in order to
change the impression of emptiness it gave to tourists.[113] In spite
of its advantages of location, facilities, and hospitality, the city
has continued to struggle with its image as a tourism destination,
and the challenge of reshaping the city to bring life to the central
business district lay ahead.[114]

8

Peaks and Valleys, 1990–1995

FOR MANY YEARS ATLANTA'S LEADERS HAD realized that the image of the Old South did not fit their city. Their vision of the city centered around a skyline with gleaming new buildings and an increasing international reputation. New hotels sprang up like mushrooms throughout the metropolitan area, accompanied by new convention and conference facilities built by the numerous cities and counties in the area. However, as the 1990s arrived, the tourism businesses in Atlanta found themselves facing new struggles as a consequence of their rapid growth. The hotel market, for instance, found itself in the doldrums of a declining occupancy rate due to overbuilding during the previous decade.

The city's residents and hospitality businesses were eager for the arrival of the 1990s. Thousands welcomed in the New Year 1990 by watching as the giant peach was lowered from the light tower at Underground Atlanta. This local version of the celebration at Times Square in New York City had begun the previous year. After the celebration at Underground was over, many of the teenage revelers returned to the Marriott Marquis Hotel, where they had rented rooms for the night. The crowd took the party into the hotel's massive atrium lobby, where the celebration took an ugly turn. People began tossing glasses, bottles, and furniture over the balconies into the lobby area below. Hotel security was overwhelmed, and before the police could arrive and calm the scene several people were injured and the hotel had sustained over $250,000 worth of damage.[1] This event provided a rather inauspicious beginning for the city's tourism businesses as they entered the 1990s.

Challenges of the New Decade

One of the first problems to surface in the new year was the need for a third expansion of the Georgia World Congress Center. A survey of convention planners across the nation indicated that the World Congress Center was the top-rated facility for meetings, but criticized the exhibition space as being too small for the city to compete for the largest shows. The survey also faulted Atlanta as being expensive to get to and unsafe because of crime. While the city featured good local transportation, shopping, and nightlife, it was not well regarded for sightseeing and as a family destination. Responding to the criticism, the head of the Atlanta Convention and Visitors Bureau, Ted Sprague, said changes needed to be made in Atlanta's downtown. "We need a walkable, livable downtown," he added. "While meeting planners love Atlanta's convention center, they are much less enthusiastic about the city as a destination."[2]

In spite of lobbying from the city and pleas from the newspaper editorials, the state general assembly turned down the request for $64 million to expand the facility. As if to confirm the worst fears of tourism business leaders, two major conventions canceled their meetings, citing the inadequate meeting space and the availability of larger facilities elsewhere. In response, the editors of the *Constitution* accused the Georgia legislature of plotting to ruin Atlanta's convention business. According to Daniel A. Graveline, executive director of the World Congress Center, the legislature's failure to fund the center's expansion would cost Atlanta at least fifteen to eighteen conventions annually.[3]

Evidence suggests there may have been some truth to the newspaper's claims. Atlanta was no longer just competing for conventions against other cities such as New York, Chicago,

Dallas, and Orlando. The city was surrounded by increasingly competitive suburban counties that had invested heavily in convention and visitor facilities during the previous decade. In 1983 the U.S. Census Bureau recognized Atlanta as an eighteen-county metropolitan area—the largest number of counties of any metropolitan area in the nation.[4] The political influence of these suburban counties was growing in the state's general assembly. Estimates for tourist expenditures for the seventeen suburban counties in the metropolitan area exceeded that of Fulton County, which contains most of the City of Atlanta.[5] This intra-urban rivalry may have played a part in the general assembly's decision to delay the expansion of the World Congress Center, since elected representatives of these suburban areas often joined with rural legislators to vote against projects that were perceived as beneficial to the City of Atlanta.[6]

During the 1990 general assembly, suburban legislators successfully promoted a bill allowing counties outside Fulton to assess an extra penny sales tax on hotel and motel rooms in order to finance the construction or expansion of convention halls.[7] The town of College Park, located near the airport, responded by issuing $28 million in bonds to finance the expansion of its convention facility. Repayment of the debt service on the bonds would come from the extra penny sales tax on hotel and motel rooms.[8] The area around Hartsfield International Airport was becoming the largest submarket in the city's hotel business. The number of hotel rooms near the airport passed the 10,000 mark in 1990, giving it more hotel rooms than downtown Atlanta for the first time. The airport area also enjoyed the highest hotel occupancy rates for the entire metropolitan area, with a rate of 64 percent in 1989, compared with the downtown rate of 61 percent (1 percent below the occupancy rate for the entire metropolitan area).[9] The low occupancy rates continued to reflect the feverish pace of hotel construction during the 1980s.

The U.S. Census for 1990 confirmed that the suburban areas were continuing to grow in population. According to the census, nearly 2.4 million people lived in the metropolitan area outside the central city. On the other hand, the report showed that the

City of Atlanta's population continued to drop, to 394,017 from 425,000 in 1980, making the city an even smaller part of the sprawling metropolitan area. The city's elected public officials responded to the news of the decline in population with a lawsuit against the Census Bureau, claiming Atlanta has been the victim of an undercount. But it was clear that the city was not growing in relation to the metropolitan area as a whole.[10]

The tourism businesses in the City of Atlanta had another reason for concern as they entered the new decade. In January 1990 the *Constitution* filed suit against the Convention Bureau for the organization's failure to make its budget available to the public. The newspaper argued successfully that the bureau received public funds from the sales tax on hotel and motel rooms and should, therefore, be subject to the state's open records law. When the budget was finally released, the high salary and lavish benefits of bureau president, Ted Sprague, led to criticism of the organization. The result was a cut in the president's expense account and increased attention placed on efforts to market the city as a convention destination.[11] These marketing activities were hurt in May 1990 when a delegate to the meeting of the American Gem Society was killed in a robbery attempt at the downtown Hilton Hotel.[12] Although the newspapers went to great lengths to offer reassurances that downtown Atlanta was generally a safe area for convention visitors, other observers noted that crime and the perception of Atlanta as unsafe were issues the city needed to address.[13]

Adding to the troubles of the Convention Bureau and the hospitality businesses in the city was the deepening recession which slowed the national economy near the end of 1990 and began to affect Atlanta early the next year. One of the first casualties of the recession was Eastern Airlines, which had been the second-largest passenger carrier at Hartsfield International Airport. With Eastern's bankruptcy and closing in January 1991, tourism businesses felt the ripple effect of fewer flights into and out of the city. The airport also lost its position as the second-busiest airport in the United States as a result of Eastern's collapse.

In anticipation of a lower budget (owing to a drop in hotel

and motel room taxes), the Convention Bureau announced plans to reduce its spending for 1991. Twelve staff positions were cut, reducing the organization's expenses by $1.5 million. Marketing efforts were also reduced (the total budget for selling the city was $1.9 million, while salaries remained at $3.7 million for 1991). To increase revenues, the bureau began publishing a visitors guide that sold advertising space to tourism businesses. This irritated the publishers of other local tourism magazines, since they claimed the Convention Bureau had an unfair advantage as a tax-supported agency. Ted Sprague also proposed raising funds by establishing a travel agency to handle airline reservations for visiting convention delegates. Not surprisingly, other travel agents and the airline companies opposed this venture.[14] After the controversy over the Convention Bureau's budget, Sprague's lavish compensation, and the fund-raising proposals that put the Convention Bureau in competition with its members, the bureau's executive board voted unanimously to fire Sprague and four senior executives. This move was intended to save the organization money, which could then be funneled into marketing the city more effectively.[15] After a lengthy search, Spurgeon Richardson, the marketing director of Six Flags Over Georgia, was hired to head the Convention Bureau. His charge was to be more aggressive in promoting Atlanta.[16]

According to Convention Bureau estimates, Atlanta was the fourth leading convention city in the United States behind New York, Dallas, and Chicago. Hospitality business officials were worried about the need for larger facilities, the crime rate, and the deepening national recession. The immediate solution they sought was more aggressive recruitment of conventions in order to fill the hotels, restaurants, amusements, and other tourism businesses. On September 18, 1990, many of their concerns were answered when the president of the International Olympic Committee announced that Atlanta was selected to host the 1996 Summer Olympic Games. For the city's tourism businesses, this was the ultimate convention. Additional good news arrived when Atlanta was chosen by the National Football League as the site of the 1994 Super Bowl. Here were two events certain to provide a lift for the city's sagging hospitality businesses.

As if buoyed by these events, Holiday Inn Worldwide announced plans to relocate its corporate headquarters to Atlanta. The city had already gained a reputation as a favorable location for tourism business headquarters. In 1970, Cecil B. Day had started his Days Inn chain of budget-priced hotels along the interstate highways in Georgia, with the corporate headquarters in Atlanta. In 1984, after Day's death, the family sold the company; however, the corporation continued to operate from the city for many years.[17] Another lower-priced hotel chain headquartered in Atlanta was the Red Carpet Inns, which were operated by Hospitality International Inc. At the opposite end of the hotel market, the luxury chain using the Ritz-Carlton name was owned by W. B. Johnson Properties, also headquartered in Atlanta. Holiday Inn Worldwide sought a corporate office building near a hotel to serve as a signature presence in the city. The company took over the Hyatt Ravinia Hotel, located in the northern part of Dekalb County known as Dunwoody, and renamed the property the Holiday Inn Crowne Plaza Ravinia.

Other new hotels opening in 1990 in Atlanta were owned by international airlines: the Hotel Nikko, owned by Japan Air Lines, in the Buckhead area; the Swissotel, owned by Swissair, also in Buckhead; and the Penta Hotel, owned by Lufthansa, in Midtown.[18] All three airlines flew into Hartsfield International Airport, making the hotels a logical place to stay for business travelers from those countries. The ownership of these hotels was part of a widespread pattern of international investment in Atlanta tourism businesses. The arrangement between the airlines and the hotels was also similar to the connection between the railroads and the first boardinghouse in the city.

In spite of the soft market and low occupancy rates, some hotel building continued in Atlanta. New suite hotels appeared throughout the metropolitan area, offering business travelers and families the advantage of extra space for little added cost. More than 1,400 suites were added to the city's hotel room inventory during

1990 and 1991. Occupancy rates for this type of accommodation were slightly higher than for traditional hotels.[19]

Low hotel occupancy rates continued into the 1990s. Hotel executives complained that even with the Olympics and the Super Bowl coming to town, the city had too many hotels. An economic recession contributed to a decline in travel and kept the occupancy rate for the city's hotels at 61.8 percent for 1990—a rate that made many hotels unprofitable. For example, the fifty-two-story Marriott Marquis, which opened in 1985 with 1,674 rooms, was the largest hotel in the South. With its large construction debt and the glut of hotel rooms in the city, the Marquis operated at a loss in 1990. John Portman, who owned 20 percent of the hotel in a limited partnership with the Marriott Corporation, had built the hotel with $195 million in adjustable-rate mortgages. Yet when the hotel opened it nearly doubled the number of convention hotel rooms in the downtown, contributing to an oversupply in the area and causing the hotel to operate at an occupancy rate that was not profitable.[20]

In 1991 the impact of the recession on travel caused the occupancy rate to drop further, to 60.1 percent.[21] Some hotels found it hard to weather the difficult times. For example, the Wyndham Hotel in Midtown was one of the new developments built in that part of the city during the 1980s. Its construction debt and low occupancy rate soon forced the hotel to seek Chapter 11 protection from its creditors.[22] The Ramada Stadium Inn suffered from a similar lack of profits resulting from low occupancy rates. The hotel was sold to a nonprofit organization known as Summerhill Neighborhood Inc., which converted the property into dormitory space for students from Georgia State University and the Atlanta University Center.[23]

Convention visitors have observed that there are relatively few restaurants in downtown Atlanta. According to urban geographer Richard Pillsbury, 95 percent of restaurants have tended to be located in clusters near other types of retail activity in cities. As a result, many restaurants in downtown areas have moved along with department stores to shopping centers in the suburbs. As banks and other types of financial institutions moved out of downtown Atlanta, many of the restaurants featuring sit-down dining left with them, relocating in Midtown and Buckhead. Most of the remaining restaurants serve the needs of office workers for sandwiches and inexpensive lunch fare. Hotel coffee shops and restaurants satisfy a large percentage of the demand for breakfast and lunch, as convention visitors and other business travelers rarely have time to explore outside their hotels for places to eat.[24] Some fine dining is available in hotel restaurants and elsewhere, but most requires a cab ride from major convention hotels. The Buckhead area offers the largest collection of fine restaurants, with another restaurant cluster in the gentrified neighborhood known as Virginia-Highland, where small cafés cater to the needs of middle-class city residents.

Atlanta's growth as a major convention city is reflected in the number and variety of restaurants in the area. According to *Restaurant Business Magazine,* in 1990 the Atlanta metropolitan area ranked high nationally in several measures of restaurant activity, including total sales and number of eating places. The magazine also compiled a Restaurant Activity Index (RAI) to overcome differences in cost of living and variations in income levels among regions of the country. Atlanta ranked among the highest in terms of RAI, which is based on an indexed ratio of restaurant sales to food store sales. This index placed the city near the top ranking with other large convention cities, resorts, and college towns.[25] The high level of restaurant activity and the large number of eating places in Atlanta suggest that the city continues to be a crossroads for travelers passing through on the interstate highway system as well as attending conventions and other events in Atlanta. The residents of the Atlanta metropolitan area are also frequent patrons.

In difficult times Atlanta's leaders have always rallied to aid the city's businesses through promotional efforts, and once again the public-private partnership turned its attention to increasing the convention business in Atlanta. In less than twelve months beginning in August 1992, the city hosted three important meetings of convention planners. The first was the American Society of Association Executives, which is the organization for the leaders of various types of nonprofit groups who have annual meetings. According to glowing press accounts, this meeting could bring in $220 million in spending by convention delegates during the following ten years.[26] Four months later, the city welcomed the International Association of Exposition Management. The members of this organization manage trade shows in various cities across the country, and impressing members of this group would bring future conventions to the city.[27] In June of the following year, Meeting Planners International, which plans conferences for large corporations, held its convention in Atlanta. Again, no expense was spared to impress the delegates to entice them to bring future meetings to the city.[28] These three meetings gave Atlanta's business and political leaders an opportunity to show off the hospitality of the city.

Under its new leadership, the Convention Bureau broadened the scope of its marketing campaign to attract visitors to the city. In 1991 the bureau targeted black tourists and conventions by developing special promotional materials and increasing the number of African Americans on their staff. Its program to promote diversity included development of a special video, "Come Home to Atlanta," and an African-American visitor guide, *Atlanta Heritage.*[29] Working with the city government, the Convention Bureau also opened a special welcome center for African Americans on Auburn Avenue, which had become a major tourist attraction. During the era of segregation, Auburn Avenue was the most prosperous street for African-American businesses in the country, but by the 1990s the combination of expressway construction, the urban renewal program, and the end of Jim Crow had severely damaged the commercial section of Auburn Avenue. Only a few of the restaurants along the Avenue were able to survive, while all of the hotels and most of the clubs closed.[30]

Auburn Avenue was known not only for its black businesses, but also for the most important African-American cultural and religious institutions in the city. One of these, Ebenezer Baptist Church, had been led by Martin Luther King, Sr., and his son, the civil rights leader who was slain in 1968. The home in which Dr. King was born, his tomb, and the Martin Luther King Center for Nonviolent Social Change (completed in 1981) became major attractions, drawing 3 million visitors in 1993.[31] The Convention Bureau's marketing efforts were designed to increase the attractiveness of the Auburn Avenue area as a tourist destination by highlighting its important role in the history of the civil rights movement. Atlanta promoted its image as a city of biracial cooperation in which black elected public officials worked with mostly white tourism business leaders to attract visitors and conventions. One of the first successes of the new campaign was the 1992 meeting of the National Baptist Convention, U.S.A., at which more than 40,000 African-American Baptists met in the Georgia Dome.[32] These biracial promotional efforts were apparently successful because in 1994 the Convention Bureau announced that a recent poll had named Atlanta as the most preferred city in which to hold nationwide black meetings and conventions.[33]

Not all of the city's marketing efforts during this period were successful. In June 1992, Mayor Maynard Jackson took the bold step of naming high-powered advertising executive Joel Babbit as Atlanta's director of communications. Babbit was to develop ways to market the city more effectively and to promote a new image for Atlanta. The press reported that Babbit took a $450,000 pay cut to take the position in city government.[34] His first action was to propose a new slogan for the city, "Atlanta: The Hometown of the American Dream." The theme failed to capture the imagination of local residents and did not take its place alongside earlier descriptions of Atlanta as the "Gate City of the South" or "The City Too Busy to Hate." City council members felt that Babbit was arrogant, and would not confirm his position until five months after his appointment.

Babbit pressed on, however, and developed a bold plan which he said would raise more money for the city than taxes. He proposed selling advertisements on public assets such as city streets, bridges, parks, airports, and buildings to corporate sponsors who would be permitted to place their names on these locations. He also developed a marketing agreement to make VISA credit cards the preferred credit card of the city. Babbit grew increasingly frustrated with local government decision making. He told the press that the VISA board approved the agreement quickly, the Convention Bureau approved the plan in fifteen minutes, but the city council took over four months and held twelve meetings before approving the arrangement.[35] His next plan was to sell advertisements in outer space on a mile-long balloon satellite that would orbit the earth over the city during the Olympic Games. This proposal was too much for the mayor, who had been Babbit's biggest supporter. The press said that Babbit had run amok and was now promoting only himself.[36] Babbit moved ahead, though, and attempted to develop an official Atlanta logo that could be emblazoned on caps, T-shirts, and coffee mugs.

While Babbit failed to advance the city's marketing efforts, he did succeed in promoting his own career, as he resigned in June 1993 to take a position in a telecommunications firm. Some charged that Babbit, rather than polishing Atlanta's image, "put the city up for sale and for ridicule." A national advertising publication suggested that Atlanta should adopt the slogan "Atlanta: The Price Is Right" rather than "Hometown of the American Dream."[37] The failure of Babbit's approach to selling Atlanta indicated the difficulty of manufacturing slogans for cities. While many objected to his "low-grade image-mongering," efforts to define Atlanta with a slogan continued as the city approached the Olympics.[38] In one respect, Babbit proved prophetic in suggesting that cities could raise needed revenue by selling marketing rights to their assets, as the now common practice of renaming of stadiums and public sports arenas reveals. The renaming of streets, bridges, parks, and other parts of urban areas may be just ahead. While this practice may prove useful to generate revenue for city governments, it nonetheless raises concerns about commercialization as well as the reduction of public space.[39]

Convention Attractions

During the early 1970s, city leaders had promoted Atlanta as a major convention destination featuring large hotels and huge exposition facilities. This approach to economic development also encouraged other tourism business entrepreneurs to open clubs for the entertainment of visitors and residents alike. In 1971, the year planning began for the Georgia World Congress Center, the city received its first nightclub featuring topless dancing. The solicitor of Fulton County promptly closed down the club, beginning a series of legal battles which resulted in a 1973 court decision that female dancers could perform their acts as long as they did not expose bare breasts.[40] This compromise led to a proliferation of clubs featuring exotic female dancers in Atlanta. In 1978 the city government closed the "She" Club on Cheshire Bridge Road and fined the owner, who promptly sued the city and reopened his club.[41] After several more years of litigation, artistic freedom for dancers and their club owners was allowed to prevail in the city. The response was a further proliferation of clubs featuring nude dancing.

In an effort to protect the morals of city residents and visitors, in 1988 the Georgia General Assembly passed legislation prohibiting the sale of alcoholic beverages in establishments offering exotic dancing. This presented tourism business owners and local public officials with a dilemma, since they were faced with the summer arrival of the Democratic National Convention. The owners of the new multimillion-dollar Gold Club on Piedmont Road in Buckhead joined with other club owners in suing the state. The courts granted an injunction halting enforcement of the state ban, and the clubs remained open for the convention.[42] They proved a popular attraction for visiting journalists. The correspondent from the British humor magazine *Punch* did his best to boost the international reputation of Atlanta's nude bars with an article that "laid bare the city's nightlife."[43]

After the legal path was cleared by a state supreme court ruling against the law in December 1989, busy investors developed a dazzling array of clubs throughout the city. With sizable amounts of money to be made and with the convention business moving to the suburbs surrounding Atlanta, the nude dancing clubs were quick to follow. The first club outside the city limits opened in neighboring Dekalb County, but others soon followed in Cobb, Clayton, Gwinnett, and Fulton Counties as well as several suburban municipalities.

In November 1993 the *Constitution* made note of the fact that Atlanta had become known as the "nation's nudie capital." The editorial observed that the city's major attraction for convention visitors, besides the major airport and fine hotels, was naked women. Club owners made sure that conventioneers had no trouble finding their way from the hotels, and paid cab drivers two to four dollars per head for every customer they transported to the nude bars.[44] Consistent with the city's reputation, one of Atlanta's establishments, the Gold Club, has been described by B.C. Hall and C. T. Wood in their book about the South as the "fanciest teatbar in the world."[45] It is no coincidence that the Gold Club is located across the street from a rapid rail station enabling patrons to take the quick ride from downtown convention hotels. Despite these developments, the city did not have the image of a party town like New Orleans or Las Vegas, so professional groups could still schedule meetings in Atlanta and maintain the "veneer of respectability."[46]

There is no question, however, that the sex industry is important to Atlanta as a convention city. Urban scholar Dennis Judd has observed that cities with a large portion of their central city devoted to tourism often have areas identified as "carousal zones"—districts that usually include strip clubs, topless bars, and stores selling sex paraphernalia and pornography. Judd adds that these are important components of a city's tourism businesses, along with convention halls, sports arenas, and festival marketplaces.[47] The clubs generally provide security forces to maintain order and to keep their highly profitable operations from being tarnished by rowdy behavior, illegal drugs, or prostitution on their property. The club owners work hard at making nude clubs seem like mainstream entertainment. "We have some of the cleanest places in the United States," one Atlanta club owner said. "It's well-controlled here."[48] Problems arise because of rivalry with similar clubs in other tourist-oriented cities. Some club owners are eager to press the limits in order to gain a competitive edge, resulting in occasional blemishes on the otherwise clean image the city seeks to convey. For example, in August 1995, two female dancers were found dead in the trunk of a car in southwest Atlanta. The women had met some customers at the Little Nikki Club and had gone to a downtown hotel with them. Although the club had policies against such meetings, the rules had not been observed in this case.[49]

In 1995 more than fifty nude dance clubs were operating in the metropolitan area, and efforts to regulate them continue. In 1994 the state general assembly passed legislation authorizing an amendment to the state's constitution giving state and local governments clear power to regulate clubs where alcohol is served. Approved by the state's voters that November, the legislation permits cities and counties to eliminate the sale of alcohol in nude dance clubs while allowing dancers' artistic freedom of expression to continue. In the metropolitan Atlanta area, only scattered efforts have been made to curb nude dance clubs using this amendment.[50]

Whether these efforts to control strip clubs will be successful is doubtful. In addition to the clubs, spas and massage parlors catering to convention visitors and residents have opened. Faced with competition from these thinly disguised prostitution shops, the strip clubs responded by offering new services such as "interactive entertainment" in private rooms. The opening of spas, massage parlors, and sex paraphernalia shops generated some opposition from neighborhood and civic groups, but little action to close them. As of 1998 there were few restrictions governing the location of strip clubs and other sex businesses in relation to schools, religious organizations, residential areas, parks, and other land uses that local governments might wish to protect. As a result, these businesses seem unlikely to go away.

Despite the opposition of the churches, sex clubs are tolerated by most elected public officials and business leaders since the clubs are another commercial application of the cultural norm of hospitality. These "carousal zones" are perhaps as important as hotels, restaurants, and other amusements in the city's competitive tourism industry, and despite occasional protests, they will continue to provide their version of Southern hospitality.

Freaknik

If nude dance clubs are the tourism businesses that will not go away, Freaknik is the event that will not disappear. Freaknik is an annual spring party held by African-American college students. It began in 1982 as a small cookout and touch football game among students attending schools in the Atlanta University Center. Inspired by a popular dance at the time known as the "Freak," the students met during their spring break for a picnic in the park. From these ingredients came the name "Freaknik."

The event did not become a mass affair until 1993, when nearly 200,000 black college students descended upon Atlanta. Concerts and various activities took place in Piedmont Park and at other locations across the city. These activities did not generate as much enthusiasm, however, as the opportunity to drive around on the streets. In the crush of traffic, residents of in-town neighborhoods near Piedmont Park found themselves unable to get out of their driveways. The following spring even more students came to Freaknik, and the resulting traffic jam tied up streets as well as the downtown connector interstate highway from Buckhead to the southside. Police efforts to control traffic broke down, and only a few citations were issued for public drinking and other violations such as riding on the tops and hoods of cars. Residents of neighborhoods near downtown reported people engaged in all sorts of lewd behavior. Convenience stores, gas stations, car rental agencies, and fast-food restaurants reported increases in sales, but other restaurants and clubs complained that customers and employees could not get to them because of the massive traffic jam. Overtime expenses for the city's police department totaled more than $300,000.[51]

Reactions to Freaknik 1994 were varied. On the one hand, the festival brought to Atlanta more than 200,000 black college

students who were the best and the brightest of their generation. The event also represented an opportunity to showcase a
majority black city. On the other hand, complaints arose from
the mostly white residents of Midtown and other neighborhoods
near Piedmont Park and from tourism businesses, especially restaurants along Peachtree Street. Faced with such strong criticism, the new mayor, Bill Campbell, decided to get tough on the
1995 Freaknik celebration as well as the Atlanta Pot Festival,
which was also held in the spring in Piedmont Park. The mayor
announced, "Our policy will be zero tolerance for any infrac-
tion." Mayor Campbell added later that Freaknik "is not an event
that we feel is appropriate for our city." He also wrote a letter to
the presidents of all the historically black colleges and universities in the country asking them to discourage their students from
coming to Atlanta for the event. He received editorial support
from the *Journal Constitution* and general praise for the decision
from business leaders and white city residents. Several black city
council members, however, denounced the mayor's decision, and
African-American college students made plans to come whether
they were welcome or not.[52] Freaknik had succeeded in polariz-
ing the city along racial lines as few other events had ever done,
and had placed a strain on the tradition of Southern hospitality.

Mayor Campbell, an African American, was caught in the middle of a storm of criticism for his decision. He had instructed his
newly appointed police chief, Beverly Harvard, the first African-
American female to head the police force of a major city, to prepare a traffic and enforcement plan for the city that would keep
Freaknik under control. Angry students vowed to come in spite
of the mayor's warning. Faced with this criticism and a loss of
support among black city residents and the African-American
majority on the city council, the mayor retreated from his earlier threats to close down the festival. Instead, he suggested that
everyone was welcome to come to Atlanta as long as they obeyed
the laws.[53]

The students selected April 21–23 as the dates for the 1995
Freaknik celebration. This caused some concern among tourism business officials because the Comdex computer show was

scheduled to begin on Sunday, April 23, and many hotel rooms were already booked for the 100,000 expected to attend the convention. For the students, the celebration of Freaknik assumed the significance of a civil rights confrontation in a city with a black mayor and chief of police as well as an African-American majority population. This equation of Freaknik with a civil rights crusade was supported and encouraged by the mayor's political opponents as well as by veterans of the civil rights movement. Some accused Mayor Campbell of changing his position on Freaknik in response to the conflict. With criticism coming from all sides, the mayor began negotiations with his counterpart in New Orleans about the possibility of moving the event to that city, but that idea found little support in either city.

Tensions ran high in Atlanta in the weeks before Freaknik. The details of the police traffic plan were not made public, giving rise to rumors about stormtrooper tactics. Fears of confrontation between students and the authorities were heightened when the state national guard announced plans to hold drills on the weekend of Freaknik. The governor delayed a trip out of the country so that he could be available if the national guard units needed to be called out. More than four hundred state law enforcement officers were placed at the disposal of the Atlanta police chief.[54]

Some local black college students attempted to change the nature of the event. They met with the organization of African-American religious organizations known as the Concerned Black Clergy and arranged to have churches open their doors and provide Freaknik participants with a place to sleep. The student leaders also met with city hall officials to proclaim a new name for the festival, "Freedomfest." The new name was designed to give the celebration a kinder, gentler image among both participating students and the public. Other events in the city, ranging from weddings and a hockey team playoff game to the annual Dogwood Festival, were rescheduled to avoid conflict with the expected traffic gridlock.[55] Restaurant owners in downtown, Midtown, and areas near Piedmont Park announced plans to close for the weekend, since, as the president of the Georgia Hospitality and Travel Association said, "Restaurants aren't going to have any business if their customers and employees can't get there."

Others feared that Freaknik would not only close restaurants, but also intimidate hotel guests and cause long-term harm to the city. Paul Karatassos, the head of the Buckhead Life Restaurant Group, announced, "If Freaknik is allowed to continue, I think the adverse effects it will have on the City of Atlanta over a period of time will become devastating and irreversible, particularly when we look at our conventions, our local businesses and the efforts to improve the image of downtown Atlanta."[56] Others wondered how Atlanta could hope to handle the crowds for a two-week mega-event like the Olympics when the city seemed unable to accommodate the partying college students for three days.

Activities for the students were minimized when the Lakewood Amphitheatre, in response to opposition from two of the three surrounding residential areas, canceled a rap music concert scheduled for Saturday. The city-owned civic center also canceled its contract for Freaknik concerts on Friday and Saturday because of concerns over security and traffic. This cancellation prompted protests near city hall against the mayor.[57]

The first groups of students began arriving on Thursday, but with police officers stationed at intersections throughout downtown, Midtown, and the Atlanta University Center, there was little disturbance. Underground Atlanta seemed the most popular destination as it remained busy throughout the evening. Street-corner T-shirt vendors did a brisk business with a shirt containing the message that became the motto for the weekend, "They Told Us Not To Come, But We Came Anyway." On Friday the crowds of students and others attracted by the event grew. Police barricades closed off most of the downtown area to automobiles, resulting in a pedestrian party as thousands paraded in the streets. Freaknik turned ugly when ten stores in Underground Atlanta were broken into and looted. Shortly after 11 P.M., when police officers attempted to close Underground Atlanta, the crowd responded by throwing bottles and rocks, injuring one officer.

Some additional looting occurred before police cleared Peachtree Street and dispersed the crowd for the night.[58]

On Saturday afternoon the students' attention turned to the
city's shopping malls. In Buckhead on the northside, students
flocked to Lenox Square and Phipps Plaza, causing traffic congestion and bringing mixed reactions from merchants as some
shops were empty, while stores selling music and sports shoes did
well. The northside malls and Underground Atlanta closed early
in the evening, forcing people to return to the streets. Many
moved to Greenbriar Mall on the southside, which had tried to
welcome the students. Around 9:00 the stores at Greenbriar Mall
closed, but as the celebration continued in the parking lot and
surrounding area looters struck again.[59]

On Sunday the visitors began leaving, with many saying the
crowds had not been as large as the year before and that Freaknik
was not as much fun. The cost to the city for overtime pay to
police and sanitation workers was estimated at $1 million. Most
of the problems of traffic gridlock were avoided, but there were
two nights of looting and, in the minds of many suburban residents, further damage to the image of Underground Atlanta. Police arrested five hundred people on charges ranging from looting to rape. Nearly half of those arrested were older than the
young college students who had come in past years.[60]

Each spring since 1995, fewer students came to Atlanta for
Freaknik in spite of an official welcome from the mayor and city
council as well as more planned activities. Departing visitors have
commented that the traffic control and police presence in the
city made Freaknik less fun than in prior years.[61] Tourism business leaders preferred that Freaknik move to another city. While
city leaders want to remain a major convention town, the festival proved that Atlanta is not a resort destination. There were
not enough leisure activities and open space to fill the weekend
for the estimated 100,000 college students and others who came
for the party. One economist estimated that the Freaknik visitors
would have a $20 million impact on the city. This amount has
to be offset, however, by the losses due to traffic problems and
business closings.[62] When the inconvenience and frustration of

local residents were added to the racial polarization from the event, many concluded that Atlanta would be better off without Freaknik. Some political leaders want the students to come back in the future, and a local poll showed that black residents overwhelmingly thought Freaknik was a good thing for the city. The mayor, hospitality business owners, and most white residents of the area, on the other hand, simply wished the event would fade away.[63]

Super Bowl XXVIII

In 1987, when the owner of the Atlanta Falcons National Football League team threatened to move the franchise elsewhere if he was not given a new stadium, the city, county, and state responded by building the indoor football arena known as the Georgia Dome. Building the new $400 million facility was almost a replay of the urban renewal program, as it destroyed a low-income black neighborhood known as Lightning. However, the community pressured the state to provide $25 million in relocation assistance for the residents, businesses, and churches in the area.[64] As soon as the new facility opened, Atlanta officials began bidding to host the annual league championship known as the Super Bowl. In 1990 the city's efforts were rewarded with the announcement that Atlanta would host Super Bowl XXVIII in January 1994. With hotel occupancy rates running low, tourism businesses were excited about the event. Public officials and other business leaders were pleased with the media spotlight that would be focused on Atlanta. Almost everyone agreed that the publicity for the city as host of the game would provide a boost to Atlanta's economic development.

The economic impact study of the Super Bowl before the game estimated that the event would add $150 million to the city's economy. Fans in town for the game would be expected to use 35,000 of Atlanta's 55,000 hotel rooms. As an added boost to the city's tourism businesses, hotels were allowed to charge their top advertised rates for guests coming to the game.[65] These forecasts were tempered by the fact that there were costs to the city, county, and state governments as well as local business supporters of the Super Bowl. In order to secure the game for the city, a number of incentives were provided to the National Football League which were not disclosed to the public until two weeks before the game. State and local governments agreed to waive more than $750,000 in sales taxes that the league would normally pay on tickets for the Super Bowl. In addition, each of the three governments was to contribute $300,000 in cash to the league to pay for the event. The National Football League also received free use of the Georgia Dome throughout the week preceding the game.

Other benefits for the league provided by the public sector included all of the novelty rights, stadium concessions, and parking revenues generated by the Super Bowl. Inside the stadium, the owners of teams and league officials were allowed to use fifty-six luxury suites during the game. Local businesses contributed 900 free room nights for the league staff and 240 free hotel rooms to be used by the participating teams for the week of the game. Training facilities for the teams were provided by the Atlanta Falcons and Georgia Tech. All these, along with several other benefits, made the total package for hosting the Super Bowl exceed $5 million.[66]

The cash payment of $300,000 from each of the three participating governments was based on a handshake agreement among the elected officials in 1990. When the time arrived for the city's payment just two weeks before the game, there was a new mayor in office and several new city council members who felt they had not been consulted on the agreement. The Georgia Dome itself was unpopular with many council members, since its construction had required the destruction of a low-income African-American neighborhood. An additional irritant was the fact that the Georgia Dome would fly the state flag, which contained the "stars and bars" of the Confederate battle flag. Efforts by the governor to change the state flag had failed earlier, but the city went ahead and removed the flag from city property. The council was now being asked to fund a third of the expenses for the Super

244

Bowl held on state property where the flag would be displayed. In spite of opposition, the city council finally approved the city's share of the expenses plus another $400,000 to cover the costs of extra police and sanitation services.[67]

The keen competition among cities to host the Super Bowl tends to drive up the cost of the bids from each city. Previous winners seem less sure of the benefits gained from the event. The mayor of Pasadena, which hosted the game in 1993, said, "In terms of the municipal balance sheet, it was a disappointment. The NFL doesn't share concessions, the NFL doesn't share rent, the NFL doesn't share parking." The mayor of 1992's host city, Minneapolis, also expressed disappointment with the economic impact of the games. The experience of other cities suggested that the immediate economic impact was slight since little of the spending by visitors stayed in the local economy. The three Super Bowl sites prior to Atlanta—Tampa, Minneapolis, and Pasadena—were all disappointed that the game did not provide an immediate boost to economic growth. Officials of these cities could only hope that the marketing effect would be more important in the long term.[68]

When the day of the game finally arrived, public interest in the event was low due to the fact that the same two teams had met the year before. Perhaps the one aspect of the game that attracted interest was the halftime show, which featured country music for the first time in Super Bowl history. Among the featured performers was a native of the Atlanta area, Travis Tritt. Although the country music theme may have validated the city's connections to the rural South, it was not well liked by some viewers outside the region. One national critic even described the show as "musical junk food."[69]

Criticism of the Southern roots of the halftime show was regarded as a breach of good manners and an insult to the city's hospitality. Southern writer George Garrett described the importance of manners (including hospitality) in the region in these words: "An act of bad manners may well be, to the Southerner, an act of violence. A violation of the code of manners may well be taken as at least *meaning* the same thing as a fist in the face or a blade between the ribs."[70] In a guest-host relationship, if hospitality was provided, it was to be received with the same graciousness with which it was given. Local civic pride was offended, as praise of the city and its hospitality in welcoming the Super Bowl was expected.

Tourism businesses were the major beneficiaries of the game. A postgame economic impact study found that the Super Bowl actually generated more spending than anticipated. The game brought nearly 75,000 visitors to the city, most of whom stayed four days. Their spending was estimated at $166 million, with $46 million generated for the hotels and entertainment establishments and $18 million for the restaurants and bars. Organizers of the event from the Chamber of Commerce considered the game a good investment for the city. They indicated that they would like to host the game again in the year 2000.[71] Mayor Campbell joined the chamber in support of another bid for the event, which was accepted by the National Football League.

Other Tourism Activities

In the years preceding Super Bowl XXVIII, as the nation emerged from the national recession, the city's hotel occupancy rate had begun to climb upward. In part this resulted from a decline in new hotel construction in the early 1990s. As Table 8.1

Table 8.1. Atlanta-Area Hotel Occupancy Rates, 1990–1995

YEAR	OCCUPANCY RATE
1990	61.8%
1991	60.1%
1992	63.2%
1993	67.4%
1994	71.7%
1995	72.9%

Source: PKF Consulting.

shows, the occupancy rate increased substantially each year from 1991 to 1995.[72] This represented a return to profitability for most of the hotels, since an occupancy rate of at least 65 percent was needed in order to make a profit in the Atlanta hotel market.[73] Considerable variation remained in the occupancy rates of the submarkets throughout the metropolitan area. Large downtown hotels depended heavily upon travelers attending major conventions and smaller meetings within the hotels. The occupancy rates for these hotels dropped as low as 58.3 percent in 1992, rising gradually to 66.2 percent in 1995. In contrast, occupancy rates for hotels in the airport area increased from 62.9 percent in 1990 to 74.7 percent in 1995. Other airline passenger carriers had moved in to make up for the loss of Eastern Airlines, and the airport was again second only to Chicago's O'Hare as the busiest in the nation. This increase in airline passengers also benefited the city's tourism businesses. Other submarkets with high hotel occupancy rates were in Buckhead and in the Cumberland Mall area of Cobb County, where hotels averaged more than 74 percent occupancy rates during 1995.[74]

During the period from 1990 to 1995, the average daily rates for hotel rooms increased from $61.52 to $73.73, helping increase profitability.[75] In spite of these price increases, hotel costs in the Atlanta area remained lower than those in many other cities. This was due in part to lower labor costs in Atlanta. In contrast to New York, Chicago, and other major hotel markets, few hotels in the Atlanta area have organized union employees. According to the Service Trades Department, American Federation of Labor–Congress of Industrial Organizers (AFL-CIO), employees in only three Atlanta hotels have a union contract. These are the Hyatt Regency, the Downtown Hilton, and the American Best Western Hotel, which are all located in the central business district. Union officials cite the low pay and high turnover rates as the reasons few hotel and restaurant employees in Atlanta are organized.[76] This is also part of a broader pattern throughout the South, where organized labor has been relatively weak. The lower labor costs of Atlanta's non-union hotels keep room rates below other cities'. This usually means that meetings

247

in the city and business travel to Atlanta can be done less expensively. Lower costs remain a powerful advantage as Atlanta competes with other cities for convention business.

A major event such as the Super Bowl can have a significant impact on a city, both economically and in terms of worldwide media coverage. However, "homegrown" events that lack the media glare of a Super Bowl can also bring significant economic benefits to the city. One event of this latter type is the Peachtree Road Race, which began as a ten-kilometer run down Peachtree Street in the Fourth of July heat more than twenty-five years ago. The race now attracts 50,000 participants and has an estimated economic impact of $9 million each year.[77] Another is the National Black Arts Festival, which began in 1988 and is held every two years. In 1994 the festival lasted ten days and offered more than 150 events in the fields of dance, film, literature, music, performance art, theater, and visual art at more than thirty venues throughout the city. Direct financial support from local government for staging the festival was less than $600,000, yet the 1994 festival drew more than a million participants.[78]

The people who attended the 1994 National Black Arts Festival came primarily from inside the state of Georgia, with most coming from the metropolitan Atlanta area. However, 25 percent of attendees came from outside the state, so they spent a considerable amount on food and lodging. Estimates for their spending on food and lodging exceeded $20 million. Total festival-related spending was estimated to be between $54 and $73 million. A higher percentage of this spending remained in the local economy than was the case with the Super Bowl because of the concessions that had been granted to the National Football League. When festival-related spending circulated through the local economy, it generated an estimated $79 to $106 million in additional business activity.[79] Therefore, the economic impact of the National Black Arts Festival was only slightly less than that of the Super Bowl, but with considerably less investment to attract the event and more local impact in terms of the dollars spent.

Although the festival did not have the media significance and image enhancement of the Super Bowl, it could be argued that it helped create a more interesting city by providing important cultural and social contributions to Atlanta. This value was recognized by city and county governments as well as the Convention Bureau and local businesses that joined in financial support and promotional activities for the festival. Among those who came to Atlanta for the festival, the favorable impression of the city formed by the event does, in its own way, help shape a positive image of the area. Survey results from the economic impact study indicated that visitors were favorably impressed by what they saw of the city and expressed an interest in returning.[80] The value of enhancing the city's reputation as a center for African-American life and culture is perhaps as important as the festival's economic benefits. While a host city for the Super Bowl cannot be considered again for at least six years, the National Black Arts Festival will return with all of its benefits every two years.

World Series

In 1990 the Atlanta Braves were mired in last place in their division. Stadium attendance was low, with the result that taxpayers in the city and in Fulton County had to pay a portion of the debt service on the bonds used to finance the stadium. The following year, the Braves made a remarkable turnaround in both their playing and in the number of fans attending the games. In a close divisional race, they beat the Los Angeles Dodgers and became the Western Division champions. In a dramatic seven-game series, the Braves beat the Pittsburgh Pirates to become the National League champions. They moved into the 1991 World Series against the Minnesota Twins of the American League. Atlantans had never experienced a major sports championship, and the seven-game series provided excitement resulting in sold-out games and enormous enthusiasm from the fans. Although the Braves lost the final game of the World Series, baseball had become a matter of deep interest for area residents.

In 1992 the Braves again provided excitement during the regular season and won the Western Division championship. Fan support was strong and sellout crowds became regular events at the stadium. The team defeated the Pirates again in the National League championship, advancing to the World Series for the second consecutive year. In a six-game series, the Toronto Blue Jays of the American League defeated the Braves, but fan interest remained at an all-time high.

The success of the Braves on the field continued in 1993 with another Western Division title. The stadium was filled to capacity for almost every game throughout the season, boosting revenues for area hotels that rented rooms to visiting fans. This time, however, the team lost to the Philadelphia Phillies in the National League championship series. Accustomed to winning teams, the fans from throughout the Southeast who supported the Braves looked forward to more success in the 1994 season. Instead, baseball players and owners were unable to agree on a labor contract, causing a strike in August that shortened the season and eliminated the playoffs. Fan support that had grown during the three previous years eroded during the strike, and when the season finally opened for 1995 there were no longer the sellout crowds of the past. There were also fewer games in the regular season, resulting in lower stadium revenues.

The Braves responded by winning their divisional championship in spite of less support from local and visiting fans. In an expanded playoff format, the Braves won the first round of playoff games against the Colorado Rockies, then swept the next series against the Cincinnati Reds, taking the National League championship. The World Series against the Cleveland Indians of the American League brought fans back to the stadium. Atlanta's team won the first two games of the best-of-seven series, and one of the next three in Cleveland. Many tourism businesses were delighted that the series returned to Atlanta because the increased spending for the extra games was estimated at $4 million per game. Restaurants, on the other hand, were anxious for the games to be over because many patrons stayed home rather than eat out during the event. Some restaurant owners reported their business was at least 35 percent lower than normal on the evenings of the World Series games. Sports bars were happy with the attention focused on the series.[81] Finally, in a dramatic sixth game, the Braves won the series, becoming the city's first major sports franchise to win a championship. Crowds of fans swelled Underground Atlanta, clubs and bars in Buckhead, and elsewhere throughout the city in celebration, and a crowd of 500,000 lined the streets of downtown for a parade honoring the team.

The baseball world championship gave the city's image a tremendous boost. After many years of sports failures, Atlanta residents could feel proud of the triumph of one of its teams. In addition, the celebration after the victory was not marred with the violence that has affected other cities. The victory was a fitting conclusion to a period of peaks and valleys for both the city and its tourism businesses. City leaders could now focus on an event that would bring international attention to Atlanta.

9

The 1996 Olympic Games

IN A LITTLE OVER 150 years since the city's founding, Atlanta's residents have turned the cultural value of Southern hospitality into a major industry. Since the opening of the first boarding-house, Atlantans welcomed visitors brought to the town, first by the railroads, then by wagons and automobiles, and more recently by airplanes. As the town grew into a metropolitan area of over 3 million people, most residents continued to share the ideal of Southern hospitality.[1] The business of welcoming visitors has also grown to the extent that perhaps 250,000 of these metropolitan residents now earn their living in tourism businesses.[2]

These tourism businesses have been important elements of the promotions that have brought growth to Atlanta. As the city's leaders have tried to attract the attention of investors through the promotion of a series of large events, a partnership between elected public officials and business leaders has helped both the growth agenda of the city and its hospitality businesses. The public sector provides the infrastructure to facilitate the welcoming of visitors and the hosting of conventions. Government resources also provide amenities, such as Underground Atlanta and the World Congress Center, which are considered crucial for the success of the private-sector tourism businesses. These businesses, in return, have had a positive effect on the local economy through the jobs created and the taxes generated, as well as the multiplier effects of money spent by visitors. Thus Atlanta's hotels, restaurants, amusements, and convention facilities have become a major source of growth, but one that depends upon continual promotion.

One way cities market themselves to visitors from all over the world is by hosting what are often called "hallmark" events, or mega-events. These are defined as major onetime or recurring events of limited duration, developed primarily to enhance the awareness, appeal, and profitability of a tourism destination. These events rely for their success on uniqueness, status, or timely significance to create interest and attract attention.[3] The mega-event is no mere festival designed to attract visitors on a regular basis. For an event to be a hallmark it must be on a scale that requires huge amounts of money spent in preparation for the event and the expectation that there will be a national and, indeed, international recognition of the host location. Without doubt, the world's largest mega-event is the Olympic Games, since few other activities have its ability to focus the attention of the world (it is estimated that 2.5 billion people around the globe watched the 1984 Olympics, held in Los Angeles). The Games provide the host city with publicity, urban renewal, the construction of physical infrastructure, and economic development on an unprecedented scale.[4] A mega-event such as the Olympics has the potential to reshape a city and its reputation in the world.

Atlanta's Bid for the Olympics

The quest to bring the Olympic Games to Atlanta began with a local attorney named Billy Payne, who had played football at the University of Georgia. He first conceived the idea in February 1987 and moved to action after reading that Nashville was also interested in hosting the Games.[5] After discussions with other business leaders, Payne forged a partnership with Mayor Andrew Young to move forward with the city's bid. Payne, Young, and a few supporters formed the Atlanta Organizing Committee (AOC) to prepare the official invitation.

In August 1987, Mayor Young sent a letter to the U.S. Olympic Committee (USOC) expressing the city's interest in hosting the Games. This was the first official step required in the lengthy bidding process. Atlanta was one of fourteen U.S. cities competing for the designation. In January 1988 the USOC's executive board chose to hold its annual meeting in Atlanta, and the hospitality extended by the city for that meeting helped to narrow the field to two cities—Atlanta and Minneapolis–St. Paul—which were invited to make presentations at the USOC's next executive board meeting in April 1988. Based on these presentations, the USOC selected Atlanta, putting the city into the international competition for the Games.[6]

The next stage was a series of formal steps in preparing the bid for the International Olympic Committee (IOC). Four other cities also wanted the Games, including Athens, Greece, the site of the revival of the modern Olympic movement in 1896. It was also a time of intense informal lobbying with the members of the IOC. Members of the AOC, such as executive vice-president Charles Battle, covered the globe, visiting over forty countries to garner support from IOC members for Atlanta's bid.[7] Financial support for these early efforts was difficult to obtain. Corporate donations were limited at first as the city was preparing to host the 1988 Democratic National Convention. Several private individuals gave $50,000 each, and salaries for AOC members were paid by their corporations. This enabled attorneys such as Payne and Battle to commit all of their time to the bid.

Atlanta's Official Bid for the 1996 Olympic Games was a two-volume document outlining details for the city's plans to host the event. The bid included proposals for all aspects of the Games, including venues for sporting competitions, financial support, and accommodations for guests. A major theme of Atlanta's bid was Southern hospitality. The estimated cost of preparing the city's bid was $7 million, which included travel to the 1988 Olympics in Seoul to observe the preparation and staging of the Games. Another expensive feature of the bid was a three-dimensional interactive video model of proposed sites for the Games in Atlanta prepared by Georgia Institute of Technology.[8]

Other local organizations also contributed to the efforts to promote Atlanta's Olympic bid. In September 1989 members of the Atlanta Track Club joined with others to stage a five-kilometer race, with all of the participants wearing AOC T-shirts in order to impress a visiting delegation of IOC members. The event was hailed as the largest race of that distance in the world and was staged to show the support of the city's amateur athletes for the Games. Momentum for hosting the Games built rapidly in the city, and other partners joined the effort. Corporate sponsors such as Coca-Cola and the Citizens and Southern National Bank (later NationsBank) provided the financial support needed to sustain the effort.

Another partner in the bidding process was the state of Georgia. In 1989 the general assembly created the Metropolitan Atlanta Olympic Games Authority (MAOGA), giving it remarkable powers to oversee the preparations for the event. MAOGA's broad oversight responsibilities included monitoring the financing for the Games, as well as issuing bonds on behalf of the Atlanta Committee for the Olympic Games (ACOG) in order to provide capital for venue construction. It was given police powers in order to coordinate Olympic security across local police jurisdictional lines, and was vested with the power of eminent domain, which could be used to assemble land for Olympics-related projects.[9] As a gesture of support, the state granted this array of power even before the bid was accepted. But, while the state was generous in granting power to MAOGA, it did not initially provide direct financial assistance for the Olympics.

In September 1990 the IOC held its selection meeting in Tokyo, where a delegation of over 350 Atlantans was on hand to represent the city in its bid for the Games. The specially selected band played, the youth choir sang, and AOC members lobbied intensely for Atlanta. Payne and the other AOC members made their presentation to the international representatives on Sunday, September 16. For the members of the Atlanta delegation the message was quite familiar. "Their most important mission," the *Constitution* noted, "is spreading Southern hospitality, a constant theme of the Atlanta bid, around the world."[10]

The IOC deliberated for two days, with many members favoring Athens as a sentimental choice over Toronto, Manchester, and Melbourne. IOC president Juan Antonio Samaranch finally made the dramatic announcement that Atlanta had been selected. A crowd of several thousand gathered at Underground Atlanta to watch the news of the announcement. As word spread through the city, thousands of others joined them in a day-long party to celebrate the awarding of the Games to Atlanta. The banner headline in the afternoon's *Journal* read, "It's Atlanta!"[11] Copies of the newspaper became immediate collector's items. The headline was also reprinted on T-shirts and bumper stickers as Atlantans cheered the news. Almost half a million people turned out for the ticker tape parade down Peachtree Street to welcome Billy Payne, former mayor Andrew Young, and the delegation returning from the selection meeting.[12] Many expected the celebration to last for six years until the arrival of the Games. There was, however, much to do in preparation for the event.

Venue Construction

The Atlanta Organizing Committee took as its model the 1984 Los Angeles Olympics, which was held at sites throughout southern California. Local planners also promised that the Atlanta Games, like the event in Los Angeles, would be financed from private sources such as sponsorships and television contracts as well as ticket sales and souvenirs. This would avoid the huge public debt that Montreal had incurred when it hosted the Olympics in 1976. However, unlike Los Angeles before the 1984 games, very few venues were already in existence in the Atlanta area, so many facilities needed to be constructed. For example, Los Angeles already had its Olympic Coliseum, which only required renovation. Atlanta had a stadium, as well as the Georgia Dome, an indoor sports facility, but neither could serve as the Olympic Stadium, which would host the opening and closing ceremonies as well as the track and field events.

The Atlanta Committee for the Olympic Games's final estimate for the cost of the event was $1.58 billion, which included nearly $170 million for building the new Olympic Stadium and over $200 million for the construction of the remaining athletic facilities. When other physical improvements financed by ACOG were added to the tally, the total construction budget was estimated to be $516.6 million.[13] This did not include, however, the cost of the Olympic Village, which was to be built by the state of Georgia at a cost of $127 million. Local governments would also pay infrastructure costs for the improvement of streets, sidewalks, and bridges. As a result, the total cost of construction for the Olympics was pegged at around $650 million.[14]

The location of venues for the Games generated considerable controversy. First, an affluent, predominantly white area of north Dekalb County known as Dunwoody resisted having the tennis venue located in their neighborhood. ACOG responded by moving the tennis center to the state-owned Stone Mountain Park. Then ACOG announced its intention to build the Olympic Stadium in the low-income black neighborhood known as Summerhill, next to the site of the Atlanta–Fulton County Stadium. The neighborhood protested the location of a second stadium in their community, but ACOG refused to budge. After an initial confrontation, a compromise was reached. The new stadium would be located just south of the Atlanta–Fulton County Stadium, but after the Games the old stadium would be demolished and the Olympic Stadium reconfigured for the use of the Atlanta Braves. The neighborhood also received promises of financial support from the business community to assist in the revitalization of Summerhill and the training and employment of area residents for construction jobs on the new stadium.

The selection of other venues also provoked conflict. Cobb County, for instance, was chosen as the location for the volleyball competition. After the Cobb County Commission passed an ordinance supporting "family values" and condemning the lifestyles of gays and lesbians, a storm of protests followed against the county and against ACOG for supporting an area practicing intolerance. ACOG decided to avoid the controversy by moving the volleyball competition to Athens. Other proposed sites, such as Tybee Island on the Georgia coast, were changed because of environmental and logistical problems.

Most of the colleges and universities in the area benefited from the Olympics by having their athletic facilities replaced or improved. Georgia Tech received a natatorium for swimming and diving events and had its basketball coliseum enlarged and air-conditioned to host the boxing matches. The University of Georgia in Athens received an indoor training facility for the volleyball competition and had its football stadium upgraded for the Olympic soccer games. At the Atlanta University complex, Morris Brown College received a new stadium for field hockey, Morehouse got a new gymnasium for Olympic basketball, and Clark-Atlanta University's football stadium was renovated for field hockey. Georgia State University received an expansion of its gymnasium to host the badminton event. Georgia State and Georgia Tech also shared use of the Olympic Village after the Games, as the buildings became dormitories for the two institutions.

The rest of the venues for the Olympics were widely dispersed. For instance, Ducktown, Tennessee, on the Ocoee River hosted whitewater canoeing and kayaking. Lake Lanier provided the site for rowing events, while Savannah provided facilities for the yachting competition. Columbus, Georgia, on the Alabama border, constructed facilities for the women's softball games, and the equestrian events were held east of Atlanta in Rockdale County.[15] Residents of each of these venue sites hoped for an increase in tourism business as a result of the Olympic preparations.

Atlanta received considerable criticism for the design of the venues. During the annual meeting of the American Institute of Architects, one member examined the local venues under construction and said, "Half a billion dollars and no architecture!" ACOG responded that its goal was to host the Games on time and under budget—an approach that left little room for virtuosity in design. Most of the structures met program requirements and did so with efficiency, but left the city only a modest legacy for the effort. This was in sharp contrast to the 1992 Barcelona Games, which provided an impressive demonstration of architecture and urban design. Atlanta's efforts were consistent with the "no-nonsense" reputation of the city as a place for business. The director of ACOG's construction effort defended his work by saying the buildings were "not necessarily unique" except for their planned adaptation for subsequent use.[16]

In one exception, ACOG attempted to develop a prominent symbol for the Games with the construction of a 132-foot-high Olympic flame cauldron. For the first time in modern Olympic history, the flame was located outside the stadium and connected to it with a bridge across the street. The artist, Siah Armajani, designed the tower holding the cauldron as a permanent legacy for the people of Georgia. Midway up the tower was a wooden house with glass windows that glowed from the inside at night. According to the artist, the house "symbolizes the warmth and hospitality of the people of Atlanta and the South." At the top of the tower, the sixteen-foot-high stainless steel cauldron was rimmed with terra-cotta made from local red clay.[17]

The designer of the flame cauldron recognized the cultural value of Southern hospitality and attempted to incorporate it into an important architectural legacy of the Olympics. Once it was completed, some critics were displeased with the flame cauldron, comparing it to a giant cardboard french fry container. The flames of controversy were further fanned when a local real estate developer decided to erect a $2 million, 123-foot torch on private property overlooking the expressway north of downtown. ACOG was quick to threaten litigation if any unauthorized use of the Olympic name was involved. The developer announced that it symbolized the torch of liberty and featured an electric flame, an observation deck from which viewers could pay to see the downtown skyline, and a souvenir shop at the base.[18] Although the torch was not located near the stadium, many visitors and residents thought it was the Olympic flame.

Economic Impact

State and local tourism officials were even more excited than most other Atlantans over the selection of the city for the Olympics. State tourism officials hoped that millions of tourists would come to Atlanta prior to the Games. These tourists were expected to spend $568 million on hotel rooms, meals, local transportation, and other items, generating an additional multiplier effect of $1.44 billion on the state's economy and creating nearly 39,000 jobs.[19] As with many other economic impact studies, these data assumed that no other events during the six-year period would bring tourists to the city. Despite the study's methodological flaws, the Olympics generated an enormous amount of publicity for the city, creating revenue and jobs for the Atlanta area.

The Atlanta Committee for the Olympic Games estimated that it spent nearly $1.7 billion to stage the event. Of this amount, over $516 million went to construction costs. ACOG officials made repeated claims that the financing would come from private sources and that there would be no cost to the public sector. The largest single source of revenue for the Games was from the sale of broadcast rights. The rights to televise the event throughout the world generated $560 million for ACOG, and ticket sales brought in $422 million.[20] Most of the remainder came from an aggressive partnership between ACOG and businesses who wished to use the Olympic theme in their advertising. The result was an array of sponsorships and official licenses granted by ACOG to 110 companies for products ranging from imported cars (BMW and Nissan), domestic cars (General Motors), watches (Swatch), salad dressing (Vidalia Onion Vinaigrette), clothing of all sorts, and sports equipment.[21] This marketing approach prompted one newspaper opinion writer to suggest that the 1996 Olympics was the "grossest commercial orgy in history," making Atlanta the "kapital of kitsch."[22]

In spite of such criticism, ACOG raised $60 million from the licensed products and $77 million from the sponsorship agreements. While the event did not run up the public debt incurred by Montreal in 1976, there was still considerable expense to the public sector. The state of Georgia spent approximately $30 million for security during the Games, as well as $127 million for the construction of the Olympic Village. The federal government spent over $92 million to provide additional security, transportation, trees, and infrastructure improvements, and the National Park Service constructed a visitors center on Auburn Avenue near the tomb of Dr. Martin Luther King, Jr. The City of Atlanta also spent $52 million for the repair of bridges, roads, sewers, and sidewalks and for other infrastructure projects. Fulton County spent an additional $11.4 million on Olympics-related projects. When other projects were added, the total public-sector expenditures grew to more than $354 million.[23] (This figure does not include the $100 million which the city received from the federal government for its Empowerment Zone program.)

Atlanta incurred costs it estimated at $13.5 million for extra municipal services used during the Games. These costs included such items as additional police and fire services, sanitation services to keep trash picked up, extended sessions for the municipal courts, and the use of city parks. After months of negotiations, the city finally reached an agreement with ACOG for repayment of most of these expenses. Under the arrangement, ACOG paid the city $8 million in direct cash payments and $1.5 million in goods and services. The city received the remainder from the federal government to pay for police overtime.[24] However, Atlanta was not content with the mere repayment of its expenses from the Games. An entrepreneur and close friend of the mayor convinced the city government that the Olympics could provide an opportunity to make money from sales in kiosks and vending carts on city property. Under the contract with the city, the sales in parks and on sidewalks were expected to return at least $2.5 million to the city. IOC officials, visiting journalists, and many of the vendors were unhappy with the program, which lined the sidewalks with stalls offering food and souvenirs. Vendors who were sold rights to locations on uncrowded streets filed claims against the city for more than $25 million.[25]

As preparations continued, the total construction costs for the Games reached $650 million.[26] Much of this was spent for labor and locally produced materials. This means that the economic impact of Olympics-related construction reached $1.2 billion for the Atlanta area and another $150 million for the surrounding region. Much of this money was spent before the start of the

Games in 1996.[27] Many new jobs were created as a result of this construction activity, and from 1992 to 1994 Atlanta led the nation's metropolitan areas in job growth.[28] In 1994 alone, an estimated 154,800 new jobs were added in the Atlanta area. While this phenomenal rate of growth slowed during 1995, there were still more than 110,000 new jobs added. Hiring for the Games themselves during 1996 meant a continued increase to around 91,700 new jobs for Atlanta. Because of the increased number of jobs in the Atlanta area, the unemployment rate declined to less than 4 percent in 1996. Employment growth for 1997 dropped to only around 40,700 new jobs for the metropolitan area, softening the economic letdown that had been forecast for the area.[29]

One immediate result of Atlanta's Olympic preparations was the increase in the cost of construction throughout the metropolitan area. As the building of venues for the Games proceeded, the price of materials and labor increased, which affected other projects in the area. For example, in the rapidly growing suburban Fayette County, a $58 million bond issue was expected to finance the building of five new schools and the renovation of eleven others. However, construction costs increased from 1.0 to 1.5 percent per month in the Atlanta area, and the school bond proceeds would not cover the 15 percent rise in costs. As a result of the increased costs, many construction projects used "value engineering," which meant cutting costs by scaling back already lean budgets. Some projects were simply delayed until Olympics-related jobs were finished.[30]

Union leaders also complained that many contractors working on Olympics projects used illegal immigrants for inexpensive labor. The construction companies responded that they had to hire workers from wherever they could be found because the construction boom had created a labor shortage. The construction activity in the area was a magnet both for workers from other parts of the country and, as raids by the Immigration and Naturalization Service showed, for illegal immigrants. This influx of workers for Olympics-related construction projects also caused crowded housing conditions in the area.

In addition to construction costs, more than $964 million was spent to operate the Olympics. This amount included the salaries of ACOG employees and the costs for communications equipment needed for the event. Again, assuming that each of these dollars added an additional dollar as it circulated through the local economy, this added more than $1.9 billion to the Atlanta area.[31]

Another significant economic impact from the Olympics came from spending by tourists. ACOG's official estimate was a $2 billion economic impact from visitors who came for the Games. Of the 11 million tickets available for all the events of the Games, ACOG sold 8.5 million, raising $422 million. Many of these were purchased by Georgians and others from the Southeast, who would commute from home and not spend large amounts in Atlanta-area tourism businesses. And a sizable number of Atlanta-area residents left town to avoid the congestion of the Olympics, displacing some of the impact of spending by visitors. With few local hotel rooms available for visitors, most lodging dollars went to a broad regional area from Birmingham to Savannah and Chattanooga. The final economic impact of tourists visiting Atlanta for the Games has not been determined, but it was most likely less than the $2 billion forecast by ACOG.[32]

Hoping to take advantage of the publicity surrounding the Olympics, the governor and Georgia Chamber of Commerce officials throughout the state worked together to lure corporate investment to the region. As part of this program, called "Operation Legacy," corporation executives were given tours of the state and tickets to the Games if they showed interest in doing business in Georgia. The budget for the program was $5 million, most of which was contributed by Georgia Power Company. Eighteen companies decided to locate operations in the state as a result of the program, bringing an investment of $130 million and 3,300 new jobs. Following this success, the program was continued into 1997, with state government assuming a larger share of its expenses.

The final economic impact of Operation Legacy and other Olympics-related business investment has not been determined. Since the program was statewide, much of the impact will not be felt in the Atlanta area.[33] It was also difficult to measure the impact of increased spending by private companies. For example, Atlanta-based Coca-Cola may have spent as much as $250 million in marketing-related activities for the Games, including a twelve-acre amusement area beside Olympic Centennial Park, sponsorship of the Olympic torch relay, vending carts throughout the city, and advertising in 135 nations. However, the company has been a long-standing sponsor of the Olympics, so it was not possible to separate the precise amount spent to support the event staged in its hometown.[34]

Neighborhood Impact

Altogether, the 1996 Olympic Games were expected to have an economic impact exceeding $5.1 billion, with most of that amount going to the Atlanta area. This rising economic tide did not lift all boats in the area. The city's low-income residents greeted the Olympics with the fear and suspicion arising from years of neglect and broken promises. During the first ten years of the urban renewal and interstate highway construction programs, the homes of more than 21,000 families were destroyed. These were the homes and neighborhoods of the city's poor, at least 79 percent of whom were African Americans.[35] Even after the abuses of these programs were curbed, construction projects such as the building of the Georgia Dome bulldozed the homes of still more low-income residents, destroying another neighborhood in the process.

The Atlanta Committee for the Olympic Games continued to foster this distrust of business and government with its initial decision concerning the Olympic Stadium in the low-income Summerhill neighborhood. Another conflict between ACOG and the city's low-income residents concerned the decision to close the Techwood Homes public housing project in order to make room for the Olympic Village. Techwood Homes was the oldest public housing project in the nation, and provided its residents with convenient access to downtown. Before the preparations for the Olympics began in 1990, more than five hundred families lived in Techwood Homes, with an occupancy rate of 92.5 percent. During the preparations for the Games, the complex was closed, the tenants relocated, and the complex reduced in size, reopening after the Games as a mixed-use apartment community with only two hundred of the original low-income families given preferential rights to return.[36]

The Atlanta Housing Authority decided to downsize four other housing projects as part of its own "Olympic Legacy Program." The Housing Authority also filed applications for funding with the federal Department of Housing and Urban Development to include nine more housing projects in this program.[37] Another housing project in the Summerhill neighborhood near the Atlanta–Fulton County and Olympic Stadiums was privatized, with the residents moved out of the buildings while the units were renovated. Once the renovations were completed, the former tenants would become owners of their individual units. The privatization of the Martin Street Plaza project was one of the centerpieces in the revitalization plans of the Summerhill neighborhood. During the Games, the Martin Street Plaza apartments were empty and awaiting renovation. With the privatization stalled, residents returned to rental homes in 1998. Martin Street Plaza was one of a total of fifteen Atlanta Housing Authority projects whose tenants were affected by the preparations for the Olympics.[38]

Public housing residents were not the only low-income residents affected by the Olympics. In an effort to spruce up the appearance of areas around the venues, more than 3,400 substandard houses were demolished.[39] Although residents received relocation assistance, most resented the disruptions of moving, since they would not be able to return. One elderly woman living in the Summerhill neighborhood told relocation officials she had only moved three times in her life—first for the construction of I-20, the second time for the construction of Atlanta–Fulton County Stadium, and finally to make way for Olympic Stadium.[40]

These relocations heightened resentment among the city's low-income residents, who received little benefit from Atlanta's hosting of the Games.

Some improvements in housing conditions were made in areas nearest Olympic venues. Prior to the Games, 336 new homes were constructed and 212 houses rehabilitated in six low-income neighborhoods, with another 800 new houses planned. Business leaders also supported efforts by nonprofit groups to rehabilitate several thousand rental properties before the Olympics. More than 80 percent of this investment went to Summerhill, the neighborhood surrounding the Olympic Stadium. Another residential area near the birthplace of Dr. Martin Luther King, Jr., also made substantial progress in restoring 75 older homes and constructing 20 new ones prior to the Games. The restoration of this area was made possible by assistance from a variety of sources, including major financial institutions and federal agencies such as the National Park Service. It was more than coincidence that the Olympic marathon course was routed past the birthplace of Dr. King and through this revitalized neighborhood. Investment in other neighborhoods seemed to be in inverse relation to their distance from Olympic venues. However, having any resources invested in the city's low-income neighborhoods was an improvement. These areas also organized themselves for what will certainly be a long-term process of community building.

Atlanta's low-income neighborhoods also received assistance from the city's designation as a federal Urban Empowerment Zone. With more than six hundred cities competing for six such designations, the selection of Atlanta had much to do with the city's Olympic preparations, as it was the only city selected with a population of less than 500,000.[41] The designation gives the targeted area $250 million in federal tax breaks over a ten-year period, as well as a Social Services Block Grant of $100 million. The Empowerment Zone application process also encourages partnerships between the public and private sectors so that federal grants and tax incentives will be able to leverage business investment in the designated area.

The Atlanta Empowerment Zone application contained commitments of more than $700 million from the private sector. The total investment in the city's designated Empowerment Zone will exceed $1 billion over ten years from the awarding of the designation in December 1994. The area selected for the Empowerment Zone in Atlanta was a collection of census tracts that wrap around the east, south, and west of the central business district. According to the 1990 census, this area had a population of 49,998 and a poverty rate of 57.4 percent.[42]

In the city's Empowerment Zone application, the goal of the program was described as the transformation of one of the most desolate areas of the city into an urban village "visibly and with an urgency established by the onrush of the Olympic Games." The policies identified to achieve this vision ranged from improving the streetscape, reclaiming abandoned properties, and providing more security for area residents, to job training and small business creation.[43]

While the Empowerment Zone programs in cities such as Detroit and Los Angeles moved quickly to implement their objectives, Atlanta's zone was delayed by friction between neighborhood residents and the executive committee of the Empowerment Zone program, which is dominated by members representing business interests. Perhaps this delay was to be expected with so much attention diverted toward other preparations for the Games. It remained to be seen, however, whether the city's business leaders could remain focused on the economic development needs of the city's poorest neighborhoods after the Olympics.

One of the main benefits of the Olympics for the city's low-income residents came from the increased availability of jobs in tourism businesses. The Games created an estimated 22,000 temporary service sector jobs, with 10,000 of these in restaurants and catering businesses. While many low-skill jobs were created, most were at the minimum wage and temporary.[44] These jobs also did not compensate area residents for their inconvenience during the construction of the venue sites and the Olympic Village.

The official agency charged with revitalizing the city's neighborhoods in preparation for the Games was the Corporation for Olympic Development in Atlanta (CODA). CODA's efforts to improve housing in low-income neighborhoods did not receive support from the private sector. The agency also aroused distrust within the neighborhoods, so that CODA's mission was limited to improving public spaces in the city by creating pedestrian corridors near Olympic venues. CODA invested more than $76 million to widen sidewalks, plant trees along streets, and improve lighting and signage on streets in downtown and in several low-income, Olympic-impact neighborhoods. They also improved six parks and supported a public arts program throughout the neighborhoods most affected by the Games.[45] There is little doubt that CODA's public spaces program made the Olympic venues more attractive for visitors during the Games. The improved pedestrian environment should benefit visitors, residents, and people who work in the city. It will take long after the Games to determine if the beautification of the streetscapes will attract additional investment to improve economic conditions in the low-income neighborhoods.

It is difficult to assess the final economic impact of the Olympics on Atlanta. One projection suggests that there will be more than 600,000 new jobs added to the metropolitan area between 1993 and 2005, which would make Atlanta the seventh-largest job market in the United States. More than half of the new jobs are expected to be in the service industry, with tourism businesses representing a large share of these positions. The increase in employment in the area will also increase the metropolitan population to more than 4 million by 2005.[46] The extensive preparations and the expected benefits more than justified the description of the Olympics as a "hallmark" event.

Tourism Businesses and the Games

Besides offering the promise of Southern hospitality, Atlanta's bid for the Olympic Games emphasized the availability of hotels, restaurants, places of entertainment, and convention facilities to host the visitors expected for the event. The athletes and officials for the competitions stayed at the Olympic Village, located between the campus of Georgia Tech and the central business district. Members of the International Olympic Committee, representatives of the various international sports federations, and Olympic committees representing the participating nations stayed at the officially designated "Olympic Family Hotel," the 1,674-room Marriott Marquis. Other official guests and visiting journalists were offered accommodations at center city hotels and apartment facilities at Emory University and other college campuses.[47]

With Atlanta as the headquarters of Holiday Inn Worldwide, the Atlanta Committee for the Olympic Games made the corporation an official Olympic sponsor. Under the arrangement, the hotel chain received publicity by providing rooms for the eighty-four-day torch relay, which began and ended each day at a Holiday Inn. Atlanta Holiday Inns were also part of the hotel network set up by ACOG to accommodate visitors.[48]

By 1990, when the Olympic bid was extended, Atlanta could boast of being one of the top three—after San Francisco and New York—conference and meeting sites in the United States. In 1989, Atlanta had attracted more than 13 million visitors, capping a decade that drew more than 100 million to the city.[49] The 1980s also brought investment in tourism businesses in Atlanta from all over the world, as Swedish, German, Swiss, Japanese, and Saudi corporations financed new hotels. This increased the supply of hotel rooms in the Atlanta metropolitan area to 50,000 by 1990. This number had increased to nearly 60,000 by 1996, providing almost 120,000 beds for the city's Olympic guests. An additional 32,000 beds were also available at nearby hotel and resort properties.[50]

Well in advance of the opening of the 1996 Games, ACOG reserved 80 percent of the hotel capacity in the Atlanta area for the use of VIPs, sponsors, and the media. Most of the rest were booked by travel agents and large tour groups, leaving few rooms in the city for the average person who wished to attend the Games. Most of these people stayed somewhere else in the region and drove as far as three hundred miles to attend the events.[51]

Anticipating that the demand for hotel space would be greater than the supply, ACOG took steps to increase the available accommodations and hold prices down. ACOG and the Atlanta Convention and Visitors Bureau joined with Convention Bureau members to avoid price increases during the Olympic Games. They also encouraged the state legislature to pass a law to restrict price gouging during this and other special events. Under this law, hotel owners, tour operators, and agents were allowed to charge up to 5.7 percent more than their published room rates in 1994. However, with ACOG taking so many available accommodations, the demand for the remainder caused hotel owners to find ways around the law. Typically, a real estate company or other company booked an entire hotel, then subleased the space to tour operators or large corporations seeking hotel space during the Olympics. Under these arrangements, rooms at an Econo Lodge near the airport that normally rented for $49 per night commanded $212. At the Presidential Hotel, which had been closed and vacant for years, rooms were renovated and rented for $400 per night. Other hotels required reservations for dates after the Olympics or packaged room deals to include meals and transportation at inflated prices. This price gouging prompted newspaper editorials and demands from the attorney general and other state officials to bring prices down.[52] In spite of their best efforts, the invisible hand of the market economy dictated that the small number of available rooms were priced at extraordinary levels and that few rooms remained for the average fan.

In order to provide additional accommodations, ACOG also established a home-listing service for homeowners to rent their houses to visitors. ACOG stated its intention to retain 65 percent of the rental fee for this service, and several individual entrepreneurs started private rental services to undercut ACOG's prices. While many homeowners fixed up their houses and hoped for extra income from Olympic visitors, the demand for rented houses was not great. To show that not all hospitality was mercenary, AT&T sponsored a program in which thousands of Atlantans opened their homes to the families of Olympic athletes, who stayed without cost.[53] Most residents did not realize that this tradition of opening private homes to visitors had a long history in Atlanta, dating back to the expositions of 1881, 1887, and 1895.

Developers of tourism businesses were attracted to Atlanta by the anticipated crowd of Olympic visitors. They planned at least three new hotel projects for the downtown area, ranging from an upscale Crowne Plaza Holiday Inn to a budget-priced Hampton Inn.[54] This development was attributable to the Olympics because occupancy rates for hotels in the downtown area were typically lower than those in the airport, Buckhead, and Cumberland Mall areas. However, the convention and tourism business was booming, with overall occupancy rates of 71.7 percent in 1994, the highest in two decades.[55] This upward trend in demand for hotel rooms in the city continued through 1995, with overall occupancy rates increasing to 72.9 percent. The occupancy rate decreased during 1996 to 70.3 percent because of an increase in the number of rooms, with more than 6,000 added since 1994. In spite of the lower occupancy rate, hotel profits rose as a result of a 12.3 percent price increase. Most of this profit was attributable to the Olympics.

Other types of tourism businesses were also busy adding new properties for the Olympics. New restaurants opened on Peachtree Street from downtown to Buckhead. These ranged from Planet Hollywood and several upscale Italian restaurants to a country-and-western imitation of the Hard Rock Café. (A Hard Rock Café was already open downtown on Peachtree Street.) National restaurant chains did not want to miss the opportunity to be in Atlanta during 1996.

While hotels profited from the Games, not all of the city's restaurants shared in the anticipated bonanza. A few restaurants, such as those owned by the Buckhead Life Group, were packed with private parties and tables reserved for corporate groups. Others, anticipating that business during the Games would be slow because local residents would stay home and visitors would not want to take the time for leisurely dining, accepted offers from national sports federations to rent their facilities for the entire Olympics period. Among these was the Mansion Restaurant in Midtown, which was leased with its staff to the German sports federation for six weeks during both the Olympics and the Paralympics which followed. Many other national sports groups also rented restaurants and other spaces for the entire period of the Games, while smaller countries made reservations for occasional private parties.[56] Although these arrangements were profitable for a few restaurants, many others suffered, and at least three of the new restaurants opened for the Olympics by national chains closed after the Games. Most downtown fast-food restaurants and smaller street vendors were busy throughout the Games serving crowds of Olympic visitors who wanted quick and inexpensive meals.

Centennial Olympic Park

Many Atlantans regarded the Olympics as a way to reshape land uses in the city. This was the same approach other Olympic cities had taken, including Barcelona. As the director of planning for Barcelona told his Atlanta counterpart, the Olympics were "Just an excuse to transform the city."[57] Numerous examples suggest that this assessment may be accurate in Atlanta as well. For example, one area of the city had long been of concern to major business and political interests. This was the area of warehouses, a few small businesses, and several shelters for the homeless located just west of downtown between the Omni Hotel and the World Congress Center and the headquarters of the Coca-Cola Company. As recently as 1992, the city's Downtown Development Authority had planned to use tax increment financing to rebuild the area and name it "Techwood Park," after the Techwood Homes housing project that formed one of its borders.

However, independent of these plans, ACOG president Billy Payne had lunch with the chairman of the Coca-Cola Company, Roberto Goizueta. They discussed the fact that the 1996 Olympics would be the centennial of the modern Olympic movement and that the city should have some permanent legacy from the Games. As a result, the two men proposed that the area near downtown and Coca-Cola headquarters be redeveloped as Centennial Olympic Park. With this strong support from the city's business leadership, the new mayor, Bill Campbell, also supported the proposal.[58]

In a complex public-private partnership, the land for the new park was acquired by the state of Georgia with funds contributed by the business community. Financial support for the development of the park also came from individual contributions through a program to sell commemorative bricks used in the sidewalks of the park. The park was located near the state-operated World Congress Center, so its construction and maintenance were the responsibility of the state. This also freed the project from any potential meddling and delay by the city. In this way, property was removed from the tax rolls of the city in order to provide open space for the Olympics and to beautify the area near the corporate headquarters of a major sponsor of the Games.

Another objective of Centennial Olympic Park was to promote the revitalization of the area around it after the Games. The city expressed the hope that upscale housing could be built in the area and that the project would be a catalyst for local economic investment. Most evidence indicates that parks do not necessarily promote economic development around them. This has been true of Woodruff Park in the Five Points area of downtown Atlanta. The creation of the park itself destroyed two city blocks of small businesses, so that the areas near the park have declined in importance due to the smaller number of people remaining downtown to use Woodruff Park. The result has confirmed Jane Jacobs's observation that parks are usually a reflection of their surroundings.[59] If this applies to Centennial Olympic Park, the site is unlikely to fulfill the expectations of its planners in stimulating the revitalization of the area.

Centennial Olympic Park was a popular gathering place for spectators during the Olympics. Unlike the competition venues, there was no price for admission, so thousands of people packed into the park from its opening in the mornings until late at night. ACOG built an Olympic "Fountain of Rings" whose jets of water were choreographed to lights and music. The fountain was also popular with children and adults as a place to splash and cool off during the hot summer days and nights. AT&T constructed a stage and amphitheater in the park for concerts. Other vendors set up a Ferris wheel and other rides near the park. The carnival atmosphere was enhanced as the city leased space in plywood booths to people selling food, Olympic T-shirts, and trading pins.

"Come and Celebrate Our Dream"

Like a typical household in the region, Atlanta fixed itself up for "company coming to town" prior to the Olympics. As part of the South, Atlanta prided itself on its reputation for hospitality and saw the Olympic Games as a way to extend a warm welcome to the world. Thus the Olympics became part of the city's history of hosting major events to lift itself up the next rung on the municipal ladder. This time, though, the city aspired to become a major player on the international stage.[60] Consistent with its aspirations, the city turned once again to slogan making. In 1992, advertising executive Joel Babbit, hired by Mayor Jackson to polish the image of the city, had proposed a new theme, "Atlanta: The Hometown of the American Dream." The local news media as well as national advertising publications criticized this slogan, saying that it was unlikely to boost the image of the city.[61]

After Babbit left his position in city government, a coalition from the mayor's office, the Atlanta Chamber of Commerce, the Convention Bureau, and several local advertising firms undertook to develop a theme for the city. The group developed five slogans which were presented to the public in the *Journal Constitution*. People were asked to vote for their favorite, and all five were resoundingly rejected.[62] After more than a year of additional work, the Atlanta office of the advertising firm McCann-Erickson Worldwide produced a new slogan and commercial featuring Mayor Campbell. The new theme invited the world to Atlanta in order to "Come and Celebrate Our Dream." In a review of the slogan and commercial, the editorial staff of *Advertising Age* said that Atlanta was really dreaming if it thought this ad would work. While conceding that holding the Olympics in a major crossroads of the richest country in the world would attract huge crowds to Atlanta, the magazine maintained that few people were likely to visit the city in order to celebrate someone else's dream.[63] The city had failed once again to manufacture an image that could be sold to the public.

With a rich and complex history as well as an increasingly diverse population, Atlanta's leadership was not able to weave together an image of the city that united its residents while captivating its potential visitors. For the civic leadership, elected officials, and tourism businesses, the Games were an opportunity to attract the attention of the world and to promote the city's growth. This process of manufacturing an image to promote the city was termed "imagineering" in a provocative book on Atlanta by urban anthropologist Charles Rutheiser, written before the Olympics. Rutheiser said that Atlanta's boosters have confused the city with the words and images they have used to describe it. As a result, Atlanta's imagineers have always promoted a wishful vision of how the city might be, rather than a realistic description of actual conditions.[64] Other scholars have observed that images manufactured to promote growth cannot replace long-held cultural values.[65] A theme chosen for a city must speak to all the inhabitants, not just those promoting growth.

It was unfortunate that the efforts to manufacture an image for Atlanta before the Olympics failed. ACOG and the city's hosting of the Games enjoyed strong popular support throughout Atlanta and the state. An ongoing public-opinion poll of a sample of residents of metropolitan Atlanta and the rest of the state was taken at six-month intervals beginning in the summer of 1992. This support for the Games was initially as high as 94 percent of those surveyed, dropping only slightly during the months before the opening of the Olympics. Among the possible benefits of the Games to the state, residents rated increased pride in Georgia higher than the potential economic benefits. This reservoir of goodwill toward the Olympics remained strong in spite of a variety of inconveniences suffered by the public during preparations for the Olympics.[66]

"Let the Games Begin"

After years of preparation, opening ceremonies finally began on Friday evening, July 19, 1996. Olympic Stadium was filled with 83,100 spectators and 172 broadcasters, and television images of the event were beamed around the world. For more than four hours, the ceremony dazzled viewers with more than 5,000 performers in a pageant honoring the one hundredth anniversary of the modern Olympic movement and Southern culture. The regional imagery portrayed in the opening ceremony was the vision of a biracial South in a post–civil rights era. Southern artists as diverse as opera star Jessye Norman and popular singer Gladys Knight performed. White dancers showed off the mountain tradition of clogging, and black fraternity members from Atlanta University Center did step dancing. Also featured were a gospel choir, chrome pickup trucks with football cheerleaders aboard, and a tribute to Dr. Martin Luther King, Jr.

Absent from the pageantry were Confederate flags and other symbols of the era of white supremacy and segregation. The images used in the opening ceremony represented a South unified by symbols of blacks and whites both contributing to a shared culture of athletics, music, and dance. In honoring the local hero, Dr. King, the pageant's organizers suggested that the civil rights movement offered Southerners a chance to replace the images of the Civil War that defeated and divided the South with the images of a region where races learned to live together.[67] Then athletes representing 197 nations marched into the stadium. The torch bearing the Olympic flame, after covering more than 15,000 miles in eighty-four days, arrived and was carried to the rim of the stadium, where former Olympic gold medalist and heavyweight champion Muhammad Ali lit the flame cauldron.

The artistic success of the opening ceremony was followed the next day by a variety of problems. While corporate sponsors and sports federation officials stayed in major downtown hotels, the press corps was scattered throughout the metropolitan area. ACOG arranged to borrow buses and drivers from transit systems across the country to convey journalists to competition sites and other destinations, such as the International Broadcast Center at the Georgia World Congress Center and the Main Press Center in Peachtree Center's Inforum building. The buses proved unreliable and lacked spare parts, while many of the drivers were unfamiliar with the Atlanta area. Through the early days of the Games, busloads of journalists were lost or late arriving at the venues. Some athletes had similar transportation problems getting from the Olympic Village to competition sites.

Members of the press and others were further inconvenienced by a failure of the IBM computer system to provide instant reporting of the results of the athletic competitions. As a major corporate sponsor of the Games, IBM had promised the most timely reporting of data from the competitions in the history of the Olympics. The failure of the system added to the frustrations of journalists from all over the world, and early press reports on the Games carried headlines such as "A Big Mess," "A Disgrace," and "Incredibly Mediocre."[68] While most of their anger was directed toward ACOG and its president, Billy Payne, the journalists also found things to criticize in their host city. They regarded the Games as too commercialized, and described Atlanta as a cheap carnival with so many vendors selling their wares to the public.

In many ways Atlanta did not compare favorably with the host city for the 1992 Olympics, Barcelona, whose history and charm had been augmented with a $10 billion makeover financed by the governments of Spain, Catalonia, and Barcelona. In comparison, Atlanta, a young city of the New South, lacked a rich architectural heritage and offered only a tourism industry focused on the convention trade. Atlanta was not a vacation destination with large numbers of attractions for visitors. It was a city built on transportation and commerce, and its businesslike approach to the task of hosting the Olympics offended many members of the international press corps.

Despite the media criticism, the athletes competed before record crowds of spectators. The traffic management plan arranged by ACOG and the city encouraged most spectators and downtown workers to use the Metropolitan Atlanta Rapid Transit Authority rail system. Operating around the clock, MARTA's trains were packed with riders. Thousands flocked downtown to the venues located nearby, to Centennial Olympic Park, and to other attractions such as Underground Atlanta. Contrary to the dour reports filed by journalists, most spectators seemed to be enjoying the Olympics and Atlanta as they filled the downtown with activity throughout the days and long into the nights.

Early in the morning of July 27, the ninth day of the Olympics, as crowds listened to a concert in Centennial Olympic Park, a pipe bomb exploded, spraying shrapnel that caused two deaths and more than a hundred injuries. The mood of the Games changed as memories were stirred of the terrorist attack on the 1972 Olympics in Munich. Competition continued the next day, but the park remained closed for three days before it reopened with a memorial ceremony led by former mayor Andrew Young. In his speech, Young explained the role of the park, saying, "This has been, in every sense of the word, the people's park. You didn't need a ticket to come here. The whole world was welcome here."[69] The crowds returned, although people faced security checks before being allowed into the park. Two days after the reopening, more than 60,000 people jammed the park to hear Ray Charles sing the state song, "Georgia On My Mind."

Those who came to the Olympics to watch world-class athletic competition were not disappointed. Almost 11,000 athletes representing 197 nations (both record numbers) participated in twenty-six sports. There were dramatic individual and team performances. Athletes from seventy-nine nations won medals at the Games, and while American fans cheered the most for the 101 U.S. medal winners, there was also celebration for the Tongan super-heavyweight boxer who won the first Olympic medal in his nation's history. Women's sports were prominent in the Games, with almost 4,000 female athletes participating. An estimated 8 million spectators attended the competition, including preliminary events held in Washington, D.C., Miami, Orlando, and Birmingham. The Atlanta games attracted a worldwide television audience estimated at 3.5 billion.[70]

As if the athletic events were not enough, the city also hosted a Cultural Olympiad that featured a variety of visual and performing arts. Some of the more important arts events were held before the Games, such as the "Celebrate Africa!" program held in collaboration with the National Black Arts Festival in 1994 and the gathering of Nobel Prize laureates in literature the following year. During the Olympics, Cultural Olympiad activities ranged from folk art installed on sidewalks to the "Rings: Five Passions in World Art" exhibit featured at the High Museum of Art. In competition with athletic events, most performances and exhibits were poorly attended, but tickets to the "Rings" exhibit were sold out during the Games. One hundred masterpieces of world art were chosen to reflect one of the Olympic ideals in the High Museum's display. During the Games, this display helped to draw crowds to the Woodruff Arts Center's other features, such as the Alliance Theater and the performances by the Atlanta Symphony Orchestra. Cultural attractions of a different sort were featured in concerts at Underground Atlanta, Olympic Centennial Park, and the "House of Blues," which opened in the Tabernacle Baptist Church in downtown. Performances at the House of Blues by artists such as Georgia native James Brown were popular throughout the period of the Games, attracting President Clinton and his family to the sold-out auditorium.

Unlike the press corps, visiting dignitaries such as corporate sponsors, IOC and national Olympic officials, and sports federation executives were treated to warm Southern hospitality. Many stayed in the official "Olympic Family Hotel," the Marriott Marquis, and other downtown luxury hotels. ACOG's staff included "guides" assigned to escort VIPs during their stay in Atlanta, as well as uniformed volunteer drivers assigned to motor pools located near hotels and venues.[71] These drivers were part of an army of more than 42,000 volunteers helping to stage the Games.

ACOG recruited volunteers to provide greetings and information, medical assistance, ticket taking, security, translating, help in athletic venues, and a variety of other tasks. Each volunteer was given training, credentials, and a uniform. In spite of the heat and humidity of the Georgia summer, the crowds of visitors, and traffic jams, the legions of blue-, green-, and white-shirted volunteers were given high praise for providing "gobs of Southern hospitality."[72] The volunteers were joined by thousands of temporary ACOG employees to make up an Olympic staff of nearly 90,000.

After seventeen days, the Olympic flame was extinguished in the closing ceremonies as another capacity crowd watched along with television audiences around the world. The event featured a Southern Jamboree of music from the region, highlighted by "Little Richard" Penniman from Macon, Georgia, whose early performances in Atlanta were in the segregated Bailey's 81 Theater on Decatur Street. As the closing ceremony neared its conclusion, the president of the IOC, Juan Antonio Samaranch, addressed the crowd and ACOG's president, Billy Payne. Samaranch said, "Well done, Atlanta!" and added that the Games were "most exceptional."

In closing the four previous Olympic games, Samaranch had proclaimed each of them to be the "best ever." Many Atlantans felt that their own efforts to host the Games were damned by his faint praise. Since guests are expected to show gratitude toward their hosts for hospitality received, the slight given to Billy Payne, ACOG, and Atlanta represented a serious violation of the Southern code of behavior governing hospitality. From Samaranch's perspective, of course, the Games were marred by terrorism as well as organizational problems resulting in the poor treatment of the press. Yet his criticisms and the reaction of Atlantans became part of the city's legacy of the Olympics.[73]

Aftermath

In the weeks after the close of the Games, debate continued over Samaranch's criticisms. President Clinton commended organizers, volunteers, and the spirit of Atlanta's people after the Centennial Park bombing: "As far as I'm concerned, these Atlanta Games were the best. They were the greatest games in the history of the Olympics."[74] Regardless of criticisms and the sensitivity to them, most Americans were favorably impressed by the friendliness and hospitality of the city's residents. According to one national survey, a majority of respondents would give Atlanta a grade of "A" as the host city of the Games. Another survey showed that the Olympics gave the majority of respondents a more favorable image of Atlanta than they held before the Games. Even more of those surveyed said Atlanta was a progressive city and a birthplace of civil rights. Only 28 percent saw the city as racially segregated, and only 16 percent observed that Atlanta has one of the highest crime rates in the United States. As one respondent commented, "The people came across as really friendly, and made it seem like a very inviting place."[75]

Georgia residents experienced a feeling of euphoria during the two weeks following the Games, with more than 94 percent indicating positive feelings about hosting the Olympics. These positive feelings remained high, as 87 percent of those surveyed in the winter 1997 Georgia State Poll felt good about hosting the Games. This unity among Georgians is perhaps one of the most important intangible benefits of the Olympics. They apparently felt good about the opportunity to show off the hospitality of the city and state in hosting the Games. Residents of the state not only attended the Olympics, but many communities participated by hosting the torch run as it moved through Georgia and by welcoming delegations of athletes from other nations as they prepared for the competition. This positive support of Atlanta was possible only because of the shared sentiment of Southern hospitality as the city played host to the world.

Members of the IOC remained critical of the commercialism surrounding the Atlanta games. Dick Pound, the IOC's chief financial officer, briefed an executive committee meeting in Switzerland and said the Atlanta organizers tarnished the image of the Olympics with "junk merchandising." He cited the marketing deals that licensed two official Olympic game shows, *Wheel of*

Fortune and *Jeopardy*, as evidence of damage to the ideals of the Olympics. He also criticized the city for allowing street vendors to turn some areas into bazaars.[76] A month later the criticism continued at the fall meeting of the IOC in Mexico. A special report issued by members of the European Olympic Committee repeated Pound's sentiments about the street vendors and added negative comments about the transportation system and the treatment of Olympic athletes. Housing conditions in the Olympic Village were described as cramped, and the food service "boring and unpalatable." In spite of negative press reports, most spectators did not share the poor impression of the Games. The IOC sponsored its own research, which indicated that the athletic competition was well done, attendance at the Games set an Olympic record, and television coverage throughout the world was well regarded by viewers.[77]

If the impressions of the Centennial Olympics were mixed, the financial report by ACOG was positive. Broadcast revenues were higher than anticipated as the NBC network sold additional advertising. This provided a revenue surplus of less than $10 million for ACOG. The surplus was divided between the IOC, the USOC, and a planned Olympic museum in Centennial Park.[78]

Although no great financial windfall resulted from the Games, many public and private academic institutions in the state received new or improved athletic facilities as well as dormitories. ACOG was also responsible for reconfiguring the Olympic Stadium, which was turned over to the Atlanta–Fulton County Recreation Authority. This group, in turn, leased the stadium for thirty years to the Atlanta Braves. The new stadium was renamed Turner Field in honor of local communications entrepreneur and former Braves owner Ted Turner.[79] The agreement called for the demolition of the old stadium next door and the paving of the area for parking. This proposal generated opposition from a group known as Save Our Stadium, which initiated legal action to stop the demolition of Atlanta–Fulton County Stadium.

There was also conflict over the future of the Olympic flame cauldron located adjacent to Turner Field. The Braves claimed that their contract to maintain the new stadium did not include upkeep on the Olympic flame cauldron. They urged that it be moved to the headquarters of the Coca-Cola Company or the Olympic Centennial Park, although neither wanted it. The artist and residents of the neighborhood around the stadium insisted that the cauldron remain in its location as a memorial to the Games. A compromise was reached that provided an endowment for the Stadium Authority to maintain the cauldron, which was moved one block and turned to face out into the surrounding neighborhood. This preserved one of the major artistic legacies of the Olympics.

Other physical legacies of the Games in the city included new park space and an improved pedestrian environment. CODA's efforts to improve sidewalks, place art in public spaces, and plant trees improved the appearance of downtown and areas adjacent to Olympic venues. The pedestrian corridors in the Atlanta University Center area benefited students and may attract investment in the future. The commercial area of Auburn Avenue also received streetscape improvements in the form of lighting, sidewalks, signage, trees, and public art. This infrastructure investment was also designed to encourage future investment in the area.

The preparations for the Olympics did not provide the catalyst for renewing Atlanta's low-income neighborhoods which some had desired. Mistakes were made as old patterns of decision making from the days of expressway construction and urban renewal were repeated. However, the Olympic preparations and the city's designation as an Empowerment Zone hold the potential for continued involvement in neighborhood revitalization by business leaders. Many low-income neighborhoods also improved their organizational capacity as they developed long-range plans for renewal. These were hopeful legacies of the Games.

There was another significant impact of the Olympics on housing in the city. A goal of Atlanta's business and government leaders since the 1971 Central Area Study had been to attract residents downtown. Efforts such as creating Residential Enterprise Zones met with limited success in attracting the development of housing in what remained largely a central business district. In preparing for the Games, developers could underwrite their costs by renting new apartments and converted lofts. More than five hundred units were renovated from commercial and office buildings in the area around Woodruff Park. The Imperial Hotel on Peachtree Street, which had been vacant for sixteen years, was reopened as single-room-occupancy apartments. In addition to renovated housing, the city leased land next door to city hall for the construction of the 100-unit apartment complex known as City Plaza. The project also featured commercial space on the street level which was occupied by a grocery store, a fast-food business, and a soul food restaurant. These projects marked progress toward city leaders' goal of having a twenty-four-hour population downtown. This would respond to criticisms raised by travel writer Arthur Frommer and others who suggested that downtown Atlanta was without life after dark.

In spite of glitches, Atlanta proved it could host a mega-event such as the Olympics. Less than two weeks after the close of the Games, Atlanta staged the Paralympic Games, in which more than 3,500 disabled athletes from 120 nations competed. The event demonstrated that Atlanta's streets and athletic venues were accessible to those with disabilities and may also contribute to the city's reputation as a convention center. The Chamber of Commerce established the Atlanta Sports Council to build upon the international exposure associated with the Olympics. Leaders of the council seek to associate Atlanta with the business of sports to attract athletic events, sports associations, and sporting goods businesses. In November 1996 the Sports Council announced that Atlanta would host the National Football League's Super Bowl in 2000 and the NCAA championship games for men's basketball in 2002.[80] The Adidas Company decided to continue using its space rented for the Olympics as a regional sales and distribution facility. In addition, the Super Show, sponsored by the Sporting Goods Manufacturing Association, continues to be one of the largest annual conventions in the city, with nearly 100,000 attending each February. The work of the Sports Council not only continues as a legacy of the Olympics, but is also another example of Atlanta's tourism businesses promoting economic growth.

While the Chamber of Commerce has focused on building on the Olympics to associate Atlanta with the business of sports, the Convention Bureau has sought to draw increased numbers of international visitors to the city. In a special promotional effort, the bureau targeted visitors from the United Kingdom, Germany, and Japan in advertisements featuring the Olympic Centennial Park and Stadium, new hotels, and downtown's improved streets and sidewalks made safer by the presence of uniformed "Atlanta Ambassadors." In addition to downtown, the promotion highlighted Hartsfield International Airport as the gateway to the Southeast. Critics of the program argued that the city lacked the cultural attractions to be a destination for international visitors.[81] As a response the Convention Bureau announced a bus service to link downtown hotels with major cultural and entertainment centers such as the Woodruff Arts Center, the Botanical Garden, the Carter Center, Auburn Avenue, and Underground Atlanta. This may be an acknowledgment that "cultural tourism" is an important method for cities to attract visitors.

The results of the Cultural Olympiad were disappointing to most supporters of the arts in Atlanta. Only the exhibits at the Atlanta History Center in Buckhead and the Woodruff Arts Center drew large audiences during the Olympics. Both institutions planned programs that would build support after the Games. For example, the High Museum of Art followed the popular "Rings: Five Passions in World Art" exhibit with two shows mounted in collaboration with New York's Museum of Modern Art. These were designed to expand the High Museum's role as a major national museum that draws audiences from local, regional, national, and, increasingly, international tourists.[82] Perhaps the new interest in promoting the arts to visitors will generate additional support for the other city's cultural institutions.

The Legacy of the Games

There is no doubt that hosting the 1996 Summer Olympic Games had a profound impact upon Atlanta. During the two weeks of the Games, an estimated 2 million people visited the city. With worldwide attention focused on Atlanta, more than 19 million visitors came to the city during 1996.[83] Some of the attention was beneficial to local tourism businesses, to the city's reputation as a place for investment, and to the growing international image of Atlanta. However, not all of the publicity was favorable. The city's controversial vending program turned the renovated streets and sidewalks into a bazaar, and ACOG's use of corporate sponsors for the Games contributed to the impression of commercialism which was denounced by the IOC and visiting journalists. The IOC reacted by proposing changes in the way future Olympic games are financed with less dependence upon corporate sponsorships, making it difficult for other U.S. cities to host the Games.

The pipe bomb that exploded in Centennial Olympic Park left a lasting imprint on the 1996 Games. Following the bombings of the World Trade Center in New York and the federal office building in Oklahoma City, the Park bombing showed that terrorism was no longer confined to cities in other parts of the world, but could be expected with little or no warning anywhere crowds gather. Although the motive for the Park bombing remains unclear, subsequent bombings in a family planning clinic and a lesbian bar in Atlanta suggest that urban terrorism is likely to continue.[84] This will affect how Atlanta and other cities plan for large events in the future.

While many hotels and some restaurants profited from the Olympics, many amusements did not. With the discretionary spending of many residents and visitors going toward Olympic tickets and souvenirs, attendance at many other types of amusements, such as concerts, theme parks, and sporting events, suffered throughout the year. The Lakewood Amphitheatre lost money in 1996 as it hosted fewer concerts and had lower attendance. Theme parks such as Six Flags Over Georgia and Whitewater Park did not attract as many patrons during the summer. The Atlanta Braves, which returned to the World Series in 1996, failed to sell out most of their games during the season. Even Stone Mountain Park, which served as the site of Olympic competition in archery, cycling, and tennis, suffered a 15 percent drop in attendance for the year and a substantial drop in revenues.[85] Although losses were expected to be temporary, they indicate that the financial benefits of the Olympics were not shared by all tourism businesses.

Because Atlanta's residents did not share equally in the benefits of the Games, fundamental questions about the nature and function of the city itself were raised. Is the city a product to be sold to visitors to the Games or to potential investors? Or, is the city a place to live and to be enjoyed by its residents and not treated as a commodity?[86] If the hosting of the Olympics in Atlanta was an attempt to reshape the city, what were the objectives of this new form? An urban geographer has noted that this type of reorganization of urban space is a mechanism for attracting capital and upper-income people to reclaim space for conspicuous consumption celebrating commodities rather than civic values. The newly built environment of the city becomes the centerpiece of "urban spectacle and display" and crowds out the routine aspect of daily life for urban residents.[87] In this sense the Olympics may be viewed as an economic development strategy designed to reshape the city and make it more attractive for international investment.

The hosting of the Olympics had little impact on the longstanding problems of poverty, unemployment, crime, and poor housing which affect large numbers of Atlanta's residents. For most people in the city's low-income neighborhoods, preparations for the Games simply meant more crowding and congestion as well as a few more low-skill, low-wage jobs in tourism businesses. Many residents also suffered the loss of the "use value" of their neighborhoods.[88] Unfortunately, these costs of Atlanta's pro-growth hospitality agenda were usually overlooked in the midst of the boosterism promoting the Olympics and Atlanta.

Throughout most of its history, the symbols of the South were tied to the Confederacy, but the Olympics offered an opportunity to celebrate a different public image of the region. The Southern symbols displayed in such events as the opening and closing ceremonies reflected the merger of cultures from Western Europe and Africa in a post-segregation South. Cultural historian Charles Reagan Wilson would argue that the South was struggling to put its best ideals into new symbols of a culture that managed to overcome legally imposed racial segregation. Perhaps this was what ACOG's chairman, former mayor Andrew Young, meant when asked before the Games if Atlanta would be ready for the Olympics. He answered that the *city* would be ready, but the real challenge was whether the *people* would be ready for the Games.[89] The public symbols used for the Games may have been ahead of the reality of residents' willingness to overcome a divided past.

Atlanta's efforts to host the Olympics reflected its leaders' hopes that after the Games more people the world over would want to come, visit, and do business in the city. Whether or not the world responds will depend upon continued hard work and promotionalism which have formed the "Atlanta Spirit" for so long.[90]

10

Conclusions

IN HIS TALE OF AN UNUSUAL murder in Savannah, *Midnight in the Garden of Good and Evil,* John Berendt tells a version of a story about Georgia's cities which says much about the character of these places. He writes that in Savannah, the first question a person asks a stranger is "What would you like to drink?" In Macon, the first question is "Where do you go to church?" In Augusta, the question is "What was your grandmother's maiden name?" But in Atlanta, the first question asked of a stranger is "What is your business?"[1] This reputation as a place for business is well established, not only within the state, but increasingly around the world.

As a city, Atlanta has come a long way in a short time. From its modest beginnings as a railroad town, the residents have used a unique combination of hard work, boosterism, and hospitality to build a metropolitan area of more than 3 million people. In this process of growth, Atlanta has become known as an ideal place for business. In 1995, *Fortune* magazine ranked Atlanta among the top locations for business in the United States and also seventh among cities in the world. Atlanta trailed only San Francisco among U.S. cities as a place for business, owing to its "gung-ho business environment," the conveniences of Hartsfield International Airport, and the "golden marketing opportunity" offered by the 1996 Summer Olympic Games. Another important factor that makes Atlanta attractive is its reputation as a great place to live. This high quality of life was noted as a major attraction for businesses seeking to relocate.[2] Such recognition is a source of pride for local public officials as well as business leaders.

Atlanta's image as a good place for business has been carefully cultivated over a long period of time. When the city was young, boosters initially sought rail lines to attract additional commerce and travelers. To promote Atlanta as a market and shipping point for the commodities of the area, the city held agricultural fairs and expositions. After the devastation of the Civil War, Atlanta residents turned their attention to efforts to attract Northern capital for manufacturing. Money for investment has always been in short supply in Atlanta, and as a young city in a poor region, Atlanta's need for capital helped the city embrace the ideals of the New South movement.[3] Here boosterism was aimed at attracting Northern investors as the city put aside the bitterness of sectional strife and sought to move away from dependence upon agriculture toward a future where commerce and manufacturing would bring prosperity to the city and the South.

With the 1895 Cotton States and International Exposition, Atlanta's leaders attempted to showcase the attractions of the city and region for potential investors. The city of fewer than 100,000 residents dared to stage the exposition in the midst of a recession with the aim of attracting the attention of the nation. This promotional activity became part of a strongly rooted pattern of boosterism which has been used throughout Atlanta's history to attract growth. These efforts to promote Atlanta were part of the culture of the Old South and were tied to an agricultural system in the region that was dependent on Northern capital. After the Civil War, the New South booster ethic helped to restore a sense of self-esteem to a defeated region. This "Atlanta Spirit" was not antagonistic to the history and culture of the South, but was always an important part of the region where the "old forms" were used in service to the new.

Early in the twentieth century, business and political leaders promoted the city as a place for conventions. The Chamber of

Commerce established a Convention Bureau to recruit a variety of organizations to hold meetings in the city. Business leaders also promoted Atlanta as a site for regional offices during the Forward Atlanta campaign. This program succeeded in attracting investment and making Atlanta a leading regional city. In spite of the Great Depression, Atlanta was able to recover because of the investments made by the federal government which provided jobs building roads, bridges, sewers, and public buildings. World War II provided additional investment to help the city grow as the home of military bases and defense industry contractors. The partnership between business leaders and local public officials remained in place after the war as Atlanta continued its role as a transportation hub both for cars and trucks on the highways and for planes at the airport. The federal government also provided financial support through the interstate highway funds as well as money for slum clearance through the urban renewal program.

Atlanta's mayors used these two federal programs to expand the area of downtown and to provide a buffer between the central business district and low-income African-American neighborhoods. Much of the land cleared through urban renewal was used for tourism businesses and infrastructure to support a growing downtown convention business. The expressway construction and urban renewal programs in Atlanta were part of an economic development strategy based on hospitality businesses supported by the private- and public-sector partnership. Working together with the regional cultural value of hospitality as the glue, Atlanta's elected public officials and business leaders developed the facilities for meetings, amusements such as Underground Atlanta, sports facilities, and an array of tourism businesses ranging from dramatic hotels to restaurants, bars, and clubs.

The accomplishments of Atlanta's public-private partnership have been impressive. The city is among the top places for conventions and annually hosts meetings for both large and small groups. Atlanta has also demonstrated the ability to prepare for and host major events such as the Democratic National Convention and the Super Bowl. This partnership also assisted the city in its successful bid to host the 1996 Olympic Games. The cooperation between business and government continued as the city prepared for the 1996 Games. The investment for this event by the Atlanta Committee for the Olympic Games, all levels of government, and the private sector exceeded $2.5 billion. As a result, Atlanta led the nation in job growth from 1992 through 1995. This expansion in employment also pushed the population of the metropolitan area to an estimated 3.4 million people.[4]

The smooth functioning between business and government in Atlanta has been described as a "regime,"[5] and Atlanta's governing regime has shown itself capable of executing complex and often controversial projects. For instance, in 1997 an agreement was made to keep the Atlanta Hawks basketball team playing in a downtown location by providing a new arena to replace the Omni. The location of the new facility, its financing, and construction were coordinated by city government working closely with the team's owner, Turner Broadcasting Corporation.[6]

Atlanta's tourism businesses have clearly benefited from this public-private partnership. The willingness of state, county, and city governments to provide infrastructure for the convention business has made the city an attractive place for private-sector investment. As a result, in 1998 the metropolitan area had over 66,000 hotel and motel rooms.[7] The prospect of Olympic visitors crowded into the city also encouraged restaurant investment as existing restaurants refurbished and national chains scrambled to add Atlanta locations. The overall occupancy rate for hotels in the metropolitan area dropped slightly during 1996 to an estimated level of 70.3 percent due to the adding of more than 6,000 new rooms since 1994.[8] The prices charged for hotel rooms also rose during 1996, making the year profitable for hotel owners. However, with so many new hotels constructed for the Olympics, occupancy rates dropped to 64.8 percent in 1997, causing financial problems for many of these tourism businesses. (A similar cycle of lower hotel occupancy rates followed the building boom of the 1970s and early 1980s.) The solution to this problem may be aggressive recruitment of new types of conventions in the city to fill hotels, restaurants, and bars. It is uncertain whether Atlanta's efforts to attract international visitors and "cultural tourism" will succeed in making the city a more attractive destination. There is also considerable concern over the future of attractions like Underground Atlanta. In 1997 there were calls for additional public-sector investments to encourage the development of other amenities in the area of Underground, including an aquarium with an estimated construction cost of $75 million.

While Atlanta's public-private partnership has produced growth for the metropolitan area and its tourism businesses, the benefits of this economic growth have not been shared by all. A combination of political, economic, and racial issues has prevented the City of Atlanta from expanding its size since 1952, and as a result the central city has not shared in the population growth that has taken place in the suburbs. According to the 1990 census, the City of Atlanta had fewer than 400,000 residents, while nearly 2.4 million lived in the surrounding suburbs.[9] This made Atlanta only the thirty-seventh-largest city in the United States, but the ninth-largest metropolitan area.

Residents of the city were also substantially different from those in the suburbs. In 1990 the central city was 67.1 percent African-American, whereas the metropolitan area as a whole was 71.3 percent white. The concentration of blacks in Atlanta's central city was second only to Detroit among the nation's cities. Residents of the central city were also poorer than those in the suburbs, with more than 27 percent living in poverty—the fifth-highest percentage in the country. The poverty rate for the Atlanta metropolitan area as a whole, on the other hand, was 10.1 percent. The City of Atlanta also had among the highest per capita rates for serious crimes of any city in the country.[10] Finally, in 1994 the median income for households in the central city was $22,275, while the median income for the entire metropolitan area was $35,606.[11]

These disparities between the central city and its suburbs are a source of concern among urban scholars. Numerous observers have pointed out that central cities and the suburban areas that surround them are interdependent parts of a regional economic area. They share the same land and labor markets, although the size of the central city relative to its suburbs varies among states and regions. Atlanta is one of the metropolitan areas where the suburbs are unusually healthy while the central city is unusually weak.[12] While this condition may not cause immediate problems, some observers feel that the downward pull of a declining central city may lead to long-term regional attrition.[13]

Although Atlanta has pursued the convention business as a part of its economic development since early in the twentieth century, tourism businesses were recognized in the city's official planning in the late 1960s as central to the future of the downtown area. This change was part of a national trend to reshape downtown areas for tourism which has been described by Sharon Zukin and Charles Rutheiser.[14] Zukin described the transformation of central cities from the manufacturing of material things to the production of culture in what she termed the "symbolic economy." Land use in downtown areas has shifted from manufacturing to the production of more abstract commodities such as stocks and bonds, real estate, and tourism.[15] Zukin's book *Loft Living* described the importance of the arts in shaping land use in cities as studios, galleries, restaurants, and other cultural activities move into former manufacturing sites.[16] Both Zukin and Rutheiser looked to the Walt Disney Corporation (and Disney World) as the symbol of the service-oriented economy of cities based on entertainment and the manipulation of images to control urban space. Zukin's works examine New York City as it was transformed into a culture capital, while Rutheiser focused on Atlanta as it prepared for the Olympic Games. Both regard the transformation of central cities as beneficial to large corporations that are able to control the reorganization of space for their own purposes at the expense of lower-class interests.[17]

Rutheiser draws upon Zukin's ideas to describe the transformation in land use that has taken place in Atlanta. The city's downtown has been converted from an area that included large numbers of low-income residents and small businesses into a major center for conventions and tourism by massive public and private investments in tourism businesses and their infrastructure.

The transformation created large numbers of jobs for many central city residents who lacked the skills and education to enter other types of employment; however, many of these jobs paid little and offered few opportunities for advancement. This contributed to the increasing disparities between wage levels of central city and suburban residents. Large numbers of poor, predominantly black residents of the central city have seen their economic conditions deteriorate, while prosperity increased for most suburban residents. Yet few other options were available for the economic development of the central city.

With Atlanta's long tradition of providing hospitality to visitors, the economic development strategy that emphasized tourism businesses was congruent with the cultural values of most of the population. Perhaps this is why there has been relatively little opposition to establishing the downtown area as a tourist center. Any inconveniences suffered by Atlanta residents tend to be overlooked as part of the cultural norm of hospitality. This is different from the cultural values of the Maryland Eastern Shore communities examined by political scientist Meredith Ramsay. When the small town of Crisfield had the opportunity to build hotels and other tourism amenities as an economic development strategy, the community rejected the prospect of new jobs in favor of retaining their traditional way of life. Their maritime economy provided for the subsistence of the many poor residents of Crisfield, who were able to defeat the development proposals of the local Chamber of Commerce.[18] In contrast, Atlantans shared a widespread agreement on the cultural value of hospitality, as well as a local government with a long history of cooperation with business leaders to promote economic development through investment in tourism businesses. This consensus on hospitality led to policy choices that built upon Atlanta's role as a transportation center. As a consequence, the commercial application of hospitality became one of the most important segments of the local economy, providing jobs for thousands of local residents.

In spite of the availability of large numbers of jobs in tourism businesses, many inner city residents face the frustrations of poor economic conditions. When combined with a regional culture that has been described by John Shelton Reed and others as willing to accept certain types of violence, the central city is a breeding place for crime.[19] While much of this criminal activity is directed against other inner-city residents who are acquaintances and family members, the fear of crime and the perception that the central city is unsafe are constant threats to the city's tourism businesses. The code words "inner-city crime" are used to emphasize racial differences between the largely white suburbs and the majority black central city.

The race and class differences between city and suburban residents pose many problems for cooperation between the two areas. For instance, any suggestions for metropolitan governance are rejected by suburban white politicians, who want little to do with the City of Atlanta, and by black political leaders in the central city, who fear the loss of their electoral strength in a consolidated government. As a consequence, problems affecting the metropolitan area as a whole, such as transportation, air quality, water supply, and sewage treatment, are difficult for the region to address. For example, inadequate transportation increases the economic isolation of low-income central city residents who are unable to commute to the suburban areas where new jobs are likely to be found.

In numerous cases the relatively small population of the central city has had to support expenditures that benefit the entire metropolitan area. Decisions to rebuild Underground Atlanta or to construct the new arena for the Atlanta Hawks placed additional financial burdens on the limited resources of the city, but provided amenities enjoyed by the residents of the entire area. Even solutions such as rental car taxes and hotel occupancy taxes, which transfer most of the cost burden to visitors, also shift resources away from other opportunities for economic development. These deferred opportunities further restrict the ability of the central city to address the needs of its poorest residents.

In spite of this, Atlanta and its suburbs have invested heavily in tourism businesses and the infrastructure required to support these businesses. Discussion is needed regarding policy options that would guide the future of these businesses and the public investments necessary for their support. For instance, if the central city cannot continue to support investments in additional amenities for hospitality businesses, should those investments automatically move toward the suburbs? This was evident in the agreement for the new home of the Atlanta Hawks. The city's political leaders felt compelled to provide the new facility, knowing that their failure to do so would result in the relocation of the team to the suburbs.

Questions also need to be addressed concerning the extent of public investment in tourism business infrastructure. Should the city use its limited debt capacity to finance new amenities for the hospitality businesses? Even new revenue streams that affect visitors reduce the funds available for other types of investments. There is a delicate balance between the needs of tourism businesses for an attractive city with appropriate amenities and the needs of local residents. Occasionally, these two sets of needs overlap. For example, a new seven-day, twenty-four-hour day care facility called Atlanta's Inn for Children opened in 1997 to provide care for the children of downtown hotel employees. The facility is owned by a nonprofit organization and supported by several of the area hotels. The Inn for Children solves a basic need for the employees, many of whom are low-income city residents, for day care as an additional benefit of their employment. It also responds to parents' needs through offering courses such as English as a Second Language. By increasing employee morale and reducing staff turnover, the day care facility should make tourism business employment more attractive to city residents. Atlanta's Inn for Children has already come to be regarded as a model facility, and plans are under way to duplicate it in other cities.

Another approach to striking a balance between the needs of central city residents and tourism businesses lies in the nature of future hospitality-related amenities. Rather than focus future policies on the large-scale investments of the past, there might be greater benefit to both existing tourism businesses and city residents by investing in smaller projects. For example, the Martin Luther King, Jr., historic site on Auburn Avenue currently attracts more than 3 million visitors per year. These visitors have little to see and do in the area besides the National Park Service's tour of Dr. King's nearby birth home and the visitors center. Most come by bus and leave the area having had little contact with the neighborhood. If the Auburn Avenue commercial area between the burial site and downtown were redeveloped and small business investment encouraged, establishments providing food, entertainment, and souvenirs could enhance the area and provide additional tourism amenities for the city. These small businesses would also provide employment opportunities for city residents. The area does not need to be completely redeveloped as a black-themed tourist attraction. Instead, it would continue to be a neighborhood commercial area serving the needs of nearby residents, students, and downtown workers as well as visitors.

Some of the work to revitalize the area is under way. Much of the residential area near the birthplace of Dr. King was rehabilitated by the Historic District Development Corporation prior to the Olympics. Also, in preparation for the Games, the Committee for Olympic Development in Atlanta worked to improve the streetscape on the commercial section of Auburn Avenue by widening the sidewalks, planting trees, and improving the lighting. Small business development loans are needed to help reopen the shops on the street. The redevelopment of the Auburn Avenue commercial area would provide a unique amenity for Atlanta's other hospitality businesses. It could emphasize the heritage of Auburn Avenue as an important center for African-American business and culture as well as the connection of the area to the history of the civil rights movement.

Unfortunately, one of Atlanta's greatest shortcomings is its residents' inability to deal with their past. The premiere of the movie version of *Gone with the Wind* identified Atlanta in the minds of many visitors with the Old South with its images of plantations and slavery. These aspects of the city's history were at odds with its image as a progressive place for business. More recently, controversy focused on the state flag, which since 1956 has featured the Confederate battle flag. Before the Olympics, Governor Zell Miller attempted to have the flag changed, arousing the anger of many whites in the state who wanted to retain this symbol of the Confederacy. Atlanta's public officials saw the flag as divisive and insulting to African-Americans. City leaders were disappointed when the general assembly rejected Miller's proposal for change, and they refused to fly the state flag on city property.

Many feared that the culture and images of the South would be kept hidden during the Olympics.[20] However, in both the opening and closing ceremonies, Southern cultural themes were used in the music, dance, and pageantry of the events. Former mayor Andrew Young said the Olympics in Atlanta would be "a celebration of the South, but not a celebration of Southern stereotypes." One of those who was uncertain how the culture of the South would be featured during the Olympics was sociologist John Shelton Reed. After the opening ceremony, Reed noted that Southern culture was very much in evidence, but commented, "New Orleans would have had more fun, Charleston would have had more class and Nashville would have had better music, but it wasn't bad for Atlanta."[21] Perhaps the prominence of Southern culture in the Olympics will enable Atlantans to begin dealing more openly with their heritage, recognizing that the history of the region does not have to be something that divides people, but is to be shared in common.

Although Atlantans have often expressed their desire to be like New York or Chicago, their city has been a role model for others in the region. Atlanta's growth and accomplishments have occasioned envy and sometimes hostility from other cities in the South. As literature professor Fred Hobson observed, "Atlanta has been the Southern City on a Hill, the city to emulate. Birmingham and Charlotte and . . . Nashville have wanted nothing more than to equal it in size, power, and sophistication."[22] These cities and others share Atlanta's dilemma over how to deal with the heritage of the South. For instance, the conflict over the public display of the Confederate battle flag has continued in Alabama, South Carolina, Kentucky, and even Maryland.

There is, however, more to the cultural heritage of the South than the symbols of the Confederacy. Scholars have sought for many years to determine what is distinctive about the region. For some it was a way of life based on agriculture, for others the distinctiveness of the South was due to white supremacy.[23] Fundamental changes in the South make these perspectives out-of-date, as the residents of the South seem more like other Americans with a majority living in urban areas and the numbers of those who farm declining to a small percentage. Despite problems that remain, the South has desegregated and seems to have no more difficulty with the relations between races than other parts of the nation.

Regardless of these and many other changes that have made cities like Atlanta appear more like those elsewhere, there remains something distinctive about the South. This difference is found in the culture of the region. The culture of a majority of Atlanta's residents has been shaped in unique ways by a core of shared meanings, understandings, and ways of doing things that are common to the region. One sociologist who has studied the South argues that white Southerners can be regarded as an ethnic group with large and persistent cultural differences between them and other Americans. Even though there are differences, many of the same cultural traits are shared by African-Americans in the South. Two of every three residents of the region live in an urban area, but most of these are only one generation removed from Southern farmlands.[24] John Shelton Reed has summarized this shared cultural experience of the South: "People who eat grits, listen to country music, follow stock car racing, support corporal punishment in the schools, hunt 'possum, go to Baptist churches, and prefer bourbon to scotch (if they drink at all) are likely to be Southerners. It isn't necessary that all or even most Southerners do these things, or that other people do not do them; if Southerners just do them more often than other Americans, we can use them to locate the South."[25] As long as these shared patterns of belief and behavior persist, there will be something distinctive about the cities of the South such as Atlanta.

This distinctiveness is not necessarily expressed in the structures that make up the city. Atlanta has most often been willing to tear down its older buildings to make way for the new, leaving

little architectural heritage that could be distinguished as Southern. Rather, the distinctive Southern culture of Atlanta resides
in its people. This culture is observable in the food, speech, music, and manners of most Atlantans. Despite the large number of
residents who were born elsewhere and relocated to the Atlanta
area, most still share the culture of the region. In a metropolitan
area of 2,833,511 residents in 1990, more than 76 percent were
born in the South, with a majority of the total population coming from Georgia.[26] These residents share the common cultural
experience of the region, which is only intensified as it comes
in contact with others who migrate to the city from outside the
South.

Among the traits held in common among the people of the
South are the manners with which folks treat one another. The
code of manners is a part of the friendliness that makes up Southern hospitality. It expresses itself in the graciousness with which
strangers are welcomed and the cordial greeting given when one
person is introduced to another. Above all, the hospitality of the
South requires that the guest is made to feel at ease. This is part
of a code of honor that has long been and continues to be characteristic of the South.[27] In a recent public-opinion poll, 91 percent of Southerners and 90 percent of non-Southerners identified the basic friendliness of the people of the South as the most
important characteristic of the area.[28] The attribute of friendliness was recognized in another national survey that ranked the
people of Atlanta as the most friendly among fifteen major cities.
A less scientific report found Atlanta to be one of six of the region's cities on the list of "most polite" cities in the United States.
According to etiquette expert Marjabelle Young Stewart, "The
South would rather give up food than manners."[29]

The cultural value of hospitality has obvious commercial importance. From the time of Atlanta's first boardinghouse, the
hospitality of the South has been an important component of the
business of welcoming people to the city. Yet there has been little
reflection upon this culture which provides the shared pattern
of beliefs and behavior that characterize the people of Atlanta.
For example, the city's business and political leaders have for

many years promoted growth through an economic development strategy based on tourism. In spite of this, there is little to distinguish the tourist attractions of Atlanta from those of other cities. After the Olympics, city leaders discussed the need to add an aquarium as another attraction to the area near Underground Atlanta, yet many other places already have festival markets such as Underground and aquariums as well. This would simply add to the homogenization of the tourist experience in Atlanta as the same amenities are available in other localities. Instead, the city ought to encourage the development of amenities that will emphasize the culture of the South. The focus could transcend the divisive issues of slavery and the Confederacy, concentrating on the music, food, and folk culture of Southern blacks and whites. By drawing upon its Southern cultural heritage, Atlanta would be emphasizing the traits that help distinguish the city from other places.

Before this change can be made, Atlantans need a better understanding of both their history and their culture. This might begin with the importance of Southern hospitality in the history of Atlanta and the South. While the tradition of hospitality has remained strong, the norms of behavior associated with Southern hospitality have not remained fixed over time. Throughout Atlanta's history, patterns of hospitality have been influenced by issues of race, ethnicity, gender, and class. For example, black tourism business employees were allowed to serve whites, but during most of the nineteenth century, African-Americans were excluded by custom, and later by law, from being customers in the city's hotels and restaurants. As a result, blacks developed a segregated group of tourism businesses. After the race riot of 1906, most of these businesses were concentrated in separate locations such as the famous "Sweet Auburn" Avenue, where a variety of hotels, restaurants, and amusements were available for African Americans. These segregated hospitality businesses also hosted conventions held for black visitors to the city and promoted these events with a fervor which matched the boosterism of white business leaders. Hospitality segregated by race lasted until the student sit-ins and other demonstrations of the 1960s and the passage of the public accommodations section of the 1964 Civil Rights Act led to changes in this pattern of Southern behavior. Since 1964, many of these black-owned tourism businesses closed as African-Americans no longer stayed in hotels or ate in restaurants restricted to their race.

Ethnicity also affected Southern hospitality in Atlanta. During the nineteenth century, Jews were welcomed to the city as a sign of prosperity and progress. As the number of Jewish immigrants increased after 1900, attitudes changed until the tragedy of the arrest, trial, and lynching of Leo Frank in 1915. Prejudice against Jews remained strong throughout all levels of Atlanta society. Even those Jewish residents who could afford to do so were not permitted to join the city's exclusive private clubs, which accepted only white gentile males into membership. The city's well-to-do Jewish citizens responded by forming their own private clubs which continue to exist today.

Throughout much of its history, Atlanta's culture has been defined by its black and white residents. Since 1980, however, new immigrants are changing the biracial makeup of the city.[30] The challenges of multiculturalism raised by these largely Hispanic and Asian immigrants are many. This increased diversity supports the claims of city leaders that Atlanta is becoming an international city. There is greater variety in the ethnic restaurants available in the city, especially in areas like the Buford Highway corridor. Many of these newly arrived immigrants are also eager for jobs such as washing dishes and cleaning rooms in the city's tourism businesses. Asians and Hispanics have become an important source of labor for these businesses. Although the Hispanic and Asian immigrants comprised less than 5 percent of the population in 1990, they represent a challenge to the culture of a region that has traditionally been defined in terms of black and white.

Southern culture has also affected the role of women in relation to tourism businesses. In the Old South, male plantation owners were expected to control the lives of others in the household, while women—both wives and slaves—performed the work required for the hospitality that was extended to guests. This pattern was replicated in Atlanta's hotels, where female slaves cooked and cleaned for white customers, a majority of whom were male. Since the Civil War, these hospitality businesses have continued to provide employment for large numbers of African-American women in low-paying jobs.

The norms of hospitality also involved issues of class, even though these frequently overlapped with race and ethnicity. Beginning in 1886, prohibition laws made the sale of liquor by the drink illegal in Atlanta. The laws were justified by the desire to restrict sales of alcohol to working-class whites and blacks. Private clubs continued to serve drinks to those who could afford membership, but with bars and saloons closed, many others turned to illegal "moonshine" whiskey, which was readily available but whose purity was unregulated. Class issues also influenced where visitors to the city stayed. During the first two decades of the twentieth century, new hotels opened for the upper-class travelers who could afford the carriage ride from the railroad station. Commercial travelers and workers of ordinary means generally stayed in hotels located closer to the noise and smoke of the railroad tracks.

Issues of race, ethnicity, and class converged in 1915 with the revival of the Ku Klux Klan in Atlanta. The city's Klan members were part of a large national movement whose members were usually working-class white men. Throughout most of the 1920s and 1930s, Atlanta's business and political leaders gave their tacit approval to the Klan, as they were generally sympathetic to its message of white supremacy and hatred of Jews and Catholics. With Atlanta as the headquarters for the Klan, there was money to be made from the group's business operations and the frequent national meetings held in the city. After the depression era, the Klan declined in popularity in Atlanta and the South, but did not disappear. However, for many years the Klan was a part of Atlanta's history, influencing Southern hospitality in the city.

Class issues have also played a role in the patronage of the arts in Atlanta. For example, wealthy patrons in 1910 began support for the annual visits of the Metropolitan Opera Company to the city. The city's elite raised funds to sponsor the event, and the extravagance of those who turned out for the opera festival made it an opportunity to showcase the wealth of the New South city.

In spite of changes in behavior over time, the norm of hospitality has remained a cultural value firmly rooted in most residents of Atlanta and the South. The city's Olympic organizers used the appeal of Southern hospitality to bid for the Games as well as to host the mega-event. Local residents showed their hospitality as more than 40,000 volunteered to help stage the event. Many Atlantans rushed to defend Billy Payne and the Atlanta Committee for the Olympic Games as they felt insulted by what was regarded as a display of bad manners by President Samaranch of the International Olympics Committee and others who criticized their hosts. Despite the transportation, communications, and other organizational problems, as well as the trauma of the Centennial Olympic Park bombing, most who visited the city during the Olympics were impressed with the friendly welcome. Atlantans once again showed their Southern hospitality, and this time they captured the attention of the world.

What role will Southern hospitality play in Atlanta's future? Its commercial application in tourism businesses will remain a significant part of the growth of the metropolitan area. These businesses must remain connected to the culture of the South; otherwise, the city and its people will lose much of what makes them distinctive.

NOTES

Introduction

1. Lewis Mumford, *The Culture of Cities* (New York: Harcourt, Brace, 1938), 3–7.

2. Louis Wirth, "Urbanism as a Way of Life," *American Journal of Sociology* 44 (1938): 1–24.

3. Peter C. Lloyd, "The Yoruba: An Urban People?" in *Urban Anthropology: Cross-Cultural Studies of Urbanization,* ed. Aidan Southall (New York: Oxford University Press, 1973), 109–12.

4. James L. Spates and John J. Macionis, *The Sociology of Cities,* 2nd ed. (Belmont, Calif.: Wadsworth, 1987), 187.

5. Blaine A. Brownell, "The Urban South Comes of Age, 1900–1940," in *The City in Southern History: The Growth of Urban Civilization in the South,* ed. Blaine A. Brownell and David R. Goldfield (Port Washington, N.Y.: Kennikat Press, 1977), 145.

6. Don H. Doyle, *New Men, New Cities, New South: Atlanta, Nashville, Charleston, Mobile, 1860–1910* (Chapel Hill: University of North Carolina Press, 1990).

7. C. Vann Woodward, *The Strange Career of Jim Crow,* 3rd ed. (New York: Oxford University Press, 1974); and Howard N. Rabinowitz, *Race Relations in the Urban South, 1865–1890* (New York: Oxford University Press, 1978).

8. Dickson D. Bruce, Jr., *Violence and Culture in the Antebellum South* (Austin: University of Texas Press, 1979); and Bertram Wyatt-Brown, *Honor and Violence in the Old South* (New York: Oxford University Press, 1986).

9. John Shelton Reed, "The Same Old Stand?" in *One South: An Ethnic Approach to Regional Culture* (Baton Rouge: Louisiana State University Press, 1982), 162–85.

10. William Alexander Percy, *Lanterns on the Levee: Recollections of a Planter's Son* (New York: Knopf, 1941).

11. William Faulkner, *Absalom, Absalom!* (1936; reprint, New York: Modern Library, 1951).

12. Joe Gray Taylor, *Eating, Drinking, and Visiting in the South* (Baton Rouge: Louisiana State University Press, 1982); Bertram Wyatt-Brown, *Southern Honor: Ethics and Behavior in the Old South* (New York: Oxford

307

University Press, 1982); and Wyatt-Brown, *Honor and Violence.* Following Wyatt-Brown, several other historians have addressed the relationship between hospitality and violence as part of the South's code of honor in the nineteenth century.

13. Robert Beverley, *The History and Present State of Virginia* (1705; reprint, ed. Louis B. Wright, Chapel Hill: University of North Carolina Press, 1947), 312–13.

14. Hugh Jones, *The Present State of Virginia* (1724; Ann Arbor, Mich.: University Microfilms, 1974), American Culture Series, reel 599.4, p. 49.

15. Rhys Isaac, *The Transformation of Virginia, 1740–1790* (Chapel Hill: University of North Carolina Press, 1982), 71.

16. Clement Eaton, *The Growth of Southern Civilization, 1790–1860* (New York: Harper & Brothers, 1961); and William R. Taylor, *Cavalier and Yankee: The Old South and American National Character* (New York: George Braziller, 1961).

17. Margaret Ripley Wolfe, *Daughters of Canaan: A Saga of Southern Women* (Lexington: University Press of Kentucky, 1995), 2–9. Wolfe uses the terms *patriarchy* and *paternalism* to describe Southern society. *Patriarchy* is defined as "the manifestation and institutionalization of male dominance over women and children in the family and the extension of male dominance over women in society in general. Although 'Paternalism' implies that men hold power in all the important institutions of society and women are deprived of access to power, . . . it does *not* imply that women are either totally powerless or totally deprived of rights, influence, and resources. 'Paternalism' is a subset of patriarchal relations."

18. Isaac, *Transformation of Virginia,* 24–46.

19. Eaton, *Growth of Southern Civilization,* 2–4. Olmsted was often met with suspicion as he traveled through the South, causing him to disparage Southern hospitality.

20. Basil Hall, *Travels in North America* (Edinburgh, 1829), in Mills B. Lane, ed., *The Rambler in Georgia* (Savannah: Beehive Press, 1973), 69.

21. Daniel R. Hundley, *Social Relations in Our Southern States* (1860; reprint, New York: Arno, 1973), 56–57, 84.

22. Wyatt-Brown, *Southern Honor,* 332–35.

23. Frederick Law Olmsted, *A Journey in the Back Country* (New York: Mason Bros., 1860), 407, quoted in Broadus Mitchell, *Frederick Law Olmsted: A Critic of the Old South* (Baltimore: Johns Hopkins University Press, 1924), 87.

24. Wyatt-Brown, *Southern Honor,* 335–37.

25. Ibid., 14, 121, 338.

26. *Atlanta Journal,* May 12, 1914, p. 11.

27. The definition of *tourism* itself is the subject of considerable debate. See Erik Cohen's "The Sociology of Tourism: Approaches, Issues, and Findings" (*Annual Review of Sociology* 10 [1984]: 373–92) for a review of some of the problems in defining the term. Douglas Pearce (*Tourism Development,* 2nd ed. [New York: Wiley, 1989], 2) identifies five components of the tourism industry: attractions, transport, accommodation, supporting facilities, and infrastructure.

28. Clare A. Gunn, *Tourism Planning: Basics, Concepts, Cases,* 3rd ed. (Washington, D.C.: Taylor & Francis, 1994), 4–5. For this work the term *tourism business* has been chosen instead of *tourism industry.* The term *tourism businesses* will sometimes be used interchangeably with the term *hospitality businesses.* Also, the use of the term *tourism business* enables the focus to be placed on four components of Atlanta's tourism industry: attractions, accommodations, supporting facilities, and infrastructure (see note 27). Less attention is paid to the remaining component, local transportation.

29. Julia Kirk Blackwelder, "Mop and Typewriter: Women's Work in Early Twentieth Century Atlanta," *Atlanta Historical Journal* 27 (Fall 1983): 24.

30. Collin Michael Hall, *Hallmark Tourist Events: Impacts, Management, and Planning* (New York: Wiley, 1992), 36.

Chapter 1

1. Edward Young Clarke, *Illustrated History of Atlanta* (1879; reprint, Atlanta: Cherokee Printing Company, 1971), 18–19.

2. Franklin M. Garrett, *Atlanta and Environs: A Chronicle of Its People and Events,* 2 vols. (New York: Lewis Historical Publishing Co., 1954), 1:130, 189, 204. In 1835 the Whitehall Tavern and Inn had been built at a road junction on the stage line in 1835. Atlanta did not develop at this location since the inn was several miles from the site of the rail line around which the new town grew. The stagecoach inn was typical of early-nineteenth-century America before the development of the railroad and the hotel.

3. William Hastings, "Early Atlanta Hotels," *Southern Hotel Journal,* June 1946, pp. 26–27, 73.

4. Pioneer Citizens' Society, *Pioneer Citizens' History of Atlanta* (Atlanta: Byrd Publishing, 1902), 24. It is interesting to note that the name "Atlanta" was given to the hotel in 1846. The state legislature did not approve the change in the town's name until the following year.

5. This pattern of investment by transportation companies in Atlanta's hospitality businesses continues today as many of the city's hotels are owned by airlines.

6. Garrett, *Atlanta and Environs,* 1:237, 248.

7. Jefferson Williamson, *The American Hotel* (1930; reprint, New York: Arno, 1975), 3–29.

8. Rupert B. Vance, "The Profile of Southern Culture," in *Culture in the South,* ed. W. T. Couch (Chapel Hill: University of North Carolina Press, 1935), 25.

9. Atlanta Historical Society, "Federal Census of Atlanta, 1850," *Atlanta Historical Bulletin* 7 (January–April 1942): 16–68.

10. U.S. Bureau of the Census, *Seventh Census of the United States, 1850,* Slave Schedule for Dekalb County, Georgia, Microfilm of manuscript census, Atlanta History Center. Although Atlanta was a small town

in 1850, it had a low percentage of slaves in its population in comparison with other cities of the South. In Charleston, for instance, blacks outnumbered whites. See Richard C. Wade, *Slavery in the Cities: The South, 1820–1860* (New York: Oxford University Press, 1964), 3, 67–68.

11. David R. Goldfield, *Cotton Fields and Skyscrapers: Southern City and Region, 1607–1980* (Baton Rouge: Louisiana State University Press, 1982), 8.

12. Garrett, *Atlanta and Environs*, 1:318.

13. Ibid., 320.

14. Clarke, *Illustrated History*, 42.

15. *Atlanta Daily Intelligencer,* June 14, 1857, quoted in James M. Russell, *Atlanta, 1847–1890: City Building in the Old South and the New* (Baton Rouge: Louisiana State University Press, 1988), 24.

16. This image of Atlanta as the Gate City is continued today, as Hartsfield International Airport functions as a major hub for air cargo and passengers.

17. U.S. Bureau of the Census, *Eighth Census of the United States, 1860,* Slave Schedule for Fulton County, Georgia. Microfilm of manuscript census, Atlanta History Center; and *Williams' Atlanta Directory, City Guide, and Business Mirror, 1859–60* (Atlanta: M. Lynch, 1859), 155. There were changes in slaveownership patterns between 1850 and 1860. Slaves remained only 20 percent of Atlanta's population in 1860, but the largest slaveowners were no longer hotelkeepers. There were eleven Atlantans who owned more than twenty slaves in 1860, and many of these owners permitted their slaves to "hire out" for wages. Most other slaves were used as domestics in households. See Wade, *Slavery in the Cities*, 38–54, for a discussion of the practice of "hiring out" slaves in the urban South.

18. Russell, *Atlanta*, 40–43; and Henry Jackson, comp., *The Code of the City of Atlanta* (Atlanta, 1870), 117.

19. Clarke, *Illustrated History*, 31.

20. Ibid., 36.

21. Garrett, *Atlanta and Environs*, 1:448–49.

22. Edward L. Ayers, *Vengeance and Justice: Crime and Punishment in the Nineteenth-Century American South* (New York: Oxford University Press, 1984), 19. For further discussion of the relationship between manners and violence in the culture of honor in the South, see Wyatt-Brown, *Southern Honor,* chap. 13; and Bruce, *Violence and Culture,* 67–88. The culture of honor in the South has also been studied by, among others, John Hope Franklin, *The Militant South* (New York: Beacon Press, 1956); Kenneth S. Greenberg, *Honor and Slavery: Lies, Duels, Noses, Masks, Dressing as a Woman, Gifts, Strangers, Humanitarianism, Death, Slave Rebellions, the Proslavery Argument, Baseball, Hunting, and Gambling in the Old South* (Princeton: Princeton University Press, 1996); and Richard E. Nisbett and Dov Cohen, *Culture of Honor* (Boulder: Westview Press, 1996).

23. Wallace P. Reed, *History of Atlanta, Georgia* (Syracuse, N.Y.: D. Mason & Co., 1889), 111; and *Atlanta Constitution*, April 8, 1894.

24. Isaac W. Avery, *The History of the State of Georgia from 1850 to 1881* (New York: Brown & Derby, 1881), 206.

25. *Gate City Guardian,* February 16, 1861.

26. Reed, *History of Atlanta,* 119.

27. *Daily Intelligencer,* May 23, 1862.

28. Pioneer Citizens' Society, *Pioneer Citizens' History,* 126.

29. *Daily Intelligencer,* January 13, July 10, 1866.

30. V. T. Barnwell, *Barnwell's Atlanta City Directory and Strangers' Guide* (Atlanta: Intelligencer Book and Job Office, 1867), 16.

31. Ibid., 115–25.

32. Goldfield, *Cotton Fields and Skyscrapers,* 3.

33. Ibid., 67.

34. Ibid., 89.

35. *Milledgeville Recorder,* quoted in Gary Pomerantz, *Where Peachtree Meets Sweet Auburn: The Saga of Two Families and the Making of Atlanta* (New York: Scribner, 1996), 53.

36. Eugene M. Mitchell, "H. I. Kimball: His Career and Defense," *Atlanta Historical Bulletin* 3 (October 1938): 253–55.

37. *Constitution,* October 18, 1870.

38. John Stainback Wilson, *Atlanta as It Is: Being a Brief Sketch of Its Early Settlers, Growth, Society, Health, Morals, Publications, Churches, Associations, Educational Institutions, Prominent Officials, Principal Business Enterprises, Public Buildings, Etc., Etc.* (New York, 1871), reprinted in *Atlanta Historical Bulletin* 6 (January 1941): 66–74.

39. Williamson, *American Hotel,* 123–25.

40. Gretchen Ehrmann Maclachlan, "Women's Work: Atlanta's Industrialization and Urbanization, 1879–1929" (Ph.D. diss., Emory University, 1992), 194–95.

41. William R. Hanleiter, *Hanleiter's Atlanta City Directory for 1871* (Atlanta: Wm. R. Hanleiter, 1871), 3–17.

42. Ibid., 3–4.

43. The Bell House passed through several generations of ownership after Emma Bell's death and did not close until 1950. See *Constitution,* December 24, 1950.

44. Maclachlan, "Women's Work," 168–70.

45. Ibid., 192–96.

46. Rabinowitz, *Race Relations,* 22.

47. For a discussion of the role of white churches in the struggle for social control in Atlanta see Harvey K. Newman, "The Vision of Order: White Protestant Churches in Atlanta, 1865–1906" (Ph.D. diss., Emory University, 1977).

48. *Daily Intelligencer,* March 14, 1868.

49. Howard N. Rabinowitz, "Southern Urban Development, 1860–1900," in Brownell and Goldfield, *City in Southern History,* 100.

50. Gaines M. Foster, *Ghosts of the Confederacy: Defeat, the Lost Cause, and the Emergence of the New South, 1865–1913* (New York: Oxford University Press, 1987).

51. Goldfield, *Cotton Fields and Skyscrapers,* 3–8.

52. Doyle, *New South,* 152.

53. *Constitution,* October 22, 1870.

54. John R. Logan and Harvey L. Molotch, *Urban Fortunes: The Political Economy of Place* (Berkeley: University of California Press, 1987), chap. 3.

55. Franklin Garrett quoted in *Constitution*, September 7, 1991.

56. Steven Hertzberg, "The Jewish Community of Atlanta from the End of the Civil War until the Eve of the Frank Case," *American Jewish Historical Quarterly* 62 (March 1973): 251.

57. Howard N. Rabinowitz, *Race, Ethnicity, and Urbanization* (Columbia: University of Missouri Press, 1994), 264–67.

58. Steven Hertzberg, *Strangers within the Gate City: The Jews of Atlanta, 1845–1915* (Philadelphia: Jewish Publication Society of America, 1978), 38–39.

59. James F. Sulzby, Jr., *Historic Alabama Hotels and Resorts* (Montgomery: University of Alabama Press, 1960). Most of these resort hotels fell victim to changing travel patterns and the widespread use of air-conditioning.

60. Garrett, *Atlanta and Environs*, 1:894.

61. *Constitution*, September 12, 1875.

62. Ibid., November 16, 1875.

63. Clarke, *Illustrated History*, 179.

64. Garrett, *Atlanta and Environs*, 1:939–40.

65. Clarke, *Illustrated History*, 108.

66. *Atlanta Daily Herald*, January 21, 1873, quoted in Russell, *Atlanta*, 118.

67. U.S. Bureau of the Census, *Tenth Census of the United States, 1880: Population*, vol. 2 (Washington, D.C.: Government Printing Office, 1883).

68. A. E. Sholes, *Sholes' Directory of the City of Atlanta, Georgia, for 1881* (Atlanta: H. H. Dickson, 1881), 103–30.

69. H. I. Kimball, *International Cotton Exposition (Atlanta, Georgia, 1881): Report of the Director-General* (New York: D. Appleton and Company, 1882), 15–17.

70. *Constitution*, November 28, 1880.

71. Alice E. Reagan, *H. I. Kimball, Entrepreneur* (Atlanta: Cherokee Publishing Company, 1983), 93.

72. Kimball, *Report of the Director-General*, 332–33.

73. Ibid., 109, 121, 332–35.

74. Reagan, *Kimball*, 100. Most of these same steps used to prepare the city for the exposition were repeated for the Olympics. See chapter 9.

75. Jack Blicksilver, "The International Cotton Exposition of 1881 and Its Impact upon the Economic Development of Georgia," *Cotton History Review* 1 (October 1960): 182.

76. Augusta Wylie King, "International Cotton Exposition, October 5th to December 31, 1881, Atlanta, Georgia," *Atlanta Historical Bulletin* 4 (July 1939): 192–93.

77. *Constitution*, October 23, 1881.

78. Kimball, *Report of the Director-General*, 105.

79. Doyle, *New South*, chap. 6.

80. Blicksilver, "International Cotton Exposition," 189–90.

81. Ibid., 188–90.
82. Doyle, *New South*, 152.
83. Reagan, *Kimball*, 106, 131.
84. *Constitution*, January 6, 1882.

Chapter 2

1. Harold E. Davis, *Henry Grady's New South: Atlanta, a Brave and Beautiful City* (Tuscaloosa: University of Alabama Press, 1990), 13–18; and Edward L. Ayers, *The Promise of the New South: Life after Reconstruction* (New York: Oxford University Press, 1992), 54.
2. Darlene R. Roth and Andy Ambrose, *Metropolitan Frontiers: A Short History of Atlanta* (Atlanta: Longstreet, 1996), 52.
3. Doyle, *New South*, 157–58.
4. This was Grady's famous description of Atlanta in the "New South" speech delivered to the New England Society of New York City on December 21, 1886. See Joel Chandler Harris, *Life of Henry W. Grady Including His Writings and Speeches* (New York: Cassel, 1890), 83.
5. Garrett, *Atlanta and Environs*, 2:59.
6. Reagan, *Kimball*, 113–14.
7. *Harper's Weekly*, May 2, 1885.
8. *Constitution*, May 19, 20, 1885.
9. *Proceedings of the National Commercial Convention of 1885, held in Atlanta, May 19, 20, and 21* (Atlanta, 1885), 1–7, quoted in Russell, *Atlanta*, 236.
10. Reagan, *Kimball*, 120.
11. There has been little scholarship to date on conventions. Geographer Wilbur Zelinsky attempts a definition of the term and describes six attributes that distinguish a convention from a meeting: (1) Conventions are carefully structured events with unique agendas that promise the dispensation of new information. (2) They are preplanned, announced beforehand, and require the services of organizers. (3) They occupy a predetermined time slot and are relatively brief in duration (half a day to two weeks). (4) Conventions contain the potential for give-and-take, for active involvement rather than passive attendance, listening, and watching. (5) Participants converge from a rather broad territory ranging from a single metropolitan area to the entire world, being drawn together because of some specialized interest. (6) Attendance is basically voluntary. Zelinsky acknowledges the difficulty drawing a clear distinction between an exposition and a convention. Most conventions observe a periodic schedule, such as an annual meeting. Expositions in the nineteenth century did not have this characteristic. I would argue that the exposition was an outgrowth of fairs, which held many of their functions outdoors and attempted to showcase a particular commodity (e.g., cotton). These events have many things in common, as both were opportunities for the host city to promote itself. Zelinsky sees the convention as

a recent phenomenon reflecting a postmodern urban system of cities which host large numbers of such events. See Zelinsky, "Conventionland USA: The Geography of a Latterday Phenomenon," *Annals of the Association of American Geographers* 84 (March 1994): 68–86.

12. Atlanta City Directories, 1859, 1867, 1871, and 1885, Atlanta History Center Collection.

13. Taylor, *Eating, Drinking, and Visiting,* 154–55.

14. For instance, in Atlanta less than 10 percent of the population were members of religious organizations from the earliest days of the city through the Reconstruction period of the 1870s. By the end of the century, a majority of the city's residents were members of a church or synagogue. See Harvey K. Newman, "Some Reflections on Religion in Nineteenth-Century Atlanta," *Atlanta Historical Journal* 27 (Fall 1983): 47–55. See also Samuel S. Hill, Jr., "The South's Two Cultures," in *Religion and the Solid South,* ed. Hill (Nashville: Abingdon, 1972), 36–37.

15. Charles Reagan Wilson, *Baptized in Blood: The Religion of the Lost Cause, 1865–1920* (Athens: University of Georgia Press, 1980), 87–88.

16. Raymond B. Nixon, *Henry W. Grady: Spokesman of the New South* (New York: Knopf, 1943), 269–70.

17. Garrett, *Atlanta and Environs,* 2:96.

18. Davis, *Grady's New South,* 46.

19. *Atlanta Evening Capitol,* November 26, 1885.

20. Ibid.

21. Doyle, *New South,* 209–11.

22. *Constitution,* January 5, 1887.

23. Jack J. Spalding, "The History of Piedmont Park," *Atlanta Historical Bulletin* 2 (September 1937): 7.

24. *Constitution,* April 20, 1887.

25. Ibid., May 22, 1887.

26. Davis, *Grady's New South,* 173–74.

27. *Constitution,* October 9, 1887.

28. Garrett, *Atlanta and Environs,* 2:149–55.

29. Rabinowitz, *Race Relations,* 314–15.

30. *Constitution,* November 27, 1887.

31. Ibid., February 11, 1893. DeGive's Grand Theatre was later converted into a movie house. In 1939 the Grand Theatre was the center of national attention as the site of the premiere of the motion picture *Gone with the Wind.* See Doyle, *New South,* 221–22, for a discussion of high culture and high society in Atlanta.

32. *Constitution,* April 29, 1895.

33. Rabinowitz, *Race Relations,* 188; and Edward R. Carter, *The Black Side: A Partial History of the Business, Religious, and Educational Side of the Negro in Atlanta, Ga.* (1894; reprint, Freeport, N.Y.: Books for Libraries Press, 1971), 201–3.

34. Garrett, *Atlanta and Environs,* 2:185–86; and *Constitution,* April 4, 1890, quoted in Rabinowitz, *Race Relations,* 190.

35. Garrett, *Atlanta and Environs,* 2:99–103. The zoo remains at Grant Park and operates as a nonprofit organization called Zoo Atlanta with

support from the city, Fulton County, businesses, foundations, member-ships, and ticket sales. The *Cyclorama* is maintained by the City of Atlanta.

36. *Constitution*, December 18, 1894. The property later became the location for the annual fair featuring agricultural exhibits as well as amusement rides and carnival attractions. The Coca-Cola Company converted the Lakewood fairgrounds into an outdoor amphitheater that continues to be a popular summer location for concerts.

37. Garrett, *Atlanta and Environs*, 1:881–83, 904. George M. Smerk, "The Decline of Public Transportation," in *Readings in Urban Transportation* (Bloomington: Indiana University Press, 1968), 6.

38. Rabinowitz, "Southern Urban Development," 114. The amuse-ment park at the Ponce de Leon Springs was rebuilt in 1906. See Garrett, *Atlanta and Environs*, 2:497–98.

39. U.S. Bureau of the Census, *Compendium of the Eleventh Census, 1890*, part 3 (Washington, D.C.: Government Printing Office, 1897), 40–41.

40. Ayers, *Promise of the New South*, 56.

41. Richard J. Hopkins, "Occupational and Geographic Mobility in Atlanta, 1870–1896," *Journal of Southern History* 34 (May 1968): 205–10; and Russell, *Atlanta*, 158–61.

42. Maclachlan, "Women's Work," 13, 17.

43. Ibid., 180–81.

44. Atlanta City Directories, 1881 and 1891, Atlanta History Center Collection.

45. James Edward Carroll, "Public Images of Atlanta, 1895–1973: Motif, Montage, and Structure" (M.S. thesis, Georgia State University, 1974), 60, observes that Atlanta's city fathers risked hubris in selecting the phoenix, as it was the ancient symbol for immortality. They also ig-nored the fact that in the legend the phoenix voluntarily consumes itself in the fire.

46. *The Atlanta Exposition and South Illustrated* (Chicago: Alder Art Publishing Company, 1895), 80.

47. Russell, *Atlanta*, 260; and Doyle, *New South*, 35–51.

48. Rabinowitz, "Southern Urban Development," 106–7.

49. Henry W. Grady, "The Farmer and the Cities Speech," *Constitu-tion*, July 26, 1889. See also his famous funeral speech for a Georgia na-tive in Goldfield, *Cotton Fields and Skyscrapers*, 121–22.

50. Russell, *Atlanta*, 252.

51. Doyle, *New South*.

52. *Report of the Board of Commissioners Representing the State of New York at the Cotton States and International Exposition Held at Atlanta, Georgia, 1895* (Albany, N.Y.: Wynkoop Hallenbeck Crawford Company, 1896), 26.

53. Walter G. Cooper, *Official History of Fulton County* (Atlanta: Walter W. Brown, 1934), 344.

54. Walter G. Cooper, *The Cotton States and International Exposition and South, Illustrated* (Atlanta: Illustrator Company, 1896), 5.

55. Ibid., 23.

56. *Atlanta Exposition and South Illustrated*, 55–80.

57. *Official Catalogue, Cotton States and International Exposition, Atlanta, Georgia, USA, September 18 to December 31, 1895, Illustrated* (Atlanta: Claflin and Mellichamp, 1895).

58. *Atlanta Exposition and South Illustrated*, 191.

59. Cooper, *Cotton States Exposition*, 65–66.

60. Rabinowitz, "Southern Urban Development," 100, 119.

61. Herman Mason, Jr., ed., *Going against the Wind: A Pictorial History of African-Americans in Atlanta* (Atlanta: Longstreet, 1992), 28.

62. Cooper, *Cotton States Exposition*, 65–66.

63. *Atlanta Exposition and South Illustrated*, 80.

64. *Constitution*, September 19, 1895.

65. Cooper, *Cotton States Exposition*, 87–88.

66. Susan Weiner, "Index to a Pictorial History of the Cotton States and International Exposition of 1895" (Atlanta: unpublished manuscript, Emory University, 1977), 4, Cotton States and International Exposition Collection, Atlanta History Center.

67. Cooper, *Cotton States Exposition*, 87–88.

68. Ibid., 72.

69. Kathleen Minnix, *Laughter in the Amen Corner: The Life of Evangelist Sam Jones* (Athens: University of Georgia Press, 1993), 99–101. The Atlanta revival of Rev. Sam P. Jones in the spring of 1896 was more successful in drawing crowds than Moody's. Minnix describes Jones as the "priest" of the New South whose crusade was used by business leaders to boost Atlanta. While Jones denounced drinking and other personal vices, he was himself a prosperous business owner in nearby Cartersville, Georgia, and shared the ideals of the New South "prophet" and Atlanta promoter Henry W. Grady. For additional discussion on Jones's influence in Atlanta, see Newman, "Vision of Order," chap. 5.

70. *Constitution*, September 19, 1895.

71. Robert W. Rydell, *All the World's a Fair: Visions of Empire at American International Expositions, 1876–1916* (Chicago: University of Chicago Press, 1984), 74.

72. *Atlanta Exposition and South Illustrated*, 80.

73. Cooper, *Cotton States Exposition*, 25–31.

74. On the other hand, Chicago used the Columbian Exposition as a means of urban redevelopment. Much of the city's south side was rebuilt for the "Great White Way," the monumental area of the fair designed by Daniel Burnham. The result was an architectural legacy for Chicago as well as an influence on other cities which became known among planners as the City Beautiful movement.

Chapter 3

1. The connection between violence and hospitality in Southern culture has been described by Bruce, *Violence and Culture;* Wyatt-Brown, *Southern Honor;* and Ayers, *Vengeance and Justice.*

2. U.S. Bureau of the Census, *Twelfth Census of the United States, 1900: Population,* vol. 2 (Washington, D.C.: Government Printing Office, 1904).

3. *Atlanta Exposition and South Illustrated,* 44, 46.

4. Atlanta City Directory, 1901, Atlanta History Center Collection.

5. *Constitution,* December 3, 1905, quoted in Doyle, *New South,* 136.

6. Blackwelder, "Mop and Typewriter," 21–30.

7. For a discussion of the term *Jim Crow* see Woodward, *Jim Crow,* 7; Rabinowitz, "Southern Urban Development," 119; John Shelton Reed and Dale Volberg Reed, *1001 Things Everyone Should Know about the South* (New York: Doubleday, 1996), 171–72; and Dana F. White, "The Black Sides of Atlanta: A Geography of Expansion and Containment, 1970–1870," *Atlanta Historical Journal* 26 (Summer–Fall 1982): 212.

8. Rabinowitz, *Race Relations,* 182–85.

9. Woodward, *Jim Crow,* 32; and Rabinowitz, *Race Relations,* 185–87.

10. Rabinowitz, *Race Relations,* 323–26, 332.

11. Russell Korobkin, "Politics of Disfranchisement in Georgia," *Georgia Historical Quarterly* 74 (Spring 1990): 28; and Ronald H. Bayor, *Race and the Shaping of Twentieth Century Atlanta* (Chapel Hill: University of North Carolina Press, 1996), 16.

12. W. E. B. Du Bois, "The Negro in Business," in *Fourth Annual Conference on the Condition of the Negro* (Atlanta: Atlanta University, 1899), 68.

13. Ibid., 8.

14. Carter, *The Black Side,* 201–3.

15. Ibid., 141–44.

16. Du Bois, "Negro in Business," 70–71. The prevailing pattern of segregation in Atlanta and the rest of the South was enforced by both law and the custom of white supremacy. However, as historian John C. Inscoe suggests, race relations in the region were complex, and there were variations, contradictions, and exceptions to the "color line." See Inscoe, ed., *Georgia in Black and White: Explorations in the Race Relations of a Southern State, 1865–1950* (Athens: University of Georgia Press, 1994), 1–12.

17. John Dittmer, *Black Georgia in the Progressive Era, 1900–1920* (Urbana: University of Illinois Press, 1977), 16–17.

18. David L. Lewis, *W. E. B. Du Bois: Biography of a Race, 1868–1919* (New York: H. Holt, 1993), 344.

19. John Hammond Moore, "Jim Crow in Georgia," *South Atlantic Quarterly* 66 (Fall 1967): 558.

20. White churches also supported the views of white supremacy in Atlanta. See Harvey K. Newman, "Piety and Segregation: White Protestant Attitudes toward Blacks in Atlanta, 1865–1906," *Georgia Historical Quarterly* 63 (Summer 1979): 238–51; and Dittmer, *Black Georgia,* 21.

21. National Negro Business League Collection, 1900 to 1906, Atlanta-Fulton Public Library System—Research Library.

22. *Atlanta Independent,* June 11, 17, August 18, 1904.

23. Ibid., August 25, p. 4, September 1, 1906, p. 1.

24. H. A. Rucker Family Papers, "Report of the Finance Committee," National Negro Business League Meeting, Atlanta, August 29–31, 1906,

Atlanta History Center Archives. Henry Rucker served from 1898 to 1909 as collector of internal revenue and was an important business leader who erected the city's first black office building on Auburn Avenue.

25. Charles Crowe, "Racial Violence and Social Reform: Origins of the Atlanta Riot of 1906," *Journal of Negro History* 53 (July 1968): 248.

26. Charles Crowe, "Racial Massacre in Atlanta, September 22, 1906," *Journal of Negro History* 54 (April 1969): 153.

27. *Constitution,* September 22, 1906, p. 7.

28. Ibid., September 23, 1906, pp. 1, 4.

29. Gregory L. Mixon, "The Atlanta Riot of 1906" (Ph.D. diss., University of Cincinnati, 1989), 592.

30. *Constitution,* September 24, 1906, pp. 1–3.

31. Ibid., September 26, 1906, p. 2.

32. Ibid.

33. Ibid., September 28, 1906, p. 6.

34. Mixon, "Atlanta Riot," 638.

35. *Constitution,* September 30, 1906, p. 4-B.

36. Ibid., September 29, 1906, p. 6.

37. Ibid.

38. Ibid., September 30, 1906, C-2, C-6.

39. The Coca-Cola Company began with the discovery of the formula for its syrup in 1886 by pharmacist and patent medicine inventor John S. Pemberton. "Doc" Pemberton and various partners operated the company before selling it to druggist Asa G. Candler in 1888. During the 1890s Coca-Cola became a popular soda fountain drink in the South, selling for a nickel a glass. Candler became wealthy, and his family sold control of the company and its product, which was now available in bottles, to a group of investors headed by Ernest Woodruff in 1919. Woodruff's son Robert took over the company in 1923 and ran it for more than fifty years, turning a local product into an international corporation. From the first convention of druggists hosted by the Candlers in 1906, the company played an influential role in the development of Atlanta and its tourism businesses. For example, three years later the company welcomed its bottlers to Atlanta, giving an additional boost to the city's young convention business. See Frederick Allen, *The Secret Formula: How Brilliant Marketing and Relentless Salesmanship Made Coca-Cola the Best-Known Product in the World* (New York: HarperCollins, 1994), for a fine review of the company's history and its impact on the city.

40. *Constitution,* September 30, 1906, D-7.

41. Ibid., October 3–6, 1906.

42. Dwight Fennell, "A Demographic Study of Black Businesses, 1905–1908, with Respect to the Race Riot of 1906" (M.A. thesis, Atlanta University, 1977), 32–45.

43. *Constitution,* October 1, 1906, p. 1.

44. Ibid., December 27, 1907, pp. 1–2.

45. Ibid., December 29, pp. 1–2, December 30, p. 5, December 31, 1907, p. 5.

46. Garrett, *Atlanta and Environs,* 2:518.

47. *Constitution,* January 28, 1909, p. 6.

48. Howard L. Preston, *Automobile Age Atlanta: The Making of a Southern Metropolis, 1900–1935* (Athens: University of Georgia Press, 1979), 24–25.

49. *Progress,* September 1909, in Preston, *Automobile Age Atlanta,* 27.

50. Ibid., 27–28.

51. Ibid., 29–44.

52. Atlanta City Directory, 1901, and Sanborn Insurance Company maps, Atlanta History Center Collection.

53. The Terminal Hotel operated at this location until it was destroyed by fire in 1938. The other three hotels on the "row" changed names and ownership frequently but remained on Mitchell Street despite the decline in railroad passengers and the closing of the Terminal Station in 1971. With another building known as Concordia Hall, the hotel was listed in 1991 on the National Register of Historic Places and designated as a Landmark District by the City of Atlanta. The three old hotels on Mitchell Street have been converted to loft apartments. Atlanta Urban Design Commission, Hotel Row District, Landmark District Nomination, N-91-11 to 16.

54. *Journal,* October 3, 1911, p. 1.

55. For a comparison of high society and culture in Atlanta and other cities, see Doyle, *New South,* chap. 8.

56. Garrett, *Atlanta and Environs,* 2:566–69; and Atlanta Chamber of Commerce, *City Builder,* April 1929, pp. 7, 48.

57. U.S. Bureau of the Census, *Thirteenth Census of the United States, 1910: Population,* vol. 2 (Washington, D.C.: Government Printing Office, 1912).

58. Garrett, *Atlanta and Environs,* 2:557–59.

59. Maclachlan, "Women's Work," 205, 208.

60. Al Rose, *Storyville, New Orleans: Being an Authentic, Illustrated Account of the Notorious Red-Light District* (Tuscaloosa: University of Alabama Press, 1974); and Neil Larry Shumsky, "Tacit Acceptance: Respectable Americans and Segregated Prostitution, 1870–1910," *Journal of Social History* 19 (Summer 1986): 665–79.

61. *Constitution,* September 25, 1912, pp. 1–2.

62. Ibid., September 29, 1912, p. 1.

63. William J. Mathias and Stuart Anderson, *Horse to Helicopter: First Century of the Atlanta Police Department* (Atlanta: Georgia State University, 1973), 70–76.

64. Timothy J. Gilfoyle, *City of Eros: New York City, Prostitution, and the Commercialization of Sex, 1790–1920* (New York: Norton, 1992), 312–15; see also Rose, *Storyville,* 166–83.

65. Rose, *Storyville,* 183.

66. Karen Luehrs and Timothy J. Crimmins, "In the Mind's Eye: The Downtown as Visual Metaphor for the Metropolis," *Atlanta Historical Journal* 26 (Summer–Fall 1982): 186–88, 197.

67. Georgina Hickey, "'Meet Me at the Arcade': Women, Business, and Consumerism in Downtown Atlanta, 1917–1964," *Atlanta History* 40 (Fall–Winter 1996–97): 5–10.

68. Cooper, *Fulton County*, 369.
69. Joseph M. Brown, 1913 and 1914, Correspondence with the Atlanta Convention Bureau and Letters of Invitation, Joseph M. Brown Collection, Atlanta History Center.
70. Minutes of the Atlanta City Council, September 20, October 4, 1909, January 2, 1911, Atlanta History Center.
71. Zelinsky, "Conventionland USA," 74–75, argues that physical facilities (i.e., meeting space and hotel capacity) and accessibility are the two most important factors in the site selection decisions of present-day convention planners. He does not consider cultural factors or organizational capacity. I would argue that the culture of Southern hospitality contributed to Atlanta's reputation as a meeting site and led to the development of the organizational capacity for the active solicitation of groups to hold their conventions in the city. This took place during the early twentieth century in spite of Atlanta's disadvantages of relatively small size and other cultural factors such as violence which might have tended to keep groups from meeting in the city.
72. *Constitution,* August 16, p. 5, August 17, 1915, p. 5.
73. This is the title of Steven Hertzberg's history of Atlanta's Jewish community.
74. Eli N. Evans, *The Provencials: A Personal History of Jews in the South* (New York: Atheneum, 1973), 273.
75. *Constitution,* August 18, 1915, pp. 1, 2, 6.
76. Ibid., August 18, 1915, p. 12.
77. Ibid., August 20, p. 4, August 22, 1915, B-1.
78. Ibid., August 28, p. 1, November 2, 1915, p. 7.
79. Hertzberg, *Strangers within the Gate City,* 213–15.
80. David M. Chalmers, *Hooded Americanism: The History of the Ku Klux Klan* (Chicago: Quadrangle, 1965), 29–30.
81. *Constitution,* August 20, p. 4, August 27, p. 2, August 29, 1915, pp. 4, B-1.
82. *Journal,* May 10, 1914, p. 1.
83. Ibid., May 14, p. 3, May 17, 1914, H-8.
84. Garrett, *Atlanta and Environs,* 2:663–65.
85. *Constitution,* November 14, 1915, pp. 6, 11.
86. Garrett, *Atlanta and Environs,* 2:666. The Lakewood fairgrounds continue to be used for smaller expositions and as the site of a major outdoor amphitheater that hosts a variety of concerts.
87. Cooper, *Fulton County,* 466–67.
88. *Journal,* August 26, 1917, p. 1. The Cecil Hotel has been enlarged and renovated several times and continues to operate as the Atlantan Hotel.
89. Ibid., October 7, 1918, p. 1.
90. Ibid., October 27, 1918.
91. Ibid., August 31, 1947, B-8. The National Linen Service Corporation is part of a large conglomerate, National Service Industries, Inc., with headquarters in Atlanta. *Constitution,* January 5, 1995, E-1.
92. U.S. Bureau of the Census, *Fourteenth Census of the United States,*

1920: Population, vol. 2 (Washington, D.C.: Government Printing Office, 1921).

93. Atlanta City Directory, 1901 and 1921, Atlanta History Center Collection.

94. Maclachlan, "Women's Work," 201–3.

95. T. Lynn Smith, "The Emergence of Cities," in *The Urban South,* ed. Rupert B. Vance and Nicholas J. Demerath (1954; reprint, Freeport, N.Y.: Books for Libraries Press, 1971), 27.

96. Ibid., 33.

97. Bradley R. Rice, "Urbanization, 'Atlanta-ization,' and Suburbanization: Three Themes for the Urban History of Twentieth Century Georgia," *Georgia Historical Quarterly* 68 (Spring 1984): 43–45.

Chapter 4

1. Louis Rubin, Jr., "Scarlett O'Hara and the Two Quentin Compsons," in *Recasting: Gone with the Wind in American Culture,* ed. Darden Asbury Pyron (Miami: University Presses of Florida, 1983), 89–95.

2. Harold K. Schefski, "Margaret Mitchell: *Gone with the Wind* and *War and Peace,*" in *"Gone with the Wind" as Book and Film,* ed. Richard Harwell (Columbia: University of South Carolina Press, 1983), 237.

3. Margaret Mitchell, *Gone with the Wind* (New York: Macmillan, 1936), 141–43.

4. Ibid., 608–9, quoted in Rubin, "Scarlett O'Hara," 96.

5. Brownell, *Urban Ethos in the South, 1920–1930* (Baton Rouge: Louisiana State University Press, 1975), xvi. I am indebted to Brownell for the use of the term *ethos.* The interpretation of Mitchell's book is based on critical essays on her work by Harold K. Schefski in Richard Harwell's *"Gone with the Wind" as Book and Film* and by Louis Rubin, Jr., in Darden Pyron's *Recasting "Gone with the Wind" in American Culture.* See also Thomas H. Pauly, *"Gone with the Wind* and *The Grapes of Wrath,*" in Harwell, *"Gone with the Wind" as Book and Film,* 220–23. Pauly suggests that both films had great appeal to a post-depression-era audience because they were "preoccupied with the problem of survival in the face of financial deprivation and social upheaval." Both showed "a nostalgic longing for the agrarian way of life which is ruthlessly being replaced by the fearful economic forces of capitalism and industrialism." *Gone with the Wind* was the more popular of the two because "it so effectively sublimated the audience's own response to the Depression." Though set in the previous century, Mitchell's novel had much to say to twentieth-century Atlantans.

6. *Constitution,* January 6, 1920.

7. Truman A. Hartshorn, Sanford Bederman, Sid Davis, G. E. Alan Dever, and Richard Pillsbury, *Metropolis in Georgia: Atlanta's Rise as a Major Transaction Center* (Cambridge, Mass.: Ballinger, 1976), 3; Numan V. Bartley, *The Creation of Modern Georgia,* 2nd ed. (Athens: University of Georgia Press, 1990), 169.

8. Anne Firor Scott, "The Study of Southern Urbanization," *Urban Affairs Quarterly* 1 (March 1966): 6.

9. Charles Reagan Wilson, *Judgment and Grace in Dixie: Southern Faiths from Faulkner to Elvis* (Athens: University of Georgia Press, 1995), 61.

10. David R. Goldfield, "Urbanization in a Rural Culture, Suburban Cities and Country Cosmopolites," in *The South for New Southerners*, ed. Paul S. Escott and David R. Goldfield (Chapel Hill: University of North Carolina Press, 1991), 92.

11. Josephine Pinckney, "Bulwarks against Change," in Couch, *Culture in the South*, 42–46.

12. *Birmingham Age-Herald*, March 14, 1920, in Brownell, *Urban Ethos in the South*, 81–82.

13. Atlanta City Directory, 1921, Atlanta History Center Collection; and Richard Pillsbury, *From Boardinghouse to Bistro: The American Restaurant Then and Now* (Boston: Unwin Hyman, 1990), 46, 61.

14. Fred Houser, "Where Do We Eat?" *City Builder*, April 1929, p. 8.

15. Ibid.

16. Pillsbury, *Boardinghouse to Bistro*, 61–62.

17. Clifford M. Kuhn, Harlon E. Joye, and E. Bernard West, *Living Atlanta: An Oral History of the City, 1914–1948* (Atlanta and Athens: Atlanta Historical Society and University of Georgia Press, 1990), 95–100. Ma Sutton's Café opened on Auburn Avenue during the 1920s and remained there until it was torn down for the construction of the downtown connector. The restaurant was a favorite of John Wesley Dobbs, the unofficial "mayor" of Auburn Avenue and grandfather of Maynard H. Jackson. John Wesley Dobbs, "Atlanta—You Ought to Know 'Ma' Sutton's Café," in *Directory of the 1937 National Negro Business League Convention*, ed. Arnett G. Lindsay, 31–32, Archive Collection, Atlanta-Fulton Public Library System—Research Library. John Wesley Dobbs is credited with giving the avenue its nickname, "Sweet Auburn." See Pomerantz, *Where Peachtree Meets Sweet Auburn*, 123–24.

18. Pillsbury, *Boardinghouse to Bistro*, 78.

19. Ibid., 37–41.

20. John Russell, "The Fundamental Purpose of the Atlanta Convention Bureau," *City Builder*, February 1923, p. 8.

21. Ibid.

22. Fred Houser, "Convention Bureau Closes Most Successful Year in Its History," *City Builder*, January 1924, p. 11.

23. *Constitution*, May 7, A-9, May 11, 1922, A-1.

24. Ibid., July 10, 1923.

25. *Journal*, July 8, 1923.

26. Houser, "Successful Year," 11.

27. Ibid.

28. Logan and Molotch, *Urban Fortunes*, 78.

29. Houser, "Successful Year," 11.

30. Logan and Molotch, *Urban Fortunes*, 70–73.

31. Ibid., 71.

32. Houser, "Successful Year," 11.

33. Ibid.

34. *Atlanta Georgian,* April 20, 1924, quoted in Garrett, *Atlanta and Environs,* 2:804.

35. Ibid., 805.

36. The Biltmore Hotel closed in 1982. Its unique design earned the hotel recognition on the National Register of Historic Places and by the City of Atlanta as an Urban Conservation and Development property. City of Atlanta, Urban Design Commission, *Atlanta's Lasting Landmarks* (1987), 74.

37. Ibid., 76.

38. The Briarcliff is listed on the National Register of Historic Properties. In the years after World War II, the Briarcliff slowly deteriorated along with the surrounding neighborhood until it was restored and opened as a home for senior citizens. Its reopening was an important step in the process of revitalizing the Ponce de Leon Avenue corridor. One of the elegant homes in the Druid Hills Neighborhood was featured in the film *Driving Miss Daisy.* Ibid., 75.

39. Eleanor Williams, *Ivan Allen: A Resourceful Citizen* (Atlanta: Ivan Allen-Marshall Company, 1950), 160–61; and Pomerantz, *Where Peachtree Meets Sweet Auburn,* 97.

40. Williams, *Ivan Allen,* 162–63.

41. Cooper, *Fulton County,* 412.

42. Roth and Ambrose, *Metropolitan Frontiers,* 98.

43. Williams, *Ivan Allen,* 65–66.

44. *Atlanta Independent,* December 16, November 27, 1926, quoted in Brownell, *Urban Ethos in the South,* 146–50.

45. Hunter Street has since been renamed Martin Luther King, Jr., Drive.

46. Mason, *Going against the Wind,* 76, 97, 100.

47. Edward Y. Clarke was the son of the *Constitution*'s managing editor and early Atlanta historian E. Y. Clarke, Sr., who died in 1910.

48. Chalmers, *Hooded Americanism,* 31–35.

49. Kenneth T. Jackson, *The Ku Klux Klan in the City, 1915–1930* (New York: Oxford University Press, 1967), 59. The Klan was never as strong in New Orleans because of the large Roman Catholic population and the city's cultural heterogeneity.

50. Ibid., 247–48; Pomerantz, *Where Peachtree Meets Sweet Auburn,* 93–94; and *Constitution,* May 7, A-1, A-6, November 28, 29, 30, 1922, A-1.

51. Frederic J. Paxon, "Atlanta Convention Bureau Re-organized," *City Builder,* January 1925, pp. 9–11, 57–59; and Garrett, *Atlanta and Environs,* 2:101–2.

52. Foster, *Ghosts of the Confederacy,* 120–22; see also Wilson, *Baptized in Blood.*

53. Preston, *Automobile Age Atlanta,* 147–48.

54. Elizabeth A. M. Lyon, "Business Buildings in Atlanta: A Study in Urban Growth and Form" (Ph.D. diss., Emory University, 1971), 309.

55. Advertisements in Lindsay, *Directory of the 1937 National Negro Business League Convention,* 69.

56. Ibid., 7.

57. Atlanta Chamber of Commerce, *City Builder,* April 1929.

58. Paxon, "Bureau Re-organized," 59. The call for the development of additional amenities to attract tourists was a major factor in the decision to redevelop Underground Atlanta and was used to promote projects such as the construction of a downtown aquarium.

59. W. G. Hastings, "Hotels Have Helped Build Atlanta," *City Builder,* April 1929, pp. 9–10, 47–48.

60. Ibid.

61. William B. Hartsfield, 1970, Airport materials, manuscript collection, Atlanta History Center; and Frederick Allen, *Atlanta Rising: The Invention of an International City, 1946–1996* (Atlanta: Longstreet, 1996), 22–24.

62. Garrett, *Atlanta and Environs,* 2:848, 851; and Norman Shavin, *Days in the Life of Atlanta* (Atlanta: Capricorn Corporation, 1987), 117.

63. *Constitution,* October 28, 1929, p. 1.

64. Douglas Lee Fleming, "Atlanta, the Depression, and the New Deal" (Ph.D. diss., Emory University, 1984), 64.

65. Lyon, "Business Buildings," 439.

66. Fleming, "Depression and New Deal," 69.

67. Atlanta City Directory, 1934, Atlanta History Center Collection.

68. Atlanta City Directory, 1931, Atlanta History Center Collection.

69. Fleming, "Depression and New Deal," 83–85; and "1936 U.S. Employment Service Report," quoted in Bayor, *Race and the Shaping of Atlanta,* 99.

70. Herbert Jenkins, *Keeping the Peace: A Police Chief Looks at His Job* (New York: Harper & Row, 1970), 5.

71. Shavin, *Life of Atlanta,* 121.

72. Roth and Ambrose, *Metropolitan Frontiers,* 101.

73. Lindsay, *Directory of the 1937 National Negro Business League Convention,* 7–12.

74. Taylor, *Eating, Drinking, and Visiting,* 140–43. Fatback refers to the strip of fat from the back of a hog that is usually dried and salted.

75. Reed and Reed, *1001 Things about the South,* 190–202. For an interesting discussion of the role of slaves in the development of a distinct cuisine in the Caribbean islands, see Sidney W. Mintz, *Tasting Food, Tasting Freedom* (Boston: Beacon Press, 1996), 33–49.

76. One indication of the continuing importance of "soul food" in Atlanta is the popularity of six restaurants that opened between 1990 and 1996 which feature "new Southern cuisine," a contemporary interpretation of traditional foods such as pork, greens, and corn bread.

77. Fleming, "Depression and New Deal," 154–59.

78. Garrett, *Atlanta and Environs,* 2:913–14.

79. *Constitution,* December 18, May 16, 1934.

80. Kuhn, Joye, and West, *Living Atlanta,* 182.

81. Garrett, *Atlanta and Environs,* 2:959–60.

82. Kuhn, Joye, and West, *Living Atlanta*, 182. In 1951 a local boot-legger brought in a bad batch of moonshine whiskey which killed or blinded dozens in the city. As late as the 1970s, Atlanta was still known as a center for white lightning sales.

83. Lindsay, *Directory of the 1937 National Negro Business League Convention*, 37–38, 55–99.

84. Garrett, *Atlanta and Environs*, 2:968–71.

85. U.S. Bureau of the Census, *Census of Business, 1939* (Washington, D.C.: Government Printing Office, 1941), 575.

86. *Journal*, May 16–18, 1938.

87. Allen, *Atlanta Rising*, 27–28; and Pomerantz, *Where Peachtree Meets Sweet Auburn*, 130–31.

88. Garrett, *Atlanta and Environs*, 2:977–91.

89. The motion picture version of *Gone with the Wind* glamorized the antebellum period more than the novel. Prior to the 1996 Olympic Games, *Gone with the Wind* did more to publicize Atlanta than anything else ever had. Many tourists know Atlanta only through its portrayal in Mitchell's novel and Selznick's motion picture.

90. This compares to the weekly wages of just over seventeen dollars per week for those employed in manufacturing during the same year. U.S. Bureau of the Census, *Census of Business, 1939*, 575.

91. Atlanta City Directories, 1931 and 1941, Atlanta History Center Collection.

92. Howard Edwin Morgan, *Motel Industry in the United States: Small Business in Transition* (Tucson: University of Arizona Press, 1964), 184–85. Motels offer sleeping accommodations as well as restaurants and lounges. They are distinguished from hotels by their lower height and accessibility by automobile.

93. Bradley R. Rice, "If Dixie Were Atlanta," in *Sunbelt Cities: Politics and Growth since World War II*, ed. Richard M. Bernard and Bradley R. Rice (Austin: University of Texas Press, 1983), 32.

94. Harold H. Martin, *William Berry Hartsfield: Mayor of Atlanta* (Athens: University of Georgia Press, 1978), 37–41.

95. Kuhn, Joye, and West, *Living Atlanta*, 353; and Harold H. Martin, *Atlanta and Environs: A Chronicle of Its People and Events*, vol. 3 (Atlanta and Athens: Atlanta Historical Society and University of Georgia Press, 1987), 3:61.

96. Lawrence H. Larsen, *The Urban South: A History* (Lexington: University of Kentucky Press, 1990), 128.

97. Martin, *Atlanta and Environs*, 3:67, 78.

98. Rice, "If Dixie Were Atlanta," 32. The plant remains an important producer of military aircraft and is a major industrial employer for the area.

99. Charles Rutheiser, *Imagineering Atlanta: The Politics of Place in the City of Dreams* (New York: Verso, 1996), 29.

100. Atlanta City Directories, 1942 to 1944, Atlanta History Center Collection.

101. Jenkins, *Keeping the Peace*, 14.

102. City of Atlanta, Urban Design Commission, Hotel Row District, Landmark District Nomination.
103. The Hotel Roxy remained open from 1939 until 1954. In 1995 the building was converted into loft apartments with the street level rented for commercial activity. One of the businesses located in the Roxy is Thelma's Kitchen, a popular soul food restaurant. Historic Preservation Division, Georgia Department of Natural Resources, National Register Announcement, September 11, 1997.
104. Garrett, *Atlanta and Environs,* 2:1004.
105. Kuhn, Joye, and West, *Living Atlanta,* 191, 358.
106. Ibid., 364.
107. Martin, *Atlanta and Environs,* 3:112–13.
108. *Constitution,* August 15, 1945, A-1.

Chapter 5

1. Martin, *Atlanta and Environs,* 3:191.
2. Atlanta City Map, 1945, Atlanta History Center Collection.
3. John M. Maclachlan and Joe S. Floyd, Jr., *This Changing South* (Gainesville: University of Florida Press, 1956), 56–58.
4. Ibid., 13–22.
5. Ibid., 44; and Goldfield, *Cottonfields and Skyscrapers,* 145.
6. Idus A. Newby, *Plain Folk in the New South: Social Change and Cultural Persistence, 1880–1915* (Baton Rouge: Louisiana State University Press, 1989), 4–5.
7. Allen, *Atlanta Rising,* 32. This compares to a failure rate of 1 percent in Ohio.
8. Newby, *Plain Folk,* 308–9, 340.
9. Atlanta University, *Business Enterprises Owned and Operated by Negroes in Atlanta, Georgia, 1944* (Atlanta: Atlanta University, 1944), 11–37; and Atlanta City Directory, 1945, Atlanta History Center Collection.
10. Robert J. Alexander, "Negro Business in Atlanta," *Southern Economic Journal* 17 (April 1951): 457–58.
11. B. B. Beamon, interview by Benjamin West, May 29, 1979, Living Atlanta Oral History Collection, Atlanta History Center transcript, 9; and Atlanta City Directory, 1945, Atlanta History Center Collection.
12. Bayor, *Race and the Shaping of Atlanta,* 58–59, 108–9.
13. Edward F. Haas, "The Southern Metropolis, 1940–1976," in Brownell and Goldfield, *City in Southern History,* 160–65.
14. In many respects Democratic Party politics, like religion, has been a deeply ingrained part of Southern culture. See David R. Goldfield, "Southern Politics, Showtime to Bigtime," in Escott and Goldfield, *South for New Southerners,* 114–34, for a useful summary of the region's political history and the role of the Democratic Party in Southern culture.
15. Haas, "Southern Metropolis," 172.

16. *Journal,* November 7, 1919.

17. Sam Heys and Allen B. Goodwin, *The Winecoff Fire: The Untold Story of America's Deadliest Hotel Fire* (Atlanta: Longstreet, 1993), 30–31.

18. Ibid., 10.

19. Ibid., 29, 40.

20. Ibid., chapters 10 and 11. The major contribution of Heys and Goodwin's book is to speculate about the origins of the fire that caused the Winecoff disaster. They name a suspect who was involved in the illegal gambling ring at the hotel.

21. *Constitution,* December 5, 1986, A-1, A-9. After closing in 1967, the Winecoff Hotel building was donated to the Georgia Baptist Convention. It was used until 1981 as a retirement home. Since then there have been numerous plans to reuse the old building, but in the late 1990s it remained closed as a sort of haunted house on Peachtree Street, empty except for some retail activity on the ground floor. In 1971 the Winecoff lost the distinction of having been the worst hotel fire in the world when 162 were killed in a blaze at the Hotel Taeyokale in Seoul, South Korea.

22. *Journal,* December 15, 1946, A-1.

23. Heys and Goodwin, *Winecoff Fire,* 168–69.

24. Ibid., 175.

25. Atlanta City Directory, 1947, Atlanta History Center Collection.

26. Allen, *Atlanta Rising,* 30.

27. U.S. Bureau of the Census, *Seventeenth Census of the United States, 1950,* vol. 2 (Washington, D.C.: Government Printing Office, 1952).

28. William B. Hartsfield, form letter to Buckhead residents, quoted in Bradley R. Rice, "The Battle of Buckhead: The Plan of Improvement and Atlanta's Last Big Annexation," *Atlanta History Journal* 25 (Winter 1981): 9.

29. Ibid., 18–19. The 1952 "Plan of Improvement" was the last substantial annexation for the central city.

30. U.S. Bureau of the Census, *Seventeenth Census of the United States, 1950: Occupations,* vol. 3 (Washington, D.C.: Government Printing Office, 1952).

31. Ibid.

32. Floyd Hunter, *Community Power Structure: A Study of Decision Makers* (Chapel Hill: University of North Carolina Press, 1953), 214–15.

33. Clarence N. Stone, *Regime Politics: Governing Atlanta, 1946–1988* (Lawrence: University Press of Kansas, 1989), 33.

34. Raymond A. Mohl, "Making the Second Ghetto in Metropolitan Miami, 1940–1960," *Journal of Urban History* 21 (March 1995): 401–2.

35. Eric Hill Associates, *City of Atlanta, Georgia, Report on the Relocation of Individuals, Families, and Businesses* (Atlanta: Community Improvement Program, 1966), iv.

36. Clarence N. Stone, *Economic Growth and Neighborhood Discontent: System Bias in the Urban Renewal Program of Atlanta* (Chapel Hill: University of North Carolina Press, 1976), 79. The literature on the federal urban renewal program is extensive. See Mohl, "Making the Second Ghetto,"

395–427, for a discussion of Miami's program. Robert A. Caro, *The Power Broker* (New York: Knopf, 1974), examines Robert Moses's role in directing New York City's urban renewal program. For a brief history of the program in general, see Heywood T. Sanders, "Urban Renewal and the Revitalized City: A Reconsideration of Recent History," in *Selected Papers from the 1979 Annual Meeting of the Council of University Institutes for Urban Affairs, Toronto, Ontario,* ed. Peter Homenuck and Harvey K. Newman (Newark: University of Delaware, 1979), 98–139.

37. Sanders, "Urban Renewal," 115–18.

38. Stone, *Economic Growth,* 94.

39. Stone, *Regime Politics,* 35–41.

40. Stone, *Economic Growth,* 93.

41. Atlanta Chamber of Commerce, "Atlanta Lands a Convention," *Atlanta,* June 1961, pp. 33, 50.

42. Dennis R. Judd, "Promoting Tourism in American Cities: A Comparative Analysis" (paper presented at the annual meeting, Urban Affairs Association, Portland, Oreg., May 1995); see also Heywood T. Sanders, "Building the Convention City: Politics, Finance, and Public Investment in Urban America," *Journal of Urban Affairs* 14 (1992): 135–59.

43. Eric Hill Associates, *Report on Relocation,* 142.

44. *Atlanta Daily World,* April 14, 1960, 1.

45. Eric Hill Associates, *Report on Relocation,* iii.

46. Atlanta City Directories, 1958–59, Atlanta History Center Collection; and Mason, *Going against the Wind,* 104–5. The site of Bailey's 81 Theater is now occupied by the Library North building of Georgia State University.

47. Rice, "If Dixie Were Atlanta," 31–32.

48. U.S. Bureau of the Census, *Eighteenth Census of the United States, 1960,* vol. 1 (Washington, D.C.: Government Printing Office, 1961).

49. Ibid., part 12, *Characteristics of the Population.*

50. Melissa Fay Greene, *The Temple Bombing* (Reading, Mass.: Addison-Wesley, 1996), 237–57.

51. James L. Townsend and Paul Hagan, eds., *Atlanta International Airport: A Commemorative Book* (Atlanta: National Graphics, 1980), 5.

52. Betsy Braden and Paul Hagan, *A Dream Takes Flight: Hartsfield Atlanta International Airport and Aviation in Atlanta* (Atlanta and Athens: Atlanta Historical Society and University of Georgia Press, 1989), 133–37.

53. Delta Airlines advertisement, *Constitution,* May 4, 1961, A-7.

54. *Journal,* May 3, 1961, p. 28. Eugene Black was president of the World Bank as well as the grandson of Henry Grady.

55. James L. Townsend, editorial, *Atlanta,* May 1961, pp. 21–22.

Chapter 6

1. Bayor, *Race and the Shaping of Atlanta,* 25–27.

2. Stone, *Regime Politics,* 29–31.

3. The six institutions are known collectively as the Atlanta University Center. In 1960 they included Morehouse, Spellman, Clark, and Morris Brown Colleges, the Interdenominational Theological Center, and Atlanta University. There are still six, although Clark College and Atlanta University merged, becoming Clark-Atlanta University, and the Morehouse School of Medicine was created.

4. Jack L. Walker, "Protest and Negotiation: A Case Study of Negro Leadership in Atlanta," in *Atlanta, Georgia, 1960–1961: Sit-Ins and Student Activism,* ed. David J. Garrow (Brooklyn: Carson Publishing Inc., 1989), 33; and "An Appeal for Human Rights," *Daily World,* March 9, 1960, p. 6.

5. *Daily World,* March 9, 1960, p. 1.

6. Ibid., March 16, 1960, p. 1.

7. This shift in tactics by the students would cost the *Daily World* advertising revenue from the targeted stores. The students, with assistance from many younger black businessmen, responded to the editorial criticism from the *Daily World* in July 1960 by launching a rival newspaper, the *Atlanta Inquirer.* See Walker, "Protest and Negotiation," 76.

8. Walker, "Protest and Negotiation," 69–82.

9. Ibid., 82–90.

10. Stone, *Regime Politics,* 49; Rice, "If Dixie Were Atlanta," 48; and Gary Orfield and Carole Ashkinaze, *The Closing Door: Conservative Policy and Black Opportunity* (Chicago: University of Chicago Press, 1991), 105–7.

11. Pomerantz, *Where Peachtree Meets Sweet Auburn,* 287–88.

12. Atlanta Chamber of Commerce, "Atlanta Lands a Convention," 50.

13. *Atlanta Inquirer,* June 17, p. 16, June 24, 1961, pp. 1, 16.

14. Ibid., March 16, 1962, pp. 1, 3.

15. *Journal,* November 16, 1961, p. 59.

16. Bayor, *Race and the Shaping of Atlanta,* 40–41.

17. *Atlanta Inquirer,* June 15, 1963, p. 10.

18. *Daily World,* July 4, pp. 1, 5, July 19, p. 1, October 6, 1964, pp. 1, 6.

19. Allen, *Atlanta Rising,* 140.

20. Roth and Ambrose, *Metropolitan Frontiers,* 202.

21. Allen, *Atlanta Rising,* 140–43.

22. Donald L. Grant, *The Way It Was in the South: The Black Experience in Georgia* (New York: Carol Publishing Group, 1993), 486–87. In 1967 the Paschal brothers opened a hotel near their restaurant and jazz club. Paschal Brothers Hotel remained in operation until 1996, when Clark Atlanta University bought the property for student housing.

23. Beamon interview transcript, 13–14, 19–20. After his hotel and restaurant closed, Beamon continued his work as an entertainment promoter and club owner.

24. Atlanta City Directories, 1960 and 1974, Atlanta History Center Collection.

25. Pomerantz, *Where Peachtree Meets Sweet Auburn,* 135.

26. The first phase of the new Forward Atlanta program was launched in 1961. There were three more three-year phases—1965–67, 1968–70, and 1971–73. Unlike the Forward Atlanta program of the

1920s, these included an economic development component that received support among black community leaders. See *Daily World,* May 1, p. 2, May 5, 1970, p. 1.

27. Pomerantz, *Where Peachtree Meets Sweet Auburn,* 130–31.

28. Chamber of Commerce, "10,000 Good Seats Up Front," *Atlanta,* August 1964, p. 62.

29. Zelinsky, "Conventionland USA," 72. These were the top-ranked cities for 1964–65 as sites for national and international conventions. Without the civic center for hosting larger meetings, Atlanta remained the "Convention City of Dixie."

30. Fred Hartley, "Young Man on the Go: John C. Portman," *Atlanta,* September 1961, p. 32.

31. John Crown, "After Forty Years: A New Hotel," *Atlanta,* February 1964, pp. 40–41.

32. John Portman and Jonathan Barnett, *The Architect as Developer* (New York: McGraw-Hill, 1976), 28.

33. Paul Goldberger, *Global Architecture: John Portman, Hyatt Regency, Atlanta, Georgia, 1967* (Tokyo: A.D.A. Edita, 1974), 2–3.

34. Portman and Barnett, *Architect as Developer,* 30–36, 193.

35. Megastructures have attracted both supporters and critics. Foremost among architects who support this type of development is Paulo Solari, whose proposals envisioned the creation of an entire city in a single structure. Critics of megastructures include former Portman associate William Conway as well as a small group of the Atlanta Society of Architects who called themselves the "Architectural Jihad" to express their opposition to Portman's Peachtree Center and similar local megastructures.

36. *Journal Constitution,* January 18, 1987, D-1, D-6.

37. Paul Goldberger, *New York Times,* March 15, 1977, p. 16, quoted in William Conway, "The Case against Urban Dinosaurs," *Saturday Review,* May 14, 1977, p. 14.

38. Conway, "Urban Dinosaurs," 12–15.

39. City of Atlanta, Civic Design Commission, "Resolution," 1966, Atlanta Urban Design Commission file.

40. Ibid.

41. Goldfield, *Cotton Fields and Skyscrapers,* 155–56.

42. Martin, *Atlanta and Environs,* 3:553–55.

43. Goldfield, *Cotton Fields and Skyscrapers,* 156.

44. William E. Kent, "Underground Atlanta: The Untimely Passing of a Major Tourist Attraction," *Journal of Travel Research* 22 (Spring 1984): 3. Proposals to revive Underground began almost immediately, and in 1989 a new version of Underground Atlanta opened.

45. Gerald Horton, "The History of Hostelry: A Century of Innkeeping in Atlanta," *Atlanta,* October 1961, p. 79.

46. Martin, *Atlanta and Environs,* 3:503–5.

47. Ivan Allen, Jr., and Paul Hemphill, *Mayor: Notes on the Sixties* (New York: Simon and Schuster, 1971), 73–74.

48. Martin, *Atlanta and Environs,* 3:494.

49. Cultural attractions include art galleries, theaters, concert halls,

museums, zoos, historic sites, and interesting architecture. See Christopher M. Law, *Urban Tourism: Attracting Visitors to Large Cities* (London: Mansell, 1993), chap. 5.

50. John Pennington, "City on the Edge of the Swamp," *Atlanta,* November 1967, p. 53.

51. The exception, of course, was caused by the VD epidemic in 1942 during World War II, when prostitution was suppressed. See Mathias and Anderson, *Horse to Helicopter,* 70–77; and Allen, *Atlanta Rising,* 33–34.

52. According to a national poll conducted by the Institute for Research in Social Science, University of North Carolina at Chapel Hill (reported in *Constitution,* July 6, 1995, B-3), sports, especially football, ranked as the second most clearly defined characteristic of the South—after hospitality.

53. Martin, *Atlanta and Environs,* 3:581–82. The debt on the stadium was finally retired early in 1997 by the Atlanta Committee for the Olympic Games as the facility was torn down and replaced by a reconfigured Olympic Stadium, now known as Turner Field, which was converted for use by the Braves.

54. Much of this literature is summarized by Mark S. Rosentraub, David Swindell, Michael Przybylsky, and Daniel R. Mullins in "Sports and Downtown Development Strategy: If You Build It, Will Jobs Come?" *Journal of Urban Affairs* 16 (1994): 221–39.

55. Law, *Urban Tourism,* 93.

56. Janet Lever, *Soccer Madness* (Chicago: University of Chicago Press, 1983).

57. In contrast, the success of both college and professional football teams in Dallas has given rise to a collective self-image that can be described as municipal hubris.

58. Martin, *Atlanta and Environs,* 3:587–88.

59. Central Area Study Policy Committee, *Central Atlanta Opportunities and Responses* (Atlanta: City of Atlanta, Central Atlanta Progress and U.S. Department of Transportation, 1971), 10.

60. City of Atlanta and Central Atlanta Progress, *Central Area Study: Atlanta, Georgia, Technical Appendix* (Atlanta: Central Atlanta Progress, 1971), 32–33. In 1970, Atlanta ranked seventh in the nation in the number of conventions hosted and the number of meeting participants.

61. Ibid., 15.

62. Ibid., 16.

63. U.S. Bureau of the Census, *Nineteenth Census of the United States, 1970,* vol. 1 (Washington, D.C.: Government Printing Office, 1972). The City of Atlanta's population in 1970 was the highest total the city would reach, as it declined in both 1980 and 1990. With continued suburban growth, the city's size as a percentage of the total metropolitan area declined to less than 14 percent in 1990.

64. Ibid. Also excluded from all occupational categories in Tables 6.3 and 6.4 are those employed in private households, e.g., household maids and cooks.

Chapter 7

1. This failure to include the entire metropolitan area continues to make regional solutions to transportation problems difficult for the Atlanta area. The 1990 census recognized twenty counties as having a substantial population that commutes to the central city for employment. Efforts since 1971 to expand MARTA outside Fulton and Dekalb Counties have been rejected by suburban voters.

2. Rice, "If Dixie Were Atlanta," 31–32.

3. Dana F. White and Timothy J. Crimmins, "How Atlanta Grew: Cool Heads, Hot Air, and Hard Work," *Atlanta Economic Review* 28 (January–February 1978): 7–15, emphasizes the roles of hard work and boosterism in Atlanta's growth; and Rutheiser, *Imagineering Atlanta*, 65–66.

4. *Constitution,* January 13, 1974, E-1, December 28, 1973, A-2.

5. Ibid., March 23, 1975, A-1.

6. Ibid., August 6, 1975, A-9. The immediate cause of the cancellation of the Elks' convention was the one published report that Peachtree Street downtown would be closed for construction of the MARTA rapid rail line. This information was not accurate, as most work would be done in a tunnel underneath Peachtree Street.

7. Grant, *The Way It Was,* 512–13. Reginald Eaves lost his position when he was linked to a scandal involving the promotion of black police officers within the department. His successor was another African American, Lee Brown, who brought to the job a reputation for integrity and a doctorate in criminology.

8. Stone, *Regime Politics,* 87–90.

9. Ayers, *Vengeance and Justice;* John Shelton Reed, *The Enduring South: Subcultural Persistence in Mass Society* (Lexington, Mass.: Lexington Books, 1972), chap. 5; Reed, *One South,* 142–45; and Christopher G. Ellison, "An Eye for an Eye? A Note on the Southern Subculture of Violence," *Social Forces* 69 (June 1991): 1223–39. The cultural explanation for violence in the South, while well documented, is a matter of considerable debate. Reed's essay "Below the Smith and Wesson Line" in *One South,* 139–53, outlines the alternative view that higher rates of violence in the South are the result of inefficient mechanisms of social control, as well as his own position, adopted here, that Southern violence is the product of regional cultural differences.

10. James C. Cobb, *The Selling of the South: The Southern Crusade for Industrial Development,* 2nd ed. (Urbana: University of Illinois Press, 1993).

11. Mayor A. J. Cervantes, *Mr. Mayor* (Los Angeles: Nash Publishing, 1974), 121, quoted in Heywood T. Sanders, "Building the Convention City: Politics, Finance, and Public Investment in Urban America," *Journal of Urban Affairs* 14 (1992): 135–36.

12. Ibid., 136–39.

13. *Constitution,* July 16, 1974, A-14.

14. Ibid., April 9, A-1, August 17, 1976, A-8.

15. Data supplied by the Atlanta Convention and Visitors Bureau.

16. *Constitution,* May 17, 1976, A-1.

17. Ibid., November 10, 1976, A-1.

18. For additional evidence of the importance of football to the culture of the region, see Wilson, "The Death of Bear Bryant: Myth and Ritual in the Modern South," in *Judgment and Grace in Dixie,* 37–51.

19. In spite of poor attendance, Turner sought a new and larger home for the Atlanta Hawks. In 1997 he negotiated a deal with the City of Atlanta and Fulton County to keep the team downtown in a new arena located on the site of the Omni. The twenty-five-year-old Omni sports arena was demolished to make way for the new facility, scheduled to open in 1999 as home to the Hawks and a new National Hockey League team, the Atlanta Thrashers (also owned by Turner).

20. Central Atlanta Progress, Inc., *Development Trends in Central Atlanta, 1987* (Atlanta: Central Atlanta Progress, 1987), 89, 94.

21. Ibid.

22. Paolo Riani, *John Portman* (Washington, D.C.: American Institute of Architects Press, 1990), 155. In 1986 the Plaza was renovated to become a luxury-class hotel. Its name was changed to the Westin Peachtree Plaza Hotel.

23. *Constitution,* April 30, 1978, A-1.

24. Ibid., December 19, C-1, December 21, 1979, C-3.

25. Braden and Hagan, *Dream Takes Flight,* 137.

26. Townsend and Hagan, *Atlanta International Airport,* 3–5.

27. Adolph Reed, Jr., "A Critique of Neo-Progressivism in Theorizing about Local Development Policy: A Case from Atlanta," in *The Politics of Urban Development,* ed. Clarence N. Stone and Heywood T. Sanders (Lawrence: University Press of Kansas, 1987), 208–11.

28. Braden and Hagan, *Dream Takes Flight,* 195–201.

29. Grant, *The Way It Was,* 487.

30. Townsend and Hagan, *Atlanta International Airport,* 6.

31. Ibid., 64.

32. Another link to *Gone with the Wind* opened in 1997, when restoration was completed on the apartment building in Midtown where Margaret Mitchell lived while writing her novel. Mitchell referred to the place as "the Dump." Its restoration was made possible by a grant from the makers of Mercedes-Benz automobiles. Scheduled to open before the Olympics, the Dump was badly damaged by an arsonist. Additional support from Mercedes-Benz restored the building again. There is also the Road to Tara Museum on Peachtree Street.

33. The closing of the Henry Grady Hotel is described in the *Constitution,* May 4, 1972, A-3. For the destruction of the hotel, see ibid., October 2, 1972, A-8.

34. Research Atlanta, Inc., *The Convention Industry in Atlanta* (Atlanta: Research Atlanta, 1982), 37–38.

35. *Constitution,* May 16, 1983, B-1.

36. Ibid., July 19, 1983, A-1.

37. Ibid., May 7, B-16, May 17, A-1, November 7, 1984, C-1.

38. Ibid., November 9, D-1. The hotel changed its name to Comfort Inn.

39. *Journal Constitution,* June 6, 1987, C-12, November 14, 1985, E-4; and *Constitution,* December 7, 1983, B-1.

40. Research Atlanta, Inc., *Convention Industry,* 23.

41. Atlanta Convention and Visitors Bureau, "Atlanta Meetings and Convention Industry Fact Sheet" (February 1982).

42. Research Atlanta, Inc., *Convention Industry,* 13.

43. Ibid., 14.

44. Central Atlanta Progress, *Development Trends, 1987,* 87.

45. Law, *Urban Tourism,* 154–55.

46. MacFarlane and Company, Inc., for the American City Corporation, *The Convention Delegate Study Report* (1982), conducted interviews with delegates to three conventions at the Georgia World Congress Center; the Center for Public and Urban Research, Georgia State University, *Guess Who's Sleeping in Atlanta Tonight* (1982), did telephone interviews with residents of three cities to gather information about their visits to Atlanta; and Research Atlanta, Inc., *Convention Industry,* also surveyed convention delegates in the city.

47. Douglas C. Frechtling, "Assessing the Impacts of Tourism," in *Travel, Tourism, and Hospitality Research: A Handbook for Managers and Researchers,* ed. J. R. Brent Ritchie and Charles R. Goeldner (New York: Wiley, 1987), 325–62.

48. Law, *Urban Tourism,* 162.

49. Douglas C. Frechtling, "Assessing the Economic Impacts of Travel and Tourism—Introduction to Travel Economic Impact Estimation," in *Travel, Tourism, and Hospitality Research: A Handbook for Managers and Researchers,* 2nd ed., ed. J. R. Brent Ritchie and Charles R. Goeldner (New York: Wiley, 1994), 363.

50. *Constitution,* September 11, 1995, C-1.

51. Frechtling, "Assessing Economic Impacts of Travel and Tourism," 363–64.

52. U.S. Bureau of the Census, *Twentieth Census of the United States, 1980,* vol. 1 (Washington, D.C.: Government Printing Office, 1984).

53. *Constitution,* February 2, 1984, I-4, March 8, 1984, I-1, October 7, 1985, C-1.

54. Joel Garreau, *Edge City: Life on the New Frontier* (New York: Doubleday, 1991).

55. *Journal Constitution,* April 25, 1985, J-3.

56. Central Atlanta Progress, *Development Trends, 1987,* 93.

57. Mayor A. J. Cervantes, quoted in Sanders, "Building the Convention City," 136.

58. Pillsbury, *Boardinghouse to Bistro,* 3–7.

59. *Constitution,* December 19, 1983, D-1.

60. Pillsbury, *Boardinghouse to Bistro,* 143, 215.

61. *Constitution,* August 1, 1995, D-1. In 1988 the local owners sold the Peasant Restaurants to a New York chain, the Quantum Restaurant Group. In January 1997 the national chain, known as Morton's Restaurant Group, sold the Peasant Restaurants to Gregory M. Buckley of At-

lanta. The headquarters of the nineteen restaurants included in the sale was returned to Atlanta. See *Constitution,* January 4, 1997, C-1.

62. Ibid., August 17, 1994, B-1, B-8. In 1994 the nine restaurants of the Buckhead Life Group earned $30 million. Prior to the 1996 Olympic Games, the chain added two other properties.

63. Pillsbury, *Boardinghouse to Bistro,* 172.

64. Thelma's Kitchen survived location changes to make way for the building of the Georgia World Congress Center and Centennial Olympic Park. Special features enjoyed by blacks and whites are fried chicken and okra cakes prepared according to owner Thelma Grundy's family recipes. Deacon Burton's Grill survived for a time the death of its founder, Lyndell "Deacon" Burton, in 1993, as well as conflict among family members over the restaurant's ownership. Finally, one claimant moved around the corner to open The Son's Place. Patrons could choose fried chicken, greens, hoecakes, etc., from either establishment, but eventually the original Deacon Burton's Grill closed. The Son's Place remained open in 1998.

65. *Constitution,* July 7, 1995, A-1.

66. Research Atlanta, Inc., *Convention Industry,* 32.

67. Ibid.; and Research Atlanta, Inc., *Atlanta Tourism and Convention Market: A Synopsis of Several Studies* (Atlanta: Research Atlanta, 1983), 37.

68. William E. Kent and J. Thomas Chesnutt, "Underground Atlanta: Resurrected and Revisited," *Journal of Travel Research* 29 (Spring 1991): 36.

69. Stone, *Regime Politics,* 138–39.

70. Harvey Newman, Barbara Ray, and Joseph Hacker, "Media, Consensus Building, Growth Machine: The Underground Atlanta Project" (paper presented at the annual meeting of the Urban Affairs Association, St. Louis, Mo., March 1988), 11–13.

71. Logan and Molotch, *Urban Fortunes,* 62–85.

72. Underground Festival Development Corporation, "Briefing Paper on the Underground Atlanta Project," December 22, 1986, 1–2.

73. Bernard J. Frieden and Lynne B. Sagalyn, *Downtown Inc.: How America Rebuilds Cities* (Cambridge: MIT Press, 1989), 155.

74. David S. Sawicki, "The Festival Marketplace as Public Policy: Guidelines for Future Policy Decisions," *Journal of the American Planning Association* 55 (Summer 1989): 348.

75. Kent and Chesnutt, "Underground Atlanta," 37–38.

76. See Joseph H. Hacker, "Recapturing Main Street: A Semiotic Analysis of Nostalgia in the Underground Atlanta Project" (M.S. thesis, Georgia State University, 1989), for a discussion of the efforts to evoke nostalgia in the design of Underground Atlanta.

77. David L. Sjoquist and Loren Williams, *The Underground Atlanta Project: An Economic Analysis* (Atlanta: Policy Research Center, Georgia State University, 1992), 29.

78. Ibid., 22–25.

79. Grant, *The Way It Was,* 506; Crime and security concerns were ac-

centuated in 1992 when violence erupted following the verdict in the trial of Los Angeles police officers accused of beating Rodney King and, again, in 1995 when looters taking part in the Freaknik celebration smashed windows and stole merchandise from ground-level stores at Underground; *Journal Constitution,* May 13, 1995, C-1.

80. *Journal Constitution,* December, 31, 1994, C-1.

81. Sjoquist and Williams, *Underground Atlanta Project,* 9.

82. *Constitution,* June 29, 1995, F-1.

83. Sjoquist and Williams, *Underground Atlanta Project,* 30–31.

84. For example, in the food court the black, female-owned Stuffen Muffin, which featured the "muffin de soul"—a corn bread muffin stuffed with collard greens and ham—failed and was replaced by a Dairy Queen.

85. The financial future of the complex is uncertain. The Rouse Company withdrew in early 1997, after seven years as the manager of Underground. Its replacement, Urban Retail Properties, manages several Atlanta-area shopping malls. *Journal Constitution,* December 25, 1996, D-1.

86. James Howard Kunstler, *The Geography of Nowhere: The Rise and Decline of America's Man-Made Landscape* (New York: Simon & Schuster, 1993), 186.

87. Wilson, *Judgment and Grace in Dixie,* 160–62.

88. *Constitution,* April 24, 1987, C-1, November 7, 1989, B-1.

89. Central Atlanta Progress, *Development Trends, 1987,* 93–94. The hotel industry came to call structures such as the Hyatt Regency "Jesus Christ" hotels because that is what visitors exclaim when they enter for the first time. "Downtown Is Looking Up," *Time,* July 5, 1976, p. 65, quoted in Frieden and Sagalyn, *Downtown Inc.,* 268, n. 4.

90. Central Atlanta Progress, *Development Trends, 1987,* 87.

91. Atlanta Convention and Visitors Bureau, "Fact Sheet," 1987.

92. J. B. Strasser and Laurie Becklund, *Swoosh: The Unauthorized Story of Nike and the Men Who Played There* (New York: Harcourt Brace Jovanovich, 1991), 630.

93. *Journal Constitution,* January 29, 1995, B-1, B-6.

94. Sanders, "Building the Convention City," 135.

95. *Constitution,* October 3, 1995, F-1.

96. Ibid., April 3, 1987, A-24.

97. Ibid., August 14, C-3, October 7, 1987, A-1.

98. Ibid., September 29, 1988, A-1.

99. Wyatt-Brown, *Southern Honor,* 335–37.

100. *Wall Street Journal,* February 29, 1988, pp. 1, 18.

101. *Constitution,* March 6, 1988, D-2.

102. *Journal Constitution,* July 17, 1988, C-1.

103. Ibid., June 11, 1988, A-1, A-8.

104. Ibid.

105. Ibid., C-14.

106. *Constitution,* July 19, 1988, C-19.

107. *Journal Constitution,* July 17, 1988, C-22.

108. Ibid.

109. *Constitution,* February 23, B-1, B-7, November 7, 1989, B-1, B-8.
110. Ibid.
111. Research Atlanta, Inc., *Convention Industry,* 1, 21–30; and Center for Public and Urban Research, *Guess Who's Sleeping,* 15.
112. *Journal Constitution,* January 18, 1987, D-1, D-6.
113. Ibid., November 5, 1988, E-1, E-7.
114. Even with the publicity of the Olympic Games, the city faces many of the same criticisms raised by Frommer and others. In the Convention Bureau's Business Plan for 1997, a major goal was to extend convention stays by focusing on spousal and family attendance.

Chapter 8

1. *Journal Constitution,* January 1, 1990, A-1; *Constitution,* January 2, A-1, January 3, 1990, A-1.
2. *Constitution,* March 13, 1990, A-1, A-7.
3. Ibid., March 13, A-1, A-7, May 23, A-1, May 24, 1990, A-26.
4. U.S. Bureau of the Census, Data Sheets for Level A (Atlanta) Metropolitan Statistical Area, March 29, 1983.
5. Georgia Department of Industry, Trade and Tourism, *Estimated Tourist Expenditures in Georgia by County, 1989* (Atlanta: Davidson-Peterson Associates, 1990), 5–7.
6. Governor Joe Frank Harris's 1990 budget proposal to the Georgia General Assembly included the proposed financing of the $70 million in bonds needed to expand the Georgia World Congress Center. The legislature approved a record budget of more than $8 billion in state spending for the year, but refused to authorize the increased debt for the expansion. The chair of the House Appropriations Committee offered the excuse that he did not want to increase the state's debt service for the bonds. Governor Harris indicated that the general assembly felt it was doing enough for Atlanta at the time with the construction of the Georgia Dome under way. *Constitution,* March 12, A-14, May 24, 1990, A-26; and author interview with Governor Joe Frank Harris, February 10, 1997.
7. Research Atlanta, Inc., *The Atlanta Report Card, 1990 Update* (Atlanta: Research Atlanta, 1990), 93.
8. *Constitution,* November 8, 1990, XK-3.
9. Research Atlanta, Inc., *Atlanta Report Card,* 93–95.
10. U.S. Bureau of the Census, *1990 Census of Population, General Population Characteristics,* part 1, *United States,* and part 12, *Georgia* (Washington, D.C.: Government Printing Office, 1993). There was some basis for the city's claim that the 1990 census undercounted its population. The Census Bureau admitted the error but refused to adjust their figures. Other major cities also participated in the litigation, but the U.S. Supreme Court refused to hear the case, letting the figures stand for the 1990 census. The suburban growth also increased the size of the metropolitan area. In 1993 the Census Bureau added three more counties to

the eighteen-county metropolitan area, bringing the total to twenty counties (Butts County was dropped from the metropolitan area because the number of people commuting from there to the central area for work dropped below the required federal limits).

11. *Journal Constitution,* January 28, 1990, H-1.

12. Ibid., May 19, 1990, A-12.

13. Research Atlanta, Inc., *Atlanta Report Card,* 108.

14. *Journal Constitution,* November 30, 1990, F-1, F-8.

15. *Constitution,* February 21, 1991, D-1, D-9.

16. Ibid., August 29, 1991, XE-9.

17. Cecil Burke Day, Jr., and John McCollister, *Day by Day: The Story of Cecil B. Day and His Simple Formula for Success* (Middle Village, N.Y.: Jonathan David Publishers, 1990), 89, 195.

18. Two of the three hotels opened by international airlines have been sold. The Hotel Nikko became the Grant Hyatt Hotel in 1997, and the Penta a Renaissance Hotel.

19. *Constitution,* May 4, 1990, F-2.

20. *Journal Constitution,* September 2, 1990, P-4. Hotel occupancy rates supplied by Atlanta Convention and Visitors Bureau, *1996 Atlanta Hotel General Managers Survey* (Atlanta: PKF Consulting, 1996), 5.

21. Atlanta Convention and Visitors Bureau, *1996 Hotel Managers Survey,* 5.

22. *Journal Constitution,* October 24, 1992, C-1.

23. *Constitution,* August 20, 1992, D-1.

24. Pillsbury, *Boardinghouse to Bistro,* 189–223.

25. Ibid., 85–86; and *Restaurant Business,* September 20, 1990, n.p. In 1990, Atlanta had an RAI of 136, compared to New York City's 138, Chicago's 123, and Dallas's 111.

26. *Constitution,* August 28, C-2, September 1, 1992, F-1.

27. Ibid., December 3, H-8, December 4, 1992, D-9.

28. *Journal Constitution,* June 26, 1993, D-12; and *Constitution,* June 30, 1993, D-2.

29. Atlanta Convention and Visitors Bureau, *Celebrating the Dream: 1996 Annual Report* (Atlanta: THP Communications Corporation, 1997), 10–11.

30. In 1966 Auburn Avenue had seventeen restaurants, four hotels, and five clubs. Twelve years later, the city directory listed fourteen restaurants, one new motel, and two clubs. City Directory Collection, Atlanta History Center. Since 1978 the number of restaurants has continued to decline and the motel has closed.

31. *Journal Constitution,* January 16, 1994, D-9.

32. Ibid., September 5, 1992, E-6.

33. *Constitution,* February 24, 1994, D-14. The city also hosted the National Conference of Black Mayors in 1996, and booked other large African-American conventions, such as the Shriners in 1997 and the NAACP in 1998.

34. Ibid., June 3, 1992, D-1.

35. Ibid., October 6, C-1, November 3, 1992, D-1; and "Babbit Kisses

Atlanta Goodbye: Marketing Czar Leaves Behind Lots of Money-Making Sponsorship Ideas," *Advertising Age,* June 21, 1993, p. 16.

36. *Constitution,* February 3, B-1, April 13, A-1, April 14, 1993, C-1.

37. "Marketing Run Amok: The Adman Who Sold Atlanta," *Advertising Age,* August 2, 1993, p. 14.

38. *Constitution,* August 22, 1993, C-1.

39. A local humorist has suggested that "Coca-Cola Peachtree Street" might be one appropriate change to generate revenue for Atlanta.

40. *Constitution,* February 11, 1971, A-8, April 30, 1973, A-31.

41. Ibid., August 9, C-1, November 3, C-1, November 17, 1978, C-6.

42. Ibid., July 14, 1988, B-8.

43. Simon Hoggart, "The Nightlife of Atlanta Laid Bare," *Punch,* July 29, 1988, pp. 21–22. In one of his less scholarly works, sociologist John Shelton Reed noted how many reporters to the 1988 convention found time to observe this "traditional Atlanta art form"—table dancing in Atlanta strip clubs. Reed added, "Yankees have always said that Southern men put women on pedestals, but I don't think this is what they meant." Reed, *Whistling Dixie: Dispatches from the South* (Columbia: University of Missouri Press, 1990), 144.

44. *Constitution,* November 12, 1993, A-13.

45. B. C. Hall and C. T. Wood, *The South* (New York: Scribner, 1995), 137.

46. *Constitution,* November 12, 1993, A-13.

47. Judd, "Promoting Tourism," 20–21.

48. *Constitution,* November 12, 1993, A-13.

49. *Journal Constitution,* August 17, 1995, H-2.

50. *Constitution,* June 7, 1995, C-6.

51. Ibid., September 23, 1994, A-1.

52. Ibid., September 23, 1994, D-3; and *Journal Constitution,* September 24, C-1, September 25, 1994, D-8.

53. *Constitution,* March 15, 1995, A-10.

54. Ibid., April 12, 1995, A-1.

55. *Journal Constitution,* March 25, 1995, B-1; and *Constitution,* March 30, C-4, April 4, 1995, C-1.

56. *Constitution,* April 13, 1995, C-1.

57. Ibid., April 19, 1995, A-14 and A-15.

58. *Journal Constitution,* April 22, 1995, A-1, D-7.

59. Ibid., A-1, D-7 to D-10.

60. *Constitution,* April 25, 1995, A-1.

61. *Journal Constitution,* April 22, 1996, A-1.

62. Ibid., April 19, 1995, C-1.

63. Ibid., May 10, 1995, B-1, B-6.

64. Harvey K. Newman, "Black Clergy and Urban Regimes: The Role of Atlanta's Concerned Black Clergy," *Journal of Urban Affairs* 16 (1994): 27–29.

65. *Constitution,* January 13, F-1, January 26, 1994, C-10.

66. Ibid., January 21, 1994, G-2.

67. *Journal,* January 19, 1994, B-2.

68. *Constitution,* January 25, 1994, B-13.

69. *Journal Constitution,* January 30, 1994, F-26.

70. George Garrett, "Southern Literature Here and Now," in *Why the South Will Survive,* ed. Clyde N. Wilson (Athens: University of Georgia Press, 1981), 138.

71. *Constitution,* April 13, 1994, B-3.

72. Atlanta Convention and Visitors Bureau, *1996 Hotel Managers Survey,* 5.

73. *Journal,* February 14, 1992, H-3.

74. Atlanta Convention and Visitors Bureau, *1996 Hotel Managers Survey,* 14–17, 32, 56, 62.

75. Ibid., 5, 14, 32, 50. As with occupancy rates, average room rates varied considerably among hotel submarkets in the Atlanta area. Buckhead hotels had the highest rates, at $108.62 per night in 1995. Large downtown hotels also had high rates, at $107.39, while hotels in the Six Flags area on the west side of Atlanta had the lowest rates, at $37.46.

76. Union Label and Service Trades Department, AFL-CIO, "Label Letter," 20, no. 5 (September–October 1995): 4–5. Conversations with state and local labor leaders in 1998 indicated that there has been little effort to organize hotels in the city. Of the three "organized" hotels, the Hilton had only a fraction of its employees who are members of the Firemen and Oilers Union; the American Hotel was sold in 1997 and closed for remodeling, so its future as an organized hotel is uncertain; and the Hyatt Regency remains as the hotel of choice for labor union functions and for visiting labor leaders.

77. Julia Emmons, Executive Director, Atlanta Track Club, author interview, October 31, 1995. The estimate is based on research by John T. McLeod, School of Economics, Georgia Institute of Technology, Atlanta, Georgia, 1994.

78. Carla J. Robinson-Barnes, John C. Thomas, and Alvin Glymph, *The Economic Impact of the 1994 National Black Arts Festival on Atlanta* (Atlanta: Applied Research Center, College of Public and Urban Affairs, Georgia State University, 1995), 2; and author interview with Linda Hall, National Black Arts Festival staff, November 17, 1997. For the 1994 festival, Fulton County contributed $549,454 (of which $174,454 was in-kind support) and the City of Atlanta contributed $37,000.

79. Ibid., 2–23.

80. Ibid., 23.

81. *Journal Constitution,* October 10, 1995, D-7.

Chapter 9

1. Poll conducted by the Institute for Research in Social Science, University of North Carolina at Chapel Hill, reported in *Constitution,* July 6, 1995, B-3.

2. Georgia Department of Labor, *Georgia Employment and Wages, 1993* (Atlanta: Georgia Department of Labor, 1994), 166.

3. J. R. Brent Ritchie, "Assessing the Impact of Hallmark Events: Conceptual and Research Issues," *Journal of Travel Research* 23 (Summer 1984): 2.

4. Hall, *Hallmark Tourist Events*, 36.

5. For a detailed discussion of the history of Atlanta's competition with Nashville, see Doyle, *New South*, chap. 6.

6. *Journal Constitution*, September 18, 1990, A-6.

7. *Constitution*, September 17, 1990, A-4.

8. Atlanta Committee for the Olympic Games, *Atlanta's Official Bid for the 1996 Olympic Games*, vol. 1, *Welcome to a Brave and Beautiful City*, and vol. 2, *Atlanta: A City of Dreams* (Atlanta: Peachtree Publishers, 1990); and *Journal Constitution*, September 23, 1990, R-4.

9. *Journal Constitution*, September 23, 1990, R-11.

10. *Constitution*, September 17, 1990, A-4.

11. *Journal*, September 18, 1990, A-1.

12. *Constitution*, September 25, 1990, A-1.

13. *Journal Constitution*, September 18, 1994, G-5 to G-8; and *Constitution*, April 14, 1995, F-3.

14. *Constitution*, March 18, C-1, April 16, 1995, R-4.

15. Ibid.

16. John Morris Dixon, "No Frills, No Thrills: Atlanta's Pragmatic Olympics," *Progressive Architecture* 76 (July 1995): 51–59.

17. Annette DiMeo Carlozzi, Visual Arts Producer, Cultural Olympiad, to Karen Hubner, Director, Atlanta Urban Design Commission, June 26, 1995. Letter presented to members of the Urban Design Commission by the artist, June 28, 1995.

18. *Constitution*, May 17, G-1, May 22, 1996, B-3.

19. Ibid., September 19, 1990, A-7.

20. Ibid., October 12, C-3, November 13, 1996, C-2.

21. Ibid., October 10, 1995, C-1.

22. Colin Campbell, *Constitution*, October 12, 1995, C-1.

23. Ibid., April 14, 1995, F-3.

24. Ibid., October 16, B-1, January 12, 1996, D-1, D-6.

25. *New York Times*, November 12, 1995, pp. 1–10; and *Atlanta Business Chronicle*, October 18–24, 1996, pp. 1–5.

26. In addition to the estimated $516 million spent on construction by ACOG, a variety of other public and private sources engaged in construction activity. See Jeffrey M. Humphreys and Michael K. Plummer, "The Economic Impact on the State of Georgia of Hosting the 1996 Olympic Games: Executive Summary," 1995 Update, prepared for the Atlanta Committee for the Olympic Games by the Terry College of Business, University of Georgia and IRE Advisors, Economic/Management Consultants.

27. Donald Ratajczak, "Impact of the Olympics," *Constitution*, April 16, 1995, R-4.

28. *Constitution*, February 22, 1995, B-3.

29. Ibid., November 11, 1995, H-1, May 17, 1996, G-1.

30. Ibid., March 23, 1995, G-1.

31. Ratajczak, "Olympic Impact"; and *Constitution,* November 13, 1996, C-2.

32. No final economic impact study has been conducted since the Olympics. One estimate for tourist expenditures for Fulton County (which includes most of the City of Atlanta) for 1996 was $4,247.84 billion. This represents an increase of $376.73 million (a 9.7 percent increase) over 1995, with most of the increase the result of the Olympics. Atlanta Convention and Visitors Bureau, "The Economic Impact of Expenditures by Tourists on Fulton County, Calendar Year 1996" (York, Maine: Davidson-Peterson Associates, Inc., 1997), 10–13.

33. *Constitution,* November 19, 1996, D-3.

34. *Journal Constitution,* January 22, 1995, A-1, A-8, A-9, June 2, 1996, H-1; and Allen, *Secret Formula,* 421. Allen suggests that having the games in Atlanta was as much a nuisance to the Coca-Cola Company as it was an opportunity. The Olympic mascot, "Whatizit" (later "Izzy"), developed in secret by ACOG and unveiled in Barcelona, featured the blue color of the company's main rival. Coke's local marketing efforts during the Games "painted the town red" with signs, banners, vending carts, and other promotions. One of the more unique displays was an exhibit of Coke bottle folk art from the 202 countries where Coca-Cola is sold. The exhibit was located in the Georgia Freight Depot near Underground Atlanta and the World of Coca-Cola.

35. Eric Hill Associates, *Report on Relocation,* iii–vii.

36. Larry Keating, Max Creighton, and Jon Abercrombie, "Essay Two, Community Development: Building on a New Foundation," in Research Atlanta, Inc., *The Olympic Legacy: Building on What Was Achieved* (Atlanta: Policy Research Center, Georgia State University, 1996), 5.

37. Author interview with the Development Director, Atlanta Housing Authority, June 4, 1996.

38. After relocating the residents of the Martin Street Plaza housing project and preparing for renovation and privatization, the Atlanta Housing Authority announced more than a year after the Olympics that the project would remain as rental housing. The residents were displaced, but in late 1997 they began returning to renovated apartments.

39. Keating, Creighton, and Abercrombie, "Community Development," 1.

40. Director of Relocation, Corporation for Olympic Development in Atlanta, author interview, May 28, 1996.

41. Robin Boyle, "Empowerment Zones: Picking the Winners," *Economic Development Quarterly* 9 (August 1995): 207, 211.

42. City of Atlanta, "Atlanta Empowerment Zone Application," *Executive Summary,* 1–7.

43. Author interview with the Special Assistant to the Mayor, who served as Director of Grants Development and Coordinator of the Empowerment Zone Project, June 3, 1996; and City of Atlanta, "Creating an Urban Village: Atlanta's Community Driven Vision for the Empowerment Zone," *Strategic Development,* vol. 1, vi.

44. *Constitution,* September 20, 1996, F-1.

45. Corporation for Olympic Development in Atlanta, *The Civic Trust: CODA Public Spaces Program* (Atlanta: CODA, 1996), 1–13.

46. U.S. Bureau of Economic Analysis, quoted in *Constitution,* May 30, 1996, F-1.

47. Atlanta Committee for the Olympic Games, *Official Bid,* vol. 2, *Atlanta: A City of Dreams,* 29.

48. *Constitution,* April 4, 1995, E-3.

49. Atlanta Committee for the Olympic Games, *Official Bid,* vol. 2, *Atlanta: A City of Dreams,* 27.

50. Ibid.

51. *Constitution,* March 2, 1995.

52. Ibid., April 7, A-1, April 13, 1995, A-16, C-4. The Presidential Hotel reopened as the Ramada Plaza Hotel.

53. Ibid., October 21, 1994, A-1.

54. Ibid., September 15, 1994, K-1, October 19, 1994, E-1, January 18, 1995, B-1.

55. Atlanta Convention and Visitors Bureau, *1996 Hotel Managers Survey,* 5.

56. For example, the Turkish Sports Federation rented Rhodes Hall, a Victorian mansion on Peachtree Street, throughout the Games. The Italians turned Callanwolde, the Candler mansion that serves as a DeKalb County arts center, into Casa Italia during the Olympics. Special hospitality centers were established by national committees seeking to host the Olympics in 2004. Puerto Rico turned the Bridgetown Grill in Midtown into Club Puerto Rico, featuring food and entertainment flown in from San Juan. Smaller nations entertained in restaurants throughout the city. For example, the Nationalist Chinese sports federation and athletes held three banquets at Frank Ma's China Express in Midtown.

57. Mary-Kate Tews, "The Mega-event as an Urban Redevelopment Strategy: Atlanta Prepares for 1996 and Beyond" (National Center for the Revitalization of Central Cities, Working Paper no. 17; New Orleans: College of Urban and Public Affairs, University of New Orleans, 1993), 3–4.

58. Rutheiser, *Imagineering Atlanta,* 259–68, regarded the development of Centennial Olympic Park as evidence that the Atlanta public-private partnership was fundamentally changed to reduce or eliminate the city's role. This overstated the case, since the state of Georgia, which developed and owned the park, had long been a participant in the partnership to redevelop the area with the Georgia World Congress Center and the Georgia Dome as evidence of its support of Atlanta's tourism industry. My interpretation of the events surrounding the development of Centennial Olympic Park owes more to Chester Hartman, *The Transformation of San Francisco* (Totowa, N.J.: Rowman & Allanheld, 1984), 319–26.

59. Jane Jacobs, *The Death and Life of Great American Cities* (New York: Modern Library, 1969), 98–99.

60. Rice, "If Dixie Were Atlanta," 31–32. Rice describes four stages in Atlanta's boosterism: its desire to become the leading city in Georgia,

the push to become the metropolis of the South, the campaign to become a national city, and, most recently, the prediction that Atlanta will become "the world's next great city."

61. *Constitution,* July 15, 1992, D-5; and "Marketing Run Amok: The Adman Who Sold Atlanta," *Advertising Age,* August 2, 1993, p. 14.

62. *Journal Constitution,* August 1, 1993, R-10. Local residents made fun of the process and suggested other slogans such as "Atlanta: Not Bad for Georgia!" and "Atlanta: We're Better Than Birmingham!" Local author Melissa Fay Greene suggested to readers of the *New York Times* that Atlanta's "hype-fest" will not end until the city proclaims itself "the Milky Way's Next Great City!" July 7, 1996, E-9.

63. Bob Garfield, "Atlanta Is Really Dreaming If It Thinks This Ad Will Work," *Advertising Age,* July 10, 1995, p. 3.

64. Rutheiser, *Imagineering Atlanta,* 4–5, 287. The stark comparison in Rutheiser's book between the image shaped by Atlanta's leaders and the realities of class and race that affect most residents was criticized for not offering solutions to the problems described. See *Constitution,* July 28, 1996, L-11. The reviewer missed the point of Rutheiser's powerful description of Atlanta's history as one of manufactured images.

65. Mark Gottdiener, "Culture, Ideology, and the Sign of the City," in *The City and the Sign: An Introduction to Urban Semiotics,* ed. Mark Gottdiener and A. P. Lagopoulos (New York: Columbia University Press, 1986), 207.

66. The state poll is conducted as an ongoing project of the Applied Research Center, Georgia State University. Olympics-related questions were asked to more than 9,500 randomly selected residents of the state as part of thirteen separate surveys conducted between summer 1992 and winter 1997 (at six-month intervals plus an additional survey before and after the Games). Respondents were asked, "All things considered, do you think it is a good idea for Georgia to host the 1996 Summer Olympic Games?" Other questions dealt with possible benefits and consequences of the Olympics and on plans to attend. The percentage of Georgia residents planning to attend dropped from an initial high of 69 percent in 1992 to a low of 28 percent just before the Games. In spite of the recognized difficulties in getting tickets, support for hosting the Games remained high.

67. Wilson, *Judgment and Grace in Dixie,* 31, 51, 161–62.

68. *Journal Constitution,* August 6, 1996, Special Edition, pp. 1–6.

69. Ibid., July 31, 1996, Special Edition, pp. 34–35.

70. Atlanta Committee for the Olympic Games, *Olympic Games Fact Book* (Atlanta: ACOG, 1996); and *Journal Constitution,* August 5, 1996, Special Edition, pp. 1–17.

71. The author served as a volunteer driver at the Olympic Family Hotel motor pool for four weeks before and during the Games. Fleets of vehicles were provided by three official sponsors—BMW, General Motors, and Nissan.

72. *New York Times,* August 4, 1996, pp. 1–23.

73. For weeks after the closing ceremony, the public discussion about

IOC president Samaranch's remark raged in the city. Atlantans felt insulted by his failure to pronounce the Games in the city as "the best ever," so he became the focus of their anger. A favorite target was President Samaranch's insistence on being addressed as "His Excellency." *Constitution* editorial writer John Head wrote, "If I hear Samaranch give Atlanta another diplomatic putdown, I'll tell His Most Exceptionalness to kiss my grits." August 16, 1996, A-22.

74. *Constitution,* August 8, 1996, C-1.

75. Ibid., August 11, 1996, A-1, C-5, February 9, 1997, C-5.

76. Ibid., October 10, 1996, B-8. Pound's opinions may have been influenced by the fact that his wife was arrested by Atlanta police in a widely publicized incident in which she was reported to have verbally abused and assaulted an officer at a street crossing late at night. ACOG responded to Pound's criticism of their commercialism by indicating all sponsorship agreements were approved by Pound and the IOC. One significant outcome of this may be to make it difficult for other U.S. cities to host the Olympics in the future. It is difficult to imagine a U.S. city raising the funds necessary to stage the Games without private-sector support.

77. Ibid., November 17, G-10, November 18, 1996, B-1.

78. Ibid., December 10, 1996, C-3.

79. The stadium was named by the Time-Warner Corporation after it acquired Turner Communications. This decision irritated IOC officials, who regarded Ted Turner as a competitor since he created and telecast the Goodwill Games. It also angered local civil rights groups who urged that the stadium be named for Braves home run hitter Hank Aaron. The City of Atlanta responded by renaming one of the streets surrounding the stadium in honor of Aaron.

80. Stan Kasten, Robert Dale Morgan, and Janet Marie Smith, "Essay Five, The Olympic Games: Seventeen Days of Sports or More?" in Research Atlanta, Inc., *The Olympic Legacy,* 4–6; and *Journal Constitution,* November 1, 1996, F-1, January 19, 1997, F-2.

81. The Atlanta Ambassador Force was the result of forming a Downtown Improvement District in 1996 which permitted area businesses to tax themselves to provide additional revenues to support the program as well as traffic control and promotional activities. The unarmed ambassadors provide information and report trouble to the police. Crime statistics for the first six months suggested that downtown crime rates did drop as criminal activity may have moved to other areas. See *Constitution,* December 12, 1996, D-1. Once again, travel writer Arthur Frommer criticized the city's promotional efforts, asking, "What in the world is there to do there?" *Journal Constitution,* November 24, 1996, H-2.

82. Michael L. Lomax, "Essay Four, The Arts: Atlanta's Missing Olympic Legacy," in Research Atlanta, Inc., *The Olympic Legacy,* 4.

83. Author interview with public relations representative, Atlanta Convention and Visitors Bureau, March 30, 1998.

84. On the morning of January 16, 1997, a bomb exploded outside the Northside Family Planning Clinic in Sandy Springs, a northern sub-

urb of Atlanta. One hour later, another bomb, probably targeted at law enforcement officers at the scene, exploded, causing injuries to four people. On Friday evening, February 21, 1997, a similar bomb with nails for shrapnel went off in the Otherside Lounge on Piedmont Road. Another explosive device was found at the scene and detonated by law enforcement officers. Unlike the Centennial Park bombing, there were no warning calls in either subsequent episode. As of early 1998, no arrests had been made in any of the attacks.

85. *Constitution,* August 14, E-2, September 28, E-3, December 17, 1996, D-1.

86. P. Bramham et al., eds., *Leisure and Urban Processes: Critical Studies of Leisure Policy in Western European Cities* (New York: Routledge, 1989), 4, quoted in Collin Michael Hall, *Tourism and Politics: Policy, Power, and Place* (New York: Wiley, 1994), 155.

87. David Harvey, "Between Space and Time: Reflections on the Geographical Imagination," *Annals of the Association of American Geographers* 80 (September 1990): 421–22; and David Harvey, "Flexible Accumulation through Urbanization: Reflections on Post-Modernism in the American City," *Antipode* 19 (1987): 275–76.

88. Logan and Molotch, *Urban Fortunes,* 103–10.

89. Wilson, *Judgment and Grace in Dixie,* 160–63; and Andrew Young, author interview, May 18, 1995.

90. These themes of promotionalism and hard work in the "Atlanta Spirit" were summarized by White and Crimmins, "How Atlanta Grew," 7–15.

Chapter 10

1. John Berendt, *Midnight in the Garden of Good and Evil: A Savannah Story* (New York: Random House, 1994), 31.

2. Suzanne Barlyn, "The Business Life: Where to Work," *Fortune,* November 13, 1995, pp. 86–87.

3. One major local developer of hotels and office parks was quoted as saying that cash for financing a building in Atlanta was so difficult to obtain that the process is the modern equivalent of sharecropping. Most financing for major projects comes from real estate investment trusts and other financing arrangements that encourage outside investment. The resulting pattern of outside ownership of hotels and other tourism businesses may contribute to what has been referred to as the "new plantation economy." See Hall, *Tourism and Politics,* 122–32.

4. Employment and population estimates are from the Economic Forecasting Center, Georgia State University.

5. Stone, *Regime Politics,* 3.

6. Turner Broadcasting Corporation and the entire corporate holdings of Atlanta's Ted Turner merged in 1996 with media giant Time-Warner. The merger did not affect the discussions between the team's owner and the city. The Omni was to be torn down and replaced by a

new 20,000 seat arena, scheduled to open in 1999. The costs of the facility were covered without increasing public debt since revenues from gate receipts will repay the funds used for construction. Any future revenue shortfall during the thirty-year life of the bonds is to be covered by the major tenants, the Hawks. Public improvements for the area were paid from a new tax on rental cars. Turner Sports was also awarded a National Hockey League franchise for the new facility.

7. *Constitution,* July 20, 1998, E-2.

8. Atlanta Convention and Visitors Bureau, *Celebrating the Dream,* 5.

9. U.S. Bureau of the Census, *1990 Census of Population, General Population Characteristics,* part 12, *Georgia* (Washington, D.C.: Government Printing Office, 1993).

10. U.S. Bureau of the Census, *1994 County and City Data Book* (Washington, D.C.: Government Printing Office, 1995).

11. Courtney M. Slater and George E. Hall, eds., *1994 County and City Extra: Annual Metro, City, and County Data Book,* 3rd ed. (Lanham, Md.: Bernan Press, 1994).

12. Edward W. Hill, Harold L. Wolman, and Coit Cook Ford III, "Can Suburbs Survive without Their Central Cities? Examining the Suburban Dependence Hypothesis," *Urban Affairs Review* 31 (November 1995): 149–52.

13. Henry V. Savitch, David Collins, Daniel Sanders, and John P. Markham, "Ties That Bind: Central Cities, Suburbs, and the New Metropolitan Region," *Economic Development Quarterly* 7 (November 1993): 347.

14. Earlier descriptions of this transformation of central cities by political scientists such as Dennis Judd and geographers such as David Harvey have been cited.

15. Sharon Zukin, *Landscapes of Power: From Detroit to Disney World* (Berkeley: University of California Press, 1991).

16. Sharon Zukin, *Loft Living: Culture and Capital in Urban Change,* 2nd ed. (New Brunswick: Rutgers University Press, 1989).

17. See Sharon Zukin, *The Cultures of Cities* (Cambridge, Mass.: Blackwell, 1995); and Rutheiser, *Imagineering Atlanta.*

18. Meredith Ramsay, *Community, Culture, and Economic Development* (Albany: State University of New York Press, 1996), 81–106.

19. Reed, "Below the Smith and Wesson Line," 139–53.

20. Former Fulton County Commission chairman Michael Lomax expressed Atlanta's dilemma when he said, "This city hasn't figured out how, at highly visible moments, to talk about its past. Talking about the past winds up being embarrassing, awkward, and it winds up being edited away." *Journal Constitution,* June 23, 1996, D-1.

21. *New York Times,* July 21, 1996, pp. 1–24.

22. Fred Hobson, "A South Too Busy to Hate," in Wilson, *Why the South Will Survive,* 48.

23. The classic statement for Southern agrarianism was made by Twelve Southerners, *I'll Take My Stand: The South and the Agrarian Tradition* (1930; reprint, Baton Rouge: Louisiana State University Press, 1970). For the role of white supremacy in defining the South, see Ulrich B. Phil-

lips, "The Central Theme of Southern History," *American Historical Review* 34 (October 1928): 30–43.

24. Reed, *One South*, 78–79, 166–69.

25. John Shelton Reed, "The South: What Is It?" in Escott and Goldfield, *The South for New Southerners*, 28.

26. U.S. Bureau of the Census, *1990 Census of Population and Housing* (Washington, D.C.: Government Printing Office, 1993).

27. For an extended discussion of this code of honor, see Wyatt-Brown, *Honor and Violence.*

28. Poll conducted by the Institute for Research in Social Science, University of North Carolina at Chapel Hill, reported in *Constitution,* July 6, 1995, B-3.

29. *Constitution,* May 21, 1996, A-1; and *Journal Constitution,* January 5, 1997, A-15. Other Southern cities on Stewart's list for 1996 included Charleston (first place), Mobile, Nashville, Memphis, and New Orleans.

30. According to the U.S. Census Bureau, the population of metropolitan Atlanta was 67.7 percent white, 27.9 percent black, 2.2 percent Hispanic, and 2 percent Asian. Between 1980 and 1990, both the Hispanic and Asian communities grew rapidly, with a 142 percent increase for Hispanics and a 338 percent increase among Asians. There is a great deal of diversity among the countries of origin among both groups.

BIBLIOGRAPHY

Alexander, Robert J. "Negro Business in Atlanta." *Southern Economic Journal* 17 (April 1951): 451–64.

Allen, Frederick. *The Secret Formula: How Brilliant Marketing and Relentless Salesmanship Made Coca-Cola the Best-Known Product in the World.* New York: HarperCollins, 1994.

———. *Atlanta Rising: The Invention of an International City, 1946–1996.* Atlanta: Longstreet, 1996.

Allen, Ivan, Jr., and Paul Hemphill. *Mayor: Notes on the Sixties.* New York: Simon and Schuster, 1971.

Atlanta City Directories. Archive collection, Atlanta History Center.

Atlanta Committee for the Olympic Games. *Atlanta's Official Bid for the 1996 Olympic Games.* Vol. 1, *Welcome to a Brave and Beautiful City.* Atlanta: Peachtree Publishers, 1990.

———. *Atlanta's Official Bid for the 1996 Olympic Games.* Vol. 2, *Atlanta: A City of Dreams.* Atlanta: Peachtree Publishers, 1990.

———. *The Official Report of the Centennial Olympic Games.* Vol. 1, *Planning and Organizing.* Atlanta: Peachtree Publishers, 1997.

———. *Olympic Games Fact Book.* Atlanta: Atlanta Committee for the Olympic Games, 1996.

Atlanta Convention and Visitors Bureau. "Atlanta Meetings and Convention Industry Fact Sheet." February 1982.

———. *Celebrating the Dream: 1996 Annual Report.* Atlanta: THP Communications Corporation, 1997.

———. "The Economic Impact of Expenditures by Tourists on Fulton County, Calendar Year 1996." York, Maine: Davidson-Peterson Associates, 1997.

———. *1996 Atlanta Hotel General Managers Survey.* Atlanta: PKF Consulting, 1996.

The Atlanta Exposition and South Illustrated. Chicago: Alder Art Publishing Company, 1895.

Atlanta Historical Society. "Federal Census of Atlanta, 1850." *Atlanta Historical Bulletin* 7 (January–April 1942): 16–68.

Atlanta University. *Business Enterprises Owned and Operated by Negroes in Atlanta, Georgia, 1944.* Atlanta: Atlanta University, 1944.

Avery, Isaac W. *The History of the State of Georgia from 1850 to 1881.* New York: Brown & Derby, 1881.

Bibliography

Ayers, Edward L. *Vengeance and Justice: Crime and Punishment in the Nine-teenth-Century American South*. New York: Oxford University Press, 1984.
———. *The Promise of the New South: Life after Reconstruction*. New York: Oxford University Press, 1992.

Barlyn, Suzanne. "The Business Life: Where to Work." *Fortune*, November 13, 1995, pp. 86–87.

Barnwell, V. T. *Barnwell's Atlanta City Directory and Strangers' Guide*. Atlanta: Intelligencer Book and Job Office, 1867.

Bartley, Numan V. *The Creation of Modern Georgia*. 2nd ed. Athens: University of Georgia Press, 1990.

Bayor, Ronald H. *Race and the Shaping of Twentieth Century Atlanta*. Chapel Hill: University of North Carolina Press, 1996.

Beamon, B. B. Interview by Benjamin West, May 29, 1979. Living Atlanta Oral History Collection, Atlanta History Center.

Berendt, John. *Midnight in the Garden of Good and Evil: A Savannah Story*. New York: Random House, 1994.

Beverley, Robert. *The History and Present State of Virginia*. 1705. Reprint, ed. Louis B. Wright, Chapel Hill: University of North Carolina Press, 1947.

Blackwelder, Julia Kirk. "Mop and Typewriter: Women's Work in Early Twentieth Century Atlanta." *Atlanta Historical Journal* 27 (Fall 1983): 21-30.

Blicksilver, Jack. "The International Cotton Exposition of 1881 and Its Impact upon the Economic Development of Georgia." *Cotton History Review* 1 (October 1960): 175–94.

Boyle, Robin. "Empowerment Zones: Picking the Winners." *Economic Development Quarterly* 9 (August 1995): 207–11.

Braden, Betsy, and Paul Hagan. *A Dream Takes Flight: Hartsfield Atlanta International Airport and Aviation in Atlanta*. Atlanta and Athens: Atlanta Historical Society and University of Georgia Press, 1989.

Brown, Joseph M. Correspondence with the Atlanta Convention Bureau and Letters of Invitation, 1913 and 1914. Archive collection, Atlanta History Center.

Brownell, Blaine A. *Urban Ethos in the South, 1920–1930*. Baton Rouge: Louisiana State University Press, 1975.

Brownell, Blaine A., and David R. Goldfield, eds. *The City in Southern History: The Growth of Urban Civilization in the South*. Port Washington, N.Y.: Kennikat Press, 1977.

Bruce, Dickson D., Jr. *Violence and Culture in the Antebellum South*. Austin: University of Texas Press, 1979.

Caro, Robert A. *The Power Broker*. New York: Knopf, 1974.

Carroll, James Edward. "Public Images of Atlanta, 1895–1973: Motif, Montage, and Structure." M.S. thesis, Georgia State University, 1974.

Carter, Edward R. *The Black Side: A Partial History of the Business, Religious, and Educational Side of the Negro in Atlanta, Ga.* 1894. Reprint, Freeport, N.Y.: Books for Libraries Press, 1971.

Central Area Study Policy Committee. *Central Atlanta Opportunities and Responses*. Atlanta: City of Atlanta, Central Atlanta Progress, and U.S. Department of Transportation, 1971.

Bibliography

Central Atlanta Progress, Inc. *Development Trends in Central Atlanta.* Atlanta: Central Atlanta Progress, 1985.

———. *Development Trends in Central Atlanta, 1987.* Atlanta: Central Atlanta Progress, 1987.

Chalmers, David M. *Hooded Americanism: The History of the Ku Klux Klan.* Chicago: Quadrangle, 1965.

City of Atlanta. Minutes of the Atlanta City Council, September 20, 1909; October 4, 1909; and January 2, 1911. Atlanta History Center.

———. Civic Design Commission. "Resolution," 1966.

———. Urban Design Commission. *Atlanta's Lasting Landmarks.* 1987.

———. Urban Design Commission. Hotel Row District, Landmark District Nomination, N-91-11 to 16, [1991].

———. *Creating an Urban Village: Atlanta's Community Driven Vision for the Empowerment Zone.* Vol. 1, *Strategic Development.*

City of Atlanta and Central Atlanta Progress. *Central Area Study: Atlanta, Georgia, Technical Appendix.* Atlanta: Central Atlanta Progress, 1971.

Clarke, Edward Young. *Illustrated History of Atlanta.* 1879. Reprint, Atlanta: Cherokee Publishing Company, 1971.

Cobb, James C. *The Selling of the South: The Southern Crusade for Industrial Development.* 2nd ed. Urbana: University of Illinois Press, 1993.

Cohen, Erik. "The Sociology of Tourism: Approaches, Issues, and Findings." *Annual Review of Sociology* 10 (1984): 373–92.

Conway, William. "The Case against Urban Dinosaurs." *Saturday Review,* May 14, 1977, p. 14.

Cooper, Walter G. *The Cotton States and International Exposition and South, Illustrated.* Atlanta: Illustrator Company, 1896.

———. *Official History of Fulton County.* Atlanta: Walter W. Brown, 1934.

Corporation for Olympic Development in Atlanta, *The Civic Trust: CODA Public Spaces Program.* Atlanta: CODA, 1996.

Couch, W. T., ed. *Culture in the South.* Chapel Hill: University of North Carolina Press, 1935.

Crowe, Charles. "Racial Violence and Social Reform: Origins of the Atlanta Riot of 1906." *Journal of Negro History* 53 (July 1968): 234–56.

———. "Racial Massacre in Atlanta, September 22, 1906." *Journal of Negro History* 54 (April 1969): 150–73.

Davis, Harold E. *Henry Grady's New South: Atlanta, a Brave and Beautiful City.* Tuscaloosa: University of Alabama Press, 1990.

Day, Cecil Burke, Jr., and John McCollister. *Day by Day: The Story of Cecil B. Day and His Simple Formula for Success.* Middle Village, N.Y.: Jonathan David Publishers, 1990.

Dittmer, John. *Black Georgia in the Progressive Era, 1900–1920.* Urbana: University of Illinois Press, 1977.

Dixon, John Morris. "No Frills, No Thrills: Atlanta's Pragmatic Olympics." *Progressive Architecture* 76 (July 1995): 51–59.

Doyle, Don H. *New Men, New Cities, New South: Atlanta, Nashville, Charleston, Mobile, 1860–1910.* Chapel Hill: University of North Carolina Press, 1990.

Bibliography

Du Bois, W. E. B. "The Negro in Business." In *Fourth Annual Conference on the Condition of the Negro*. Atlanta: Atlanta University, 1899.

Eaton, Clement. *The Growth of Southern Civilization, 1790–1860*. New York: Harper & Brothers, 1961.

Ellison, Christopher G. "An Eye for an Eye? A Note on the Southern Subculture of Violence." *Social Forces* 69 (June 1991): 1223–39.

Eric Hill Associates. *City of Atlanta, Georgia, Report on the Relocation of Individuals, Families, and Businesses*. Atlanta: Community Improvement Program, 1966.

Escott, Paul S., and David R. Goldfield, eds. *The South for New Southerners*. Chapel Hill: University of North Carolina Press, 1991.

Evans, Eli N. *The Provencials: A Personal History of Jews in the South*. New York: Atheneum, 1973.

Faulkner, William. *Absalom, Absalom!* 1936. Reprint, New York: Modern Library, 1951.

Fennell, Dwight. "A Demographic Study of Black Businesses, 1905–1908, with Respect to the Race Riot of 1906." M.A. thesis, Atlanta University, 1977.

Fleming, Douglas Lee. "Atlanta, the Depression, and the New Deal." Ph.D. diss., Emory University, 1984.

Foster, Gaines M. *Ghosts of the Confederacy: Defeat, the Lost Cause, and the Emergence of the New South, 1865–1913*. New York: Oxford University Press, 1987.

Franklin, John Hope. *The Militant South*. New York: Beacon Press, 1956.

Frechtling, Douglas C. "Assessing the Impacts of Tourism." In *Travel, Tourism, and Hospitality Research: A Handbook for Managers and Researchers*, ed. J. R. Brent Ritchie and Charles R. Goeldner, 325–62. New York: Wiley, 1987.

———. "Assessing the Economic Impacts of Travel and Tourism—Introduction to Travel Economic Impact Estimation." In *Travel, Tourism, and Hospitality Research: A Handbook for Managers and Researchers*, 2nd ed., ed. J. R. Brent Ritchie and Charles R. Goeldner, 359–65. New York: Wiley, 1994.

Frieden, Bernard J., and Lynne B. Sagalyn. *Downtown Inc.: How America Rebuilds Cities*. Cambridge: MIT Press, 1989.

Garreau, Joel. *Edge City: Life on the New Frontier*. New York: Doubleday, 1991.

Garrett, Franklin M. *Atlanta and Environs: A Chronicle of Its People and Events*. 2 vols. New York: Lewis Historical Publishing Co., 1954.

Georgia Department of Industry, Trade and Tourism. *Estimated Tourist Expenditures in Georgia by County*. Atlanta: Davidson-Peterson Associates, 1990.

Georgia Department of Labor. *Georgia Employment and Wages, 1993*. Atlanta: Georgia Department of Labor, 1994.

Georgia Department of Natural Resources. National Register Announcement, September 11, 1997.

Georgia State University. *Guess Who's Sleeping in Atlanta Tonight*. Atlanta: Center for Public and Urban Research, 1982.

Gilfoyle, Timothy J. *City of Eros: New York City, Prostitution, and the Commercialization of Sex, 1790–1920.* New York: Norton, 1992.

Goldberger, Paul. *Global Architecture: John Portman, Hyatt Regency, Atlanta, Georgia, 1967.* Tokyo: A.D.A. Edita, 1974.

Goldfield, David R. *Cotton Fields and Skyscrapers: Southern City and Region, 1607–1980.* Baton Rouge: Louisiana State University Press, 1982.

Gottdiener, Mark, and A. P. Lagopoulos, eds. *The City and the Sign: An Introduction to Urban Semiotics.* New York: Columbia University Press, 1986.

Grant, Donald L. *The Way It Was in the South: The Black Experience in Georgia.* New York: Carol Publishing Group, 1993.

Greenberg, Kenneth S. *Honor and Slavery: Lies, Duels, Noses, Masks, Dressing as a Woman, Gifts, Strangers, Humanitarianism, Death, Slave Rebellions, the Proslavery Argument, Baseball, Hunting, and Gambling in the Old South.* Princeton: Princeton University Press, 1996.

Greene, Melissa Fay. *The Temple Bombing.* Reading, Mass.: Addison-Wesley, 1996.

Gunn, Clare A. *Tourism Planning: Basics, Concepts, Cases.* 3rd ed. Washington, D.C.: Taylor & Francis, 1994.

Hacker, Joseph H. "Recapturing Main Street: A Semiotic Analysis of Nostalgia in the Underground Atlanta Project." M.S. thesis, Georgia State University, 1989.

Hall, B.C., and C. T. Wood. *The South.* New York: Scribner, 1995.

Hall, Collin Michael. *Hallmark Tourist Events: Impacts, Management and Planning.* New York: Wiley, 1992.

———. *Tourism and Politics: Policy, Power, and Place.* New York: Wiley, 1994.

Hanleiter, William R. *Hanleiter's Atlanta City Directory for 1871.* Atlanta: Wm. R. Hanleiter, 1871.

Harris, Joel Chandler. *Life of Henry W. Grady Including His Writings and Speeches.* New York: Cassel, 1890.

Hartman, Chester. *The Transformation of San Francisco.* Totowa, N.J.: Rowman & Allanheld, 1984.

Hartsfield, William B. Airport materials, 1970. Archive collection, Atlanta History Center.

Hartshorn, Truman A., Sanford Bederman, Sid Davis, G. E. Alan Dever, and Richard Pillsbury. *Metropolis in Georgia: Atlanta's Rise as a Major Transaction Center.* Cambridge, Mass.: Ballinger, 1976.

Harvey, David. "Flexible Accumulation through Urbanization: Reflections on Post-Modernism in the American City." *Antipode* 19 (1987): 260–86.

———. "Between Space and Time: Reflections on the Geographical Imagination." *Annals of the Association of American Geographers* 80 (September 1990): 418–34.

Harwell, Richard, ed. *"Gone with the Wind" as Book and Film.* Columbia: University of South Carolina Press, 1983.

Hastings, William. "Early Atlanta Hotels." *Southern Hotel Journal,* June 1946, pp. 26–27, 73.

Hertzberg, Steven. "The Jewish Community of Atlanta from the End of the Civil War until the Eve of the Frank Case." *American Jewish Historical Quarterly* 62 (March 1973): 250–85.

——. *Strangers within the Gate City: The Jews of Atlanta, 1845–1915.* Philadelphia: Jewish Publication Society of America, 1978.

Heys, Sam, and Allen B. Goodwin. *The Winecoff Fire: The Untold Story of America's Deadliest Hotel Fire.* Atlanta: Longstreet, 1993.

Hickey, Georgina. "'Meet Me at the Arcade': Women, Business, and Consumerism in Downtown Atlanta, 1917–1964." *Atlanta History* 40 (Fall–Winter 1996–97): 5–15.

Hill, Edward W., Harold L. Wolman, and Coit Cook Ford III. "Can Suburbs Survive without Their Central Cities? Examining the Suburban Dependence Hypothesis." *Urban Affairs Review* 31 (November 1995): 147–74.

Hill, Samuel S., Jr., ed. *Religion and the Solid South.* Nashville: Abingdon, 1972.

Hopkins, Richard J. "Occupational and Geographic Mobility in Atlanta, 1870–1896." *Journal of Southern History* 34 (May 1968): 200–213.

Horton, Gerald. "The History of Hostelry: A Century of Innkeeping in Atlanta." *Atlanta,* October 1961, p. 44.

Humphreys, Jeffrey M., and Michael K. Plummer. "The Economic Impact on the State of Georgia of Hosting the 1996 Olympic Games: Executive Summary." 1995 Update, prepared for the Atlanta Committee for the Olympic Games. Athens: Terry College of Business, University of Georgia and IRE Advisors, Economic/Management Consultants.

Hundley, Daniel R. *Social Relations in Our Southern States.* 1860. Reprint, New York: Arno, 1973.

Hunter, Floyd. *Community Power Structure: A Study of Decision Makers.* Chapel Hill: University of North Carolina Press, 1953.

Inscoe, John C., ed. *Georgia in Black and White: Explorations in the Race Relations of a Southern State, 1865–1950.* Athens: University of Georgia Press, 1994.

Isaac, Rhys. *The Transformation of Virginia, 1740–1790.* Chapel Hill: University of North Carolina Press, 1982.

Jackson, Henry, comp. *The Code of the City of Atlanta.* Atlanta, 1870.

Jackson, Kenneth T. *The Ku Klux Klan in the City, 1915–1930.* New York: Oxford University Press, 1967.

Jacobs, Jane. *The Death and Life of Great American Cities.* New York: Modern Library, 1969.

Jenkins, Herbert. *Keeping the Peace: A Police Chief Looks at His Job.* New York: Harper & Row, 1970.

Jones, Hugh. *The Present State of Virginia.* 1724. Ann Arbor, Mich.: University Microfilms, 1974. American Culture Series, reel 599.4.

Judd, Dennis R. "Promoting Tourism in American Cities: A Comparative Analysis." Paper presented at the annual meeting of the Urban Affairs Association, Portland, Oreg., May 1995.

Kent, William E. "Underground Atlanta: The Untimely Passing of a Major Tourist Attraction." *Journal of Travel Research* 22 (Spring 1984): 2–7.

Kent, William E., and J. Thomas Chesnutt. "Underground Atlanta: Resurrected and Revisited." *Journal of Travel Research* 29 (Spring 1991): 36–39.

Bibliography

Kimball, H. I. *International Cotton Exposition (Atlanta, Georgia, 1881): Report of the Director-General.* New York: D. Appleton and Company, 1882.

King, Augusta Wylie. "International Cotton Exposition, October 5th to December 31, 1881, Atlanta, Georgia." *Atlanta Historical Bulletin* 4 (July 1939): 181–98.

Korobkin, Russell. "Politics of Disfranchisement in Georgia." *Georgia Historical Quarterly* 74 (Spring 1990): 20–58.

Kuhn, Clifford M., Harlon E. Joye, and E. Bernard West. *Living Atlanta: An Oral History of the City, 1914–1948.* Atlanta and Athens: Atlanta Historical Society and University of Georgia Press, 1990.

Kunstler, James Howard. *The Geography of Nowhere: The Rise and Decline of America's Man-Made Landscape.* New York: Simon & Schuster, 1993.

Lane, Mills B., ed. *The Rambler in Georgia.* Savannah: Beehive Press, 1973.

Larsen, Lawrence H. *The Urban South: A History.* Lexington: University of Kentucky Press, 1990.

Law, Christopher M. *Urban Tourism: Attracting Visitors to Large Cities.* London: Mansell, 1993.

Lever, Janet. *Soccer Madness.* Chicago: University of Chicago Press, 1983.

Lewis, David L. *W. E. B. Du Bois: Biography of a Race, 1868–1919.* New York: H. Holt, 1993.

Lindsay, Arnett G., ed. *Directory of the 1937 National Negro Business League Convention.* Archive collection, Atlanta-Fulton Public Library System—Research Library.

Lloyd, Peter C. "The Yoruba: An Urban People?" In *Urban Anthropology: Cross-Cultural Studies of Urbanization,* ed. Aidan Southall, 107–23. New York: Oxford University Press, 1973.

Logan, John R., and Harvey L. Molotch. *Urban Fortunes: The Political Economy of Place.* Berkeley: University of California Press, 1987.

Luehrs, Karen, and Timothy J. Crimmins. "In the Mind's Eye: The Downtown as Visual Metaphor for the Metropolis." *Atlanta Historical Journal* 26 (Summer–Fall 1982): 177–98.

Lyon, Elizabeth A. M. "Business Buildings in Atlanta: A Study in Urban Growth and Form." Ph.D. diss., Emory University, 1971.

MacFarlane and Company, Inc., for the American City Corporation. *The Convention Delegate Study Report.* Atlanta, 1982.

Maclachlan, Gretchen Ehrmann. "Women's Work: Atlanta's Industrialization and Urbanization, 1879–1929." Ph.D. diss., Emory University, 1992.

Maclachlan, John M., and Joe S. Floyd, Jr. *This Changing South.* Gainesville: University of Florida Press, 1956.

Martin, Harold H. *William Berry Hartsfield: Mayor of Atlanta.* Athens: University of Georgia Press, 1978.

———. *Atlanta and Environs: A Chronicle of Its People and Events.* vol. 3 Atlanta and Athens: Atlanta Historical Society and University of Georgia Press, 1987.

Mason, Herman, Jr., ed. *Going against the Wind: A Pictorial History of African-Americans in Atlanta.* Atlanta: Longstreet, 1992.

Mathias, William J., and Stuart Anderson. *Horse to Helicopter: First Century of the Atlanta Police Department.* Atlanta: Georgia State University, 1973.

Minnix, Kathleen. *Laughter in the Amen Corner: The Life of Evangelist Sam Jones.* Athens: University of Georgia Press, 1993.

Mintz, Sidney W. *Tasting Food, Tasting Freedom.* Boston: Beacon Press, 1996.

Mitchell, Broadus. *Frederick Law Olmsted: A Critic of the Old South.* Baltimore: Johns Hopkins University Press, 1924.

Mitchell, Eugene M. "H. I. Kimball: His Career and Defense." *Atlanta Historical Bulletin* 3 (October 1938): 249–83.

Mitchell, Margaret. *Gone with the Wind.* New York: Macmillan, 1936.

Mixon, Gregory L. "The Atlanta Riot of 1906." Ph.D. diss., University of Cincinnati, 1989.

Mohl, Raymond A. "Making the Second Ghetto in Metropolitan Miami, 1940–1960." *Journal of Urban History* 21 (March 1995): 395–427.

Moore, John Hammond. "Jim Crow in Georgia." *South Atlantic Quarterly* 66 (Fall 1967): 554–65.

Morgan, Howard Edwin. *Motel Industry in the United States: Small Business in Transition.* Tucson: University of Arizona Press, 1964.

Mumford, Lewis. *The Culture of Cities.* New York: Harcourt, Brace, 1938.

National Negro Business League Collection, 1900 to 1906. Atlanta-Fulton Public Library System—Research Library.

Newby, Idus A. *Plain Folk in the New South: Social Change and Cultural Persistence.* Baton Rouge: Louisiana State University Press, 1989.

Newman, Harvey K. "The Vision of Order: White Protestant Churches in Atlanta, 1865–1906." Ph.D. diss., Emory University, 1977.

———. "Piety and Segregation: White Protestant Attitudes toward Blacks in Atlanta, 1865–1906." *Georgia Historical Quarterly* 63 (Summer 1979): 238–51.

———. "Some Reflections on Religion in Nineteenth-Century Atlanta." *Atlanta Historical Journal* 27 (Fall 1983): 47–55.

———. "Black Clergy and Urban Regimes: The Role of Atlanta's Concerned Black Clergy." *Journal of Urban Affairs* 16 (1994): 23–33.

Newman, Harvey, Barbara Ray, and Joseph Hacker. "Media, Consensus Building, Growth Machine: The Underground Atlanta Project." Paper presented at the annual meeting of the Urban Affairs Association, St. Louis, Mo., March 1988.

Nisbett, Richard E., and Dov Cohen. *Culture of Honor.* Boulder: Westview Press, 1996.

Nixon, Raymond B. *Henry W. Grady: Spokesman of the New South.* New York: Knopf, 1943.

Official Catalogue, Cotton States and International Exposition, Atlanta, Georgia, USA, September 18 to December 31, 1895, Illustrated. Atlanta: Claflin and Mellichamp, 1895.

Orfield, Gary, and Carole Ashkinaze. *The Closing Door: Conservative Policy and Black Opportunity.* Chicago: University of Chicago Press, 1991.

Pearce, Douglas. *Tourism Development.* 2nd ed. New York: Wiley, 1989.

Percy, William Alexander. *Lanterns on the Levee: Recollections of a Planter's Son.* New York: Knopf, 1941.

Phillips, Ulrich B. "The Central Theme of Southern History." *American Historical Review* 34 (October 1928): 30–43.

Bibliography

Pillsbury, Richard. *From Boardinghouse to Bistro: The American Restaurant Then and Now.* Boston: Unwin Hyman, 1990.

Pioneer Citizens' Society. *Pioneer Citizens' History of Atlanta.* Atlanta: Byrd Publishing, 1902.

Pomerantz, Gary. *Where Peachtree Meets Sweet Auburn: The Saga of Two Families and the Making of Atlanta.* New York: Scribner, 1996.

Portman, John, and Jonathan Barnett. *The Architect as Developer.* New York: McGraw-Hill, 1976.

Preston, Howard L. *Automobile Age Atlanta: The Making of a Southern Metropolis, 1900–1935.* Athens: University of Georgia Press, 1979.

Pyron, Darden Asbury, ed. *Recasting "Gone with the Wind" in American Culture.* Miami: University Presses of Florida, 1983.

Rabinowitz, Howard N. *Race Relations in the Urban South, 1865–1890.* New York: Oxford University Press, 1978.

———. *Race, Ethnicity, and Urbanization.* Columbia: University of Missouri Press, 1994.

Ramsay, Meredith. *Community, Culture, and Economic Development.* Albany: State University of New York Press, 1996.

Reagan, Alice E. *H. I. Kimball, Entrepreneur.* Atlanta: Cherokee Publishing Company, 1983.

Reed, Adolph, Jr. "A Critique of Neo-Progressivism in Theorizing about Local Development Policy: A Case from Atlanta." In *The Politics of Urban Development,* ed. Clarence N. Stone and Heywood T. Sanders, 199–215. Lawrence: University Press of Kansas, 1987.

Reed, John Shelton. *The Enduring South: Subcultural Persistence in Mass Society.* Lexington, Mass.: Lexington Books, 1972.

———. *One South: An Ethnic Approach to Regional Culture.* Baton Rouge: Louisiana State University Press, 1982.

———. *Whistling Dixie: Dispatches from the South.* Columbia: University of Missouri Press, 1990.

Reed, John Shelton, and Dale Volberg Reed. *1001 Things Everyone Should Know about the South.* New York: Doubleday, 1996.

Reed, Wallace P. *History of Atlanta, Georgia.* Syracuse, N.Y.: D. Mason & Co., 1889.

Report of the Board of Commissioners Representing the State of New York at the Cotton States and International Exposition Held at Atlanta, Georgia, 1895. Albany, N.Y.: Wynkoop Hallenbeck Crawford Company, 1896.

Research Atlanta, Inc. *The Convention Industry in Atlanta.* Atlanta: Research Atlanta, 1982.

———. *Atlanta Tourism and Convention Market: A Synopsis of Several Studies.* Atlanta: Research Atlanta, 1983.

———. *The Atlanta Report Card, 1990 Update.* Atlanta: Research Atlanta, 1990.

———. *The Olympic Legacy: Building on What Was Achieved.* Atlanta: Policy Research Center, Georgia State University, 1996.

Riani, Paolo. *John Portman.* Washington, D.C.: American Institute of Architects Press, 1990.

Rice, Bradley R. "The Battle of Buckhead: The Plan of Improvement and

Atlanta's Last Big Annexation." *Atlanta History Journal* 25 (Winter 1981): 5–22.

———. "If Dixie Were Atlanta." In *Sunbelt Cities: Politics and Growth since World War II,* ed. Richard M. Bernard and Bradley R. Rice, 31–57. Austin: University of Texas Press, 1983.

———. "Urbanization, 'Atlanta-ization,' and Suburbanization: Three Themes for the Urban History of Twentieth Century Georgia." *Georgia Historical Quarterly* 68 (Spring 1984): 40–59.

Ritchie, J. R. Brent. "Assessing the Impact of Hallmark Events: Conceptual and Research Issues." *Journal of Travel Research* 23 (Summer 1984): 2–11.

Robinson-Barnes, Carla J., John C. Thomas, and Alvin Glymph. *The Economic Impact of the 1994 National Black Arts Festival in Atlanta.* Atlanta: Applied Research Center, College of Public and Urban Affairs, Georgia State University, 1995.

Rose, Al. *Storyville, New Orleans: Being an Authentic, Illustrated Account of the Notorious Red-Light District.* Tuscaloosa: University of Alabama Press, 1974.

Rosentraub, Mark S., David Swindell, Michael Przybylsky, and Daniel R. Mullins. "Sports and Downtown Development Strategy: If You Build It, Will Jobs Come?" *Journal of Urban Affairs* 16 (1994): 221–39.

Roth, Darlene R., and Andy Ambrose. *Metropolitan Frontiers: A Short History of Atlanta.* Atlanta: Longstreet, 1996.

Rucker, H. A. Family Papers. "Report of the Finance Committee." National Negro Business League Meeting, Atlanta, August 29–31, 1906. Archive collection, Atlanta History Center.

Russell, James M. *Atlanta, 1847–1890: City Building in the Old South and the New.* Baton Rouge: Louisiana State University Press, 1988.

Rutheiser, Charles. *Imagineering Atlanta: The Politics of Place in the City of Dreams.* New York: Verso, 1996.

Rydell, Robert W. *All the World's a Fair: Visions of Empire at American International Expositions, 1876–1916.* Chicago: University of Chicago Press, 1984.

Sanders, Heywood T. "Urban Renewal and the Revitalized City: A Reconsideration of Recent History." In *Selected Papers from the 1979 Annual Meeting of the Council of University Institutes for Urban Affairs, Toronto, Ontario,* ed. Peter Homenuck and Harvey K. Newman, 98–139. Newark: University of Delaware, 1979.

———. "Building the Convention City: Politics, Finance, and Public Investment in Urban America." *Journal of Urban Affairs* 14 (1992): 135–59.

Savitch, Henry V., David Collins, Daniel Sanders, and John P. Markham. "Ties That Bind: Central Cities, Suburbs, and the New Metropolitan Region." *Economic Development Quarterly* 7 (November 1993): 341–57.

Sawicki, David S. "The Festival Marketplace as Public Policy: Guidelines for Future Policy Decisions." *Journal of the American Planning Association* 55 (Summer 1989): 347–61.

Scott, Anne Firor. "The Study of Southern Urbanization." *Urban Affairs Quarterly* 1 (March 1966): 5–14.

Shavin, Norman. *Days in the Life of Atlanta.* Atlanta: Capricorn Corporation, 1987.

Sholes, A. E. *Sholes' Directory of the City of Atlanta, Georgia, for 1881.* Atlanta: H. H. Dickson, 1881.

Shumsky, Neil Larry. "Tacit Acceptance: Respectable Americans and Segregated Prostitution, 1870–1910." *Journal of Social History* 19 (Summer 1986): 665–79.

Sjoquist, David L., and Loren Williams. *The Underground Atlanta Project: An Economic Analysis.* Atlanta: Policy Research Center, Georgia State University, 1992.

Slater, Courtney M., and George E. Hall, eds. *1994 County and City Extra: Annual Metro, City, and County Data Book.* 3rd ed. Lanham, Md.: Bernan Press, 1994.

Smerk, George M. *Readings in Urban Transportation.* Bloomington: Indiana University Press, 1968.

Spalding, Jack J. "The History of Piedmont Park." *Atlanta Historical Bulletin* 2 (September 1937): 5–13.

Spates, James L., and John J. Macionis. *The Sociology of Cities.* 2nd ed. Belmont, Calif.: Wadsworth, 1987.

Stone, Clarence N. *Economic Growth and Neighborhood Discontent: System Bias in the Urban Renewal Program of Atlanta.* Chapel Hill: University of North Carolina Press, 1976.

———. *Regime Politics: Governing Atlanta, 1946–1988.* Lawrence: University Press of Kansas, 1989.

Strasser, J. B., and Laurie Becklund. *Swoosh: The Unauthorized Story of Nike and the Men Who Played There.* New York: Harcourt Brace Jovanovich, 1991.

Sulzby, James F., Jr. *Historic Alabama Hotels and Resorts.* Montgomery: University of Alabama Press, 1960.

Taylor, Joe Gray. *Eating, Drinking, and Visiting in the South.* Baton Rouge: Louisiana State University Press, 1982.

Taylor, William R. *Cavalier and Yankee: The Old South and American National Character.* New York: George Braziller, 1961.

Tews, Mary-Kate. "The Mega-event as an Urban Redevelopment Strategy: Atlanta Prepares for 1996 and Beyond." National Center for the Revitalization of Central Cities, Working Paper no. 17. New Orleans: University of New Orleans, 1993.

Townsend, James L., and Paul Hagan, eds. *Atlanta International Airport: A Commemorative Book.* Atlanta: National Graphics, 1980.

Twelve Southerners. *I'll Take My Stand: The South and the Agrarian Tradition.* 1930. Reprint, Baton Rouge: Louisiana State University Press, 1970.

Underground Festival Development Corporation. "Briefing Paper on the Underground Atlanta Project." December 22, 1986.

Union Label and Service Trades Department, AFL-CIO. *Label Letter* 20, no. 5 (September–October 1995): 4–5.

U.S. Bureau of the Census. *Seventh Census of the United States, 1850,* Slave Schedule for Dekalb County, Georgia. Microfilm of manuscript census, Atlanta History Center.

———. *Eighth Census of the United States, 1860,* Slave Schedule for Fulton County, Georgia. Microfilm of manuscript census, Atlanta History Center.

———. *Tenth Census of the United States, 1880: Population,* vol. 2. Washington, D.C.: Government Printing Office, 1883.

———. *Compendium of the Eleventh Census, 1890,* part 3. Washington, D.C.: Government Printing Office, 1897.

———. *Twelfth Census of the United States, 1900: Population,* vol. 2. Washington, D.C.: Government Printing Office, 1904.

———. *Thirteenth Census of the United States, 1910: Population,* vol. 2. Washington, D.C.: Government Printing Office, 1912.

———. *Fourteenth Census of the United States, 1920: Population,* vol. 2. Washington, D.C.: Government Printing Office, 1921.

———. *Census of Business, 1939.* Washington, D.C.: Government Printing Office, 1941.

———. *Seventeenth Census of the United States, 1950: Population,* vol. 2, and *Occupations,* vol. 3. Washington, D.C.: Government Printing Office, 1952.

———. *Eighteenth Census of the United States, 1960,* vol. 1. Washington, D.C.: Government Printing Office, 1961.

———. *Nineteenth Census of the United States, 1970,* vol. 1. Washington, D.C.: Government Printing Office, 1972.

———. *Twentieth Census of the United States, 1980,* vol. 1. Washington, D.C.: Government Printing Office, 1984.

———. *1990 Census of Population, General Population Characteristics,* part 1, *United States,* and part 12, *Georgia.* Washington, D.C.: Government Printing Office, 1993.

———. *1990 Census of Population and Housing.* Washington, D.C.: Government Printing Office, 1993.

———. *1994 County and City Data Book.* Washington, D.C.: Government Printing Office, 1995.

Vance, Rupert B., and Nicholas J. Demerath. *The Urban South.* 1954. Reprint, Freeport, N.Y.: Books for Libraries Press, 1971.

Wade, Richard C. *Slavery in the Cities: The South, 1820–1860.* New York: Oxford University Press, 1964.

Walker, Jack L. "Protest and Negotiation: A Case Study of Negro Leadership in Atlanta." In *Atlanta, Georgia, 1960–1961: Sit-Ins and Student Activism,* ed. David J. Garrow, 31–58. Brooklyn: Carson Publishing Inc., 1989.

Weiner, Susan. "Index to a Pictorial History of the Cotton States and International Exposition of 1895." Unpublished manuscript, Emory University, 1977. Archive collection, Atlanta History Center.

White, Dana F. "The Black Sides of Atlanta: A Geography of Expansion and Containment, 1970–1870." *Atlanta Historical Journal* 26 (Summer–Fall 1982): 199–225.

White, Dana F., and Timothy J. Crimmins. "How Atlanta Grew: Cool Heads, Hot Air, and Hard Work." *Atlanta Economic Review* 28 (January–February 1978): 7–15.

Williams, Eleanor. *Ivan Allen: A Resourceful Citizen.* Atlanta: Ivan Allen-Marshall Company, 1950.

Williams' Atlanta Directory, City Guide, and Business Mirror, 1859–60. Atlanta: M. Lynch, 1859.

Williamson, Jefferson. *The American Hotel.* 1930. Reprint, New York: Arno, 1975.

Wilson, Charles Reagan. *Baptized in Blood: The Religion of the Lost Cause, 1865–1920.* Athens: University of Georgia Press, 1980.

———. *Judgment and Grace in Dixie: Southern Faiths from Faulkner to Elvis.* Athens: University of Georgia Press, 1995.

Wilson, Clyde N., ed. *Why the South Will Survive.* Athens: University of Georgia Press, 1981.

Wilson, John Stainback. *Atlanta As It Is: Being a Brief Sketch of Its Early Settlers, Growth, Society, Health, Morals, Publications, Churches, Associations, Educational Institutions, Prominent Officials, Principal Business Enterprises, Public Buildings, Etc., Etc.* 1871. Reprint, *Atlanta Historical Bulletin* 6 (January and April 1941): 11–144.

Wirth, Louis. "Urbanism as a Way of Life." *American Journal of Sociology* 44 (1938): 1–24.

Wolfe, Margaret Ripley. *Daughters of Canaan: A Saga of Southern Women.* Lexington: University Press of Kentucky, 1995.

Woodward, C. Vann. *The Strange Career of Jim Crow.* 3rd ed. New York: Oxford University Press, 1974.

Wyatt-Brown, Bertram. *Southern Honor: Ethics and Behavior in the Old South.* New York: Oxford University Press, 1982.

———. *Honor and Violence in the Old South.* New York: Oxford University Press, 1986.

Zelinsky, Wilbur. "Conventionland USA: The Geography of a Latterday Phenomenon." *Annals of the Association of American Geographers* 84 (March 1994): 68–86.

Zukin, Sharon. *Loft Living: Culture and Capital in Urban Change.* 2nd ed. New Brunswick: Rutgers University Press, 1989.

———. *Landscapes of Power: From Detroit to Disney World.* Berkeley: University of California Press, 1991.

———. *The Cultures of Cities.* Cambridge, Mass.: Blackwell, 1995.

INDEX

371